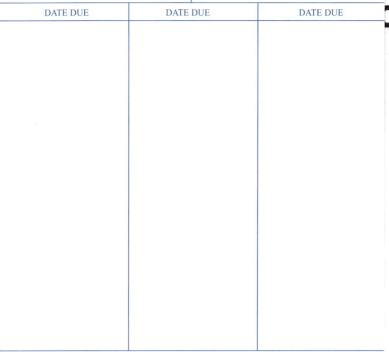

ch in

chnology

Current Research in Decision Support Technology

Robert W. Blanning and David R. King

IEEE Computer Society Press
Los Alamitos, California

Washington • Brussels • Tokyo

IEEE COMPUTER SOCIETY PRESS TUTORIAL

Library of Congress Cataloging-in-Publication Data

Blanning, Robert W.
　　Current research in decision support technology / Robert W. Blanning and
　　David R. King.
　　　　　　　　　　p. cm. -- (IEEE Computer Society Press tutorial)
　　Includes bibliographical references.
　　ISBN 0-8186-2806-5. -- ISBN 0-8186-2807-3 (case)
　　1. Decision support systems.　2. Management--Data processing.
　I. King, David R.　II. IEEE　III. Series.
　T58.62.B55　　1993
　658.4' 03--dc20　　　　　　　　　　　　　　　　　CIP 92-41031

Published by the
IEEE Computer Society Press
10662 Los Vaqueros Circle
PO Box 3014
Los Alamitos, CA 90720-1264

IEEE Computer Society Press Order Number 2807
Library of Congress Number 92-41031
ISBN 0-8186-2806-5 (microfiche)
ISBN 0-8186-2807-3 (case)

Additional copies can be ordered from

IEEE Computer Society Press
Customer Service Center
10662 Los Vaqueros Circle
PO Box 3014
Los Alamitos, CA 90720-1264

IEEE Computer Society
13, avenue de l'Aquilon
B-1200 Brussels
BELGIUM

IEEE Computer Society
Ooshima Building
2-19-1 Minami-Aoyama
Minato-ku, Tokyo 107
JAPAN

Technical editors: Barry W. Johnson and Ralph H. Sprague, Jr.
Editorial production and copyediting: Robert Werner
Cover designed by Joseph Daigle/Schenk-Daigle Studios
Printed in the United States of America by Braun-Brumfield, Inc.

 The Institute of Electrical and Electronics Engineers, Inc.

Foreword

This is the second text in the IEEE Computer Society Press Information Systems Series addressing the use of communication and computer technology to operate and manage organizations. The first book in this series (*Information Systems and Decision Processes*, by Edward Stohr and Benn Konsynski) presented the results of a five-year project assessing the status and charting the future of decision support systems. This text focuses on technologies that will be crucial in developing these systems and assesses current foundations of research and development supporting these technologies.

Blanning and King have collected an important set of papers on this topic and have organized those papers into several primary themes. The introductory chapter integrates these themes and shows how the technologies will improve decision making and problem solving in the management of organizations.

First labeled as business data processing, and later as management information systems, this field is now known as information systems (IS). "Systems" is the operative word, since the field includes not only technologies, but people, processes, and organizational mechanisms as well, combined as systems to improve organizational performance.

In effect, management becomes the dominant use of information technology. While we use communication and computer technologies in space exploration, weapons systems, medicine, entertainment, and most other aspects of human activity, the major use of information technology is to run and manage organizations.

The IEEE Computer Society Press Information Systems Series will provide an ongoing stream of high-quality, up-to-date books on information technologies and their use in organizations. Drawing on the best papers from conferences and special research projects, this series will select, combine, and disseminate valuable material that is otherwise difficult to find and assemble. It will focus simultaneously on the technology and its organizational usage. Most publications emphasize a single technology or application in a specific industry. The unique emphasis of this series, viewing both areas simultaneously, represents a significant contribution to the literature.

Ralph H. Sprague, Jr.
Consulting Editor
January 28, 1993

Preface

When electronic digital computers were invented approximately 50 years ago, it was assumed that they would be used for three purposes. The first was to perform scientific and engineering calculations — for example, the numerical solution of systems of nonlinear differential equations that simulated physical processes, such as the flight of projectiles through the atmosphere or the flow of neutrons through absorbing and reflecting barriers. The second was to route electronic communications (which, at the time, meant voice telephone calls) rapidly, efficiently, and reliably. This was a much more specialized application, initially resulting in the development of switching circuits for local telephone calls, and eventually resulting in the routing of messages in global computer networks. The third purpose, known to only a few people at the time, was the breaking of encrypted communications.

As computers became less expensive and more reliable, additional purposes emerged. One was commercial data processing, which included the production of financial documents (bills and paychecks, for example), the preparation of summary financial reports, and the calculation of statistical (census) data. Another was to perform the non-numeric symbolic calculations needed to simulate intelligent behavior. A third was data management, in which computers were viewed not as algorithmic machines with data as input but rather as mechanisms for organizing and maintaining data to which algorithms might be applied. As time passed, still more applications (interactive computing and computer graphics, for example) presented themselves, and the hardware and software needed to realize them were developed.

Approximately 20 years ago, these various purposes began to coalesce into yet another purpose — to support the decision processes of line managers and their staff analysts. Systems that performed such functions were called decision support systems (DSSs). One example was interactive decision models, such as spreadsheet models that calculated pro forma financial and operating statements. These and other DSSs sometimes contained graphics interfaces so that users could easily compare alternative scenarios, and a few even contained intelligent procedures for analyzing scenarios and procedures for interfacing with local and remote databases. Systems like these are in widespread use today, and more sophisticated applications are under development.

As the DSS area began to grow, three important issues in DSS development were identified by practitioners and were seized upon by academics as opportunities for research. These issues continue to be essential to DSS progress and form the foundation for this book. The first is model management, which is an extension of data management to cases in which information resources being organized and processed are not stored data but decision models, such as linear programming models and simulations. The second is the incorporation of expert knowledge to DSSs. This includes the development of expert systems for decision support (for example, in production planning, portfolio management, and auditing) as well as the development of intelligent systems for constructing various types of decision models and interpreting their output. The third issue is the relationship of DSSs to individual and group behavior. This research began with attempts to relate behavioral characteristics of individual DSS users to the effective use of the DSS, but now focuses on the use of DSSs in integrating the efforts of decision maker teams.

There is every indication that these three areas of research will continue to yield fruitful results for years to come. For example, innovations in model management will include new model types, such as logic-based models based not only on first-order logic but also on nonstandard logics (multivalued logics and logics of permission and obligation, for instance). Artificial intelligence will continue to provide important foundations for DSS research — especially in the areas of DSS construction and evaluation. That is, we may expect to see knowledge-based DSSs that will help their users to evaluate and modify themselves and that may even learn to perform certain modifications automatically. The organizational aspects of DSSs will continue to be a research focus, especially in the areas of DSSs to support team knowledge acquisition, team learning, and inter-organizational decision support.

We prepared this book to communicate the results of current research in DSSs that will form the foundations for future research. The papers included in this volume — representing some of the most innovative DSS research — were taken from the annual *Hawaii International Conference on System Sciences (HICSS)* proceedings, and in some cases from HICSS papers that were revised and published in the *Decision Support Systems* journal and the *Journal of Management Information Systems*. These papers span the fields of model management, intelligent DSSs, and organizational aspects of DSSs. We feel that this work will be of interest to students, faculty, and DSS researchers and also to practitioners wishing to stay current with DSS research.

Finally, we would like to thank Ralph Sprague, who has organized HICSS for many years, for encouraging us to prepare this book.

Robert W. Blanning and David R. King
January, 1993

Table of Contents

Chapter 3: Organizational issues in DSS development

*Note: Those papers marked with " * " were specially revised and expanded for this tutorial.*

Introduction: The Growth of Decision Support Technology

To understand the significance of current research in decision support technology it is useful to understand the history of decision support systems (DSS), including the considerations that gave rise to the DSS movement and the changes that have occurred in this movement during the past two decades. In summarizing this history we emphasize the growth of model management and other types of information management as a form of decision support, the application of artificial intelligence to decision support, and certain organizational issues in DSS. We then introduce the papers in this special issue.

The origins of DSS

The DSS movement grew out of dissatisfaction with two earlier and very successful applications of technology to management. The first was operations research and management science (OR/MS), and the second was management information systems (MIS). By 1970 both of these technologies were viewed as too limited to (1) meet the growing demand of managers for more effective decision support and (2) make proper use of the expanding capabilities of information processing technology, especially in such areas as information management and interactive computing.

The principal concern about OR/MS was that it was directed to the construction of decision models and to the development of model solution techniques (for example, in mathematical programming and stochastic processes), but that there was insufficient attention paid to the implementation of these models and almost no attention paid to the ongoing use of models by practicing managers. The first significant attempt to address these issues was made by Michael Scott Morton in 1971 under the rubric of management decision systems. Morton [1971] implemented a model of the production/distribution network of a major manufacturing company so that the managers could perform *what if* analyses of possible changes in production, distribution, and marketing efforts. In doing this he focused on two issues that had not been well addressed in previous studies. The first was the development of a convenient interface (primarily an interactive graphics interface, which was quite innovative at the time) between the managers and the management decision system. The second was the impact of the system, which was used by several managers in the logistical network, on the effectiveness of their decision processes. The principal improvement in effectiveness came about because several managers responsible for critical points in the network were able rapidly and conveniently to analyze the impact of their decisions on their own operations and on those of their colleagues. In other words, a management decision system was intended not only to improve the effectiveness of decisions with regard to individual operations but also to identify intra-organizational externalities and thus to improve the aggregate performance of integrated operations within the firm.

The principal concern about the second area, MIS, was that it focused on support for structured decision processes rather than semistructured or unstructured processes. MIS technology generally used byproduct information from transaction processing systems to provide summary reports for repetitive decision processes. The processes for which this type of information was appropriate were typically well structured in terms of their objectives, the procedures to be used, and the constraints involved. Examples of these reports were summaries of payments made to employees, lists of suppliers that had failed to settle delinquent accounts within a specified period, and descriptions of shipments from suppliers or to customers that had failed to arrive. In the same year that Morton introduced the concept of a management decision system, Gorry and Morton [1971] suggested that MIS technology be enhanced to include an emphasis on semistructured and unstructured decision tasks and examined the way in which these tasks arose at different levels of an organization.

These notions were consolidated seven years later when Keen and Morton [1978] published their seminal book on DSS. They identified three purposes of a DSS. The first was to *assist managers in their decision processes in semistructured tasks*. They suggested that this could be done by providing interactive access to stored data and decision models with a convenient user interface. The second was to *support, rather than replace, managerial judgment*. They suggested that the interactive capabilities and convenient user interfaces provided by DSS allowed managers to exert more control over the application of technology to decision making than was previously available. The third purpose of DSS was to *improve the effectiveness of decision making rather than its efficiency*. This was done by *extending the range and capability of managers' decision processes*, — for example, by means of user-friendly interfaces to rapid analyses of decision problems.

In retrospect some of these purposes were not clearly stated and caused confusion. For example, the phrase *rather than replace* suggested that OR/MS and MIS technologies were attempts to replace decision makers, which was not an accurate description of the intentions of most OR/MS and MIS developers. The phrase *rather than its efficiency* ignored the fact that improvements in efficiency often by themselves led to improved effectiveness by giving managers and analysts the freedom to think about the unstructured (or less-structured) aspects of their problems, even when no support was directly provided for these aspects. Even focusing on semistructured tasks caused some confusion, since all computational processes are structured. The important point was that a DSS invokes well-structured processes to support less-structured ones, and the challenge in DSS development is to figure out how to do this. However, these observations are made with the benefit of hindsight; a more elaborate description of purpose would probably have obscured the fundamental changes that were taking place in the application of information processing technology to decision making.

Decision support as information management

Much of the early research on DSS was strongly influenced by the progress in data management that had begun in the late 1960's and was establishing itself as a productive area of research and practice during the 1970's. This establishment consisted of the development and commercial implementation of hierarchical and network (especially CODASYL DBTG) database management systems, along with the development of a solid theoretical foundation for relational data management, which eventually saw widespread commercial implementation with the explosive growth in microcomputers in the 1980's.

The appeal of data management as an inspiration for research in decision support was that it offered a framework (in fact, several competing frameworks) for integrating data files and that it resulted in several widely used software systems. Much of the early research in DSS consisted of attempts to enlarge the scope of these systems to include decision models and user interfaces. For example, Alter [1980] surveyed 56 different implemented DSS and classified them into seven types, consisting of various data-based systems and model-based systems. Bonczek, Holsapple, and Whinston [1982] described DSS as an evolution from data management to model management and suggested that a DSS consists of a knowledge system, for example, data, models, and descriptions of the relationships among them, a problem processing system, that is, procedures for organizing, maintaining, and processing these information types, and a language system, for the user interface. In addition, Sprague and Carlson [1982] defined a DSS in terms of three functions that it performs for a user: data base management, model management, and dialog management.

Of these three functions — the management of stored data, the management of decision models, and management of the user interface — the one that has received the most attention in DSS research is model management. The reason is that data management and dialog management (for example, computer graphics, windowing, and iconic interfaces) have many applications outside of DSS and are generally treated as separate research topics. Model management, on the other hand, owes its existence to the need to support management decision processes, and research in model management is based directly on the requirements of line managers and staff analysts for decision support [Blanning, 1989].

Research in model management began in 1975 with the suggestion that decision models, like data, are an important organizational resource and that software systems, called model management systems, should be constructed to assist in organizing and utilizing this resource [Sprague and Watson, 1975; Will, 1975]. The purpose of a model management system is to make the organization and processing of models transparent to the users of a DSS, just as the purpose of a data management system is to make the organization and processing of stored data transparent to those who wish to maintain and process formatted data files. The earliest work on model management grew out of existing work on CODASYL DBTG database systems [Bonczek, Holsapple, and Whinston, 1976; Konsynski, 1980; Stohr and Tanniru, 1980]. Some of the files in a data management system were replaced with models, and the linkage between files and models and between the models themselves were provided by the model management

2

system. Thus, model management was viewed as an extension of data management with the result that some information sources were algorithms rather than files. A more recent innovation in this area is structured modeling, in which real-world entities and linkages are arranged into a directed acyclic graph, which is then mapped into a hierarchical decomposition of models and their components [Geoffrion, 1987].

Yet another perspective is that of relational model management. Models are viewed as a system of virtual relations — relations that do not exist in stored form [Blanning, 1986b]. The tuples of these relations, that is, the records in the virtual files are generated on demand when the user initiates a request for information that requires the execution of a model. User queries are processed by performing the relational operations of selection, projection, and join on these virtual relations in a manner analogous to, but not identical with, that of relational data management. For example, the integration of models, in which the outputs of one model or set of models are the inputs of another model or set of models, is accomplished by executing a join across the virtual relations representing the models [Blanning, 1985]. An important purpose of this research is to integrate data management and model management into a single framework, and it has been suggested that this framework might be extended to include other information increasingly found in some DSS, such as statements of logical relationships among variables [Blanning, 1986a].

Knowledge-based DSS

Model management, along with data and dialog management, continues to be an important focus of DSS research. However, all three are being strongly influenced by developments in artificial intelligence, and especially inexpert, or knowledge-based, systems. This is occurring in two ways. First, some DSS contain knowledge bases and the inferential procedures needed to apply them to a specific decision problem. In other words, they are in part expert systems, but the expertise is applied to management problems rather than to problems in engineering design, chemical spectroscopy, medical diagnosis, etc. Examples are DSS for intelligent production scheduling, portfolio management, underwriting, and financial statement analysis [Hertz, 1988; Blanning, 1990; Turban, 1990].

Second, artificial intelligence techniques are being used to improve the management of data, models, and dialog in a DSS. One of the early improvements was in the integration of files and models in a DSS. Bonczek, Holsapple, and Whinston [1981] developed procedures, based on inferential techniques such as logic programming, for identifying and assembling the collection of files and models needed to respond to a specific user query. Thus, a DSS was viewed as a collection of information sources, coupled with a collection of procedures for integrating them and an interface that allowed the user to communicate with the procedures.

Another area of improvement is in the construction of the DSS itself. The most prominent work in this area is the development of expert systems for the construction of linear programming models [Ma, Murphy, and Stohr, 1989; Krishnan, 1991]. The builder of a linear programming model, and by extension, other components of a DSS, is viewed as an expert some of whose knowledge and experience might be captured by an intelligent component of a DSS, and the purpose of the DSS is to help novices to perform the model building task more effectively.

Yet another area is improvement in the user interface — for example, natural language front ends for the variety of information sources found in a DSS [Blanning, 1984]. Although a few such front ends with limited capabilities exist, most of the research in this area is devoted to the explanation of outputs of a DSS. For example, ERGO is a system that explains anomalies in spreadsheet outputs [King, 1986]. If a *what if* query produces counterintuitive results, ERGO attempts to find a simple explanation. ANALYZE is a software system that performs a similar task with regard to linear programming models [Greenberg, 1987]. In this case the anomalies are infeasibilities that suggest an overconstrained problem, unbounded solutions that suggest an inappropriate or mistaken objective function, and the use of costly resources in a cost minimization problem that might be caused by unintended or unrecognized constraints on the less expensive resources.

An unresolved issue is the application of machine learning to data, model, and dialog management. As a DSS is being used, data is generated as to the accuracy of its data, the validity of its models, and the convenience of its dialog. At present, any learning is generally done by the people who use or maintain

3

the system. But it might eventually be possible to incorporate learning procedures into a DSS [Shaw, Tu, and De, 1988], thus allowing the DSS to improve its performance over time and even to adapt its procedures to the requirements of its various users.

Organizational issues in DSS development

From the earliest days of the DSS movement it was recognized that one could not properly study the technology of decision support without understanding the organizational setting in which the technology is implemented [Keen and Morton, 1978]. While some researchers were focusing on issues in information management and knowledge-based decision support, others were turning their attention to such issues as DSS development frameworks, human information processing and problem solving styles, manager-analyst interactions, and the impact of decision support technology on organizational decision processes [House, 1983]. However, this research has undergone a significant change in orientation — from concerns about individual use of DSS to concerns about the joint use of DSS by members of teams, groups, departments, and entire organizations.

Much of the early research in this area focused on the impact of individual behavioral characteristics, such as risk preference and cognitive style, on the use of information systems for decision making [Benbasat and Taylor 1978; Zmud, 1979]. It was felt that significant results in this area might have important implications for DSS design, since they would suggest ways in which systems could be adapted to the needs of the individual managers and analysts using them. Even for standardized systems that are not conveniently adapted to the characteristics of their individual users, such results would alert selected users to difficulties they might encounter with the systems, ways in which they might use the systems more effectively, and biases introduced into their decision processes resulting from the uses of these systems. There was much enthusiasm for these ideas during the formative years of DSS research, since they suggested a framework for examining jointly both technological and human issues. However, five years after the publication of the Keen and Morton book, substantial skepticism about this line of research began to surface, especially as it related to cognitive style [Huber, 1983]. People doing research in this area began to feel that many variables, behavioral and technological, affect the successful use of DSS, and isolating a few significant behavioral variables appeared less promising than was originally thought. As a result, most behavioral research in DSS is now being directed away from analyses of individual users and towards the use of DSS by groups of people and by entire organizations.

The application of DSS to groups began with the notion of a *decision room*, in which teams of managers and analysts addressing a problem communicated through a network of workstations containing decision models, and also by means of a display screen visible to all [Gray, Berry, Aronofsky, Helmer, Kane, and Perkins, 1981]. Although the original purpose of the decision rooms was to facilitate division of intellectual labor, it soon became apparent that they had other advantages as well. One advantage is simultaneity: people with different points of view can *talk* simultaneously by editing their comments at their workstations and then sending them to the display screen for all to see. Another advantage is anonymity: personality and power relationships that often inhibited the face-to-face exchange of ideas are themselves inhibited by anonymity in the decision room. These features led to an explosion of research under the terms *group DSS* [DeSanctis and Gallupe, 1987] and *organizational DSS* [Lee, McCosh, and Migliarese, 1988]. The former, which accounts for most of the literature to date, is concerned with the use of DSS by teams working on specific problems, even when they are not in the same location and are not working on the problem simultaneously. The latter, which is far more recent, is concerned with organization-wide and multi-functional uses of DSS and with the application of DSS to environmental interfacing, such as in negotiation support.

The trend towards group-based and organization-wide applications of DSS will certainly continue as organizations evolve towards less hierarchical and more flexible forms. It has been suggested that in the future managers will coalesce into a variety of time-varying problem-specific *cluster organizations* [Applegate, Cash, and Mills, 1988] and that analysts will form temporary *scenario analysis units* to address changing problems [Huber 1984]. It has even been suggested that concepts of artificial intelligence might be enlarged to include organizations as well as computers [Marsden and Pingry, 1988] and that organization design and development might be considered a form of *organizational knowledge engineering* [Blanning, 1991]. Thus, research on knowledge-based DSS might be enlarged to include organizational issues as well.

Purpose

The purpose of this book is to present outstanding recent work on decision support systems and thereby identify research issues of current interest that also offer promise for further development. The papers are from the Decision Support and Knowledge-Based Systems Track of the Hawaii International Conference on System Sciences (HICSS), 1989. All of these papers were refereed and revised for publication in the conference proceedings, and some of them have been revised substantially for publication in this book. Thus, the papers represent outstanding innovative work in the major subspecialties of DSS, and each has been subjected to a thorough peer review process.

The field of DSS is sufficiently new and the technology on which it is based is changing sufficiently rapidly that the subspecialties have fluid boundaries. Still, it is possible to identify three major areas of current research similar to those identified above. These are also growing areas of application development, as well as fruitful areas for future research and applications. This book is partitioned into three chapters, each corresponding to one of these areas.

The first area is advanced decision modeling and model management. DSS have long contained decision models, such as linear programming models, logistical simulations, and spreadsheet models. Recent research has emphasized two additional topics. The first is logic modeling — that is, decision modeling in which the variable types and model structures differ from the conventional quantitative decision models pioneered by operations researchers and management scientists. This topic is examined in the first two papers by Kimbrough and Thornburg and by Blanning. Kimbrough and Thornburg develop a formal language for business communication in an electronic-messaging environment, while Blanning develops a theory of propositional expressions based on the operations of relational database theory performed on the truth tables of the expressions. The second topic is model management — that is, an extension of the concepts of database management to include decision models. This is described in the paper by Geoffrion. A related issue is the economics of designing and using systems containing models and other decision support tools, examined in the paper by Richmond, Moore, and Whinston.

The second area is knowledge-based decision support. The field of artificial intelligence is beginning to have a significant impact on DSS. Most of the work being done in this area is in the development of intelligent models of decision problems, such as the diagnosis of equipment failures or the preparation of tax returns. However, three new topics are becoming prominent. The first is the use of expert systems in DSS construction. The designer of a DSS might be considered an expert, and it is possible to develop expert systems to assist in this task. Examples are given in the papers by Krishnan and Dolk and Kridel. In addition, it might be necessary to use such a system episodically — that is, in response to sudden opportunities or problems — in which case the construction of a reusable system is not at issue. An example is found in the paper by Elofson and Konsynski. (This paper was published in the proceedings of HICSS 1990, and was included to provide an example of a DSS used to solve ad-hoc problems.) The second topic is the application of connectionist architectures, and especially neurocomputers, to decision support. This is described by Trippi and Turban. The third topic is the development of active DSS that adapt themselves to the needs of their users — for example, by intervening in the decision process when support is needed. Two such systems are described by Raghavan and Chand, and by Fischer and Mastaglio.

The third area concerns organizational issues in DSS development. There are three principal topics in this area. The first is group DSS — that is, DSS that support groups of decision makers and analysts both by supporting individual members of the group and by helping them to integrate their efforts. An example is described by Vogel, et al. The second topic is determining the organizational impact of DSS, which is illustrated in the paper by Sviokla. The third topic is the application of computer science and cognitive science concepts to the understanding of organizational information processing and decision making. Two such articles, both based on object-oriented design, are by McIntyre and Higgins, and Chen and Nunamaker, Jr. Another approach, based on cognitive learning theory, is outlined by An, Hunt, and Sanders.

These papers are important not only because of the quality of their contributions, but also because they demonstrate a continuation of three basic research themes established early in the DSS movement. These themes — information management, knowledge-based decision support, organizational support — have shown remarkable consistency over the past 15-20 years, even though there have been remarkable changes in information processing technology during that time. They are also discussed in a companion volume analyzing the decision support movement and its likely future [Stohr and Konsynski, 1992]. In large measure this consistency results from the willingness of those doing DSS research to not only pursue basic themes but also to adapt their research to changes in information processing technology and its applications.

References

[1] Alter, S.L., *Decision Support Systems: Current Practice and Continuing Challenges*, Addison-Wesley Publishers, Reading, Mass., 1980.

[2] Applegate, L.M., Cash, J.I., Jr., and Mills, D.Q., "Information Technology and Tomorrow's Manager," *Harvard Business Review*, November-December 1988, pp. 128-136.

[3] Benbasat, I. and Taylor, N., "The Impact of Cognitive Styles on Information Systems Research," *MIS Quarterly*, Vol. 2, No. 2, June 1978, pp. 43-54.

[4] Blanning, R.W., "Organization Design as Expert Systems Design," *Proceedings of the 24th Hawaii International Conference on Systems Sciences (HICSS)*, Vol. IV: Organizational Systems and Technology Track, 1991, pp. 3-12.

[5] Blanning, R.W., "Expert Systems for Managers: Design Issues," *Concise Encyclopedia of Information Processing in Systems and Organizations*, ed. by Andrew B. Sage, Pergamon Press, Oxford, 1990, pp. 67-174.

[6] Blanning, R.W., "Model Management Systems," *Decision Support Systems: Putting Theory into Practice*, (2nd ed.), ed. by Ralph H. Sprague, Jr. and Hugh H. Watson, Prentice-Hall, Englewood Cliffs, New Jersey, 1989, pp. 156-169.

[7] Blanning, R.W., "A Relational Framework for Information Management," *Decision Support Systems: A Decade in Perspective*, ed. by Ephraim R. McLean and Henk G. Sol, North-Holland Publishers, Amsterdam, 1986a, pp. 25-40.

[8] Blanning, R.W., "An Entity-Relationship Approach to Model Management," *Decision Support Systems*, Vol. 2, No. 1, March 1986b, pp. 64-72.

[9] Blanning, R.W., "A Relational Framework for Join Implementation in Model Management Systems," *Decision Support Systems*, Vol. 1, No. 1, January 1985, pp. 69-81.

[10] Blanning, R.W., "Conversing with Management Information Systems in Natural Language," *Communications of the ACM*, Vol. 27, No. 3, March 1984, pp. 201-207.

[11] Bonczek, R.H., Holsapple, C.W., and Whinston, A.B., "The Evolution from MIS to DSS: Extension of Data Management to Model Management," in *Decision Support Systems*, ed. by Michael J. Ginzberg, Walter Reitman, and Edward A. Stohr, North-Holland Publishers, Amsterdam, 1982, pp. 61-78.

[12] Bonczek, R.H., Holsapple, C.W., and Whinston, A.B., *Foundations of Decision Support Systems*, Academic Press, New York, 1981.

[13] Bonczek, R.H., Holsapple, C.W., and Whinston, A.B., "Data Management Techniques in Mathematical Programming," *Proceedings of the SIGMAP Bicentennial Conference on Mathematical Programming*, November 1976.

[14] DeSanctis, G. and Gallupe, R.B., "A Foundation for the Study of Group Decision Support Systems," *Management Science*, Vol. 33, No. 5, May 1987, pp. 589-609.

[15] Geoffrion, A.K., *An Introduction to Structured Modeling*, Management Science, Vol. 33, No. 5, May 1987, pp. 547-588.

[16] Gorry, G.A. and Morton, M.S. Scott, "A Framework for Management Information Systems," *Sloan Management Review*, Vol. 13, No.1, Fall 1971, pp. 55-70.

[17] Gray, P., Berry, N.W., Aronofsky, J.S., Helmer, O., Kane, G.R., and Perkins, T.E., "The SMU Decision Room Project," *DSS-81 Transactions*, June 1981, pp. 122-129.

[18] Greenberg, H.J., "A Natural Language Discourse Model to Explain Linear Programming Models and Solutions," *Decision Support Systems*, Vol. 3, No. 4, December 1987, pp. 333-342.

[19] Hertz, D.B., *The Expert Executive*, John Wiley & Sons, Inc., New York, 1988.

[20] House, W.C., *Decision Support Systems: A Data-Based, Model-Oriented, User-Developed Discipline*, Petrocelli, New York, 1983.

[21] Huber, G.P., "The Nature and Design of Post-Industrial Organizations," *Management Science*, Vol. 30, No. 8, August 1984, pp. 928-951.

[22] Huber, G.P., "Cognitive Style as a Basis for MIS and DSS Designs: Much Ado About Nothing?" *Management Science*, Vol. 29, No. 5, May 1983, pp. 567-579.

[23] Keen, P.G.W., and Morton, M.S.S., *Decision Support Systems: An Organizational Perspective*, Addison-Wesley Publishers, Reading, Mass., 1978.

[24] King, D., "The ERGO Project: A Natural Language Query Facility for Explaining Financial Results," *DSS-86 Transactions*, April 1986, pp. 131-150.

[25] Konsynski, B.R., "On the Structure of a Generalized Model Management System," *Proceedings of the 14th Hawaii International Conference on Systems Sciences (HICSS)*, 1980, pp. 630-636.

[26] Krishnan, R., "PDM: A Knowledge — Based Tool for Model Construction," *Decision Support Systems*, Vol. 7, No. 4, November 1991, pp. 301-314.

[27] Lee, R.M., McCosh, A.M., and Migliarese, P. (eds.), *Organizational Decision Support Systems*, North-Holland Publishers, Amsterdam, 1988.

[28] Ma, P.-C., Murphy, F.J., and Stohr, E.A., "A Graphics Interface for Linear Programming," *Communications of the ACM*, Vol. 32, No. 8, August 1989, pp. 996-1012.

[29] Marsden, J.R. and Pingry, D.E., "The Intelligent Organization: Some Observations and Alternative Views," *Proceedings of the 21st Hawaii International Conference on System Sciences (HICSS)*, Vol.III: Decision Support and Knowledge-Based Systems Track, 1988, pp. 19-24.

[30] Morton, M.S.S., *Management Decision Systems: Computer Based Support for Decision Making*, Division of Research, Harvard University, Cambridge, 1971.

[31] Shaw, M.J., Tu, P.-L., and De, P., "Applying Machine Learning to Model Management in Decision Support Systems," *Decision Support Systems*, Vol. 4, No. 3, September 1988, pp. 285-305.

[32] Sprague, R.H., Jr. and Carlson, E.D., *Building Effective Decision Support Systems*, Prentice-Hall, Englewood Cliffs, New Jersey, 1982.

[33] Sprague, R.H., Jr., and Watson, H.J., "Model Management in MIS," *Proceedings of the Seventeenth National AIDS*, 1975, pp. 213-215.

[34] Stohr, E.A. and Konsynski, B.R. (eds.), *Information Systems and Decision Processes*, IEEE Computer Society Press, Los Alamitos, California, 1992.

[35] Stohr, E.A. and Tanniru, M.R., "A Database for Operation Research Models," *International Journal of Policy Analysis and Information Systems*, Vol. 4, No. 1, 1980, pp. 105-121.

[36] Turban, E., *Decision Support and Expert Systems*, (2nd ed.), Macmillan, New York, 1990.

[37] Will, H.J., "Model Management Systems," in *Information Systems and Organization Structure*, ed. by Edwin Grochla and Norbert Szyperski, Walter de Gruyter, Berlin, 1975, pp. 468-482.

[38] Zmud, R.W., "Industrial Differences and MIS Success: A Review of the Empirical Literature," *Management Science*, Vol. 25, No. 10, October 1979, pp. 966-979.

CHAPTER 1
ADVANCED DECISION MODELING AND MODEL MANAGEMENT

Kimbrough and Thornburg

Blanning

Geoffrion

Richmond, Moore, and Whinston

On Semantically–Accessible Messaging in an Office Environment

Steven O. Kimbrough

Michael J. Thornburg

University of Pennsylvania, Department of Decision Sciences/6366
Philadephia, PA 19104-6366

abstract: Electronic messaging in an office environment is normally carried out in natural language. For a variety of reasons it would be useful if electronic messaging systems could have semantic access to, i.e. access to the meanings and contents of, the messages they processes. Given that natural language understanding is not a practicable alternative, there remain three approaches to delivering systems with semantic access: electronic data interchange, tagged messages, and the development of a formal language for business communication (FLBC). We favor the latter approach. In this paper we compare and contrast these three approaches, present a theoretical basis for an FLBC (speech act theory), and describe a prototype implementation.

1. Introduction

Electronic messaging in an office environment is normally carried out in natural language. Electronic mail systems, for example, typically have functionality that is in the main limited to transmitting, storing, and retrieving natural language text, which text is atomic to, and neither parsed nor processed by, the systems. In such cases, we say that the system does not have *semantic access* to the messages it handles.

For a variety of reasons—including filtering out unimportant messages, issuing alerts in response to important messages, and initiating responses to messages—it would be useful if, somehow, electronic messaging systems could have at least partial access to the meanings of the messages they send and deliver. In recognition of this fact, EDI (electronic data interchange) protocols have been developed and implemented, and an attendant industry has sprung up [Frost & Sullivan, Inc., 1988]. We discuss EDI in §2. Further, a number of researchers (cf. §3, below) have developed and experimented with electronic messaging systems in which messages are tagged with meaning indicators that can be employed by the system to provide certain features for subscribers. Experiments with these prototype systems have demonstrated the usefulness of having semantic access to the messages in an electronic messaging system. The aim of the work reported on here is to develop and explore a deeper, more thoroughgoing, theoretically–grounded means of providing semantic access to the messages in an electronic messaging system.

There are essentially four strategies for obtaining semantic access to electronic messages. First, and most obviously, is to use natural language techniques to parse and process the messages. Just as obviously, this is not presently feasible and researchers have generally not taken this strategy. Second, message forms, called *documents*, may be standardized and proto-cols developed for representing document contents. This is the strategy behind EDI, which we discuss briefly in §2. Third, as noted above, is to tag or structure messages in a way that can be used by the system for inferencing. We briefly review efforts in this direction in §3. Although there is much to be said for EDI and tagged–message strategies, we find them basically *ad hoc*. We seek a theoretical view of messages, of what they may be, of how they are interrelated and of how we can make inferences on them. The fourth basic strategy for semantic access is, then, to develop a formal language for messaging, called a formal language for business communication (FLBC). Such a language would subsume both the EDI and the tagged–message approaches, would be machine readable, and could be theoretically grounded. The research reported here is an effort in that direction.

In what follows (after reviewing previous work in §§2-3), we present (in §4) some very general and powerful theoretical approaches, developed in philosophy and linguistics, that are, we believe, highly applicable to messages, or expressions, in an FLBC. Further, we sketch a theory of how these expressions can be represented in FOL (first order logic), which representation techniques will be instrumental for the results that follow. In §5, we discuss a context, Army office work, for which we have developed a prototype FLBC system, called Stella and in §6 we develop a logic model for FLBC messages in this context. §7 describes and discusses the prototype. Finaly, in §8, we conclude by summarizing our findings and by indicating matters for future research.

2. Previous Work: EDI

EDI (electronic data interchange) protocols were, and are being, developed for the purpose of replacing the interfirm (and intrafirm) flow of standard paper documents—such as purchase orders and bills of lading—with computer–to–computer exchange of information. (See [Edwards, 1987; Frost & Sullivan, Inc., 1988] for general information on EDI in practice.) Such protocols are quite commonly used in the grocery, automotive, warehousing, transportation, distribution, and general manufacturing industries, and use of these protocols is growing.

There are at least five major EDI protocol standards, but there is a general movement towards a common EDI standard, called X.12, which is under development by ANSI (American National Standards Institute: ANSI Accredited Standards Committee X12, Alexandria, VA). In the case of X.12, and all the other existing EDI standards, various paper documents—e.g., purchase orders, invoices—are identified and carefully structured definitions are developed for the sake of representing them electronically. Once the standards are in place, organizations

Reprinted from the *Proceedings of the 22nd Annual Hawaii International Conference on System Sciences*, 1989, pages 566-574. Copyright © 1989 by the Institute of Electrical and Electronics Engineers, Inc. All rights reserved.

write software for creating and interpreting documents conforming to the standards. Given an existing protocol, an EDI implementation has the information systems architecture described in Figure 2:1 (cf. [Frost & Sullivan, Inc., April 1988]).

Figure 2:1

1. **application (source).** This is a process—perhaps manual, perhaps computerized—that may generate information to be sent via EDI. Purchasing, order entry, and accounts payable are typical applications that firms have found it useful to be sources of EDI messages.

2. **application–generator link.** This is the process that extracts needed information from the application source and forwards it for further EDI processing. Forwarding may be performed by producing an ouput file to be read by the translator, or by calling the translator as a procedure and passing it parameters. Typically, implementation of the application–generator link requires modification of the application source program. There are cases, however, in which the application naturally produces needed data in a usable way, and the link may be built without modifying the application.

3. **message generator.** This process accepts the output of the application–generator link and produces messages (or documents) conforming to the EDI standard in use. The generator may also perform validity–checking tasks and may communicate back to the application or to a human supervisor. Generated documents may be forwarded, again, either by calling procedures or by file.

4. **telecommunications.** This element of the information system is responsible for delivering the sender's document (message) error–free to the proper receiver. In terms of the ISO OSI reference model, EDI standards are level 7 (application level) protocols. The telecommunications component handles the first six levels in the reference model (and possibly more), and may be said to stradle both the sender and the receiver. Possible physical and institutional arrangements are manifold, including: simple communications software, plus modems and telephone line; host–to–host communications using value–added networks (VANS); and industry networks with centralized 'post office' features.

5. **message interpreter.** On the receiver's end, the telecommunications module must, having received a message, forward the document/message to the message interpreter, which interprets and analyzes the message/document. The output of the message interpeter is data that is forwarded to the interpreter–application link.

6. **interpreter–application link.** This process tailors output from the interpreter, which is normally application–nonspecific, for the particular application (sink) at hand, and forwards the results to the application.

7. **application (sink).** This process—perhaps manual, perhaps computerized—uses information received via EDI. As a result of receiving and processing EDI messages, the application may initiate additional EDI messages.

Although EDI systems have been extensively and successfully implemented, and are growing in popularity, it is clear that (1) the protocol orientation of EDI continues to be a hindrance to further use because of inflexibility; and (2) the document—as opposed to message—orientation of EDI protocols also hinders flexibility and expressive power. While EDI is a good and growing thing, other technical approaches may yield greater functionality.

3. Previous Work: Tagged Messages and Languages

There is an intriguing literature emerging, focused on computer–mediated communications in which messages are tagged (the term is ours) in some way and the tags used for various purposes. Much of this work is oriented towards developing intelligence–based electronic mail systems [Malone et al., 1987a, b; Case, 1982; Chang and Leung, 1987; Comer and Peterson, 1985, 1986; Hiltz and Turoff, 1985]. A general complaint with existing electronic mail systems has been that they foster "information overload" by inundating the subscriber with "junk mail." By tagging messages and giving subscribers procedures for processing the tags, one could hope that the resulting system would help subscribers to "filter, sort, and prioritize messages that are already addressed to them, and...[help] them find useful messages they would not otherwise have received" [Malone et al., May 1987]. The state of the art here is that a number of prototype systems have been built, installed, and studied (with generally quite positive results), but the widely–used electronic mail (and more inclusively, electronic mail, computer conferencing, and electronic bulletin board) systems do not make significant use of information about messages, and what use is made of such information is limited to data stored in the message header and is normally not available to a user's procedures.

A second area, outside electronic mail systems, in which the tagged message idea has been explored may loosely be described as office support. There has been some (indirect) speculation in the literature of group decision support system research that message properties need to be captured and processed (e.g., [DeSanctis and Gallupe, 1987]). Others (e.g., [Kaye and Karam, October 1987]) have designed and developed prototype office support systems that can direct and coordinate the functioning of multiple, distributed processes in support of a given office task. The state of the art is here much less advanced than that for electronic mail systems.

Finally, there is a small but growing literature aimed at developing what we call a formal language for business communication (e.g. [Lee, 1981; McCarthy, 1982; Kimbrough and Lee, 1986; Lee 1988; Kimbrough, 1988]). The differences between a tagged message system, an EDI system, and an FLBC system may be described as follows. Typically, in a tagged–message system, a message consists of two elements: the message header and the message body (cf. [Chang and Leung, July 1987]). The message body may be processed only in the most rudimentary ways; it may be displayed, copied, and forwarded, but cannot be used for inferencing. The message header contains, in our terminology, a series of tags, normally including such information items as the message type, a unique message identifier, and various associated key words that serve as message descriptors. The elements in the header—the tags—are available for processing by an inferencing procedure. We can think of the EDI approach as a tagged message in which all the information has been moved out of the body and into the header. In an FLBC system, a message consists of a series of assertions, or declarations, each of which is, typically, a possible input to an inferencing procedure. We can think of such a system as an EDI system that replaces the header (expressed as a data structure) with a series of individually–meaningful and arbitrarily orderable declarations, or statements.

The state of the art for FLBC systems is best described as being in the exploratory phase. This paper represents an effort to explore the idea somewhat further and to do so by tying the effort to develop an FLBC to a solid theoretical base. We now turn to a short discussion of our theoretical outlook.

4. Theory: Speech Acts and Representations

Recent work in linguistics and philosophy of language—aimed at developing theories of how language understanding and communication works—has emphasized the rôle of inference and context (e.g. [Levinson, 1983; Bach and Harnish, 1979]). In concert with this work, and beginning, roughly, with the publication of Austin's *How to Do Things with Words* [1962], a theory of—or theoretical approach to—linguistic communication has been under more or less continual development by linguists, philosophers, psychologists, and cognitive scientists generally. (Of course, there is precursor work, particularly [Strawson, 1950].) This theoretical approach is called *speech act theory*, in part because its adherents take as their starting point for their theorizing about linguistic communication that fact that to say something is, among other things, to take an action. (The term action is, of course, being used in a technical and theory-laden, if not altogether clear, way. Briefly, to act is more than to do something; it is to do something with an appropriate attendant intention. Falling down is usually not an action, pulling a lever in a polling booth normally is.) Although there is no generally accepted full description of the theory, since different authors tend to emphasize the details of their differences with other writers on speech acts, there are two core ideas broadly accepted by speech act theorists and it is these two core ideas that prove most useful for developing a formal language for business communication.

The first core idea of speech act theory is the notion that every (or nearly every) speech act involves an expression by the speaker of a propositional attitude towards some (possibly complex) proposition. For example, if the speaker says "It will rain," then typically the speaker is asserting that it will rain. Here, then, the proposition is that it will rain and the propositional attitude is that of an assertion. On the other hand, if the speaker says, "Will it rain?" then typically the speaker is asking whether it will rain. In this case, the proposition is the same— that it will rain—and the propositional attitude expressed is that of a question. In both cases the underlying proposition is the same, but the propositional attitude is different. In the first case, we have that the attitude is that of an assertion and in the second case that of a question. Because propositional attitudes arise in other contexts (particularly in psychological explanation), those associated with speech acts have been given a special name. They are called *illocutionary forces*. This first core idea is summarized by saying that every speech act may be analyzed formally as having the structure, $F(P)$, where F is an illocutionary force applied to a proposition, P, called the *propositional content* of the act. Thus, this first core idea may be called the *F(P) framework*.

The second core idea of speech act theory is the idea that every speech act may be understood as consisting of several distinct actions. The idea and most of the terminology come from Austin [1962], although both have been developed in an extensive subsequent literature. Recognizing that different authors

distinguish somewhat differently among the various constituent acts and even recognize different acts, for present purposes we may understand a speech act as representable by four distinct actions. Suppose that a speaker, s, succeeds in saying something to a hearer, h, in a given context, c, then we may distinguish the following acts: (1) *utterance act* :: the uttering by s to h in c of a particular expression from a given language; (2) *locutionary act* :: the actual saying of something by s to h in c; (3) *illocutionary act* :: the doing of something by s in c, in virtue of having performed the utterance act; (4) *perlocutionary act* :: h's being affected by s in c, in virtue of s's utterance act

The general picture of communication and understanding that emerges is this. A linguistic communication—a successful *speech act*—between a speaker, s and a hearer, h, may be viewed as a sequence of four steps, which (after [Bach and Harnish, 1979]) we shall call the *speech act scenario*. It begins with a *speech event* [Levinson, 1983] or *utterance act* [Bach and Harnish, 1979] consisting of an *utterance, u*, and a *context, c*. The utterance, u, may be many things, including a sentence from a given language (e.g. English), a sentence fragment (e.g. "She's in the (pointing to the living room)"), or a sign designating a sentence (e.g., nodding assent, giving a 'thumbs down' to reject an offer to sell stock). The context, c, may include: (1) certain conventions and assumptions (e.g. that English is the primary language presently in play; that this is the serious business of buying and selling equities and not, for example, a game of charades), (2) certain gestures and inflections of speech, e.g. pointing and emphasis, (3) relevant history relating to a conversation, e.g., to fix the reference of a pronoun, and (4) relevant ambient facts, e.g. "I'll see you in an hour" means the speaker will see the hearer at 3:00 p.m., given that it is now, at the time of the utterance act, 2:00 p.m. (Just what, in a given situation, should be included in the relevant context is a problem for which there is presently no broadly satisfactory answer. We shall proceed workman–like, putting into the context whatever we need to perform the job at hand.)

The second stage of the speech act scenario is called the *locutionary act*. Our hearer, h has heard the utterance act, that is, has heard s utter u in c. Now h has the problem of figuring out, inferring, what the utterance means. If, for example, h has just asked s if he will be home Tuesday night and s has responded with a nod (the utterance act in question), then h might infer that the content of s's utterance is that he will be home on Tuesday night. Let P be this inferred (propositional) content of s's utterance act. If P is what s intended his utterance to mean, then we say that the locutionary act aspect of s's speech act (begun with s's utterance act) has succeeded. (Notice that P is abstract. The utterance act is (a sentence) in a particular language, while (the proposition) P is what is said. For example, "If pleut" and "Es regnet" are two different utterance acts having, as it were, a common locutionary act, that it is raining.)

The third stage of the speech act scenario is called the *illocutionary act*. Our hearer has heard, or observed, the utterance act and has successfully interpreted it: s's utterance means that he will be at home Tuesday night. But, what is s really saying? Is s predicting that he will be home Tuesday night, or is he promising it? There is a difference and the difference is important. If h succeeds in correctly inferring the attitude (promising, predicting, etc.) towards P that s intended to communicate, then we say that the illocutionary act aspect of s's speech act has succeeded. Following Searle [Searle, 1979; Searle

12

and Vanderveken, 1985], let F—for illocutionary force—be this inferred attitude towards the content, P, and we say that what s has said can be represented as $F(P)$, an illocutionary force, F, applied to a content, to a true–or–false statement, P.

Finally, the *perlocutionary act* aspect of the speech act includes the effects that s's utterance act has on h. For example, if the illocutionary act is a promise (to be home on Tuesday night), then h might come to rely on the promise and consequently cancel a previous commitment in order to visit.

In what follows, we shall not be much concerned with the perlocutionary act aspects of speech acts. Instead, we shall focus on developing representations for utterance acts, for a formal language for business communication (FLBC), such that the inferences needed to produce the locutionary and illocutionary acts—and to reason with the results—are correct and transparent. Our strategy is: (1) to accept the $F(P)$ framework for all speech acts; (2) to provide a means of translating $F(P)$ expressions into first order logic (FOL); and (3) to develop explicit conventions for representing $F(P)$ in an FLBC.

Our general strategy for translating $F(P)$ expressions into FOL is discussed at length in [Kimbrough, 1988]. Schematically, we say that:

$$\mathbf{Trans}(F(P)) = \forall w(A(a^*, w) \wedge F(w, \alpha, \beta, \nu) \rightarrow$$

$$\mathbf{Rel}(P, w)) \qquad (4:1)$$

For example, if Wahl asserts to Lane that she (Wahl) will be absent from August 8, 1988 to August 15, 1988, then we have $F = Assert$ and $P = Absent(wahl, 8\text{-}8\text{-}88, 8\text{-}15\text{-}88)$, and translating our $F(P)$ expression yields:

$$\forall w(A(a*, w) \wedge Assert(w, wahl, lane, id) \rightarrow$$

$$Absent(wahl, 8\text{-}8\text{-}88, 8\text{-}15\text{-}88, w)) \qquad (4:2)$$

where id is a unique identifier for the utterance act associated with (4:2). Then, (4:2) reads "In every possible world, w, accessible from the actual world, a^*, if Wahl asserts the truth to Lane with respect to utterance act id, then in that world, Wahl is absent from August 8, 1988 to August 15, 1988." Thus, in (4:1) α is the speaker, β is the hearer, and ν is the name of (unique identifier for) the associated utterance act. Expressions (4:1) and (4:2) represent five essential elements in an utterance act: the speaker, the hearer, the utterance act identification token, the illocutionary force, and the propositional content. The context of the utterance is a sixth essential element in need of representation. It may logically be interpreted as a relevant collection of statements, distinct from the utterance act expression representation, (4:1). For present purposes, the only contextual item we shall consider is the date of the utterance, which is represented in accordance with the following schema:

$$\mathrm{Date}(\nu, \delta) \qquad (4:3)$$

where ν is an utterance act identifier (a logical term) and δ is a date identifier (logical term).

In sum, an utterance act, ν, is to be represented in FOL by the conjunction of the context description (here, an FOL expression of the form (4:3)) and the utterance act expression representation (an FOL expression of the form (4:1)). We shall now discuss a specific application area and, following that, develop a partial FLBC and associated FOL translations for the application area.

5. Application Area: Army Office Work

We chose the Army office environment to test the application of the formal language approach to business communications because we are familiar with it and because the clear lines of authority in an Army office present opportunities for computerized inferencing on messages.

In an Army office, paths of command and responsibility can easily be delineated. Within such an office, each dialog carries with it information on its own implied force, based on the rank and relationship of the individuals involved. While rank may not be the sole guide of who works for whom, a combination of rank and job position reflect the lines of communication used within the office. Furthermore, the rigidity of the military chain of command clearly reinforces the comprehension of how illocutionary force is applied to various message types. For example, when a military commander issues a directive for an appointment with a subordinate, virtually all military personnel construe that request as an order, rather than a suggestion, polite request, or invitation. While the perception of an analogous situation in the civilian world between a supervisor and subordinate may be similar, the exact underlying force of the message may not be as obvious and is likely more variegated.

We have identified seven general message types for the Army office context. The names we have selected for these seven are not formal names adhered to by the official military community. Instead, in the day–to–day functioning of many military staff officers, the names reflect what a staff officer might use as a subject heading on a written memorandum to a commander, co-worker, or subordinate. The seven message types are, we believe, capable of facilitating a broad spectrum of communication between military personnel. They are as follows: (1) read/review/comment; (2) appointment; (3) dissemination of information; (4) staff action; (5) query for information; (6) absence; (7) statement.

We shall now briefly discuss each of these seven message types. We give further analysis, specific to our prototype implementation, in §6.

5.1 read/review/comment

Much of an officer's day is taken up with reading documents or with writing critiques of, or comments on, documents. Read/review/comment (RRC) provides the speaker with the capability to distribute documents and messages to people and to assign one or more people to read, act upon as appropriate, and possibly critique a document. The message type conveys the force of a directive and the speaker may optionally require a response and set a date and time when some specified action is to be completed. Further, recipients of an RRC message may be required to send an acknowledgement when the material is read. Records of each acknowledgement may be maintained by the sender (speaker), indicating the personnel who have read and complied with the message. This type of message is used extensively by military organizations and government agencies in distributing requirements set by military regulations, Federal guidelines, and Privacy Act requirements.

5.2 appointment

In all professional environments, the ability to manage appointments is required to schedule events, ranging from major meetings to minor social gatherings. Just as in any face–to–face encounter, a request for an appointment requires the hearer to respond to the speaker's request. How elaborate the response is, especially a negative response, depends upon the relationship between the speaker and hearer. If the speaker is the commander, a simple "no" will not be sufficient. Instead, an explanation would probably be required. The explanation may also contain a question. If a colonel asks to see a major at 2 p.m. on Thursday, the major may reply negatively, explaining that he will be in a meeting with another offfer at that time. Depending upon circumstances, the major may wish to include a question, e.g., "Do you want me to change my meeting with Major Amos?"

5.3 dissemination of information

Every office has a bulletin board with notices whose posters are suggesting may be of interest to various readers. Further, every office circulates, e.g. with routing slips, documents that may be of interest to, or were requested with a standing order by, their recipients. From the sender's point of view, this is a "send and forget" message. It is the responsibility of the hearer to read and act—or not—on the message.

5.4 staff action

One of the main work horses of this system is the staff action message type. In a staff action, one person might be assignment to attend a meeting, or an entire office might be directed to work on a high–priority project. Normally, one or more responses by the hearer are required. Often the required response comprehends the requested action. For example, if a report is to be written and delivered by a particular time to a particular officer, then the required response includes the report. When the speaker desires additional responses, such as message receipt confirmation, capability of meeting project due date, and acknowledgement of intermediate due dates (milestones), then these must be explicitly requested by the speaker.

5.5 query for information

A query for information is, from the point of view of speech act theory, closely related to a staff action. In the Army office context, the difference between a query and a staff action is genuine, but one of degree. The information requested in a query is expected to exist already and the effort to collect the information is thought to be minor. A staff action would be used to produce, or substantially process, the information, while a query is intended to result in a relatively easy retrieval of information.

5.6 absence

The absense message type allows speakers to give notification of planned and authorized future absences. When such an announcement is appropriately made, office procedures may be more or less automatically altered in order to maintain office functionality at a high level. Through checking announced absences, supervisors may know where their people are, messages can be rerouted to alternate personnel who are not absent, and scheduling meetings may be made simplified by looking ahead at the availability of various participants.

5.7 statement

Similar to dissemination of information, the statement message type is used to convey information. While a dissemination of information carries with it only the implication that the

speaker thinks the content might be of interest to the hearer, a statement message is an assertion by the speaker, to the hearer, that the content of the message is in fact true.

Given this general description of the seven message types and their uses in existing (not automated) Army office contexts, we now proceed to an implementation–directed analysis, in light of the theory discussed in §4.

6. Logic Model of Office Messages

We now consider how to represent the seven message types in an FLBC and in first order logic (FOL). Recall, from §4, that our general strategy in representing a speech act is to identify: (1) the speaker; (2) the hearer (addressee); (3) the message (utterance act) identification token; (4) the context; (5) the illocutionary force; (6) the propositional content.

For present purposes, again, assume that the only aspect of context that is to be captured is the time at which the utterance act takes place. Then, the form of an FLBC message is:

$$\texttt{message(<id>,<s>,<h>,<f>,<p>,<c>)} \qquad (6{:}1)$$

where: message ID :: `<id>`; speaker :: `<s>`; hearer :: `<h>`; force :: `<f>`: propositional content :: `<p>`; context :: `<c>`

To illustrate with an earlier example, suppose that on August 2, 1988 Wahl asserts to Lane that she (Wahl) will be absent from August 8, 1988 to August 15, 1988. Then, we could have in our FLBC:

$$\texttt{message(id,wahl,lane,assert,}$$
$$\texttt{absent(wahl,8-8-88,8-15-88), date(8-2-88))} \quad (6{:}2)$$

and the FOL translation of (6:2) would be (4:2) conjoined with:

$$Time(id, 8\text{-}2\text{-}88) \qquad (6{:}3)$$

We now turn to examining the seven message types explicitly. Each case is a fairly direct analog of (6:1) and its FOL translation. Because of space limitations, our discussion will be limited to indicative sketches.

6.1 statement

A statement, in terms of speech act theory, is an assertion. In making a statement, the speaker is asserting that what he is stating (i.e. the propositional content of the statement) is true. The FLBC representation of a statement message type is (6:1), with `assertive` replacing `<f>`. Permitted propositional content is implementation–specific. In a particular implementation, a lexicon of predicates and terms is developed. Any expression that is logically well–form and composed of predicates and terms from the lexicon is a valid propositional content, here and for all other message types.

6.2 absence

A speaker's announcement of impending absence is an assertion whose associated content is a predication of the predicate `absent(<person>,<from>,<to>)`, whose FOL translation is $Absent(x, y, z, w)$, where x is a person, y the from time, z the to time, and w a possible world. (6:2) is an example of an absence message in our FLBC.

6.3 dissemination of information

In disseminating an item of information, the speaker is asserting that the information in question is interesting to the hearer. Let `interesting(<i>,<h>)` belong to our FLBC lexicon with the intended interpretation that information item named by `<i>` is interesting to person `h`. Then one form of a dissemination of information message is:

$$\texttt{message(<id>,<s>,<h>,assert,}$$
$$\texttt{interesting(<i>,<h>),<c>)} \qquad (6.3{:}1)$$

A second form for dissemination of information, dissemination of information that, allows us to put messages within messages. In (6.3:1) we replace `interesting` with `interesting_that`, and `<i>` with `<i that>`, the syntax for the latter being that of any valid FLBC message (i.e. (6:1)). In this way, 'that' iterations (e.g. "Bob said that Mary said Sue said she would be home tonight") in natural language can be modeled in our FLBC.

6.4 appointment

An appointment message type is a directive to the effect that the hearer have a meeting with certain specified individuals at some time and place in order to discuss a certain topic. When rank matters—as it does here and almost always elsewhere—it is important to qualify the strength of the directive (cf. [Searle and Vanderveken, 1985]). Thus, we use `directive(<n>)` to indicate illocutionary force in our message, where n ranges from -5 (pleading, beseeching) to +5 (commanding, giving an ultimatum), and 0 represents a polite request. The bulk of the content for an appointment message is carried in `meeting(<m id>,<h>,<date>,<time>,<place>,<re>)`, where `<m id>` is a unique token to identify the meeting; `<h>`, is a person, normally the hearer; `<date>,<time>,<place>` have the obvious interpretation; and `<re>` names the subject of the meeting. Attendees may be indicated by a separate predicate, `attendee(<m id>,<attendee>)`.

6.5 query for information

There are different ways in which questions might be handled. The method we use deviates somewhat from the taxonomy of Searle and of some (but not all) others, in which a question is a kind of directive. Our method is simply to treat a query as its own illocutionary force and to place the knowledge of what to do in response to a question in the programs that use and process the FLBC messages. Full analysis and defense of this approach must wait for future work. In short, then, a query looks like a statement message, with `query` replacing `assertive`.

6.6 staff action

We model a staff action message as a directive. The key to successful automation of this message type is to develop a useful (concise yet powerful) lexicon for representing the content of such messages. Our initial investigations lead us to believe this can be done. A great many message contents have to do with project status reporting, task assignment, and alteration of task priorities. Full discussion of this matter is beyond the scope of the present paper.

6.7 read/review/comment (RRC)

In terms of speech act theory, we model an RRC message as a directive. The speaker is directing the hearer to read a particular document, to review it (act appropriately, depending on the content of the document), and to reply with comments on the document as appropriate. We distinguish two types of RRC message. RRC-1 is used when a speaker desires some sort of response but does not specify any additional actions. For example, if a project officer sends a document to an assistant, either via office hard copy distribution or through electronic mail, the officer may transmit a request that the assistant acknowledge the receipt of the document.

RRC-2 is used by a speaker when he wants both a response and some specified actions by the hearer. The actions may be specified explicitly by the speaker or may be contained within the document in question. For example, a new administrative requirement could be sent to the appropriate department responsible for implementing such requirements. Within the document is contained what to implement, how to implement it, and when to do so. A commander who transmits this message as an RRC may merely ask the hearer to reply whether or not the required implementation date can be met. A similar message may involve sending a document that only contains what to implement and when implementation is required to be complete. In addition to inquiring whether the implementation date can be met, the speaker may include in the message information on how to implement the new procedures, a request to prepare an additional briefing or report, and so forth.

To illustrate, suppose that Colonel Wahl sends an RRC-1 message to Major Lane to the effect that Lane is to read a particular document, implement its directives by a given date, and to respond immediately whether the implementation can be effected a week earlier. Specifically, let: speaker :: `wahl` :: Colonel G. Wahl; hearer :: `lane` :: Major M. Lane; message ID :: `id(123)`; context :: `date(8-31-88)` :: date the message is sent; force :: `rrc` :: read/review/comment; content :: `read(x,y)` :: `x` reads `y`; content :: `doc(37)` :: document number 37; content :: `implement(x,y,z)` :: `x` implements applicable directives in `y` at time `z`; content :: `before(t)` : a time on or before time `t`; content :: `reply(x,y,S)` :: `x` replies to `y`, stating whether or not statement `S` is true; content :: `doable(S,t)` :: Situation `S` can be brought about at time `t`.

Given this, Colonel Wahl's message is as follows:
$$\texttt{message(id(123),wahl,lane,rrc,} \Phi, \Psi \texttt{)}$$
where Ψ is
$$\texttt{date(id(123),8-31-88)}$$
and Φ is

$$\texttt{read(lane,doc(37)), implement(lane,doc(37),}$$
$$\texttt{before(date(8-16-88))),}$$
$$\texttt{reply(lane,wahl,doable(implement(lane,doc(37),}$$
$$\texttt{before(date(9-16-88)))))}$$

Having presented these rudiments of our FLBC, and the theory behind it, we shall now discuss our prototype implementation.

7.0 Implementation and Inferencing

The principal benefit of the syntactic articulation of messages in a business communications context is that the messages become semantically accessible. By expressing the messages in a theoretically sound language, provably correct inferencing can be performed on them. In order to illustrate this concept, we have developed a prototype FLBC system, called Stella, written in Prolog. Our main purpose, in this section, is to sketch a description of Stella with enough detail that the feasibility and usefulness of (correct) inferencing on messages in a business communication context is made plausible. Space limitations prevent a more thorough presentation.

In our FLBC system concept, there are four main rôles for inferencing related to messaging. First, during message initiation, inferencing is performed in order validate the message before it is sent. We construe validation in a broad sense. It includes such matters as issuing a directive to a superior and issuing a directive to do something in the past. Second, upon receipt, the message must be interpreted and handled appropriately. Unlike in an EDI system, the message interpreter has, again, semantic access to the message; it can make inferences and initiate responses based on what the message means. The third sort of inferencing is what we call *system–level inferencing*. Using records of messages sent and received, various sorts of useful inferences may be drawn. For example, a user may inquire whether a directive he has issued has been responded to, or what directives addressed to him are outstanding. Finally, *application–level inferencing* may be performed by an application, treating messages sent and received as facts in a knowledge base.

The remainder of this section is organized as follows. In §7.1, we describe our FLBC system architecture on analogy with the EDI system architecture. In §7.2, we sketch a message communication scenario, using the discussion to illustrate how the system works and where inferencing is performed. Space limitations prevent a more complete discussion. The FLBC for our prototype is just that discussed above, which is syntactically proper Prolog.

7.1 FLBC System Architecture

Our FLBC system architecture is similar to, but a generalization of, that for EDI (recall Figure 2:1) and is given in Figure 7:1, below, including comments regarding the current state of our prototype, Stella.

Figure 7:1

1. **application (source).** This is a process—partially manual, partially computerized—that may generate information to be sent in FLBC format. Our current (prototype) implementation is tailored for messaging in an Army office context.

2. **application–generator link.** This is the process that extracts needed information from the application source and forwards it to the message generator. Forwarding (in our prototype) is performed by passing parameters. The application and the application–generator link are tightly coupled in our implementation. They may be characterized as a simple front end to the message generator.

3. **message generator.** This process accepts the output of the application–generator link and produces messages (not documents) conforming to our FLBC standard. The generator performs validity–checking tasks and communicates back to the application. Generated messages are forwarded by being written to a file.

4. **telecommunications.** This element of an FLBC information system is not implemented in our prototype, but need in principle be no different than its analog in an EDI sys-

tem. (Because of the semantic articulation of the messages, however, there is opportunity for enhanced functionality.)

5. **message interpreter.** On the receiver's end, the telecommunications module must, having received a message, forward the message to the message interpreter, which interprets and analyzes the message. In Stella, the message interpreter simply gets the message by consulting the output file from the message generator.

6. **translator–application link.** This process tailors output from the interpreter, which is normally application-nonspecific, for the particular application (sink) at hand, and forwards the results to the application.

7. **application (sink).** This process—perhaps manual, perhaps computerized—uses information received via EDI. As a result of receiving and processing EDI messages, the application may initiate additional EDI messages, and may invoke system–level or application–level inferencing procedures.

7.2 Message Communication Scenario

We shall now describe, in outline, the communication of a message under Stella. After starting the program, a user may choose to send a message and is given a menu of message types, specifically, the seven message types discussed above. Upon choosing a particular type, say RRC, the procedure compose_rrc is called. This procedure, which is part of the application–generator link, works interactively with the user to elicit the various elements of the message, performs elementary error checking, composes a message in application–generator link format, and returns the formatted message. For example, if compose_rrc(X) is called and if the user successfully inputs a message, then compose_rrc will succeed, instantiating X to, e.g.

```
[[force,rrc], [speaker,wahl], [hearer, lane]]....
```

At this point, the user is given the option of formatting and validating the message. Choosing this option leads to the calling of the message generator, the generator(X,Y) procedure, which takes X (now instantiated) as its input and returns a validity message, Y, as output.

The message generator procedure consists of two subprocedures. The first, which we shall not discuss further for lack of space, creates a message in the FLBC format and asserts it into the working knowledge base. The second generator procedure uses a metainterpreter on the asserted (candidate) message in order to perform inferencing for validity checking on the message. Results of the validity checking inferences are accumulated in much the way explanations are developed in Prolog expert system inference engines. For example, suppose only two validity tests are performed, called the faut pas test and the past time test. One commits a faut pas by issuing a directive to a superior officer. One fails the past time test by issuing a directive or commissive for a prior state of affairs. (One should not be able to order someone to do something in the past.) Validity testing is called with:

```
valid(<message>,<result>)
```

If neither faut pas nor past time is found, <result> is instantiated to [[faut_pas,ok], [past_time, ok]]. Continuing with this example, the faut pas inference, in ordinary language, goes like this. The message is an RRC messasge, and any RRC message is a directive, so this message is a directive; further any directive in which the speaker is rank–inferior to the hearer is a faut pas, and not if otherwise; but here the speaker is not rank–inferior to the hearer, hence the message is not faut pas invalid. In emulating this deduction in code, three bodies of clauses (statement expressions) are used: the message itself, various general knowledge bases (containing, e.g., information about the ranks of network subscribers), and the validity metainterpreter plus its various called validity predicates, e.g., faut_pas. Call these, respectively, Λ, Θ, Γ and call the result returned by the validity check δ, then we can say that Λ, Θ, Γ computationally imply δ, or in symbols:

$$\Lambda, \Theta, \Gamma \vdash_{comp} \delta \qquad (7.2{:}1)$$

But, given our theory, we are now in position to prove that the computational implication is correct. We do this by translating the expressions in (7.2:1), each of which is in our FLBC, into FOL, using a revised **Trans** operator, and then proving the resulting sequent in FOL. See [Kimbrough, 1988] for a discussion of a full example, which lack of space prevents here.

Once validity checking is performed by the generator procedure, the results are returned to the user in the application. Assuming, for present purposes, that the message passes the validity tests, the user is given the option of sending the message. Taking this option, in the current prototype, results in the message being written to a communications file, as well as to the the user's file of sent messages. This completes the message-initiation sequence.

Handling of the received message begins when the prototype informs the user that a new message is awaiting receipt processing and presents the user with the option to process the message. After the user opts to process the new message, the message is read into working memory and inserted into the received messages file, and the message interpreter is called for the purpose of generating a report and taking action on the message.

Like the validity checker under the generator process, the message interpreter performs a series of deductions, using the message plus various environmental knowledge bases (plus inference engines as appropriate), and reports to the application. It may, in addition, respond directly with a message in reply. For example, if the hearer (addressee) is presently absent and the message is a directive, then the interpreter will, among other things, reply with an assertion to the effect that the message was received, but the hearer is absent and is expected to return at a given time. The inferencing and action taken by the message interpreter can be made arbitrarily rich and complex, but the underlying principles are simple and are the ones we have described already. Given semantic access to the message and environmental knowledge, provably correct inferencing procedures may be added more or less at will.

Finally, abbreviated versions of system–level and of application–level inferencing procedures have been implemented. Stella is a working, but sketchy, prototype. She illustrates these concepts and is undergoing further growth.

8. Conclusion and Discussion

We have, in the above, sketched results from a much more extensive project on formal languages for business communications. The basic findings and ideas may be summarized as follows.

1. The value, in a business communications context, of syntactically articulating messages, for the purpose of supporting processing and inferencing on the messages (i.e. for semantic access), has been amply demonstrated by experience with EDI and by prototype tagged–message electronic messaging systems. The full value of this idea, however, is far from being realized.

2. The idea of an FLBC (formal language for business communication) is a generalization of EDI and tagged–message electronic mail systems, and promises to provide the basis for expressively- and inferentially–rich computerized messaging systems.

3. Any FLBC implementation ought to be theoretically motivated. Recent theoretical work in philsophy of language and linguistics—in pragmatics generally and speech act theory particularly—holds great promise of providing an adequate theoretical basis for FLBCs.

4. Kimbrough's representation scheme for representing speech act expressions in first order logic [Kimbrough, 1988] may be used to prove the theoretical correctness of inferences in an FLBC based on the scheme.

5. The architecture of an FLBC system may be thought of as a generalization of the EDI architecture. In the prototype, discussed here, of such an FLBC system, four main rôles were found for inferencing on messages: (1) validation during message generation, (2) message interpretation, and (3) system–level inferences, and (3) application–level inferences, where (3) and (4) may integrate knowledge about messages with application–specific knowledge.

6. Programming methods for the prototype, Stella, relied on standard, non–exotic Prolog and expert systems techniques.

This said, much remains to be done. Theory needs to be broadened and deepened. FLBCs need to be defined and studied more systematically. Prototypes need to be used and experimented with. But these are topics for other papers.

acknowledgements: Thanks to Ron Lee and two anonymous referees for useful suggestions and comments.

References

Austin, John L., *How to Do Things with Words,* Oxford at the Clarendon Press, Oxford, England, 1962.

Bach, Kent and Robert M. Harnish, *Linguistic Communication and Speech Acts,* The MIT Press, Cambridge, Massachusetts, 1979.

Camurait, Paolo and Paolo Prinetto, "Formal Verification of Hardware Correctness: Introduction and Survey of Current Research," *Computer,* **21**, no. 7, (July 1988), 8-19.

Case, G. R., "Feedback on Electronic Junk," *Communications of the ACM,* **25**, no. 6, (1982), 378-398.

Chang, S. K. and L. Leung, "A Knowledge–Based Message Management System," *ACM Transactions on Office Information Systems,* **5**, no. 3, (1987), 213-236.

Comer, D. E. and L. L. Peterson, "Conversations—An Alternative to Memos and Conferences," *Byte,* **10**, no. 13, (1985), 263-272.

Comer, D. E. and L. L. Peterson, "Conversation Based Mail," *ACM Transactions on Computer Systems,* **4**, no. 4, (1986), 299-319.

DeSanctis, G. and R. B. Gallupe, "A Foundation for the Study of Group Decision Support Systems," *Management Science,* **33**, no. 5, (1987), 589-609.

Edwards, Daniel W., "Electronic Data Interchange: A Senior Management Overview," International Center for Information Technologies, 2000 M Street, N.W., Washington, D.C. 20036, 202-659-1314, 1987.

Frost & Sullivan, Inc., *The Electronic Data Interchange (EDI) Market in the U.S.*, Frost & Sullivan, Inc., 106 Fulton Street, New York, NY 10038, 212-233-1080, April 1988.

Hiltz, S.R. and M. Turoff, "Structuring Computer–Mediated Communications Systems to Avoid Information Overload," *Communications of the ACM*, **28**, no. 7, (1985), 680-9.

Johnson-Laird, Philip N., *The Computer and the Mind*, Harvard University Press, Cambridge, MA, 1988.

Kaye, A. Roger and Gerald M. Karam, "Cooperating Knowledge–Based Assistants for the Office," *ACM Transactions on Office Information Systems*, **5**, no. 4, (October 1987), 297-326.

Kimbrough, Steven O., "On Representation Schemes for Electronic Speech Acts," University of Pennsylvania, Department of Decision Sciences working paper, 1988; forthcoming in *Decision Support Systems*.

Kimbrough, Steven O. and Ronald M. Lee, "On Illocutionary Logic as a Telecommunications Language," *Proceedings of the Seventh International Conference on Information Systems*, Leslie Maggi et al., eds., San Diego, CA, (December 15-7, 1986), 15-26.

Lee, Ronald M., "CANDID—A Logical Calculus for Describing Financial Contracts," Ph.D. thesis, University of Pennsylvania, Department of Decision Sciences, working paper 80-06-2, 1980.

Lee, Ronald M. and Ranjit Bose, "Deontic Reasoning in Bureaucratic Systems," *Proceedings of the 21st Hawaii International Conference on System Sciences*, (January 1988).

Levinson, Stephen C., *Pragmatics*, Cambridge University Press, Cambridge, England, 1983.

Malone, Thomas W., Kenneth R. Grant, Franklyn A. Turbak, Stephen A. Brobst, and Michael D. Cohen, "Intelligent Information–Sharing Systems," *Communications of the ACM*, **30**, no. 5, (1987a), 390-402.

Malone, Thomas W., Kenneth R. Grant, Kum–Yew Lai, Ramana Rao, and David Rosenblitt, "Semistructured Messages Are Surpirsingly Useful for Computer–Supported Coordination," *ACM Transactions on Office Information Systems*, **5**, no. 2, (1987b).

McCarthy, John, "The Common Business Communication Language," in *Textverarbeitung und Bürosysteme*, Albert Endres and Jürgen Reetz, eds., R. Oldenbourg Verlag, Munich and Vienna, 1982.

Searle, John R., *Speech Acts*, Cambridge University Press, Cambridge, England, 1969.

Searle, John R., *Expression and Meaning*, Cambridge University Press, Cambridge, England, 1979.

Searle, John R., and Daniel Vanderveken, *Foundations of Illocutionary Logic*, Cambridge University Press, Cambridge, England, 1985.

Strawson, P. F., "On Referring," *Mind*, LIX, no. 235 (1950), 320-44; reprinted in *Readings in the Philosophy of Language*, Jay F. Rosenberg and Charles Travis, eds., Prentice-Hall, Inc., Englewood Cliffs, New Jersey, 1971.

A RELATIONAL ALGEBRA FOR ASSERTION MANAGEMENT

Robert W. Blanning
Owen Graduate School of Management

Vanderbilt University
Nashville, Tennessee 37203

ABSTRACT

We extend the established relational theory of stored data to encompass logical assertions. Since the truth table for an assertion is a virtual relation, relational database theory can be extended to include assertion management. We establish a correspondence between the relational algebra, as applied to the management of stored data, and the same algebra, as applied to the management of logical assertions and thus, present a single comprehensive framework for the management of these two important types of information.

I. INTRODUCTION

An important purpose of the research being done on decision support systems is to develop a theory of information management that is as independent as possible of the way in which the information is stored and processed. Two types of information that have been examined in some detail are stored data and decision models. We are concerned here with a third type of information - logic statements (which we will call assertions) that may be true or false. We will show that a simple and elegant theory that has been developed for the management of stored data, one based on the mathematics of relations, can also fruitfully be applied to the management of assertions.

A substantial amount of effort has been devoted to the development of a relational theory of stored data [8, 9] and, to a lesser extent, of decision models [2]. In the latter work, a model is viewed as a virtual relation whose tuples do not exist in stored form but are generated on demand by a stored algorithm, and the input and output attributes of the model correspond to the key and content attributes of a file. Some attention has also been paid to the development of a relational view of assertions - that is, of well-formed expressions in two-valued sentential

calculus [4]. In the latter work assertions are represented both intensionally (i.e., by expressions in sentential calculus) and extensionally (in the form of simplified truth tables). It was shown that two important relational operations, projection and join, performed on the extensions correspond to two simple intensional operations. In this paper we consider a complete set of relational operations, called the relational algebra of relational database theory, and derive the corresponding intensional operations. The purpose of this effort is to extend the relational view of data to encompass a simple form of logic. Thus, we hope to integrate, from a theoretical perspective, two important types of information, (stored) data and (logical) assertions, used in decision support.

II. A RELATIONAL VIEW OF ASSERTIONS

In this section we present briefly some of the definitions and theorems of [4]. We do this in order to introduce the interpretation of the complete relational algebra in Sections III and IV below.

We begin by considering a set of variables, which we will call assertions, that may take on the values 1 (true) or 0 (false). These may be combined by certain operations to produce more complex assertions, which will also take on the values of 1 or 0. The operations are (1) conjunction, $(x \wedge y) = 1$ iff $x = 1$ and $y = 1$, (2) disjunction $(x \vee y) = 0$ iff $x = 0$ and $y = 0$, (3) implication $(x \rightarrow y) = 0$ iff $x = 1$ and $y = 0$, (4) equivalence, $(x \equiv y) = (x \rightarrow y) \wedge (y \rightarrow x)$, and (5) negation $\bar{x} = 1$ iff $x = 0$. Thus, for example, $(x \wedge y) \rightarrow (z \vee w)$ is also an assertion.

We now define an a-relation (assertion relation) as follows:

DEFINITION I: An a-relation scheme, S, is a set of assertion names - for example, $S = \{x, y, z\}$. An a-relation, A, defined over S, is a subset of the Cartesian product of domains of the elements of S. Thus, if S contains N assertion names, then $A \subseteq \{0, 1\}^N$.

The correspondence between an (intensional) expression involving assertions and an (extensional) a-relation is established as follows:

Reprinted from the *Proceedings of the 22nd Annual Hawaii International Conference on System Sciences,* 1989, pages 560-565. Copyright © 1989 by the Institute of Electrical and Electronics Engineers, Inc. All rights reserved.

ALGORITHM I: Given an expression involving an a-relation scheme S = {x, y, ...}, we construct the corresponding a-relation A over S by including in A all tuples <x, y, ...> containing values of the variables for which the expression is true.

For example, the a-relations for the expressions x ∨ y and y $\equiv$ z appear in Figures 1 and 2. All tuples in the Cartesian products for these two schemes are represented, except for those for which the expressions are false. We note that an a-relation is similar to a truth table [5] except that (1) all rows corresponding to the value "false" of the expression are missing and (2) the column containing the value of the expression (which would then take on the value "true" for each tuple) is missing. Thus, truth tables and a-relations are isomorphic up to an ordering of their rows and columns. Finally we note that an a-relation is a relation, on which the operations of relational database theory can be performed. Our purpose here is to uncover the intensional meaning of these extensional operations.

To do so, we define transformations between the extensional and intensional representations of assertions, as follows:

DEFINITION II: Given an expression K defined over a set of an a-relation scheme S, its <u>extension</u> E(K) is an a-relation over S that can be derived from K by Algorithm I. Given an a-relation A over S, its <u>intension</u> I(A) is an expression containing members of S from which A can be generated by Algorithm I.

We note that the symbolic representations of intensions and extensions are not unique. For example, since an a-relation is a relation, it is unique (with respect to an intension) up to an ordering of its rows and (labelled) columns. Similarly, an intension is unique up to logical equivalence. For example, if A is the a-relation in Figure 1, then I(A) = x ∨ y, but we could also write I(A) = $\overline{\overline{x} \land \overline{y}}$. We note that E(I(A)) = A and I(E(K)) = K.

Since a-relations are relations, it is possible to define the relational operations of (natural) join and projection, as follows:

DEFINITION III: Let A and A' be a-relations with schemes S and S'. The <u>join</u> of A and A', J(A, A'), is the subset of the Cartesian product of A and A' for which the attribute values of S ∩ S' in A equal the attribute values of S ∩ S' in A'.

DEFINITION IV: Let A be an a-relation on S and let S' ⊆ S. The <u>projection</u> of A along S', P(A, S'), is formed by deleting from A all columns belonging to S \ S' and then eliminating duplicate tuples.

We note that (1) the join of any two a-relations is an a-relation, (2) the projection of an a-relation along any subset of its scheme is an

relation along its scheme is the relation itself (i.e., P(A, S) = A). We now state and illustrate two results (proven in [4]) that reveal the intensional meaning of these two relational operations:

THEOREM I: Let A and A' be a-relations such that I(A) = K and I(A') = K'. Then I(J(A, A')) = K ∧ K'. Similarly, E(K ∧ K') = J(A, A'). (Proven in [4].)

In other words, extensional join corresponds to intensional conjunction. For example, the a-relation in Figure 3, whose intension is (x ∨ y) ∧ (y $\equiv$ z), is the join of the two a-relations in Figures 1 and 2, whose intensions are x ∨ y and y $\equiv$ z.

THEOREM II: Let A and A' be a-relations on S and S' such that S' ⊆ S and A' = P(A, S'). Then:

    a.   I(A) → I(A')
    b.   If K is an assertion such that I(A) → K, then I(A') → K.
(Proven in [4].)

Thus, extensional projection corresponds to intensional inference. For example, the projection of the a-relation in Figure 3 - whose intension is (x ∨ y) ∧ (y $\equiv$ z) - along the scheme {x, z} is the a-relation in Figure 4, the intension of which is x ∨ z. This is the most that we can infer about the relationship between x and z, given that (x ∨ y) ∧ (y $\equiv$ z) is true, without any information about the value of y. Of course, if we knew the value of y, then we could state an additional assertion. For example, if y were known to be false, then the first and third rows of Figure 3 would be eliminated, and we could assert that x is true and z is false.

Although we have not yet presented the entire relational algebra as applied to assertions, it should be apparent that there are three differences between the relational views of data and of assertions. First, the notion of functional dependency does not arise in assertion management - for example, if x → y, y is not functionally dependent on x. Second, the tuples in an a-relation are not time varying - that is, they are not individually updated. Thus, notions of storage anomalies and normal forms do not arise in assertion management. (However, another important issue in information organization, that of lossy and lossless joins, does arise and has been addressed in [4].) Third, a-relations have an elegant intensional representation (i.e., the sentential calculus), which makes it possible to interpret the relational algebra in logical terms - thus, making it possible to establish a correspondence between the algebras of these two important types of information. We have begun to do this in this section, and will complete it in the two following sections.

III. THE RELATIONAL ALGEBRA OF ASSERTIONS

We are now ready to present and interpret the full complement of the operations that make up the relational algebra of relational database theory [8, 9] in the context of a-relations. The operations are as follows:

1. Projection and join
2. Selection
3. The set operations of union, intersection, difference, and complementation
4. Renaming
5. Division

The first of these was presented in the previous section of this paper, and the fourth is trivial. The second and third are straightforward, once their meaning is clear. The fifth, relational division, is more complicated, and we will examine it separately in the following section.

Selection is accomplished by limiting the tuples in a relation to those that meet the restrictions of a logical expression containing assignments or comparisons (i.e., equalities or inequalities) - such as $(x = 1)$, $(x \geq y)$, $(x = 1$ AND $y = 0)$, etc. Strictly speaking, inequalities do not apply to assertions, since the domain {1, 0} is not an integer domain; it could be denoted {true, false}. However, 0 and 1 are sometimes in the domains of both integer and logic operators (such as in APL), and we will allow that interpretation here. We now present the intensional analogue of extensional selection:

THEOREM III: Let A be an a-relation, and let k be a logical expression containing assignments or comparisons. Let K be an assertion derived from k as follows: $x = 1$ is replaced by $\underline{x}$, $x = 0$ is replaced by $\overline{x}$, $x < y$ is replaced by $x \wedge y$, $x \leq y$ is replaced by $x \rightarrow y$, $x = y$ is replaced by $x \equiv y$, AND is replaced by $\wedge$, OR is replaced by $\vee$, and NOT is replaced by negation. Then the intension of the selection of A, restricted by k, is $I(A) \wedge K$.

PROOF: The tuples that remain after a selection operation has been performed on a relation are those that satisfy exactly two criteria. First, they must have been in the original relation. Therefore, their intension can be true only if $I(R)$ is true. Second, they must satisfy the selection criteria. Therefore, their intension can be true only if a logic statement equivalent to the selection criteria is true. The rules for deriving K from k ensure that this logic statement is K. Therefore, the intension of R selected by k is $I(R) \wedge K$.

The set operations of union (denoted $\cup$), intersection (denoted $\cap$), and difference (denoted $\setminus$), are performed on the tuples of relations that are union compatible - that is, on the tuples of relations that have the same schemes. The complement of a relation, which is denoted by the same symbol (A) as the negation operator, is the

set of tuples in the Cartesian product of the domains of the relation that are not the relation itself. The correspondence between intensional logical operations on assertions and extensional set operations on relational tuples is demonstrated in:

THEOREM IV: If A and A' are union-compatible a-relations with intensions $K = I(A)$ and $K' = I(A')$, then:

1. $I(A \cup A') = K \vee K'$
2. $I(A \cap A') = K \wedge \underline{K'}$
3. $I(\underline{A} \setminus \underline{A'}) = K \wedge \overline{K'}$
4. $I(\underline{A}) = \overline{K}$

PROOF: Since the tuples in an a-relation correspond to the sets of values of the scheme assertions for which the intension of the relation is true, the union (resp., intersection) of two sets of tuples corresponds to the sets of values for which both (resp., either) of the intensions are true, and hence, to $K \vee K'$ (resp., $K \wedge K'$). Similarly, since the tuples in the complement of an a-relation correspond to the sets of values of the scheme assertions for which the intension of the relation is false, complementation corresponds to negation and set subtraction to intersection and negation.

The fourth operation, renaming, consists of changing the name of a varible to another name (i.e., changing x to w) in the labelled column of an a-relation. This corresponds to making the same change in the intension of the a-relation.

IV. RELATIONAL DIVISION

Relational division is a more complex operation and is defined as follows:

DEFINITION V: Let A and A' be a-relations defined over S and S', where $S' \subset S$. A will be called dividend and A' will be called the divisor. Q is the quotient of A and A', written $Q = A \div A'$, if Q is defined over $S \setminus S'$ and the tuples in Q are the largest subset of $P(A, S \setminus S')$ such that $J(Q, A') \subseteq A$. The remainder, R, is defined by $R = A \setminus J(Q, A')$. We note that Q and R are a-relations, and that $R \div A'$ is a null relation over S.

Before describing relational division in the context of assertion management and presenting its intensional interpretation, we illustrate its use in relational database management. Consider the data relation in Figure 5, which contains the names of three programmers and the names of the programming languages in which they are skilled. We will divide this by the relation in Figure 6, which is defined over the skill attribute and contains two tuples, corresponding to two elements in the language domain - LISP and PROLOG. The quotient, displayed in Figure 7, is defined over all of the attributes (i.e., NAME) not in the divisor. The quotient is the largest subset of the NAME elements for which there is both a LISP and a PROLOG tuple in the dividend. In other words, it consists of the names of all people who program both in LISP and in PROLOG. The remainder is a subset of the dividend; it consists of all tuples except JONES's LISP and PROLOG records. We note that if JONES were also skilled in another language (e.g., APL), then a ⟨JONES, APL⟩ tuple would appear in the dividend and also in the remainder. Finally, we note that there is no person in the remainder who programs in both LISP and PROLOG (although BROWN programs in LISP).

When the dividend and the divisor are a-relations, the interpretation is the same, except that it can be represented intensionally. Let the dividend be the a-relation in Figure 9, which is the extension of $(x \vee y) \wedge (y \equiv z)$. (This is the same as Figure 3.) Let the divisor be the a-relation in Figure 10, which is the extension of z (i.e., the statement that z is true). The quotient, given in Figure 11, is the extension of y. (In other words, y is true and nothing is known about x.) The intensional interpretation of the quotient operation is that y is the most general assertion that one can make about the relationship between x and y such that if the assertion is true and z is true, then $((x \vee y) \wedge (y \equiv z))$ is true (i.e., $I(A)$ is true). By the most general assertion we mean the one with the largest number of tuples in its extension. We now demonstrate formally these properties of a-relational division:

THEOREM V: Let A, A', Q, and R be a-relations over S, S' ⊆ S, S \ S', and S, respectively, such that $Q = A \div A'$ and $R = A \setminus J(Q, A')$. Then:

1. $((I(Q) \wedge I(A')) \vee I(R)) \equiv I(A)$
2. $I(R \div A') = 0$

PROOF: #1 holds because (1) the tuples in A consist of both the tuples in J(Q, A') and the tuples in R, and (2) the union of the tuples in two union-compatible relations corresponds to an intensional OR (∨) operation (Theorem IV-1). #2 holds because R ÷ A' is the null relation over S - that is, all of the rows in the truth table for I(R) result in the value "false."

From Theorem V one can derive:

COROLLARY I: If the conditions of Theorem V obtain, then:

1. $(I(Q) \wedge I(A')) \rightarrow I(A)$
2. $I(R) \rightarrow I(A)$

For example, in the example of Figures 9-12, we have:

1. $I(Q) = y$
2. $I(A') = z$
3. $I(A) = (x \vee y) \wedge (y \equiv z)$
4. $I(R) = x \wedge y \wedge z$

and therefore,

5. $(y \wedge z) \rightarrow ((x \vee y) \wedge (y \equiv z))$
6. $(x \wedge y \wedge z) \rightarrow ((x \vee y) \wedge (y \equiv z))$

V. A RELATIONAL VIEW OF INFORMATION RESOURCES

We stated at the beginning of this page that an important purpose of the research being done on decision support systems is to develop a theory of information management that is as independent as possible of the way in which the information is stored and processed. A promising framework for such a theory is one based on the mathematics of relations, and this has been applied to stored data, decision models, and assertions.

Three principal issues have been investigated as a part of this theoretical development [3]. The first is the nature of the relations themselves - that is, whether they are stored or virtual. The tuples in a stored relation exist in stored form, whereas those in a virtual relation do not exist in stored form but are generated on demand by a stored algorithm. Thus, data relations are stored, and model and assertion relations are virtual. The concept of functional dependency is important in data relations, where the content attributes are functionally dependent on the key attributes, and in model relations, where the output attributes are functionally dependent on the input attributes. This concept does not arise in assertion management. For example, $x \rightarrow y$ (i.e., x implies y) does not mean that y is functionally dependent on x.

The second issue is that of information organization. There are two sub-issues here, the first concerning normal forms and the second concerning lossy joins. The need for normal forms (i.e., permissible assignments of attributes to relations) arise in data management because of storage anomalies - problems that can arise in adding, deleting, or changing individual tuples in a stored relation. By projecting relations into the appropriate normal forms, certain storage anomalies are eliminated. The need for normal forms also arises in model management, but for different reasons. Since model relations are virtual, tuples are not individually updated, and no storage anomalies exist. If a parameter in a model is changed, then the entire virtual relation is changed, but this does not lead to storage anomalies. However, other anomalies, called processing anomalies, are found in model management. These anomalies arise from the ways in which models are used, rather than the ways in which they are maintained, and they lead to normal forms that are similar, but not identical, to the normal forms of relational database theory. The sub-issue of normal forms does not arise in relational assertion management.

The other sub-issue is that of lossy joins. This occurs when a relation is projected into a set of two or more smaller relations in such a way that information is lost. This will occur when the join of the smaller relations is not equal to the original relation, and it means that information about individual attributes or the relationships between some of the attributes has been lost. This a problem in relational database theory, and substantial efforts have been directed toward addressing it. It is not a problem in relational model management, because the output attributes of models in a model bank are pairwise disjoint. That is, if one model in a set of models used to respond to a query has net income as an output attribute, then no other model in the same set can have net income as an output attribute: there can be only one net income. It has been shown that this eliminates the lossy join problem. The lossy join problem can arise in relational assertion management, but a simple necessary and sufficient condition for its existence has been identified [4].

The third issue is the criteria for completeness of query languages for relational information structures. It has been shown the that linear (e.g., SQL) and graphical (e.g., QBE) language structures that have been developed for database management can also be applied, with modification, to model management. A linear structure for assertion management would be a sequence of extensional operations of the type specified in Sections II-IV above, and a graphical structure is given in [4].

Finally, we note that the type of information used to support decision making is not confined to data, models, and assertions. It may also include data analysis procedures (e.g., statistical packages), text files, sensory information, knowledge bases, and human information resources (e.g., people, committees, departments, etc.). This more global view of information is being addressed by the emerging discipline of information resources management (IRM) [6, 7], and it has been suggested that a relational framework may be useful in IRM [1]. There are two principal differences between a relational framework for IRM and the more restricted relational framework summarized above. First, a relational framework for IRM must allow for unnormalized relations, so that relations can be among the inputs and outputs of other relations. For example, one of the inputs to a statistical analysis procedure (a virtual relation) is a data file (a stored relation). Similarly, if a human information resource (e.g., a committee) creates another such resource (e.g., a subcommittee), then one of the outputs of the former relation is the latter relation. Second, it will probably be necessary to enhance the relational approach with a semantic extension, such as the entity-relationship approach, in order to facilitate the process of information resource organization. Although it is not clear where this is leading, it appears possible to develop a comprehensive framework for managing many of the variety of information resources used in decision support.

VI. CONCLUSION

Decision makers are being given access to an increasing variety of information sources - such as stored data, decision models, and expert knowledge - and it is important that a common framework be developed for as many of these sources as possible. We have suggested elsewhere that the established relational framework for stored data be enlarged to encompass decision models [3], and we suggest in [4] and here that it be further enlarged to encompass logic statements as well.

ACKNOWLEDGEMENTS

This research was supported by the Dean's Fund for Faculty Research of the Owen Graduate School of Management of Vanderbilt University.

REFERENCES

[1] Blanning, Robert W., "An Entity-Relationship Framework for Information Resource Management," Proceedings of the First International Conference on Information Resource Management, The Hague, May 1988 (also to appear in Information & Management, 1989).

[2] Blanning, Robert W., "A Relational Theory of Model Management," in: Decision Support Systems: Theory and Application, ed. by Clyde W. Holsapple and Andrew B. Whinston, Springer-Verlag, Berlin, 1987, pp. 19-53.

[3] Blanning, Robert W., "A Relational Framework for Information Management," in: Decision Support Systems: A Decade in Perspective, ed. by Ephraim R. McLean and Henk G. Sol, North-Holland, Amsterdam, 1986, pp. 25-40.

[4] Blanning, Robert W., "A Relational Framework for Assertion Management," Decision Support Systems, Vol. 1, No. 2, April 1985, pp. 167-172.

[5] Hilbert, D. and Ackerman, W., Principles of Mathematical Logic, Chelsea, New York, 1950.

[6] Horton, Forest W., Information Systems Management: Concepts and Cases, Association for Systems Management, Cleveland, 1979.

[7] Khosrowpour, Medhi, "Preface," Information Resources Management Journal, Vol. 1, No. 1, Fall 1988.

[8] Maier, David, The Theory of Relational Databases, Computer Science Press, Rockville, 1983.

[9] Yang, Chao-Chih, Relational Databases, Prentice-Hall, Englewood Cliffs, 1986.

x	y
1	1
1	0
0	1

FIGURE 1: The Extension of x ∨ y

y	z
1	1
0	0

FIGURE 2: The Extension of y ≡ z

x	y	z
1	1	1
1	0	0
0	1	1

FIGURE 3: The Join of Figures 1 and 2

x	z
1	1
1	0
0	1

FIGURE 4: The Projection of Figure 3 along {x, z}

NAME	SKILL
SMITH	SMALLTALK
JONES	LISP
JONES	PROLOG
BROWN	LISP

FIGURE 5: Data Example – The Dividend (A)

SKILL
LISP
PROLOG

FIGURE 6: Data Example – The Divisor (A')

NAME
JONES

FIGURE 7: Data Example – The Quotient (Q)

NAME	SKILL
SMITH	SMALLTALK
BROWN	LISP

FIGURE 8: Data Example – The Remainder (R)

x	y	z
1	1	1
1	0	0
0	1	1

FIGURE 9: Assertion Example – The Dividend (A)

z
1

FIGURE 10: Assertion Example – The Divisor (A')

x	y
1	1
0	1

FIGURE 11: Assertion Example – The Quotient (Q)

x	y	z
1	0	0

FIGURE 12: Assertion Example – The Remainder (R)

Reusing Structured Models via Model Integration

Arthur M. Geoffrion

Western Management Science Institute, University of California, Los Angeles

Abstract

This paper begins with a review of reusability and modularity ideas from the software engineering literature, most of which are applicable to the modeling context. Many features of structured modeling support reusability and modularity, and these are noted. The main focus of the paper, however, is on achieving reusability and modularity via the integration of two or more model schemas. A five step approach for integrating schemas written in structured modeling language (SML) is proposed for this purpose. Examples are given to illustrate this approach, and the pros and cons of structured modeling for reuse are discussed at some length.

Acknowledgments

I gratefully acknowledge the helpful comments of Gordon Bradley, Dan Dolk, Sergio Maturana, Laurel Neustadter, Yao-Chuan Tsai, and Fernando Vicuña. Supported partially by the National Science Foundation, the Office of Naval Research, and the Navy Personnel Research and Development Center (San Diego). The views contained in this paper are those of the author and not of the sponsoring agencies.

"Reusability" and "modularization" concepts play a key role in the part of software engineering that is concerned with improving software development productivity. The analogies between programming and modeling suggest that some of what software engineers have learned about these concepts might be adapted to improve model development productivity.

Reusability need not involve model integration, but integration is an important way in which reuse can occur in the context of modeling. Reuse via model integration is the central focus of this paper.

In particular, we treat this topic from the viewpoint of *structured modeling* (Geoffrion [1987] [1989a]). It would be impossible to give an adequate introduction to structured modeling within the confines of this paper, and so we must presume prior knowledge on the part of the reader. In a nutshell, however, one can say that structured modeling aims to provide a formal conceptual framework of considerable generality for modeling, within the broader task of laying the foundation for a new generation of modeling environments. The framework uses a hierarchically organized, partitioned, and attributed acyclic graph to represent the semantic as well as mathematical structure of a model. A language called SML has been designed and implemented to support this framework (Geoffrion [1991], [1992]).

The organization of this paper as follows. Section 1 reviews reusability and modularity ideas from the software engineering literature for the benefit of readers who might not be familiar with these ideas. Section 2 presents a procedure for integrating the general structure of two distinct models written in SML. Section 3 and a series of examples in Appendices 1-3 illustrate this approach in simple but instructive settings. The last section discusses some of the issues that arise when one considers structured modeling in the context of the ideas presented in the prior sections.

Papers by other authors on model integration include Blanning [1986], Bradley and Clemence [1988], Kottemann and Dolk [1992], Liang [1986], Muhanna and Pick [1988], Murphy et al. [1990], Tsai [1987], and Zeigler [1984] (Chaps. 4, 5). Each adds a dimension not treated here. For example, Kottemann and Dolk [1990] addresses the integration of model manipulation operations, whereas we limit consideration to model definition alone. For a more general discussion of model integration, see Geoffrion [1989b]. That paper distinguishes several different kinds of model integration and assesses the strengths and weaknesses of structured modeling in support of each.

1. Selected Ideas from Software Engineering

Reusability is a prominent topic in software engineering because being able to use previously created and (presumably) debugged code saves work that is expensive and for which skilled personnel are in short supply. Advantages accrue not only to the initial development activity, but also to the very important activities of maintenance and modification. Moreover, code is not the only thing that can be reused; it can be advantageous also to reuse data, program and system designs and architecture, specifications, test plans, and so on. See Freeman [1987] for an excellent collection of readings on reusability.

As might be expected, different authors focus on different aspects of reusability. Here is a selected sample of points and opinions.

One leading expert on software engineering cites "reusing components" as one of six primary options for improving software productivity (Boehm [1987]). To Boehm, reusability is most closely related to two things: libraries of software components (like mathematical and statistical routines) and 4GL/application generators (like Focus and Nomad). The justification for the second item appears to be that various of the software components constituting a 4GL processor or application generator are reused at each application in place of writing a program in a traditional language. Reuse is by reconfiguring the preexisting components into a relatively special purpose software system, or by using them in lieu of a special purpose software system by "executing" a high level specification of functionality.

Near the end of the article, Boehm offers this opinion:

> "Thus, for the 1995-2000 time frame, we can see that two major classes of opportunities for improving software productivity exist: providing better support systems for broad-domain applications, involving fully integrated methods, environments, and modern programming languages such as Ada; and extending the number and size of the domains for which we can use domain specific fourth generation languages and application generators."

If transposed from the context of programming to the context of modeling, this view is very much in the spirit of structured modeling.

Another view of reusability is provided by Balzer, Cheatham, and Green [1983]. Their basic approach is that software should be produced by end users who write formal specifications that can be transformed more or less automatically by computer into the desired software. Maintenance would not be done on source code, as is the usual case today, but rather on the formal specification; revised code would be regenerated as needed. This automation-based paradigm for software development admittedly is idealistic: the necessary technology is not yet adequate for many applications. Thus the authors accept skilled intervention with respect to strategic implementation decisions. However, they argue that both the documentation of these decisions (they call this the "development") and their execution should be automated. The authors claim important advantages for the automation-based paradigm, among which is software reusability. To quote:

> "Software libraries — with the exception of mathematical subroutine libraries — have failed because the wrong things are in those libraries. They are filled with implementations, which necessarily contain many arbitrary decisions. The chance that such an implementation is precisely right for some later application is exceedingly small. Instead, we should be placing specifications and their recorded development in libraries. Then, when a module is to be reused, the specification can be modified appropriately — that is, maintained — and its development changed accordingly. Thus, maintenance of both the specification and its development becomes the basis of reuse, rather than a fortuitous exact match with a previously stored implementation."

There seems to be a strong connection between the automation-based paradigm and the 4GL/application generators advocated by Boehm: the latter can be viewed as domain-specific examples of the former.

A third article discussing reusability, Kartashev and Kartashev [1986], takes the position that the reuse of software components is one of only two main options for reducing software costs. Within this option, two approaches are noted:

"...The *composition approach* provides for some abstract initial representation of reused program modules, then the use of a composition technique such as parameterized programming, the UNIX pipe mechanism, or special specification techniques to construct a complex program from reusable modules with the interfaces specified by the composition technique. The second approach involves the creation of libraries of reused components that do not need preliminary specifications to be connected to each other."

Goguen [1986] develops the first approach in detail. He gives this brief and tantalizing synopsis at the outset:

"...The goal is to make programming significantly easier, more reliable, and cost effective by *reusing* previous code and programming experience to the greatest extent possible. Suggestions given here include: systematic (but limited) use of semantics, by explicitly attaching *theories* (which give semantics, either formal or informal) to software components with *views* (which describe semantically correct interconnections at component interfaces); use of *generic* entities, to maximize reusability; a distinction between *horizontal* and *vertical* composition; use of a *library interconnection language*, called LIL, to assemble large programs from existing entities; support for different levels of formality in both documentation and validation; and facilitation of program understanding by animating abstract data types and module interfaces."

Several of these ideas have analogues in structured modeling.

Goguen's most intriguing ideas, and his main focus, are those relating to LIL. The structured modeling analogue of LIL would be a language for integrating models (schemas or even fully specified structured models). No such language presently exists for structured modeling. In the modeling literature more generally, the only efforts I know of along these lines are the contributions by Bradley and Clemence [1988] and by Muhanna and Pick [1988]. Since such a language could greatly facilitate model reuse through integration, this is a potentially fruitful area for research. Some inspiration might be found in the literature on module interconnection languages, which has been surveyed by Prieto-Diaz and Neighbors [1986].

A topic in software engineering closely related to reusability is *modularization*. The connection is that well modularized code is easier to reuse than code that is poorly modularized. Presumably, the same statement is true of models. See, for example, the classic paper by Parnas [1972], which cites these benefits for a modular style of programming:

•shorter development time is possible because different people can work simultaneously on separate program modules;
•evolutionary flexibility is improved because drastic changes can be made to one module
without impacting the others;
•understandability is improved because it should be possible to study the system one module at a time.

That paper champions information hiding as a criterion that often leads to better modularization than more traditional criteria. That is, each module "hides some design decision from the rest of the system," with its interfaces crafted "to reveal as little as possible about its inner working." The design decisions worth modularizing are those which are difficult or likely to change.

Modularization ideas play a major role in the thinking of many leading authors in the area of program and system design. For example, Yourdon and Constantine [1979] describe the central focus of their book as follows:

"Our concern is with the architecture of programs and systems. How should a large system be broken into modules? *Which* modules? Which ones should be subordinate to which? How do we know when we have a 'good' choice of modules? and, more important, How do we know when we have a 'bad' one? What information should be passed between modules? Should a module be able to access data other than that which it needs to know in order to accomplish its task? How should the modules be 'packaged' into efficient executable units in a typical computer?" [page xvi]

Much of the book's discussion of such questions can be translated easily into provocative positions about analogous questions in modeling. These positions deserve to be studied.

One of the most fashionable manifestations of modularization and related ideas in the service of reusability (and other popular goals) is *object oriented programming*. A particularly vigorous presentation from this point of view is found in the book by Cox [1987]. He argues that it is possible to develop software counterparts of integrated circuits; counterparts in that they can be reused readily by programmers much as integrated circuits are reused readily by hardware designers. Here are two intriguing passages to provide a taste of Cox's viewpoint:

"Objects are tightly encapsulated and thus relatively independent of their environment. They can be designed, developed, tested, and documented as stand-alone units without knowledge of any particular application, and then stockpiled for distribution and reuse in many different circumstances. A reusable module acquires value unto itself, while the value of application dependent code has no value beyond that of the application as a whole. It can be tested and documented to much higher standards than has been done in the past." [page 26]

"These concepts, working together, put reusability at the center of the programming process. Encapsulation raises fire walls around the objects within a system, so that if they change, other parts of the system can remain unchanged. Inheritance does the converse, by spreading decisions implemented in generic classes automatically to each of their subclasses. The net effect is making libraries of reusable code, called Software IC libraries, a central feature of the system building shop." [page 91]

This completes the review of reusability and modularization ideas from the software engineering literature.

We turn now to a step-by-step approach for integrating two structured modeling schemas. This is one way in which reuse can occur in modeling. Each participating schema can be viewed as a module.

2. A Procedure for Model Intergration

This section explains a procedure for integrating the general structure of two models. Let two SML model schemas be given.

By necessity, we presume that the reader is acquainted with the basic technical terms of SML (Geoffrion [1992]). For example, the reader should know that an SML *schema* represents a model's general structure; that *Schema Properties* are context sensitive syntax rules associated with the schema; and that it falls to SML's *elemental detail tables* to instantiate a schema to a specific model instance. In what follows, a "structural change" is any change other than simple renaming or changing an interpretation.

Step 1. Customize the two schemas to the roles that they will play in the integrated model, but do not violate the syntax or Schema Properties of SML. For example, achieve consistency in units of measurement.

      a. Make any appropriate structural changes.

b. Customize the genus names, module names (including the root module name), key phrases, and interpretations of each schema as appropriate. Often this helps to reduce the amount of work that must be done at Step 3a.

Step 2. Make technical preparations for joining the two schemas, but do not violate the syntax or Schema Properties of SML.

a. Anticipate duplicate genus names, module names, key phrases, indices, functional and multivalued dependency names, and symbolic parameter stems, that will occur at Step 3, and eliminate all conflicts.

b. Usually there is at least one pair of genera, one from each schema, that needs to be "merged." Identify all such pairs. Make ready for the merges by making both genus paragraphs as similar as possible for each merging genus pair. Sometimes they can be made identical, but not always. Structural changes are allowed.

c. Optionally, put the "inputs" and "outputs" of each schema in special modules. This might not be possible to do in a fully satisfactory way. Structural changes are allowed.

Step 3. Join the two schemas. This step can cause Schema Property violations.

a. Concatenate the two schemas. Choose an order that preserves monotonicity of the modular structure if possible.

b. Continue the work begun in Step 2b, if necessary, until each merging genus pair is identical. Drop the second genus replicate for each merging genus pair.

c. Make any other structural changes necessary for proper joining.

Step 4. Revise the integrated schema as necessary, structurally or non-structurally, to restore satisfaction of all Schema Properties. For example, it might be necessary to revise the modular structure so as to restore monotonicity.

Step 5. Optionally, make any desired final cosmetic or structural changes, being sure to observe the syntax and Schema Properties of SML.

The next section presents an illustrative application of this approach. Actually, the approach is carried out three times in a cumulative way that culminates in the integration of four distinct models.
Additional illustrative applications are given in the first three appendices. They apply the approach to three simple situations. The first integrates a forecasting model with the classical transportation model. The second integrates the transportation model with a multi-item economic order quantity model. The third integrates two transportation models to produce a two-echelon transshipment model.
All examples treat model schemas, not specific model instances. It would be worth examining these examples at the level of fully detailed instances, but that is not done here.

3. An Example

This section illustrates the approach of Section 2 with a small but richly instructive example that has been used by several authors. The example is due to Blanning, who discusses model integration at some length in several of his papers (e.g., Blanning [1986], Blanning [1987]). A recurring example in his papers is the "CORP" model, which has been discussed also by other authors (e.g., Muhanna [1987]).
One of the interesting things about this model is that it can be viewed as four interconnected submodels. The development of this section explains how the appropriate interconnections can be accomplished by applying the integration procedure of Section 2 to SML representations of the component submodels.

29

The CORP model is discussed at length in Geoffrion [1988] because although it appears to be cyclic, closer inspection re veals that it need not be. The Third Formulation therein repairs certain anomalies of the original model and presents it as a genuine SML schema. That is the version used here. It can be considered to be what the final integrated model should look like, except perhaps for its overly simple modular structure.

Original Component Models

There are four component models. The first estimates demand.

&MKT DEMAND ESTIMATION

> **PROD /pe/** There is a certain PRODUCT.
>
> **P (PROD) /a/ : Real+** The PRODUCT has a unit PRICE.
>
> **V (P) /f/ ; 800000 - 44000 * P** The PRODUCT has a sales VOLUME given by a certain linear demand function in terms of PRICE.

The second model analyzes markup. It is the only component model that differs significantly from the corresponding one of Blanning. It does not calculate **P** from the values of **M**, **V**, and **E**. However, that value of **P** can be calculated by a solver for the satisfaction problem of finding **P** such that **M_VAR** is zero.

&MAR MARKUP ANALYSIS

> **PROD /pe/** There is a certain PRODUCT.
>
> **P (PROD) /va/ : Real+** The PRODUCT has a unit PRICE.
>
> **V (PROD) /a/ : Real+** The PRODUCT has a sales VOLUME.
>
> **E (PROD) /a/ : Real+** There is a total MANUFACTURING EXPENSE associated with the PRODUCT.
>
> **M (P,V,E) /f/ ; P * V / E** The actual MARKUP for the PRODUCT is total revenue (PRICE times VOLUME) divided by total MANUFACTURING EXPENSE.
>
> **M_VAR (M) /f/ ; M - %M_TARGET** The actual MARKUP less a certain target value is called the MARKUP VARIANCE.

The third component model predicts manufacturing cost.

&MFG MANUFACTURING

> **PROD /pe/** There is a certain PRODUCT.
>
> **U (PROD) /a/ : Real+** The PRODUCT has a UNIT COST of manufacture, exclusive of fixed manufacturing expenses.
>
> **V (PROD) /a/ : Real+** The PRODUCT has a sales VOLUME.
>
> **E (U,V) /f/ ; 1000000 + U * V** The total MANUFACTURING EXPENSE for the PRODUCT is fixed manufacturing expenses plus UNIT COST times VOLUME.

The fourth model one calculates a key financial quantity.

&FIN <u>FINANCIAL</u>

     PROD /pe/ There is a certain <u>PRODUCT</u>.

     P (PROD) /a/ : Real+ The PRODUCT has a unit <u>PRICE</u>.

     V (PROD) /a/ : Real+ The PRODUCT has a sales <u>VOLUME</u>.

     E (PROD) /a/ : Real+ There is a total <u>MANUFACTURING EXPENSE</u> associated with the PRODUCT.

     N (P,V,E) /f/ ; P * V - E The <u>NET INCOME</u> obtained for the PRODUCT is total revenue (PRICE times VOLUME) less total MANUFACTURING EXPENSE.

It is straightforward to interconnect these four components into a single composite model provided there is sufficient compatibility among definitions that appear in more than one component model. This is a critical requirement whenever component models are to be interconnected. Care has been taken to ensure that it holds here. The following interconnection diagram is adapted from Muhanna and Pick [1986].

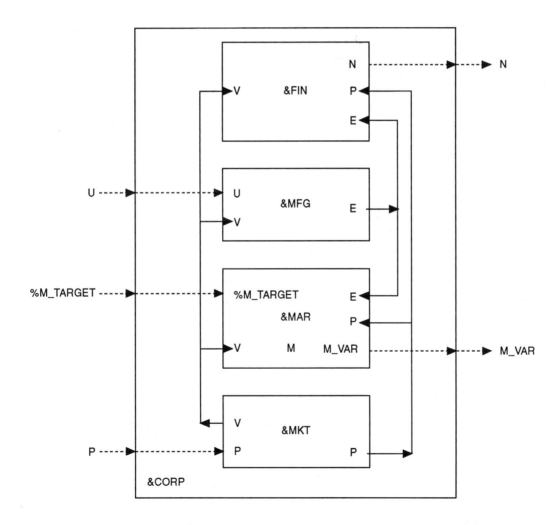

Note that **&MKT** has the task of supplying the value of **V** to the other three models, **&MFG** the value of **E** to two of the other models, **&FIN** the value of **N**, and **&MAR** the value of **M_VAR**. All these are obvious roles because **V, E, N,** and **M_VAR** are computed only once in the four models. **U** is not computed at all, and so must be supplied externally. The same is true for the symbolic parameter %M_TARGET. In addition, **&MKT** passes on the externally supplied value of **P**, which is modeled as a variable attribute, to the two other models that need it. This is one of two significant differences between the above diagram and the Muhanna-Pick diagram on which it is based; their diagram would receive and distribute **P** from **&MAR** (which they call "PRI") instead of from **&MKT**. If our diagram did it this way, it would be cyclic rather than acyclic. The second significant difference is noted in the next paragraph.

Thus **&CORP** can be viewed as having three inputs, **U**, %M_TARGET, and **P**, and two outputs, **N** and **M_VAR**. If a value of **P** is desired such that **M_VAR** is zero, then finding such a value is the task of a solver external to **&CORP**. Please note that this viewpoint differs from that of Blanning and Muhanna, who both appear to view **&CORP** itself (as a model) as bearing the responsibility for finding such a value. I believe that such a viewpoint confuses the notion of model and solver.

There is nothing to prevent the four component models from being interconnected per the diagram by some mechanism underlined external to the SML notational system. Perhaps a capability of this sort should be provided by a modeling environment based on structured modeling; a formal interconnection language would be one possibility. If so, however, some defenses are needed to detect and repair definitional incompatibilities when similar model elements appear in multiple component models. (This is not unlike the problems that arise in information systems when distinct data bases are to be integrated with one another; see, e.g., Batini, Lenzerini, and Navathe [1986]).

That is not the approach taken here. In what follows, we integrate the four models by stages into a single composite SML schema. First, **&MKT** and **&MAR** will be integrated. Then **&MFG** will be folded in. Finally, **&FIN** will be integrated with the result of the previous two integrations.

It is evident from the partial ordering of the component models (such an ordering is obvious from the interconnection diagram) that it would be wiser to interchange the integration order of **&MAR** and **&MFG**, for the former depends on the latter. Wiser in the sense that monotonicity would be easier to maintain. We choose the less favorable order to help dispel the reader's possible suspicion that choosing the order of integration requires divine guidance.

Integrate &MKT and &MAR

Step 1. Null.

Step 2a. Null.

Step 2b. The merging genus pairs are PROD, P, and V in &MKT and, respectively, PROD, P, and V in &MAR. The PROD pair already has identical genus paragraphs. The P paragraphs differ only in that the first is /a/ and the second is /va/; make the first identical to the second. The V paragraphs differ substantially; make the second identical to the first (since the second paragraph will be dropped at Step 3b, it is not truly necessary to make this change).

Step 2c. Omit.

Step 3a. Concatenate in the order &MKT, &MAR. Call the new module &MKT_MAR.

Step 3b. Drop the PROD, P, and V paragraphs from &MAR.

Step 3c. Null.

Step 4. Null.

Step 5. Omit.

The result is as follows.

&MKT_MAR

&MKT <u>DEMAND ESTIMATION</u>

PROD /pe/ There is a certain <u>PRODUCT</u>.

P (PROD) /va/ : Real+ The PRODUCT has a unit <u>PRICE</u>.

V (P) /f/ ; 800000 - 44000 * P The PRODUCT has a sales <u>VOLUME</u> given by a certain linear demand function in terms of PRICE.

&MAR <u>MARKUP ANALYSIS</u>

E (PROD) /a/ : Real+ There is a total <u>MANUFACTURING EXPENSE</u> associated with the PRODUCT.

M (P,V,E) /f/ ; P * V / E The actual <u>MARKUP</u> for the PRODUCT is total revenue (PRICE times VOLUME) divided by total MANUFACTURING EXPENSE.

M_VAR (M) /f/ ; M - %M_TARGET The actual <u>MARKUP</u> less a certain target value is called the <u>MARKUP VARIANCE</u>.

Integrate &MKT_MAR and &MFG

Step 1. Null.

Step 2a. Null.

Step 2b. The merging genus pairs are PROD, V, and E in &MKT_MAR and, respectively, PROD, V, and E in &MFG. The PROD paragraphs already are identical. The V paragraphs differ substantially; the second needs to be made like the first, but this cannot be accomplished until Step 3b because &MFG has no P genus. The E paragraphs also differ substantially; the first needs to be made like the second, but this cannot be accomplished until Step 3b because &MKT_MAR has no U genus. Thus no changes at all are made at this substep.

Step 2c. Omit.

Step 3a. Concatenate in the order &MKT_MAR, &MFG. Call the new module &MKT_MAR_MFG.

Step 3b. Drop the second PROD paragraph. Make the second V paragraph identical to the first, then drop the second (obviously, it is not truly necessary to change V before dropping it). Make the first E paragraph identical to the second, then drop the second one.

Step 3c. Null.

Step 4. There is only one Schema Property violation, the one caused by the forward reference to U by the E paragraph. Cure it by moving the &MFG module to the position between &MKT and &MAR.

Step 5. Move the E paragraph to the position immediately after the U paragraph. This is more in keeping with the scopes of &MAR and &MFG. Change the modular structure (here we do not bother to list the genera)

	&MKT_MAR_MFG		&MKT_MFG_MAR
	&MKT_MAR		&MKT
from	&MKT	to	&MFG
	&MFG		&MAR.
	&MAR		

The result is as follows.

&MKT_MFG_MAR

&MKT DEMAND ESTIMATION

PROD /pe/ There is a certain <u>PRODUCT</u>.

P (PROD) /va/ : Real+ The PRODUCT has a unit <u>PRICE</u>.

V (P) /f/ ; 800000 - 44000 * P The PRODUCT has a sales <u>VOLUME</u> given by a certain linear demand function in terms of PRICE.

&MFG MANUFACTURING

U (PROD) /a/ : Real+ The PRODUCT has a <u>UNIT COST</u> of manufacture, exclusive of fixed manufacturing expenses.

E (U,V) /f/ ; 1000000 + U * V The total <u>MANUFACTURING EXPENSE</u> for the PRODUCT is fixed manufacturing expenses plus UNIT COST times VOLUME.

&MAR MARKUP ANALYSIS

M (P,V,E) /f/ ; P * V / E The actual <u>MARKUP</u> for the PRODUCT is total revenue (PRICE times VOLUME) divided by total MANUFACTURING EXPENSE.

M_VAR (M) /f/ ; M - %M_TARGET The actual <u>MARKUP</u> less a certain target value is called the <u>MARKUP VARIANCE</u>.

Integrate &MKT_MFG_MAR and &FIN

Step 1. Null.

Step 2a. Null.

Step 2b. The merging genus pairs are PROD, P, V, and E in &MKT_MFG_MAR and, respectively, PROD, P, V, and E in &FIN. The PROD and P pairs already have identical genus paragraphs. The V paragraphs differ substantially; make the second identical to the first (since the second paragraph will be dropped at Step 3b, it is not truly necessary to make this change). The E paragraphs also differ substantially; the second needs to be made like the first, but this cannot be accomplished until Step 3b because &FIN has no U genus.

Step 2c. Omit.

Step 3a. Concatenate in the order &MKT_MFG_MAR, &FIN. Call the new module &CORP.

Step 3b. Drop the second PROD and P paragraphs. Drop the second V paragraph. Make the second E paragraph identical to the first, then drop the second one (obviously, it is not truly necessary to change E before dropping it).

Step 3c. Null.

Step 4. Null.

Step 5. Change the modular structure

	&CORP			&CORP
	&MKT_MFG_MAR			&MKT
from	&MKT	to		&MFG
	&MFG			&MAR
	&MAR			&FIN.
&FIN				

The result is as follows. Clearly it is consistent with the interconnection diagram given earlier. In fact, the diagram gives an accurate view of **&CORP**.

&CORP

&MKT DEMAND ESTIMATION

PROD /pe/ There is a certain <u>PRODUCT</u>.

P (PROD) /va/ : Real+ The PRODUCT has a unit <u>PRICE</u>.

V (P) /f/ ; 800000 - 44000 * P The PRODUCT has a sales <u>VOLUME</u> given by a certain linear demand function in terms of PRICE.

&MFG MANUFACTURING

U (PROD) /a/ : Real+ The PRODUCT has a <u>UNIT COST</u> of manufacture, exclusive of fixed manufacturing expenses.

E (U,V) /f/ ; 1000000 + U * V The total <u>MANUFACTURING EXPENSE</u> for the PRODUCT is fixed manufacturing expenses plus UNIT COST times VOLUME.

&MAR MARKUP ANALYSIS

M (P,V,E) /f/ ; P * V / E The actual <u>MARKUP</u> for the PRODUCT is total revenue (PRICE times VOLUME) divided by total MANUFACTURING EXPENSE.

M_VAR (M) /f/ ; M - %M_TARGET The actual MARKUP less a
certain target value is called the <u>MARKUP VARIANCE</u>.

&FIN FINANCIAL

N (P,V,E) /f/ ; P * V - E The <u>NET INCOME</u> obtained for the
PRODUCT is total revenue (PRICE times VOLUME) less total
MANUFACTURING EXPENSE.

Modular structure aside, **&CORP** is indeed exactly the same as the Third Formulation in Geoffrion
[1988], as predicted at the outset of this section.

This completes our application, thrice in succession, of the SML schema integration approach given in
Section 2.

4. Discussion

This section discusses reusability and related ideas sketched in Section 1 from the point of view of
structured modeling and the examples of model integration provided in Section 3 and the appendices.

**ISSUE: How well does structured modeling support "information hiding" and
"modularization"?**

Several features of structured modeling promote the objectives of information hiding and modularization:

(1) the core concept of hierarchical *modular structure* (Definition 12 of Geoffrion
[1989a]);

(2) the concepts of *views* and *modular outlines* (Definitions 20 and 23 of Geoffrion
[1989a]), and the closely related notion of using outline processor functions to conceal
and reveal different portions of modular structure depending on the intended audience
(Geoffrion [1991]);

(3) the sharp distinction between models and solvers (Section 2.3 of Geoffrion [1987])
helps to keep the internal concerns of each away from the other;

(4) model and solver libraries (Section 2.4 of Geoffrion [1987], and Geoffrion [1991])
achieve a kind of information hiding and modularization at the macroscopic level,
although some of the models in a model library could be relatively small reusable
fragments;

(5) the distinction in SML between the general structure of the schema and the detailed
data of the elemental detail tables enables users to be insulated from an excessive
volume of problem specifics when that is appropriate;

(6) the distinction in SML between the formal part and the interpretation of each genus
and module paragraph helps to insulate technical users from excessive problem domain
information, and non-technical users from excessive technical details; and

(7) each individual element in a structured model is, in effect, a module (e.g., the
details of the rule of a function element are totally localized).

These features might not go as far toward the support of information hiding and modularization as some
people might wish (cf. Muhanna and Pick [1986]). Certainly they do not go as far as the notion of a
"black box," taken here to mean a hiding or module so secure that special authority is required before one

is permitted to look inside it. Black boxes don't make sense in the context of modeling if integration is to be an important kind of reuse. The reason is that *almost any part of a model can serve as the focus of integration with another model.* Since integration is difficult or impossible if the focal part is inaccessibly hidden, it follows that virtually no part of a model can be black boxed without limiting the possibilities for integration. Obviously, to limit the possibilities for integration is to limit the possibilities for reuse.

To illustrate that almost any part of a model can serve as the focus of integration, consider the case of the classical transportation model. The development of Appendix 1 illustrates that the demand portion can be the focus of integration (with a forecasting model). The development of Appendix 2 illustrates that the transportation links can be the focus of integration (with an economic order quantity model). The development of Appendix 3 illustrates that the origins and their supply capacities can be the focus of integration (with another transportation model on the front end), and that the destinations and their demands can be the focus of integration (with another transportation model on the back end). It would be easy to develop other examples in which the transportation cost rate is the focus of integration with a freight rate estimation model, or in which the supply capacities are integrated with a more detailed supply capacity estimation model. Thus *every* part of the classical transportation model can serve as the focus of integration.

The most extreme form of information hiding is close to the idea of a "black box." How does one know whether a black box contains something that is truly consistent with what it is connected to? This is a particularly difficult worry in the realm of modeling, where model elements often have subtle definitions. The only way to know for sure is for the modeler to *inspect the contents of the box.* The contents alone suffice to explain the complete function of the box. **Unit of measurement**? Look inside to find out whether it is pounds, hundredweight, tons, or some other unit. **Demand point**? Look inside to find out whether it is an individual customer, all customers of a given class of trade in a certain area, etc. **Product**? Look inside to find out whether gray and black products are grouped, whether standard attachments are included with the basic product itself, and so on. **Cost**? Only a look inside will tell you whether it is book, actual, incremental, fully or partially loaded, etc. It would be grossly redundant to attach all this information to the "inputs" and "outputs" of a black boxed model, which would have to be done to accommodate all possible kinds of reuse.

This establishes that information hiding and modularization ought not to be taken to the black box extreme in the context of modeling. However, I accept these as criteria to help guide the practical use of features (1) through (4) listed above.

The foregoing discussion also establishes that *visibility of all model parts and explicit representation of their interconnections* are important objectives in support of reuse through integration.

Structured modeling comes close to making a fetish of these objectives. For example, the core concept of a *calling sequence* (Definition 6 of Geoffrion [1989a]) renders interconnections explicit, and the interpretation part of genus and module paragraphs in SML help to make all model parts visible to users who might find difficulty in reading the more formalistic parts of SML. "Input" modules or interfaces are not necessary because calling sequences in effect play this role. The generic calling sequence in SML does the same thing at the level of an entire genus. Nor are "output" modules or interfaces necessary in structured modeling, because any element or genus can be called by any other (subsequent) one that needs it as input.

The above comments have to do with how structured modeling relates to some of the ideas reviewed in Section 1. What about the model integration approach of Section 2? A brief answer is that Step 2c can increase the degree of modularization, but that Step 3b tends to decrease it by increasing the level of structural connectivity. It is not clear whether the latter effect is good or bad on balance, as its negative effects on maintainability and reusability are offset by positive effects on efficiency and avoidance of redundancy.

ISSUE: To what extent can the 5 step approach of Section 2 be automated?

The approach detailed in Section 2 and illustrated in Section 3 and Appendices 1-3 evidently is quite labor intensive. Certain standard capabilities of ordinary word processors, like the search/replace and block move features, have obvious uses for carrying out many of the substeps, but a higher degree of automation seems essential to facilitate model integration in general.

A tree-oriented editor, otherwise known as an "outliner," would be helpful. (We note that one is available in FW/SM, the prototype structured modeling implementation.) It would be much more helpful to employ a SML syntax-directed (structure) editor of the type developed in Vicuña [1990]: such an editor can detect or even preclude the violations of SML syntax or Schema Properties prohibited in Steps 1, 2, and 5, and can detect the violations that must be fixed at Step 4.

The diagnostic part of Step 2a lends itself particularly well to automation, as does — although it is more difficult — the diagnostic part of Step 4. Moreover, specialized search-and-replace capabilities for changing names, indices, and key phrases would be helpful for Steps 1b, 2a, and perhaps other steps.

A good implementation of all or even most of these possibilities would greatly facilitate the integration of structured model schemas. However, there will remain a certain amount of modeler's discretion that must be exercised at most of the steps. For example, only the modeler can decide at Step 1a exactly what structural changes are appropriate. Similar discretion is needed at the other steps, except for 3a, 2a (probably), and 3b (possibly). That discretion, incidentally, is what an integration language like that of Bradley and Clemence [1988] must express.

The last-mentioned reference, and Murphy, Stohr, and Ma [1990], are examples of recent work that offer intriguing prospects for automating some of what we have called "modeler's discretion" by more deeply exploiting the syntactic and semantic information available in (or attachable to) two SML schemas.

ISSUE: Within the context of SML, is it easier to reuse schemas per the integration approach of Section 2, or to build monolithic schemas from scratch?

I believe that reuse will be significantly more efficient than ground-up development in most cases. The amount of work that must be done with each approach in a particular application depends on the special facilities available in the modeling environment and the answer to the previous issue.

It should be possible to address this issue experimentally by counting operations (or actions, or deliberate decisions that must be made, or the amount of time consumed) for each approach for different modelers in a controlled setting. This is an attractive research topic.

There might be some modifications to SML that would reduce the total amount of work that must be done in reuse via model integration. For example, it can be a nuisance to have to avoid duplication of names for genera, modules, indices, functional and multi-valued dependencies, and symbolic parameter stems. It might be feasible to allow selected modules to limit the scope of the names defined within them, so that all external references would have to include the name of the defining module in order to gain access. Duplicate names could then be allowed because references could be unambiguous. Such an extension of SML would be well worth working out.

ISSUE: Within the context of FW/SM, the prototype structured modeling implementation, does structured modeling put the "right" things put in libraries in the sense of Balzer, Cheatham, and Green [1983]?

Structured modeling puts model schemas, elemental detail tables, and solvers in libraries.

A schema is an analog of a "specification" in the sense of Balzer, Cheatham, and Green [1983]. Putting a schema in a library seems appropriate to the extent that FW/SM facilitates revising it and integrating it with other schemas, provided that it is of possible future interest. See Sections 3.1 and 3.2 of Geoffrion [1987] and the appendices of this paper.

Putting not only a schema, but also associated elemental detail, in a library makes as much sense as putting just the schema in the library in some situations. One such occurs when the elemental detail is a commercial or private database with multiple potential applications, such as an air freight rate database that is of possible use in any logistics model involving air freight. Another such situation occurs when the aim is to set the stage for model integration within the context of the original application. Of course, there could not be many more than one reuse of elemental detail in this case.

There can be little question about the appropriateness of putting solvers in libraries, as the function they perform is useful over the entire class of models to which they are intended to apply.

While on the subject of libraries, it should be noted that a library is of little use if users cannot easily find out what is in it. This suggests that a structured model of the contents would be useful. More generally, it could be useful to have computer-based tools to support library management and access. One paper dealing specifically with libraries in the context of model management is Mannino, Greenberg, and Hong [1990]. Related papers in the context of software, such as Prieto-Diaz and Freeman [1987], might be inspirational.

ISSUE: In programming, the goals of reusability, maintainability, and modifiability usually are pursued by adhering to strict disciplines like structured programming, structured design, etc. that impose order on the otherwise chaotic process of programming. Similar goals for modeling would seem to imply the need for comparably strict disciplines that impose order on the otherwise chaotic process of modeling. Does structured modeling impose such discipline?

Yes, structured modeling does indeed impose a great deal of discipline on the modeler by comparison with what would be the case if, say, ordinary mathematics were used in the usual *ad hoc* fashion to express models. Consider:

- All definitional dependencies among model elements are supposed to be explicit (in the calling sequences).
- Circular definitional dependencies are supposed to be avoided.
- All values are supposed to have an explicit range.
- Modular structure is supposed to reflect the natural conceptual groupings of model elements.
- Model elements are supposed to be arranged in a sequence such that there are no forward definitional references.
- Model instances are supposed to be viewed in terms of a general class of model instances that are all isomorphic in a certain sense.
- Models are supposed to be sharply distinguished from problems posed on models, and both of these from solvers.

These conventions are imposed by the core concepts of structured modeling (Geoffrion [1989a]). SML either enforces or is consistent with all of these conventions, and lays down others as well (e.g., the strict separation of general structure from detailed data, and the provision for informal interpretation as an integral part of formal specification).

The overall intended effect of these and other conventions is to bring order to the modeling process in a way that will advance the goals of reusability, maintainability, and modifiability.

References

Balzer, R., T.E. Cheatham, Jr., and C. Green [1983] "Software Technology in the 1990's: Using a New Paradigm," *Computer*, 16:11 (November), pp. 39-45.

Batini, C., M. Lenzerini, and S.B. Navathe [1986], "A Comparative Analysis of Methodologies for Database Schema Integration," *ACM Computing Surveys*, 18:4 (December), pp. 323-364.

Blanning, R.W. [1986], "A Relational Framework for Information Management," in E.R. McLean and H.G. Sol (eds.), *Decision Support Systems: A Decade in Perspective*, Elsevier Science Publishers B.V. (North Holland), Amsterdam.

Blanning, R.W. [1987], "A Relational Theory of Model Management," in C.W. Holsapple and A.B. Whinston (eds.), *Decision Support Systems: Theory and Application*, Springer Verlag.

Boehm, B.W. [1987], "Improving Software Productivity," *Computer*, 20:9 (September), pp. 43-57.

Bradley, G.H. and R.D. Clemence, Jr. [1988], "Model Integration with a Typed Executable Modeling Language," *Proceedings of the Twenty-First Hawaii International Conference on System Sciences*, Vol. III, 1988, pp. 403-410.

Cox, B.J., Jr. [1987], *Object-Oriented Programming*, Addison Wesley, Reading, MA.

Freeman, P. [1987], *Software Reusability*, Computer Society Press, Los Alamitos, CA.

Geoffrion, A. [1987], "An Introduction to Structured Modeling," *Management Science*, 33:5 (May), pp. 547-588.

Geoffrion, A. [1988], "A 'Cyclic' Model Discussed by Blanning and Muhanna," Informal Note, UCLA, 10 pages, August 4.

Geoffrion, A. [1989a], "The Formal Aspects of Structured Modeling," *Operations Research*, 37:1 (January-February), pp. 30-51.

Geoffrion, A. [1989b], "Integrated Modeling Systems," *Computer Science in Economics and Management*, 2:1, pp. 3-15.

Geoffrion, A. [1990], "A Library of Structured Models," *Informal Note*, UCLA, 275 pages, August.

Geoffrion, A. [1991], "FW/SM: A Prototype Structured Modeling Environment," *Management Science*, 37:12 (December), pp. 1513-1538.

Geoffrion, A. [1992], "The SML Language for Structured Modeling," *Operations Research*, 40:1 (January- February), pp. 38-75.

Goguen, J.A. [1986], "Reusing and Interconnecting Software Components," *Computer*, 19:2 (February), pp. 16-28. Reprinted in Freeman [1987].

Kartashev, S. and S. Kartashev [1986], "Guest Editors' Introduction," *Computer*, 19:2 (February), pp. 9-13.

Kottemann, J.E. and D.R. Dolk [1992], "Model Integration and Modeling Languages," *Information Systems Research*, 3:1, March, pp. 1-16.

Liang, T.P. [1986], *Toward the Development of a Knowledge-Based Model Management System*, PhD Dissertation, University of Pennsylvania.

Mannino, M., B.S. Greenberg, and S.N. Hong [1990], "Model Libraries: Knowledge Representation and Reasoning," *ORSA J. on Computing*, 2:3 (Summer), pp. 287-301.

Muhanna, W. [1987], "Composite Models: Hierarchical Construction, Circularity, and Deadlocks," *Working Paper*, University of Wisconsin-Madison, 52 pages, October.

Muhanna, W.A. and R.A. Pick [1986], "A Systems Framework for Model Management," School of Business, Univ. of Wisconsin-Madison, December. Revised August, 1988.

Muhanna, W.A. and R.A. Pick [1988], "Composite Models in SYMMS," *Proceedings of the Twenty-First Hawaii International Conference on System Sciences*, Vol. III, January, pp. 418-427.

Murphy, F.H., E.A. Stohr, and P. Ma [1990], "Composition Rules for Building Linear Programming Models from Component Models," Working Paper, Information Systems Area, Graduate School of Business Administration, New York University, 21 pages, March.

Parnas, D.L. [1972], "On the Criteria To Be Used in Decomposing Systems into Modules," *Comm. ACM*, 15:12 (December), pp. 1053-1058.

Prieto-Diaz, R. and J.M. Neighbors [1986], "Module Interconnection Languages," *J. Systems and Software*, 6:4 (November), pp. 307-334. Reprinted in Freeman [1987].

Prieto-Diaz, R. and P. Freeman [1987], "Classifying Software for Reusability," *IEEE Software*, January, pp. 6-16. Reprinted in Freeman [1987].

Tsai, Y. [1987], "An Operational Approach to Model Integration Using a Structured Modeling Framework," Research Paper, Anderson Graduate School of Management, UCLA, 60 pages, December. Revised 2/88.

Vicuña, F. [1990], "Semantic Formalization in Mathematical Modeling Languages," Ph.D. Thesis, Computer Science Department, UCLA, 189 pages, 1990.

Yourdon, E. and L.L. Constantine [1979], *Structured Design*, Prentice Hall, Englewood Cliffs, NJ.

Zeigler, B. P. [1984], *Multifaceted Modeling and Discrete Event Simulation*, Academic Press, London.

Appendix 1

First example: FCAST2 + TRANS2

TRANS2 (see Appendix 4) is the classical Hitchcock-Koopmans transportation model and FCAST2 (see Appendix 5) is a simple exponential smoothing model. Our aim is to reuse these by integration so that the demands in TRANS2 are produced by FCAST2.

Notice that FCAST2 is designed to forecast one item, not several. So it is necessary to make a multi-item forecasting model out of FCAST2. This means replacing PROD by CUST in FCAST2, with quite a few corresponding induced changes. This is a structural change because it introduces a new index. Assume that the same ALPHA is used for each CUSTOMER. Also, we must redefine F so that it produces a forecast only for the last time period. This is also a structural change. Rename F to DEMF and revise its defined key phrase accordingly. Rename the root module to &FORECAST.

The result of Step 1 applied to FCAST2 is as follows. Step 1 does nothing to TRANS2 except to rename the root module to &TRANSP.

&FORECAST FORECASTING SECTOR

> **TIME t /pe/ 2 <= Size {TIME}** There is an ordered list of at least 2 TIME periods.

> **CUSTj /pe/** There is a list of CUSTOMERS.

> **ALPHA (CUST) /a/ : 0 <= Real <= 1** There is a SMOOTHING CONSTANT to be used for all CUSTOMERS.

> **D (CUSTj, TIMEt) /a/ {CUST} x {TIME}** For each CUSTOMER and TIME period there is a DEMAND level.

> **E (ALPHA, Dj<1:t>) /f/ {CUST} x {TIME} ; @IF (t>1, ALPHA * Djt + (1-ALPHA) * Ej<t-1>, Dj<1>)** For each CUSTOMER and TIME period there is an EXPONENTIAL AVERAGE based on smoothed DEMAND history.

> **S (ALPHA, Ej<1:t>) /f/ {CUST} x Filter(t>1) {TIME} ; @IF (t>2, ALPHA * (Ejt - Ej<t-1>) + (1 - ALPHA) * Sj<t-1>, Ejt - Ej<t-1>)** For each CUSTOMER and TIME period after the first there is a SMOOTHED TREND based on the EXPONENTIAL AVERAGES for the TIME period at hand and all of the ones before that.

> **DEMF (ALPHA, Ej<-1>, Sj<-1>) /f/ {CUST} ; Ej<-1> + Sj<-1>/ALPHA** For each CUSTOMER there is a one-ahead DEMAND FORECAST.

Step 2a. The key phrase DEMAND is not unique; change the one in &FORECAST to HISTORICAL DEMAND.

Step 2b. The merging genus pairs are {CUST in &FORECAST, CUST in &TRANSP} and {DEMF in &FORECAST, DEM in &TRANSP}. The first pair of genus paragraphs is already identical, since we imported CUST into &FORECAST. The second pair cannot be made identical because DEM would have to become DEMF, which is not possible since DEMF calls some genera that are not in &TRANSP (remember, the schemas have not been joined yet).

Step 2c. Put DEMF into its own output module and annotate &CDATA that it is an input module.

Step 3a. Concatenate &FORECAST and &TRANSP in that order.

Step 3b. Replace the DEM paragraph in &TRANSP by the DEMF paragraph. Be sure to change all calls to it. Drop CUST and DEMF in &CDATA.

Step 3c. Null.

The result is as follows (the new root module is not shown).

&FORECAST FORECASTING SECTOR

TIME t /pe/ 2 <= Size {TIME} There is an ordered list of at least 2 TIME periods.

CUSTj /pe/ There is a list of CUSTOMERS.

ALPHA (CUST) /a/ : 0 <= Real <= 1 There is a SMOOTHING CONSTANT to be used for all CUSTOMERS.

D (CUSTj, TIMEt) /a/ {CUST} x {TIME} For each CUSTOMER and TIME period there is a HISTORICAL DEMAND level.

E (ALPHA, Dj<1:t>) /f/ {CUST} x {TIME} ; @IF (t>1, ALPHA * Djt + (1-ALPHA) * Ej<t-1>, Dj<1>) For each CUSTOMER and TIME period there is an EXPONENTIAL AVERAGE based on smoothed HISTORICAL DEMAND.

S (ALPHA, Ej<1:t>) /f/ {CUST} x (Filter(t>1) {TIME}) ; @IF (t>2, ALPHA * (Ejt - Ej<t-1>) + (1 - ALPHA) * Sj<t-1>, Ejt - Ej<t-1>) For each CUSTOMER and TIME period after the first there is a SMOOTHED TREND based on the EXPONENTIAL AVERAGES for the TIME period at hand and all of the ones before that.

&F FORECAST (output module)

DEMF (ALPHA, Ej<-1>, Sj<-1>) /f/ {CUST} ; Ej<-1> + Sj<-1> / ALPHA For each CUSTOMER there is a one-ahead DEMAND FORECAST.

&TRANSP TRANSPORTATION SECTOR

&SDATA SOURCE DATA

PLANTi /pe/ There is a list of PLANTS.

SUP (PLANTi) /a/ {PLANT} : Real+ Every PLANT has a SUPPLY CAPACITY measured in tons.

&CDATA CUSTOMER DATA (input module)

&TDATA TRANSPORTATION DATA

LINK (PLANTi, CUSTj) /ce/ Select {PLANT} x {CUST} where i covers {PLANT}, j covers {CUST} There are some transportation LINKS from PLANTS to CUSTOMERS. There must be at least one LINK incident to each PLANT, and at least one LINK incident to each CUSTOMER.

FLOW (LINKij) /va/ {LINK} : Real+ There can be a nonnegative transportation FLOW (in tons) over each LINK.

COST (LINKij) /a/ {LINK} Every LINK has a <u>TRANSPORTATION COST RATE</u> for use in $/ton.

$ (COST, FLOW) /f/ 1 ; @SUMi SUMj (COSTij * FLOWij) There is a <u>TOTAL COST</u> associated with all FLOWS.

T:SUP (FLOWi., SUPi) /t/ {PLANT} ; @SUMj (FLOWij) <= SUPi Is the total FLOW leaving a PLANT less than or equal to its SUPPLY CAPACITY? This is called the <u>SUPPLY TEST</u>.

T:DEM (FLOW.j, DEMFj) /t/ {CUST} ; @SUMi (FLOWij) = DEMFj Is the total FLOW arriving at a CUSTOMER exactly equal to its DEMAND FORECAST? This is called the <u>DEMAND TEST</u>.

Step 4. It is only necessary to delete the degenerate module &CDATA.

Step 5. This step can be null. Alternatively, one could restore the &CDATA module, move CUST inside it, and move the entire remains of the &FORECAST module inside of it right after CUST. The modular outline of the result would be as follows. (The complete schema can be found in Geoffrion [1990] under the name T_FCAST.)

&TRANSP <u>TRANSPORTATION SECTOR</u>
    &SDATA <u>SOURCE DATA</u>
        PLANT
        SUP
    &CDATA <u>CUSTOMER DATA</u> (input module)
        CUST
        &FORECAST <u>FORECASTING SECTOR</u>
            TIME
            ALPHA
            D
            E
            S
            &F <u>FORECAST</u>
        DEMF
    &TDATA <u>TRANSPORTATION DATA</u>
        LINK
        FLOW
        COST
    $
    T:SUP
    T:DEM

An interesting observation is that this schema can be viewed as a *refinement* of the original TRANS2 schema rather than an integration of it with FCAST2; of course, the reconciliation of these two viewpoints is that the refinement has been accomplished via integration.

Appendix 2

Second Example: TRANS2 + MEOQ1

This example is the one treated in Section 3.2 of Geoffrion [1987]. The discussion there was at a fairly high level of abstraction; here we consider details according to the step step approach suggested in Section 2. The motivation for this example will not be repeated. See Appendix 4 for the TRANS2 schema and Appendix 6 for the MEOQ1 schema. See also Tsai [1987], who treats the same example in detail.

Step 1a. Null.

Step 1b. Rename both root modules. Rename SETUP$ to REC$ and change the word "setup" to the word "receipt" in several paragraphs. It would be desirable to do more customization, but not much more can be done without referencing one schema in the other. Change "units" to "tons" in the second schema for consistency with the first. No structural changes are necessary.

Step 2a. Null. There is a duplicate index; this conflict could be eliminated, but the work to do this would be undone at Step 3b.

Step 2b. The merging genus pairs are {LINK, ITEM} and {FLOW, D}. Nothing can be done (without calling the first schema from the second) to make them more similar.

Step 2c. Put LINK and FLOW in &OUTPUT and put ITEM and D in &INPUT.

The two schemas after Step 2 are as follows.

&TRANS <u>TRANSPORTATION SECTOR</u>

    &SDATA <u>SOURCE DATA</u>

        PLANTi /pe/ There is a list of <u>PLANTS</u>.

        SUP (PLANTi) /a/ {PLANT} : Real+ Every PLANT has a <u>SUPPLY CAPACITY</u> measured in tons.

    &CDATA <u>CUSTOMER DATA</u>

        CUSTj /pe/ There is a list of <u>CUSTOMERS</u>.

        DEM (CUSTj) /a/ {CUST} : Real+ Every CUSTOMER has a nonnegative <u>DEMAND</u> measured in tons.

    &TDATA <u>TRANSPORTATION DATA</u>

        &OUTPUT

            LINK (PLANTi, CUSTj) /ce/ Select {PLANT} x {CUST} where i covers {PLANT}, j covers {CUST} There are some transportation <u>LINKS</u> from PLANTS to CUSTOMERS. There must be at least one LINK incident to each PLANT, and at least one LINK incident to each CUSTOMER.

FLOW (LINKij) /va/ {LINK} : Real+ There can be a nonnegative transportation <u>FLOW</u> (in tons) over each LINK.

COST (LINKij) /a/ {LINK} Every LINK has a <u>TRANSPORTATION COST RATE</u> for use in $/ton.

$ (COST, FLOW) /f/ 1 ; @SUMi SUMj (COSTij * FLOWij) There is a <u>TOTAL COST</u> associated with all FLOWS.

T:SUP (FLOWi., SUPi) /t/ {PLANT} ; @SUMj (FLOWij) <= SUPi Is the total FLOW leaving a PLANT less than or equal to its SUPPLY CAPACITY? This is called the <u>SUPPLY TEST</u>.

T:DEM (FLOW.j, DEMj) /t/ {CUST} ; @SUMi (FLOWij) = DEMj Is the total FLOW arriving at a CUSTOMER exactly equal to its DEMAND? This is called the <u>DEMAND TEST</u>.

&EOQ <u>EOQ SECTOR</u>

    &ITEMDATA Certain <u>ITEM DATA</u> are provided.

        &INPUT

            ITEMi /pe/ There is a list of <u>ITEMS</u>.

            D (ITEMi) /a/ {ITEM} : Real+ Every ITEM has a <u>DEMAND RATE</u> (tons per year).

            H (ITEMi) /a/ {ITEM} : Real+ Every ITEM has a <u>HOLDING COST RATE</u> (dollars per ton per year).

            F (ITEMi) /a/ {ITEM} : Real+ Every ITEM has a <u>FIXED RECEIPT COST</u> (dollars per receipt).

        Q (ITEMi) /va/ {ITEM} : Real+ The <u>ORDER QUANTITY</u> (tons per order) for each ITEM is to be chosen.

        &OPCON <u>OPERATING CONSEQUENCES</u> of ORDER QUANTITY choices.

            FREQ (Di, Qi) /f/ {ITEM} ; Di / Qi Every ITEM has a <u>RECEIPT FREQUENCY</u> (average number of receipts per year) equal to DEMAND RATE divided by ORDER QUANTITY.

            REC$ (FREQi, Fi) /f/ {ITEM} ; FREQi * Fi Every ITEM has an <u>ANNUAL RECEIVING COST</u> (dollars per year) equal to the RECEIPT FREQUENCY times the FIXED RECEIPT COST.

            CARRY$ (Hi, Qi) /f/ {ITEM} ; Hi * Qi / 2 Every ITEM has an <u>ANNUAL CARRYING COST</u> (dollars per year) equal to its HOLDING COST RATE times one half of its ORDER QUANTITY (which estimates average inventory level).

ITEM$ (REC$i, CARRY$i) /f/ {ITEM} ; REC$i + CARRY$i
Every ITEM has an <u>ANNUAL ITEM COST</u> (dollars per year) equal to its ANNUAL RECEIPT COST plus its ANNUAL CARRYING COST.

TOT$ (ITEM$) /f/ 1 ; @SUMi (ITEM$i) The <u>TOTAL ANNUAL COST</u> (dollars per year) is the sum of all ANNUAL ITEM COSTS.

Step 3a. Concatenate, with &TRANS coming first.

Step 3b. Change ITEM to LINK and D to FLOW, with all the ramifications that this entails. Drop the second replicates.

Step 3c. Null.

The result is as follows (the new root module is not shown).

&TRANS <u>TRANSPORTATION SECTOR</u>

    &SDATA <u>SOURCE DATA</u>

        PLANTi /pe/ There is a list of <u>PLANTS</u>.

        SUP (PLANTi) /a/ {PLANT} : Real+ Every PLANT has a <u>SUPPLY CAPACITY</u> measured in tons.

    &CDATA <u>CUSTOMER DATA</u>

        CUSTj /pe/ There is a list of <u>CUSTOMERS</u>.

        DEM (CUSTj) /a/ {CUST} : Real+ Every CUSTOMER has a nonnegative <u>DEMAND</u> measured in tons.

    &TDATA <u>TRANSPORTATION DATA</u>

        &OUTPUT

            LINK (PLANTi, CUSTj) /ce/ Select {PLANT} x {CUST} where i covers {PLANT}, j covers {CUST} There are some transportation <u>LINKS</u> from PLANTS to CUSTOMERS. There must be at least one LINK incident to each PLANT, and at least one LINK incident to each CUSTOMER.

            FLOW (LINKij) /va/ {LINK} : Real+ There can be a nonnegative transportation <u>FLOW</u> (in tons) over each LINK.

        COST (LINKij) /a/ {LINK} Every LINK has a <u>TRANSPORTATION COST RATE</u> for use in $/ton.

$ (COST, FLOW) /f/ 1 ; @SUMi SUMj (COSTij * FLOWij) There is a <u>TOTAL COST</u> associated with all FLOWS.

T:SUP (FLOWi., SUPi) /t/ {PLANT} ; @SUMj (FLOWij) <= SUPi Is the total FLOW leaving a PLANT less than or equal to its SUPPLY CAPACITY? This is called the <u>SUPPLY TEST</u>.

T:DEM (FLOW.j, DEMj) /t/ {CUST} ; @SUMi (FLOWij) = DEMj Is the total FLOW arriving at a CUSTOMER exactly equal to its DEMAND? This is called the <u>DEMAND TEST</u>.

&EOQ <u>EOQ SECTOR</u>

> **&ITEMDATA** Certain <u>ITEM DATA</u> are provided.

> > **&INPUT**

> > **H (LINKij) /a/ {LINK} : Real+** Every LINK has a <u>HOLDING COST RATE</u> (dollars per ton per year).

> > **F (LINKij) /a/ {LINK} : Real+** Every LINK has a <u>FIXED RECEIPT COST</u> (dollars per receipt).

> > **Q (LINKij) /va/ {LINK} : Real+** The <u>ORDER QUANTITY</u> (tons per order) for each LINK is to be chosen.

> > **&OPCON** <u>OPERATING CONSEQUENCES</u> of ORDER QUANTITY choices.

> > > **FREQ (FLOWij, Qij) /f/ {LINK} ; FLOWij / Qij** Every LINK has a <u>RECEIPT FREQUENCY</u> (average number of receipts per year) equal to FLOW divided by ORDER QUANTITY.

> > > **REC$ (FREQij, Fij) /f/ {LINK} ; FREQij * Fij** Every LINK has an <u>ANNUAL RECEIVING COST</u> (dollars per year) equal to the RECEIPT FREQUENCY times the FIXED RECEIPT COST.

> > > **CARRY$ (Hij, Qij) /f/ {LINK} ; Hij * Qij / 2** Every LINK has an <u>ANNUAL CARRYING COST</u> (dollars per year) equal to its HOLDING COST RATE times one half of its ORDER QUANTITY (which estimates average inventory level).

> > > **ITEM$ (REC$ij, CARRY$ij) /f/ {LINK} ; REC$ij + CARRY$ij** Every LINK has an <u>ANNUAL LINK COST</u> (dollars per year) equal to its ANNUAL RECEIPT COST plus its ANNUAL CARRYING COST.

> > > **TOT$ (ITEM$) /f/ 1 ; @SUMi SUMj (ITEM$ij)** The <u>TOTAL ANNUAL COST</u> (dollars per year) is the sum of all ANNUAL LINK COSTS.

Step 4. Drop the degenerate module &INPUT.

Step 5. Change the name of $ to TRANS$, ITEM$ to LINK$, and TOT$ to INV$ for cosmetic reasons; change the associated key phrases also. Create a new genus TOTCOST to sum up TRANS$ and INV$; put it at the very end as a sibling of the two first level modules. The complete schema can be found in Geoffrion [1990] under the name T_MEOQ.

Appendix 3

Third Example: TRANS2 + TRANS2

The aim is to take two classical transportation models and connect them so that the output of the first becomes the input to the second. The result will be a two echelon transshipment problem. See Appendix 4 for the TRANS2 schema. Incidentally, this is the same example as the one worked in Bradley and Clemence [1988].

Step 1a. Copy TRANS2 to the workspace. Rename its root module to "&FIRST_ECHELON." Specialize its structure to its intended use as the first echelon: drop DEM and T:DEM (outputs will go to the 2nd echelon). Copy TRANS2 to the workspace. Rename its root module to "&SECOND_ECHELON." Specialize its structure to its intended use as the second echelon: drop SUP and T:SUP (inputs will come from the 1st echelon).

Step 1b. In &FIRST_ECHELON: rename CUST to DC, LINK to IBLINK, &TDATA to &IBDATA, FLOW to IBFLOW, COST to IBCOST; and change key phrases accordingly. In &SECOND_ECHELON: rename PLANT to DC, LINK to OBLINK, &TDATA to &OBDATA, FLOW to OBFLOW, COST to OBCOST; and change key phrases accordingly. Change the key phrase for $ in both schemas. Change the name of DC's module to &DCDATA in both schemas; change the corresponding key phrases to match.

The two schemas at this point are as follows.

&FIRST_ECHELON <u>FIRST ECHELON</u>

    &SDATA <u>SOURCE DATA</u>

        PLANTi /pe/ There is a list of <u>PLANTS</u>.

        SUP (PLANTi) /a/ {PLANT} : Real+ Every PLANT has a <u>SUPPLY CAPACITY</u> measured in tons.

    &DCDATA <u>DC DATA</u>

        DCj /pe/ There is a list of <u>DCS</u>.

    &IBDATA <u>INBOUND TRANSPORTATION DATA</u>

        IBLINK (PLANTi, DCj) /ce/ Select {PLANT} x {DC} where i covers {PLANT}, j covers {DC} There are some transportation <u>INBOUND LINKS</u> from PLANTS to DCS. There must be at least one INBOUND LINK incident to each PLANT, and at least one INBOUND LINK incident to each DC.

        IBFLOW (IBLINKij) /va/ {IBLINK} : Real+ There can be a nonnegative transportation <u>INBOUND FLOW</u> (in tons) over each INBOUND LINK.

        IBCOST (IBLINKij) /a/ {IBLINK} Every INBOUND LINK has an <u>INBOUND TRANSPORTATION COST RATE</u> for use in $/ton.

    $ (IBCOST, IBFLOW) /f/ 1 ; @SUMi SUMj (IBCOSTij * IBFLOWij) There is a <u>TOTAL INBOUND COST</u> associated with all INBOUND FLOWS.

T:SUP (IBFLOWi., SUPi) /t/ {PLANT} ; @SUMj (IBFLOWij) <= SUPi Is the total INBOUND FLOW leaving a PLANT less than or equal to its SUPPLY CAPACITY? This is called the <u>SUPPLY TEST</u>.

&SECOND_ECHELON <u>SECOND ECHELON</u>

&DCDATA <u>DC DATA</u>

DCi /pe/ There is a list of <u>DCS</u>.

&CDATA <u>CUSTOMER DATA</u>

CUSTj /pe/ There is a list of <u>CUSTOMERS</u>.

DEM (CUSTj) /a/ {CUST} : Real+ Every CUSTOMER has a nonnegative <u>DEMAND</u> measured in tons.

&OBDATA <u>OUTBOUND TRANSPORTATION DATA</u>

OBLINK (DCi, CUSTj) /ce/ Select {DC} x {CUST} where i covers {DC}, j covers {CUST} There are some transportation <u>OUTBOUND LINKS</u> from DCS to CUSTOMERS. There must be at least one OUTBOUND LINK incident to each DC, and at least one OUTBOUND LINK incident to each CUSTOMER.

OBFLOW (OBLINKij) /va/ {OBLINK} : Real+ There can be a nonnegative transportation <u>OUTBOUND FLOW</u> (in tons) over each OUTBOUND LINK.

OBCOST (OBLINKij) /a/ {OBLINK} Every OUTBOUND LINK has an <u>OUTBOUND TRANSPORTATION COST RATE</u> for use in $/ton.

$ (OBCOST, OBFLOW) /f/ 1 ; @SUMi SUMj (OBCOSTij * OBFLOWij) There is a <u>TOTAL OUTBOUND COST</u> associated with all OUTBOUND FLOWS.

T:DEM (OBFLOW.j, DEMj) /t/ {CUST} ; @SUMi (OBFLOWij) = DEMj Is the total OUTBOUND FLOW arriving at a CUSTOMER exactly equal to its DEMAND? This is called the <u>DEMAND TEST</u>.

Step 2a. There is a pair of genera with the duplicated name $; change to IB$ and OB$ respectively. There are two pairs of indices with duplicate names: i and j. Change j in &SECOND_ ECHELON to k, and change i in &SECOND_ECHELON to j since that will serve the purposes of Step 2b. There are two identical module paragraphs named &DCDATA. It does no harm to leave them as is.

Step 2b. The two schemas will be merged on the genus pair {DC, DC}. Both genus paragraphs are already identical.

Step 2c. Skip this option.

Step 3a. Concatenate in the order &FIRST_ECHELON, &SECOND_ECHELON.

Step 3b. The merging genus pair is already identical. Drop the second DC genus.

Step 3c. Introduce a material balance genus T:DC that checks whether total inflow equals total outflow at the DCs.

The integrated schema is as follows.

&FIRST_ECHELON <u>FIRST ECHELON</u>

    &SDATA <u>SOURCE DATA</u>

        PLANTi /pe/ There is a list of <u>PLANTS</u>.

        SUP (PLANTi) /a/ {PLANT} : Real+ Every PLANT has a <u>SUPPLY CAPACITY</u> measured in tons.

    &DCDATA <u>DC DATA</u>

        DCj /pe/ There is a list of <u>DCS</u>.

    &IBDATA <u>INBOUND TRANSPORTATION DATA</u>

        IBLINK (PLANTi, DCj) /ce/ Select {PLANT} x {DC} where i covers {PLANT}, j covers {DC} There are some transportation <u>INBOUND LINKS</u> from PLANTS to DCS. There must be at least one INBOUND LINK incident to each PLANT, and at least one INBOUND LINK incident to each DC.

        IBFLOW (IBLINKij) /va/ {IBLINK} : Real+ There can be a nonnegative transportation <u>INBOUND FLOW</u> (in tons) over each INBOUND LINK.

        IBCOST (IBLINKij) /a/ {IBLINK} Every INBOUND LINK has an <u>INBOUND TRANSPORTATION COST RATE</u> for use in $/ton.

    IB$ (IBCOST, IBFLOW) /f/ 1 ; @SUMi SUMj (IBCOSTij * IBFLOWij) There is a <u>TOTAL INBOUND COST</u> associated with all INBOUND FLOWS.

    T:SUP (IBFLOWi., SUPi) /t/ {PLANT} ; @SUMj (IBFLOWij) <= SUPi Is the total INBOUND FLOW leaving a PLANT less than or equal to its SUPPLY CAPACITY? This is called the <u>SUPPLY TEST</u>.

&SECOND_ECHELON <u>SECOND ECHELON</u>

    &DCDATA <u>DC DATA</u>

    &CDATA <u>CUSTOMER DATA</u>

        CUSTk /pe/ There is a list of <u>CUSTOMERS</u>.

        DEM (CUSTk) /a/ {CUST} : Real+ Every CUSTOMER has a nonnegative <u>DEMAND</u> measured in tons.

    &OBDATA <u>OUTBOUND TRANSPORTATION DATA</u>

OBLINK (DCj, CUSTk) /ce/ Select {DC} x {CUST} where j covers {DC}, k covers {CUST} There are some transportation <u>OUTBOUND LINKS</u> from DCS to CUSTOMERS. There must be at least one OUTBOUND LINK incident to each DC, and at least one OUTBOUND LINK incident to each CUSTOMER.

OBFLOW (OBLINKjk) /va/ {OBLINK} : Real+ There can be a nonnegative transportation <u>OUTBOUND FLOW</u> (in tons) over each OUTBOUND LINK.

OBCOST (OBLINKjk) /a/ {OBLINK} Every OUTBOUND LINK has an <u>OUTBOUND TRANSPORTATION COST RATE</u> for use in $/ton.

OB$ (OBCOST, OBFLOW) /f/ 1 ; @SUMj SUMk (OBCOSTjk * OBFLOWjk) There is a <u>TOTAL OUTBOUND COST</u> associated with all OUTBOUND FLOWS.

T:DEM (OBFLOW.k, DEMk) /t/ {CUST} ; @SUMj (OBFLOWjk) = DEMk Is the total OUTBOUND FLOW arriving at a CUSTOMER exactly equal to its DEMAND? This is called the <u>DEMAND TEST</u>.

T:DC (IBFLOW.j, OBFLOWj.) /t/ {DC} ; @SUMi (IBFLOWij) = @SUMk (OBFLOWjk) Is the total INBOUND FLOW arriving at each DC exactly equal to the total OUTBOUND FLOW leaving it? This is called the <u>DC MATERIAL BALANCE TEST</u>.

Step 4. Delete the vestigial module &DCDATA in &SECOND_ECHELON.

Step 5. Add a new genus TOT$ to add up the two cost subtotals. Make it a sibling of &FIRST_ECHELON and &SECOND_ECHELON. This paragraph is:

TOT$ (IB$, OB$) /f/ 1 ; IB$ + OB$ The <u>TOTAL COST</u> is the sum of the TOTAL INBOUND COST and TOTAL OUTBOUND COST.

The complete schema can be found in Geoffrion [1990] under the name TRANS_2E.

Appendix 4

Classical Transportation Model

&SDATA <u>SOURCE DATA</u>

    PLANTi /pe/ There is a list of <u>PLANTS</u>.

    SUP (PLANTi) /a/ {PLANT} : Real+ Every PLANT has a <u>SUPPLY CAPACITY</u> measured in tons.

&CDATA <u>CUSTOMER DATA</u>

    CUSTj /pe/ There is a list of <u>CUSTOMERS</u>.

    DEM (CUSTj) /a/ {CUST} : Real+ Every CUSTOMER has a nonnegative <u>DEMAND</u> measured in tons.

&TDATA <u>TRANSPORTATION DATA</u>

    LINK (PLANTi, CUSTj) /ce/ Select {PLANT} x {CUST} where i covers {PLANT}, j covers {CUST} There are some transportation <u>LINKS</u> from PLANTS to CUSTOMERS. There must be at least one LINK incident to each PLANT, and at least one LINK incident to each CUSTOMER.

    FLOW (LINKij) /va/ {LINK} : Real+ There can be a nonnegative transportation <u>FLOW</u> (in tons) over each LINK.

    COST (LINKij) /a/ {LINK} Every LINK has a <u>TRANSPORTATION COST RATE</u> for use in $/ton.

$ (COST, FLOW) /f/ 1 ; @SUMi SUMj (COSTij * FLOWij) There is a <u>TOTAL COST</u> associated with all FLOWS.

T:SUP (FLOWi., SUPi) /t/ {PLANT} ; @SUMj (FLOWij) <= SUPi Is the total FLOW leaving a PLANT less than or equal to its SUPPLY CAPACITY? This is called the <u>SUPPLY TEST</u>.

T:DEM (FLOW.j, DEMj) /t/ {CUST} ; @SUMi (FLOWij) = DEMj Is the total FLOW arriving at a CUSTOMER exactly equal to its DEMAND? This is called the <u>DEMAND TEST</u>.

Appendix 5

Exponential Smoothing Model

TIME t /pe/ 2 <= Size {TIME} There is an ordered list of at least 2 <u>TIME</u> periods.

PROD /pe/ There is a <u>PRODUCT</u> whose demand process is to be forecasted.

ALPHA (PROD) /a/ : 0 <= Real <= 1 There is a <u>SMOOTHING CONSTANT</u> to be used for the PRODUCT.

D (PROD, TIMEt) /a/ {TIME} For each TIME period there is a <u>DEMAND</u> level for the PRODUCT.

E (ALPHA, D<1:t>) /f/ {TIME} ; @IF (t>1, ALPHA * Dt + (1-ALPHA) * E<t-1>, D<1>) For each TIME period there is an <u>EXPONENTIAL AVERAGE</u> based on smoothed DEMAND history.

S (ALPHA, E<1:t>) /f/ Filter(t>1) {TIME} ; @IF (t>2, ALPHA * (Et - E<t-1>) + (1 - ALPHA) * S<t-1>, Et - E<t-1>) For each TIME period after the first there is a <u>SMOOTHED TREND</u> based on the EXPONENTIAL AVERAGES for the TIME period at hand and all of the ones before that.

F (ALPHA, Et, St) /f/ Filter(t>1) {TIME} ; Et + St/ALPHA For each TIME period after the first there is a one-ahead <u>FORECAST</u> of DEMAND.

Appendix 6

Multi-Item EOQ Model

ITEMi /pe/ There is a list of <u>ITEMS</u>.

&ITEMDATA Certain <u>ITEM DATA</u> are provided.

    D (ITEMi) /a/ {ITEM} : Real+ Every ITEM has a <u>DEMAND RATE</u> (units per year).

    H (ITEMi) /a/ {ITEM} : Real+ Every ITEM has a <u>HOLDING COST RATE</u> (dollars per unit per year).

    F (ITEMi) /a/ {ITEM} : Real+ Every ITEM has a <u>FIXED SETUP COST</u> (dollars per setup).

Q (ITEMi) /va/ {ITEM} : Real + The <u>ORDER QUANTITY</u> (units per order) for each ITEM is to be chosen.

&OPCON <u>OPERATING CONSEQUENCES</u> of ORDER QUANTITY choices.

    FREQ (Di, Qi) /f/ {ITEM} ; Di / Qi Every ITEM has a <u>SETUP FREQUENCY</u> (average number of setups per year) equal to DEMAND RATE divided by ORDER QUANTITY.

    SETUP$ (FREQi, Fi) /f/ {ITEM} ; FREQi * Fi Every ITEM has an <u>ANNUAL SETUP COST</u> (dollars per year) equal to the SETUP FREQUENCY times the SETUP COST.

    CARRY$ (Hi, Qi) /f/ {ITEM} ; Hi * Qi / 2 Every ITEM has an <u>ANNUAL CARRYING COST</u> (dollars per year) equal to its HOLDING COST RATE times one half of its ORDER QUANTITY (which estimates average inventory level).

    ITEM$ (SETUP$i, CARRY$i) /f/ {ITEM} ; SETUP$i + CARRY$i Every ITEM has an <u>ANNUAL ITEM COST</u> (dollars per year) equal to its ANNUAL SETUP COST plus its ANNUAL CARRYING COST.

    TOT$ (ITEM$) /f/ 1 ; @SUMi (ITEM$i) The <u>TOTAL ANNUAL COST</u> (dollars per year) is the sum of all ANNUAL ITEM COSTS.

An Economic Framework for Computing

William B. Richmond
William E. Simon Graduate School of Business Administration
University of Rochester, New York

James C. Moore and Andrew B. Whinston

1. Introduction

Most computer systems, including decision support systems (DSS) and executive information systems (EIS), are based on algorithms. We can define an algorithm as a series of actions for solving a problem or accomplishing some goal. As such, we view an algorithm as the formalization of (part of) a decision strategy or as a description of (part of) a firm's production process, whose output has some value (for example, it improves decision making). Viewing algorithms in this light, requires the development of an economic based model for constructing and analyzing algorithms. We use a decision theoretic model developed by Moore and Whinston [15,16] to look at the cost and the value of computations and select the sequence that maximizes the net payoff (gross value-cost). The economic model addresses the issue of how precise an answer or solution should be for any particular problem. Greater precision is more attractive (has a higher value) from a decision theoretic view; however, greater precision is costlier.

In this paper, we survey some recent and on-going research. We provide a link between algorithm construction and optimal (economic) decision processes. We use a decision model that incorporates the cost of the decision process in determining an optimal decision, and we model decision making as a two stage process — gathering information about the world and selecting an alternative. When making a decision, the decision maker successively refines his or her knowledge by performing information gathering actions, which we call experiments. Each experiment sends a signal that allows the decision maker to more accurately characterize the true state of the world (for example, the requested record is in the lower half of the file, or the value of an integral is between 10 and 10.5, etc.). The experiment taken at each step depends on the outcomes or signals of the previous experiments. The decision to obtain more information is based on the trade-off between the cost of obtaining the information and the expected value of the information. The final decision depends on the decision maker's information. We view the final choice as being one of choosing a decision function defined on an "information set" (which we make explicit later in the paper). What constitutes a good decision function depends upon the cost of obtaining information, so what appears to be a mediocre decision function might dominate what appears to be an excellent decision function if the latter requires more extensive information than the former.

From a computer science perspective, we are formulating a model whose solution is an optimal algorithm (optimal for the given parameters of the decision problem for example, the cost function). The optimization approach to algorithm construction is an alternative to the more intuitive discovery approach commonly used in computer science, but it is not amenable to all problem domains.

In Section 2, we motivate the use of the decision theoretic approach to algorithm construction. In Section 3, we present the decision model. In Section 4, we provide a sufficient condition for using dynamic programming to construct an optimal algorithm, and we relate this condition to the construction of an optimal binary search tree. In Section 5, we discuss a generalization of file search where we optimize over a payoff function that reflects the user's valuation of the information provided by the search. We call this the common index problem. In Section 6, we discuss a variant of this problem that generalizes the common index to multiple attributes. Section 7 provides more sufficient conditions for using dynamic programming to construct an optimal algorithm and describes the relationship between these conditions and parallel processing.

56

2. Algorithm Evaluation and Design

In computer science, theoreticians primarily rank algorithms using a worst-case-order-of measure. New algorithms are evaluated, at least in part, by the degree to which their worst-case-order-of time bests the worst-case-order-of time of the current reigning algorithm.

The worst-case-order-of measure is pervasive because it is machine independent, and relatively easy to calculate and interpret. Many of the complexity results are both mathematically complex and elegant. The elegance of these results, however, seems to outshine the simplicity of the ranking measure. Theorists implicitly acknowledge that the worst-case-order-of analysis is too simplistic, through their use of probalistic and heuristic algorithms. Practitioners implicitly acknowledge its inappropriateness by using algorithms, such as quick sort, which are suboptimal under this ranking procedure. To some degree, the drawbacks of the worst-case-order-of analysis are explicitly acknowledged and work is proceeding in the development of new complexity measures. Karp [7] advocates using an average case analysis; Tarjan & Sleator [23] have introduced amortized complexity; and Traub and Wozniakowski [25] have done extensive work on ε-complexity.

All complexity measures have a common goal — to effectively evaluate and rank algorithms, and therefore prescribe what algorithms are good for certain classes of problems. The importance of the predominant ranking method cannot be underestimated, since the ranking method guides algorithm research by defining the focus of what an algorithm must accomplish to be considered good.

To define the appropriate measure for ranking algorithms, we must first define the purpose of an algorithm and the desired characteristics of the ranking measure. To the extent that an algorithm serves different purposes, different algorithm hierarchies (ranking methods) might be appropriate. Ideally, the ranking measure will be independent of the idiosyncrasies of computation (for example, what machine the algorithm is running on, the implementation of the algorithm, the other processes being run, etc.). It also needs to to be highly discriminatory — ideally a weak order over the class of algorithms for a given problem. Unfortunately, these two goals are contradictory. Independence from the computations' idiosyncrasies is obtained by abstracting away from the details of computation, and it is these details that make possible the discrimination among algorithms.

The third characteristic that the ranking measure should have is to measure the degree to which the algorithm accomplishes its purpose. The traditional approach to complexity analysis assumes that an algorithm's purpose is to solve the problem exactly (although for some problems, approximation algorithms are used [13]). Traub's ε-complexity implies that the purpose of an algorithm is to provide information at some sufficient level of detail (error < ε) at a minimum cost.

Although algorithms are designed to provide information, the information itself has a purpose — to aid in decision making. We therefore claim that the purpose of many algorithms is to aid in some decision process. The appropriate measure of an algorithm must be related to the net payoff from the decision. The trade-off between the cost and the value of information determines the degree to which a problem is solved. This is similar to ε-complexity, except that in the decision theoretic approach the ε is not ad hoc, but is based on the trade-off between the cost and the value of the information.

The decision process framework for studying algorithms has its advantages and disadvantages. Its primary disadvantage is that the analysis of algorithms can become much more complex than in the traditional approach. The advantages, of course, arise from this additional complexity. The more detailed evaluation of the algorithms will provide a bridge between theorists and practitioners. Using the economic approach could help practitioners choose an algorithm for a given environment, and might eventually enable an expert operating system to chose algorithms from an algorithm data base.

3. Decision Model

We view an algorithm as a formalization of part of the decision process. To model the process, we use the decision model developed by Moore and Whinston [15,16]. In this model a decision is a function of eight parameters.

$$D = < X, \phi, D, \omega, A, M_a, c, r >$$

where:

X is the state space.

ϕ is a probability distribution over X. $\phi(x)$ is the probability that x is the true state of the world, where $x \in X$

D is the set of final decisions.

ω is the gross payoff function.

A is the set of allowable experiments.

M_a is the information partition of X resulting from experiment a, $a \in A$.

c is the cost function. c(a) is the cost of executing experiment a.

r is the maximum allowable number of experiments.

The state space, X, represents all of the possible states of the world. It embodies all of the relevant aspects of the decision about which the decision maker is uncertain. In file search, X represents the records and gaps in the file, and $x_i \in X$ is the true state of the world if the requested element, b, corresponds to x_i (i.e., if x_i is a record then $b = x_i$ and if x_t is a gap then $b \in x_i$). For linear programming, X, represents the basic feasible solutions, and $x_i \in X$ is the true state of the world if it is the solution to the linear program.

ϕ is the probability distribution over the state space, X. In the file search problem, $\phi(x)$ is the probability that x is the requested record or that the requested record lies in a particular gap. In the linear programming problem, although there is only one true state, the decision maker's a priori probabilities are what are important. It is therefore reasonable to assume that $\phi(x) = 1/n$ where $n = |X|$.

D is the set of final decisions. This is the set of possible responses that the computer system might make. In the file search problem, $D = \{0,1,...,n\}$ where $d = 0$ is the decision that the requested record is not in the file and $d = i$ is the decision that the requested record is the ith record in the file. In a linear programming problem, D is the set of basic feasible solutions.

$\omega = \omega^*(x,d,c)$ is the payoff function. We use $\omega^*(x,d,c)$ as part of the objective function for evaluating the different decision strategies available to the decision maker. By altering $\omega(x,d,c)$, we can reflect the priorities of the decision maker. We will frequently assume that the payoff function is separable, so that $\omega^*(x, d, c) = \omega(x, d) - c$. In this case, $\omega(x,d)$ is the gross payoff resulting from decision d when x is the true state of the world.

If $\omega^*(x, d, c) = \omega(x, d) - c$ and

$$\omega(x, d) = \begin{cases} \omega > 0 \text{ if the correct decision is made} \\ \\ 0 \text{ otherwise} \end{cases}$$

then for sufficiently large ϖ, the optimal algorithm minimizes expected cost. A large ϖ is necessary to guarantee that complete information is obtained, which is generally assumed within the computer science literature. Whether complete information (distinguishing between each element of the state space for every request, or solving the problem exactly) is obtained in the decision theoretic approach, however, depends on ω, c, ϕ, and r and is not assumed to optimal a priori.

$$\text{If } \omega^*(x,d,c) = \begin{cases} \varpi - \max_{B \in B_{r+1}} \{C(B)\} \text{ if the correct decision is made} \\ \\ - C(B) \text{ otherwise} \end{cases}$$

then for sufficiently large ϖ, the optimal algorithm minimizes the maximum cost (i.e., minimizes the worst case). $B_{r+1} = \{B_1,...,B_n\}$ is the final partition of the state space resulting from the decision strategy. If ϖ is sufficiently large, then each partition element, B_i, contains a single state, x, (i.e., complete information is obtained), and the payoff is a function of the highest cost of reaching any state x.

Other payoff functions that reflect an organization's or individual's priorities are possible and from a decision theoretic stand point are more interesting. In the case of large linear programming problems, the simplex algorithm might approach the final solution asymptotically. A payoff function that mirrors the objective function might be appropriate. In this case, the linear program might halt before reaching the solution that maximizes the objective function.

A is the set of available experiments or computations used to obtain information about the state space. An experiment can be viewed as an abstract unit of computation. Depending on the level of investigation, an experiment can range from a machine instruction to a program to an information system. We assume that each experiment partitions the state space and reduces the set of possible true states of the world. $A = \{a_0, ...,a_n\}$, where a_0 represents the null experiment - do nothing; and a_i represents an experiment that partitions the state space. In the file search problem, a_i corresponds to comparing the requested record with the ith record in the file.

For each experiment there is a set of possible outcomes, or signals, and associated with each possible signal is a set of states. A different set of experiments or signals could result in a different optimal algorithm, and might also require a different formulation of the state space.

$\mathbf{M}_a$ is the partition of the state space resulting from experiment a. For example, in the file search problem,

$\mathbf{M}_a = \{ M_{a1}, M_{a2}, M_{a3}\}$ where:

$M_{a1} = \{z_0, y_1,...z_{a-1}\}$ - the states (records and gaps) less than a.

$M_{a2} = \{y_a\}$ - the state (record) equal to a.

$M_{a3} = \{z_a, y_{a+1},...,z_n\}$ - the states (records and gaps) greater than a.

Once a signal is received, the decision maker knows which set of states contains the true state. In general,
$M_{ai} = \{x \in X: \text{if } x \text{ is the true state of the world, then executing experiment a results in signal i}\}$

c is the cost function. c(a) is the cost of executing experiment a. Different experiments can have different costs.

r is the maximum number of experiments allowed.

4. Optimality

Being rational decision makers, we want to use an optimal decision process. In a decision theoretic approach, decision strategies are evaluated on their resulting expected net payoff. The goal, therefore, is to choose the decision strategy, σ^*, that maximizes the expected net payoff. In the decision theoretic setting, the optimization problem is:

$$\text{maximize } \Omega^*(\sigma)$$
$$\sigma$$

where:

$$\Omega^*(\sigma) = \underbrace{\sum_{B \in B_{r+1}} \underbrace{\sum_{x \in B} \phi(x)\big[\omega[x,\delta(B)] - C(B)\big]}_{U}}_{V}$$

C(B) is the cost of executing the sequence of experiments that results in partition element B.

U is the expected net payoff if the state of the world is $x \in X$. (Note that we are using a separable payoff function here.)

V is the expected net payoff for a subset, B, of the state space. If B contains only a single element, then U = V.

The question that arises is when can we effectively use an optimization approach to construct optimal algorithms and decision processes?

One approach for determining an optimal strategy is to represent the strategies as a decision tree and evaluate each strategy using backward induction (averaging out and folding back) [20]. Backward induction calculates the expected value of a strategy starting at the most refined level of the decision tree (the leaves), and progresses backwards up the tree until a final evaluation for the full set of strategies is reached. To use the averaging out and folding back method, we have to first construct every possible strategy. For many problems, the number of strategies is too large for this to be effective.

Dynamic programming can provide a systematic method for using backward induction to evaluate the alternative strategies. Knuth was one of the first to look at constructing optimal algorithms using dynamic programming [8]. In constructing an optimal binary search tree, Knuth followed (established?) the traditional approach of assuming the algorithm obtains complete information and then minimized the expected cost of the algorithm. Knuth noted that constructing an optimal binary search tree satisfies the principal of optimality and that the number of subproblems is small $((n+2)(n+1)/2)$, but he did not explain why dynamic programming was an efficient method for constructing an optimal binary search strategy.

According to Bradley, et al., [3]:

> "Usually, creativity is required before we can recognize that a particular problem can be cast effectively as a dynamic program; and often subtle insights are necessary to restructure the formulation so that it can be solved effectively."

We can effectively use dynamic programming if we can characterize which subsets of the state space are feasible, i.e., which subsets of the state space can be generated by some set of experiments. If for each partition element, we know which experiments result in a refinement of the partition element, what the refinement is and the value of each refinement, and if the number of efficient strategies is much less than the total number of strategies (the number of subproblems is much less than the number of elements in the power set of X).

Moore and Whinston [15,16] show that when the payoff function is linearly separable (i.e., $\omega(x,d,c) = \omega(x,d) - c$) then the decision problem satisfies the principal of optimality. They continue by proving that a sufficient condition for dynamic programming to be efficient is the existence of a linear ordering over the experiment set A. A linear ordering, $\geq$, exists over $A = \{a_1,...,a_n\}$ if every experiment $a \in A$ partitions X into two sets M_{a1} and M_{a2} and $a_i \geq a_j \Leftrightarrow M_{ai1} \supseteq M_{aj1}$ for all pairs of experiments a_i and a_j. Alternatively, a linear ordering, $\geq$, exists over $A = \{a_1,...,a_n\}$ if every experiment $a \in A$ partitions X into three sets M_{a1}, M_{a2}, and M_{a3} and $a_i \geq a_j \Leftrightarrow M_{ai1} \supseteq M_{aj1} \cup M_{aj2}$ for all pairs of experiments a_i and a_j. Figure 1 shows how $M_{2,1} \cup M_{2,2} \subseteq M_{3,1}$ implying $a = 2 \leq a = 3$.

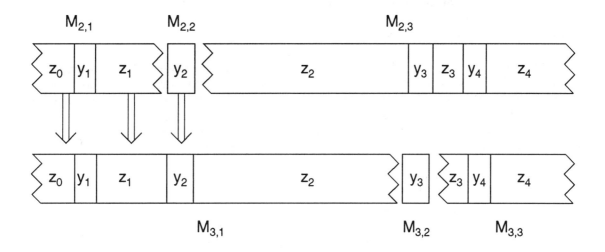

Figure 1. Linear ordering condition

The linear ordering lets us characterize the feasible subsets as $B_{ij} = M_{i3} \cap M_{j1}$ and M_{k2} in the case of trinary experiments, and as $B_{ij} = M_{i2} \cap M_{j1}$ in the case of binary experiments. We can also define the efficient experiments on each feasible subset, B_{ij}, as those a_k such that $i<k<j$. Finally, the number of subproblems is fewer than $|X| + (|A| \cdot (|A|+1))/2$.

We can use the decision model to formulate the optimal binary search problem so that the linear ordering condition is satisfied. We can, therefore, use dynamic programming to construct the same optimal binary search tree arrived at by Knuth.

The linear ordering is a sufficient condition, but not a necessary one [18]. In general, assume D^1 is a decision problem with experiment set A^1 and information partitions M_a^1. Suppose that an optimal strategy for D^1 is myopic, and that the value of the optimal experiment at each stage is unique (for example, in sequential search, the probabilities are unique). Now let D^2 be the same decision problem as D^1 except it has experiment set A^2 and information partitions M_a^2. Suppose that there is a linear ordering, $\geq$, over A^2. Then dynamic programming can effectively be used to construct an optimal algorithm for the decision problem D^* that differs from D^1 and D^2 in A^* and M_a^* and where $A^* = A^1 \cup A^2$, or $A^* = A^1 + A^2$. Under this generalization, we can construct optimal split trees and an optimal search strategy that uses split comparisons and node value comparisons in any order.

In the optimal binary search problem discussed in the computer science literature, the optimization process only allows the access probabilities to change. Using the decision theoretic approach, we can also vary the cost function and the payoff function to incorporate the value of time, the relative importance of certain requests, the relative importance of certain users and the cost of inexact answers. In [17], we use a payoff function that depends on how close the choice made is to the best available alternative to investigate the problem of choosing the best available alternative from a set.

5. Information Retrieval and the Common Index Problem

In the common index problem and in the multi-attribute choice problem we view information retrieval as a choice problem because in many decision situations, the decision maker wants to know what the best available alternative is, not if there are alternatives with properties (A and B and C) or (D and E and F). Data base systems are designed to support all or nothing retrievals where either the requested record exists and is returned or the null response is made. To find the best available record in a traditional data base system, the decision maker must design his or her own search strategy. He or she must:

1. Determine a characterization of the best available alternative.

2. Formulate a query that determines if the characterization exists or not.

3. If the characterization does not exist or if it matches too many records, the decision maker must repeat steps 1 and 2 until a suitable solution is found.

Both the efficacy and efficiency of this method depend on the user's knowledge of the contents of the data base, and on the user's willingness to spend his/her mental resources. By treating queries as choice problems, the data base system becomes responsible for evaluating the information and presenting a manageable set of information that is relevant to the choice problem.

The fields of economics, computational geometry and information retrieval (IR) all study the search process involved in choosing the best alternative from a set. The economic literature focuses on the strategy a rational individual uses in making a choice; whereas, the IR literature and the computational geometry literature attempt to formulate strategies that are good for a class of users.

The economic literature generally assumes that the decision maker either has all of the information necessary for making an optimal choice, or that the decision maker sequentially searches through the set of alternatives until the expected cost of looking at the next alternative exceeds the expected value of the alternative [1,9,28]. This literature either ignores the choice process — the process of gaining information on the alternatives — or examines only a single type of information acquisition experiment — examining an alternative.

The IR and computational geometry literature generally assume a fixed similarity or dissimilarity measure [2,10,11]. The goal is to find a good search strategy (one that requires a relatively small amount of computation) given the fixed (dis)similarity measure. The use of a fixed (dis)similarity measure for all users and all requests might return the worst available alternative rather than the best.

The common index problem [17] is a step towards applying a decision theoretic approach to constructing an algorithm (decision strategy) that focuses on the choice process and is embedded within the foundations of economic theory. In the common index problem, each member of a group wants to select the best available alternative from a set, which we refer to as the choice set. The set of alternatives is drawn from a known, linearly ordered universal set (i.e., each individual knows the domain from which the choice set is drawn, but does not know which alternatives are in the choice set). The decision maker's task is to search through the choice set to find the best available alternative.

The set of alternatives is represented by a file — each record of the file represents one alternative of the set. Instead of each individual developing his/her own search strategy, we introduce a search intermediary (the searcher). The searcher's task is to find the best available alternative for each individual of the group. The information acquisition and decision strategy that the searcher uses corresponds to the retrieval algorithm employed by the computer system.

An alternative interpretation is that the group wants a single choice process that is socially optimal for the group. The problem of determining an optimal resource allocation for a group of people is studied in welfare economics. A social welfare function aggregates the individual utility functions to come up with some sort of social utility, and the search algorithm should be designed to maximize the social utility.

To determine the best available element in the file, we make several assumptions. The first assumption is that the index associated with each record has an intrinsic meaning and that it captures all of the information relevant for choosing between records. This assumption implies that the choice can be based upon the value of a single attribute. This assumption is not as restrictive as it first appears. For example, Coombs [4] shows that if preferences are over two dimensions (attributes), if good things satiate and bad things escalate (apparently a behaviorally and economically reasonable assumption), and if the set of alternatives is an efficient set, then preferences are ordered over one attribute and, additionally, preferences are single-peaked.

The second assumption is that there exists an individual utility function associated with each potential user and that the utility function is a function of the index. The utility functions measure the individuals' preferences over the elements in the file, and can be interpreted as measuring the amount or quality of information in a record, or the desirability of the object that the record represents. (See Debreu [6] for the conditions necessary for the existence of a utility function.)

We can formulate the common index problem using the Moore and Whinston decision model. In one formulation, there is a linear ordering, $\geq$, over the experiment set, A. Moore, Richmond and Whinston [17] develop a dynamic programming solution to the common index problem. Additionally, an example is given where the optimal strategy does not obtain complete information. Since complete information is neither guaranteed nor assumed in the decision theoretic approach, a sufficient condition for obtaining complete information is derived. Moore, et al. show that if the payoff function is user sovereign, and single peaked in d, and if

$$\min \phi(x) \, [\omega(x,\delta^*(x)) - \omega(x,\delta^*(x)\pm1)] > c$$

then the optimal strategy results in complete information.

6. Multi-attribute Choice Problem

The most restrictive assumption in the common index problem is the assumption that the user's preferences are a single peaked function of the index. Richmond [21] investigates the problem of choosing the best alternative form a set where each alternative is represented by m attributes and the decision maker's utility is a linear function of the attributes. This is consistent with the economic model proposed by Lancaster [12] and the psychological models proposed by Tversky [26,27]. In Lancaster's model, an individual consumer chooses the bundle of characteristics, rather than goods, that maximizes utility. The goods are determined indirectly through the choice of characteristics. In Tversky's EBA and HEM models, an alternative is also chosen based on its characteristics. To select an alternative, the decision maker selects a desired characteristic, and eliminates from further consideration all alternatives that do not have the desired characteristic. A second characteristic is chosen and the alternatives still under consideration that do not have this second characteristic are eliminated. This process continues until a single alternative remains.

In many choice situations, the decision maker does not know which alternatives have which characteristics. Making a choice consists of obtaining information on the alternatives, evaluating the alternatives and then selecting an alternative. In general, the decision maker does not obtain complete information on the alternatives before evaluating and selecting the final choice. There is a tradeoff between the cost of obtaining more information and the expected improvement in the choice that might result from the additional information. A consumer selecting a durable good is one example of this type of choice situation. If, for example, I am looking for a car, and my ideal choice is a 1964 red convertible E-type Jaguar that costs nothing, and I have found a 1964 red convertible E-type Jaguar that costs one dollar, it is unlikely that getting more information on the other available cars will result in a better choice.

In this formulation of the multi-attribute choice problem, the elements of the state space, X, are mxn matrices, Z, where there are m objects or alternatives, each represented by a row of Z, and there are n attributes that the alternatives might possess, each represented by the columns of Z. As is evident by this formulation of the state space, the multi-attribute choice problem is related to the problem of searching a table for the best alternative.

As an example, consider an individual who wants to purchase a car, and assume that Table 1 represents the alternatives and their attributes. The decision maker knows the different possible attributes that are relevant to his/her choice, and he/she knows that the ideal car has a price less than $10,000, has four seats, get more than 40 miles per gallon, is a convertible, and has manual transmission. The decision maker also realizes that this combination is unlikely to exist. In general, the decision maker knows what he/she wants in a car, but does not know which attribute combinations exist or the attributes that any particular car embodies.

To determine which cars are available, the decision maker must gather information. The decision maker goes to a car lot and drives a Honda to find that it has great suspension. He/she reads Car and Track magazine to find that Hondas are reliable, but Fiats are not, etc. As the decision maker gathers information, he/she fills in the information matrix, Z. At some point, the decision maker makes a decision — usually before the matrix is completely filled in.

One of the goals of many choice models is to predict the probability that a decision maker will select a particular alternative. Some choice models (for example, the logit model [24]) assume that the decision maker's choice is deterministic, i.e., the decision maker selects an alternative that maximizes utility. The choice model provides only a probability that a particular alternative will be chosen, but this is because the outside researcher lacks information about the alternatives and the decision maker; therefore, the outside researcher cannot accurately predict what choice will be made.

Table 1. Set of possible cars

	Price A B C D	# Seats E F G H	MPG I J K L	Roof M N	Transmission O P
Honda Accord	0 1 0 0	0 1 0 0	0 0 0 1	0 1	1 0
Yugo	1 0 0 0	0 1 0 0	0 0 1 0	0 1	1 0
BMW 320i	0 0 0 1	0 1 0 0	0 1 0 0	0 1	0 1
Corvette	0 0 0 1	1 0 0 0	1 0 0 0	1 0	1 0
Chevette	1 0 0 0	0 1 0 0	0 0 1 0	0 1	1 0
Town&Country	0 0 1 0	0 0 0 1	1 0 0 0	0 1	0 1
Fierro	0 1 0 0	1 0 0 0	0 1 0 0	1 0	1 0
LTD	0 0 1 0	0 0 1 0	0 1 0 0	0 1	0 1

A = <$10,000	E= 2I= <20	M= Convertible
B = $10-15,000	F= 4J= 20-30	N= Hardtop
C = $15-20,000	G= 5K=30-40	0=Manual
D = >$20,000	H= 6L=>40	P=Automatic

Other models (for example, Tversky's HEM model [26]) assume that the choice mechanism itself is probabilistic. In a repeated choice problem, a decision maker might select different alternatives under seemingly identical conditions. The question of whether the probabilistic nature of choice is due to the inadequacies of the researcher or to the inherent nature of the choice mechanism is important to issues that arise in validating the choice model, but it is also somewhat philosophic in nature.

In Richmond [21], the choice mechanism might be either probabilistic or deterministic. Probabilistic choice occurs when the decision maker does not have enough information about the alternatives to distinguish the unique alternative that will maximize utility.

The probability of any alternative, x_i, being selected depends entirely on the strategy the decision maker uses to make the choice — not on the decision maker's preferences — we assume, however, that the decision maker will use a strategy that results in choices that reflect his or her preferences, and when describing an economically rational agent, the strategy maximizes expected utility. Assume that the decision maker has a linear utility function represented by:

$$u(x) = \begin{aligned} &30A + 15B + 5C + OD + \\ &5E + 10F + 0G + 0H + \\ &0I + 0J + 25K + 45L + \\ &10M + 20N + 20O + 0P. \end{aligned}$$

The probability of choosing any of the cars is unknown at this point (or can be considered random), because the probability depends on the information that the decision maker has about the alternatives. Thus the probability of choosing any alternative will depend on the information acquisition and decision strategy. We use the car example and a decision function that selects the alternative with the highest expected utility.

A (not necessarily optimal) strategy of testing the columns in decreasing order of their weights results in the following choice probabilities:

After one experiment (column L)

$P(Honda) = 1$

After two experiments (column L and A)

$P(Honda) = 1$

after three experiments (columns L,A,K)

$P(Honda) = 0$

$P(Yugo) = 1/2$

$P(Chevette) = 1/2.$

For a utility maximizing individual, the probability of selecting an alternative changes with the information on the alternatives. It is no wonder, then, that people show inconsistencies in making choices, since their information rarely stays constant. Note that in each case, the probability of choosing an alternative, x, given the known information, will always be either 0 or $1/k$, where k is the number of alternatives that have the same, maximum expected utility. This symmetry in the choice probabilities results from our assumption that an individual will use an economic choice model and will select the alternative that maximizes his/her expected utility given the information. The choice probabilities will rarely, if ever, coincide with the choice probabilities generated by the psychological choice models. In part this is because we assume (as a first step) that the information acquisition process and the final decision are separate and that the cost of making the final choice is zero. To the extent that these assumptions are invalid, the choice probabilities will be invalid.

We want to look for optimal information gathering strategies, given an individual's preference function, and assuming that the final choice maximizes expected utility. Under certain conditions [21], the optimal information acquisition strategy, is to obtain information about the alternatives' attributes in decreasing order of the attributes weights. At each step, an attribute's value is ascertained for every alternative. Changes to the cost function imply that in some cases an EBA-like strategy — reducing the set of considered alternatives at each step to those that have the selected attribute — can dominate the strategy that obtains the attribute's value for all alternatives.

7. Parallel Optimization

In sections 4, 5, and 6 we discussed using the decision theoretic model to construct optimal decision strategies or algorithms. In each case, the optimal strategy was sequential. As shown in [19], a sequential strategy is not always optimal — especially when the value of time is incorporated into the objective function. The question that we now ask is "Under what conditions can we effectively construct an optimal parallel decision strategy for a decision problem?"

The answer to this questions has repercussions in economics as well as in computing. In economics, a major issue is when can tasks be efficiently broken down and delegated to other people. An organization can be viewed as having analogies to a parallel (or distributed) computing system, with each role in the organization corresponding to a processor. Under what conditions, then, can we construct an optimal strategy for problem solving in parallel?

From a computing stand point, we are dealing with an abstract parallel machine. To illustrate, we take the case of optimal binary search and optimal split tree search. Each experiment can be viewed as being a composite experiment built up from two primary experiments. In both cases, the primary experiments are:

1. compare b with y_i
with result $b = y_i$ or $b \neq y_i$

2. compare b with y_j
with result $b > y_j$ or $b \mid y_j$

where y_i is the ith record in the file, y_j is the jth record in the file and b is the element requested by the user.

For optimal binary search, an optimal experiment is a combination of an experiment of type 1 and an experiment of type 2 under the restriction that the y_i in part 1 is the same as the y_j in part 2. For optimal split tree search, an experiment is a combination of an experiment of type 1 and an experiment of type 2 without any restriction on the value of y_i or y_j.

In general, assume $\mathbf{D}_1$ is a decision problem with experiment set A_1 and information partitions $\mathbf{M}_a^1$. Suppose that an optimal strategy for $\mathbf{D}_1$ is myopic, and that the value of the optimal experiment at each stage is unique (for example, in sequential search, the probabilities are unique). Now let $\mathbf{D}_2$ be the same decision problem as $\mathbf{D}_1$ except it has experiment set A_2 and information partitions $\mathbf{M}_a^2$. Suppose that there is a linear ordering, $\geq$, over A^2. Then dynamic programming can effectively be used to construct an optimal algorithm for the decision problem D^* that we construct from D^1 and D^2 by defining $\mathbf{M}_a^* = \mathbf{M}_a^1 \cap \mathbf{M}_a^2$ and $A^* = A^1 \times A^2$ subject to the condition that on any subset, only the optimal first experiment from A^1 is considered. Under this generalization, we can construct optimal split trees [18].

For the split tree algorithm, we can envision two processors — one with experiment set A^1 and the other with experiment set A^2. Each processor is trying to solve the same problem optimally using its own set of experiments, but with common or shared information. Under what conditions will individuals using their own optimal strategy execute a strategy that is optimal for the group or organization?

Another case where we can effectively use dynamic programming to construct an optimal decision strategy is: when D^1 is a decision problem with experiment set A^1 and information partitions $\mathbf{M}_a^1$, and there is a linear ordering, $\geq_1$, over A^1. Now let D^2 be the same decision problem as D^1 except it has experiment set A^2 and information partitions $\mathbf{M}_a^2$. Suppose that there is a linear ordering, $\geq_2$ over A^2. Then dynamic programming can effectively be used to construct an optimal algorithm for the decision problem D^* that we construct from D^1 and D^2 by defining $A^* = A^1 \times A^2$ and $\mathbf{M}_a^* = \mathbf{M}_a^1 \cap \mathbf{M}_a^2$.

A special case is when $A^1 = A^2$ and $\geq_1 = \geq_2$, and we can extend this special case to where $A^1 = A^2 = \ldots = A^n$, $\geq_1 = \geq_2 = \ldots = \geq_n$, and $A^* = A^1 + A^2 + \ldots + A^n$. Using the experiments that form this special case, we can construct an optimal k-ary search tree.

We can again view this as k processors each executing an individually optimal strategy. Since each processor has the same experiment set, payoff function, information, etc., each processor will execute the same strategy. To keep the processors from executing the same strategy, each processor must have common knowledge of the other processors and their relative positions (i.e., the processors have to be numbered, and the ith processor must know that its experiment must be a lower numbered experiment than the $i+1^{st}$ processor's experiment).

The ability to effectively determine an optimal decision strategy for the composite experiments enables us to investigate the conditions under which a particular experiment set is optimal. Sheil [22] claims that median split trees are superior to optimal binary search trees. What Sheil implicitly assumes is that the cost of a split tree experiment is the same as the cost of a binary search tree experiment. Cunto and Gascon [5] show that generalized binary search trees are superior to binary search trees. Again, using the decision theoretic approach, we can investigate the conditions under which this statement is true. By investigating the conditions on the cost functions that make a particular formulation optimal, we can select algorithms that are appropriate for specific machines. Eventually, we might design specialized hardware to support a particular class of composite experiments.

A natural extension of this line of reasoning is under what conditions is parallel processing superior to traditional sequential processing? Parallel processing can be viewed as executing a particular class of composite experiments. An instruction executed by a SIMD machine with n processors can be viewed as the execution of an n-ary experiment, with each of the n processors executing one primary instruction at each step. For decision processes that are inherently sequential, executing one n-ary experiment causes up to n-1 more primary instructions to be executed than might be required by a sequential strategy that uses primary instructions. Although a strategy based on k-ary experiments might appear optimal, the cost and method of communication among processors must be included.

For decision processes that are inherently parallel (for example, convolution), n-ary experiments are efficient (i.e., the same experiments would be executed in a sequential strategy), but the cost of communication among processors is still an issue. For a parallel strategy to be optimal, the expected value of the time saved must exceed the expected incremental cost associated with parallel computation.

8. Conclusion

Incorporating the cost of information acquisition into the decision process enables us to treat many computer algorithms as a formalization of the decision process. By looking at algorithms and information systems as part of the decision process, we can build algorithms to reflect an individual's or organization's preferences.

From an economic view point, incorporating the cost of information acquisition into the choice process should bring the normative, economic choice models and the descriptive, psychological choice modes closer together. It will allow us to investigate the conditions under which the psychological choice models are optimal. At the same time it opens up the field of constructive economics. It can enable us to teach people rational processes for specific scenarios, and to embed rational (optimal) strategies within information retrieval and decision support systems.

Bibliography

1. Benhabib, J. and Bull, C., (1983). "Job Search: The Choice of Intensity," *Journal of Political Economy*, Vol. 91, No. 5. (pp. 747-765) .

2. Bookstein, A. (1983), "Outline of a General Probabilistic Retrieval Model," *Journal of Documentation*, Vol. 39, No. 2, (pp. 63-72).

3. Bradley, S.P., Hax, A.C., and Magnanti, T.L., (1977), *Applied Mathematical Programming*, Addison-Wesley, New York.

4. Coombs, C.H., (1983), *Psychology and Mathematics*, The University of Michigan Press, Ann Arbor, Michigan.

5. Cunto, W. and Gascon, J.L., (1987), "Improving Time and Space Efficiency in Generalized Binary Search Trees," *Acta Informatica*, Vol. 24, (pp. 583-594).

6. Debreu, G., (1959), *Theory of Value: An Axiomatic Analysis of Economic Equilibrium,* Yale University Press, New Haven, CT.

7. Frenkel, K.A., (1986), "Complexity and Parallel Processing: An Interview with Richard Karp," *Communications of the ACM*, Vol. 29, No. 2, (pp. 112-117).

8. Knuth, D.E., (1970), "Optimum Binary Search Trees," *Acta Informatica*, Vol. 1, (pp. 14-25).

9. Kohn, M.G. and Shavell, S., (1974), "The Theory of Search," *Journal of Economic Theory*, Vol. 9, (pp. 93-123).

10. Kraft, D.H., (1978), "A Threshold Rule Applied to the Retrieval Decision Model," *Journal of the American Society for Information Science*, Vol. 29, No. 3 (pp. 77-80).

11. Kraft, D.H. and Bookstein, A., (1978), "Evaluation of Information Retrieval Systems: A Decision Theory Approach," *Journal of the American Society for Information Science*, Vol. 29, No. 1, (pp. 31-40) .

12. Lancaster, K.J., (1966), "A New Approach to Consumer Theory," *Journal of Political Economy*, Vol. 74, No. 2 (pp. 132-157).

13. Melhorn, K., (1984), *Data Structures and Algorithms 2: Graph Algorithms and NP-Completeness*, Springer-Verlag, Berlin.

14. Moore, J.C., Richmond, W.B., and Whinston, A.B., (1988), "A Decision Theoretic Approach to File Search," *Computer Science in Economics and Management*, Vol 1, No.1, (pp. 3-20).

15. Moore, J.C. and Whinston, A.B., (1986), "A Model for Decision-Making with Sequential Information-Acquisition — Part 1," *Decision Support Systems*, Vol. 2 (pp. 285-307).

16. Moore, J.C. and Whinston, A.B., (1987), "A Model for Decision-Making with Sequential Information-Acquisition — Part 2," *Decision Support Systems*, Vol. 3 (pp. 47-72).

17. Moore, J.C., Richmond, W.B., and Whinston, A.B., (1990), "A Decision Theoretic Approach to Information Retrieval, *ACM Transactions on Database Systems*, Vol. 15, No. 3 (pp. 311-340).

18. Moore, J.C., Richmond, W.B. and Whintston, A.B., (1990), "Optimal Decision Processes and Algorithms," *Journal of Economic Dynamics and Control*, 1990, Vol. 14, (pp. 375-417).

19. Morgan, P. and Manning, R., (1985), "Optimal Search," *Econometrica*, Vol. 53, No. 4, (pp. 923-944).

20. Raiffa, H. (1968), *Decision Analysis Introductory Lectures on Choice Under Uncertainty*, Addison-Wesley, New York.

21. Richmond, W.B., (1988), *Choice, Information, and Computing*, PhD dissertation, Krannert Graduate School of Management, Purdue University, 1988.

22. Sheil, B.A., (1978), "Median Split Trees: A Fast Lookup Technique for Frequently Occurring Keys," *Communications of the ACM*, Vol. 21, No. 11, (pp. 947-958) .

23. Tarjan, R.E. and Sleator, D.D., (1985), "Self—Adjusting Binary Search Trees," *Journal of the ACM*, Vol. 32, No. 3, (pp. 652-686).

24. Train, K., (1986), *Qualitative Choice Analysis: Theory, Economics, and an Application to Automobile Demand*, The MIT Press, Cambridge, Massachusetts.

25. Traub, J.F. and Wozniakowski, H., (1984), "Information and Computation," *Advances in Computers*, Vol. 23, (pp. 35-92).

26. Tversky, A. and Sattath, S.,(1979), "Preference Trees," *Psychological Review*, Vol. 86, No. 6, (pp. 542-573).

27. Tversky, A., "Elimination by Aspects: A Theory of Choice," *Psychological Review*, Vol. 79, (pp. 281-299).

28. Weitzman, M.L., (1979), "Optimal Search for the Best Alternative," *Econometrica*, Vol 47, No. 3, (pp. 641-654).

CHAPTER 2
KNOWLEDGE-BASED DECISION SUPPORT

Krishnan

Dolk and Kridel

Elofson and Konsynski

Trippi and Turban

Raghavan and Chand

Fischer and Mastaglio

PDM: A knowledge-based tool for model construction

Ramayya Krishnan

Decision Systems Research Institute, School of Urban and Public Affairs, Carnegie-Mellon University, Pittsburgh, PA 15213, USA

This paper describes PDM, a knowledge-based tool designed to help non-expert users construct Linear Programming (LP) models of Production, Distribution and Inventory (PDI) planning problems. PDM interactively aids users in defining a qualitative model of their planning problem, and employs it to generate problem-specific inferences and as input to a model building component that mechanically constructs the algebraic schema of the appropriate LP model. Interesting features of PDM include the application of domain knowledge to guide user interaction, the use of syntactic knowledge of the problem representation language to effect model revision, and in the use of a small set of primitive modeling rules in model construction.

Keywords: Artificial intelligence, Model management.

Ramayya Krishnan is Assistant Professor of Management Science and Information Systems at Carnegie Mellon University. He has a B. Tech in Mechanical Engineering from the Indian Institute of Technology, a M.S. in Operations Research, and a Ph.D. in Information Systems from the University of Texas at Austin. His research interests are in the application of symbolic and qualitative reasoning techniques. His recent work has used these techniques to develop computer-based environments that support model development activities.

1. Introduction

Models play an important role in decision support. While models drawn from several modeling traditions have been successfully integrated into computer-based decision support systems, Linear Programming (LP) models have been among the most widely used. While the quality of system support for LP modeling has improved considerably in recent years, the need to conceptualize a real-world problem in terms of abstract concepts and mathematical notation has inhibited their use by non-expert users. Several knowledge-based systems have been proposed to address these shortcomings (Binbasioglu and Jarke, 1986; Bu-Halaiga and Jain, 1988; Ma, Murphy and Stohr, 1986; Murphy and Stohr, 1986; Krishnan, 1987,1988; Muhanna and Pick, 1988).

This paper describes PDM, a knowledge-based tool that has been designed to help non-expert users construct LP models of Production, Distribution and Inventory (PDI) planning problems. PDM interactively aids users in defining a logic model of their planning problem which is used to provide qualitative [1] insights, and as input to a model building component that mechanically constructs the corresponding LP model through the application of a small set of primitive modeling rules such as material balance. The ability to construct a quantitative LP model from high level qualitative specifications is an important feature of the PDM system.

PDM has been implemented in Prolog and the chief purpose of this paper is to describe its key modules in order to document the lessons learnt in designing and implementing a knowledge-based model construction system. PDM employs alter-

---

[1] By qualitative, we imply a focus on representations and inferences which deal with objects, their inter-relationships, and their attributes as opposed to representations that employ numeric relationships and emphasize numeric reasoning.

nate knowledge sources (domain knowledge and model building knowledge) and a variety of knowledge representation schemes. Thus the primary focus of the paper is on the functionality to be gained from both the structure and the content of the knowledge used in PDM and the means employed to integrate the alternate knowledge sources and representation schemes.

The rest of the paper is organized as follows. Section 2 introduces the key features and components of the PDM system. Section 3 and 4 detail knowledge representation and control issues in two principal components: the front end and the model construction module. Section 5 draws conclusions and describes some avenues for future research in light of current limitations.

2. PDM: The system

PDM was designed to support non-expert users who lacked the familiarity with mathematical modeling to construct a model appropriate to their needs. The ability of non-expert users, by virtue of their familiarity with their problem, to provide qualitative problem descriptions is an important assumption underlying the approach in PDM. These qualitative descriptions when formalized within the syntax of a logical language result in a logic model of the problem. Since all the inferences flow from this representation, key features in the PDM system revolve around the processes used to obtain, represent and manipulate it. Figure 1 illustrates the important features of PDM which are summarized in the following.

(a) Qualitative descriptions of PDI planning problems are represented in a domain-specific logic-based language called PM (Krishnan, 1988). PM allows problems to be described in vocabulary familiar to the user and employs domain-specific axioms to provide problem-specific inferences. A specification in PM defines a logic model of the problem.

(b) To render the syntax of PM transparent to the user, an object-oriented dialogue system has been designed to interactively aid the user in problem description. This system employs knowledge of PM to assert sentences in response to answers obtained from the user, and domain-specific knowledge to aid problem elicitation by focusing

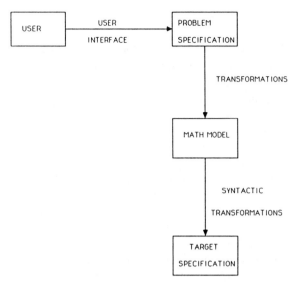

Fig. 1. The PDM system.

the users attention on processes implied by the evolving description (i.e. the logic model) of the problem.

(c) The knowledge base employed by the dialogue system also explicitly encodes syntactic interdependencies between elements that make up the logic model enabling structural revision of PM problem specifications in the event of change. An important implication of this feature is the ability to structurally revise LP models, since structurally revised PM specifications yield structurally revised LP models.

(d) The algebraic schema of the LP model is constructed from the PM problem specification through the application of primitive modeling rules such as material balance. The application of these primitive modeling rules, stated in domain-independent terms, to a specific logic model in PM is facilitated by transformation rules which represent knowledge about the relationships between the generic processes that underlie the modeling rules and the specific processes that underlie PDI planning. The output of the model construction component is the LP model represented in an embedded list notation which is subsequently transformed to sentences of a mathematical modeling language called Structured Modeling (SM) (Geoffrion, 1987).

3. PDM architecture

Components in the PDM system have been grouped together and implemented as three distinct modules. (See fig. 2.) They are the front end, the model construction module and the back end. While user interaction, query answering, and model revision are handled by the front end, model building is performed by the model construction module, and syntactic transformations of the constructed LP models to Structured Modeling implemented in the back end.

The modules employ distinct knowledge sources. The front end employs domain-specific knowledge to guide user interaction and query answering, and syntactic knowledge of PM to effect model revision. On the other hand, the model construction module employs model building knowledge. The modules also use different knowledge representation schemes. While the front end employs an object-oriented scheme, the model construction component employs a forward chaining rule-based system and a set of procedures that manipulate certain object-types to perform equation building. The back end which implements a straightforward syntactic transformation into Structured Modeling is implemented as a set of Prolog procedures. The alternative knowledge representation schemes and knowledge sources employed in these modules are integrated within a blackboard type architecture, i.e., all communication between them is channeled exclusively through changes to a global database of facts.

The rest of the paper focusses on the two most important features of PDM: (a) the ability to interactively aid a user in defining and revising a high level qualitative specification of a planning problem and (b) the ability to construct the LP

model from these high level specifications. Readers interested in a complete treatment of the PDM system are referred to Krishnan (1987, 1988).

3.1. The front end

The two important kinds of functionality offered by the front end are: (a) interactive support in the definition of a PM problem specification and (b) management and control of revisions to existing PM problem specifications. Both these features are directly influenced by the problem representation language PM. The following briefly introduces PM with a view to motivate the discussion on the knowledge base employed in the front end module.

3.2. The PM language

PM (Krishnan, 1988) is a logic-based language designed to logically model the PDI planning domain. An important feature in PM is the ability to introduce specific vocabulary as and when necessary to describe particular problems that arise in PDI planning. These user-introduced terms form the open vocabulary of PM while the rich set of generic concepts about PDI planning form part of its closed vocabulary. The following specifies a subset of the closed vocabulary of PM.

object constants: products, machines, raw-materials, regular-labor, overtime-labor, production-process, plant, distribution-center, warehouse, customer-site, purchase-yard, time, real-number, used-in, produced-by, purchased-at, stored-at, sold-at, available-at, shipped-from, unit-process-cost, unit-process-price, process-level, utilization-rate, availability, min-level, max-level

primitive predicates: basic-type, type, ftype, subtype, fsubtype, fdomain, fapply, ins-of, index, = , ! =

Object constants in PM are used to name the various objects, processes and relationships that characterize the PDI domain. For example, constants such as **product** and **raw-material** name sets of objects, while others such as **purchased-at** and **stored-at** are used to name relationships. Examples of constants used to name functions are **process-level** and **unit-process-cost**. These different types of object constants in PM are distinguished and

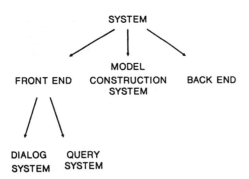

Fig. 2. System architecture.

explicitly inter-related using declarations in PM. Three important declarations are introduced using examples.

basic-type (product)
All object constants that name sets are declared using the predicate **basic-type**. The statement shown above declares that product is a type of set.

type (purchased-at, [raw-material, purchase-location, time])
Object constants that name relations are declared using the predicate **type**. The predicate is interpreted as declaring that the domain of the relation named in the first argument is defined by the cross product of the sets named in the second argument. Thus, **purchased-at** names a relation that is the purchase of **raw-materials** at **purchase-locations** across **time**.

ftype (process-cost, [commodity, location, time], [real-number])
Object constants that name functions (i.e. attributes of objects or their relationships) are declared using the predicate **ftype**. The predicate is also used to declare the domain and range of the named function. Thus, **process-cost** names a function that measures the cost of performing a given task or process using some **commodity** at a particular **location** and **time-period**.

The declarations shown above explicitly relate object constants **within** the closed and open vocabulary respectively. Relationships **between** elements of the open and closed vocabulary are declared as shown below. Object constants that name sets and relations in the open and closed vocabulary are related using the predicate **subtype**. This predicate plays a role that is similar to the generalization/specialization declarations in frames and semantic networks.

subtype (steel, product)
The example declares that the set named by **steel**, an object constant of the open vocabulary, is a subset of the set named by **product**, an object constant of the closed vocabulary. Similarly, object constants used to name functions in the open and closed vocabulary are related using the predicate **fsubtype**.

fsubtype (coal-purchase-cost, process-cost)
This predicate is interpreted as declaring that **coal-purchase-cost** is a type of **process-cost**.

Sets, relations, and functions that are named in PM are defined using the predicates **ins-of** and **fapply**.

ins-of([brown-coal], coal)
The example declares that **brown-coal** is an element of the set named by **coal**. Elements of sets and relations are declared using the predicate **ins-of**.

fapply (coal-purchase-cost, [brown-coal, dallas, 1980], 12.25)
The predicate **fapply** is interpreted as applying the function named in the first argument to a list of constants in the second argument. The output of the function application is the third argument.

A fragment of PM specification of a production problem in the steel industry is shown below.

An Example in PM
basic-type (steel)
basic-type (coal)
basic-type (coal-mines)
basic-type (weeks)

subtype (steel, product)
subtype (coal, raw-material)
type (coal-purchase, [coal, coal-mines, weeks])
subtype (coal-purchase, purchased-at)
ftype (coal-purchase-cost, [coal, coal-mines, weeks, [real-number])
fsubtype (coal-purchase-cost, process-cost)

ins-of ([brown-coal], coal)

The example consists of a set of declarations which specify the production of steel in a production process utilizing coal as a raw-material. An important feature of the specification is its focus on representing qualitative relationships at a high level of abstraction.

3.3 Knowledge base

As previously mentioned, helping the user define his problem in PM and managing structural revisions to a PM specification are the two important tasks performed by the front end module.

Since elements of the closed vocabulary represent generic objects, processes and attributes in PDI planning, defining a specific problem in PM requires the identification of those problem-specific concepts that are specializations of the generic domain-specific concepts. Thus aiding problem definition requires the ability to "visit" each generic concept and generate a question regarding its relevance to the users problem situation. The knowledge base (KB) in PDM enables this by structuring the domain-specific elements in PM into a graph of objects. [2] Each individual constant in PM used to name sets, relations, and functions is treated as an object. The object-based representation of the constant **purchased-at** is shown below.

purchased-at
⟨related-objects⟩:
    value: [raw-material, purchase-location, time]
⟨inv-related-to-prod⟩:
    value: [purchase-cost, purchase-level]
⟨inv-related-to-dis⟩:
    value: [purchase-cost, purchase-level, shipping-plan]
⟨process-relations⟩:
    value: [used-in, stored-at, supplied-from]
⟨to-fill-in⟩:
    rule-action: should-we-proceed
⟨if-confirmed⟩:
    rule-action: perform-tasks

Each object has five slots. The first three slots represent information about the syntactic inter-dependencies between the elements in PM. These inter-dependencies are used to effectively link the various objects in the KB to create an object graph. Each leaf node of this object graph corresponds to a constant used to name a set (i.e., declared using the predicate **basic-type**). Internal nodes of this object graph such as the example object correspond to constants used to name relations and functions (i.e., declared using the predicate **type** and **ftype** respectively). A fragment of the object graph that corresponds to the closed vocabulary is shown in fig. 3.

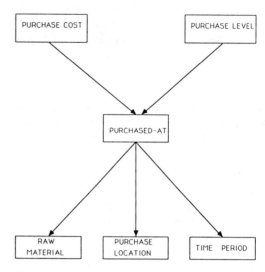

Fig. 3. An object graph.

The value fillers of the first three slots associated with an object are derived directly from the **type**, **fdomain** [3], and **joint-domain** declarations in PM. The close relationship between the object-based representation and the language is illustrated with a simple example. Consider the type declaration in PM of the purchased-at predicate shown below.

type (purchased-at, [raw-material, purchase-location, time])

The declaration relates the object constant **purchased-at** to a list of object constants that define its domain. This list of object constants is used as the filler of the **related-objects** slot of the purchased-at object.

The next two slots, **inv-related-to-prod** and **inv-related-to-dis**, represent the "inverse" of the linkages represented in the **related-objects** slot. These slots represent the set of all object constants whose type/fdomain/joint-domain declarations contain the object under consideration. Thus for example, the purchased-at object would be part of the inverse pointer slots of the raw-material, purchase-location and time objects. Specifically, the inverse pointers associated with an object, say Y, in the

---

[2] The term objects is used in the object-oriented programming sense. While the objects we use in PDM resemble frames in their use of slots and procedural attachments, no use is made of either inheritance or defaults.

[3] fdomain and joint domain are declarations in PM. While fdomain explicitly relates functions to its domain, joint-domain relates three relations X, Y and Z such that X names the join of the relations named by Y and Z.

object graph can be defined set theoretically as shown below.

$$\text{Inv}(Y) := \{X: \text{type } (Y, L) \, \& \, X \in L \, | \, \text{fdomain } (Y, X) \, | \, \text{joint-domain } (Y, U, V) \, \& \, X = U \text{ or } V\}$$

This set of inverse pointers is partitioned into two non-disjoint sets as a function of the problem contexts that arise in PDI planning. Thus, the **inv-related-to-prod** slot of the purchased-at object that represents the inverse pointers in the production planning context has a filler that consists of purchase-level and purchase-cost while the equivalent **inv-related-to-dis** slot for the distribution planning context additionally consists of the shipping-plan object. The rationale is that while distribution contexts may involve both purchase and shipping, production contexts only involve purchase. This partitioning of the inverse pointers as a function of the problem context enables the selective traversal of objects in the object graph as a function of problem context enabling a focussed and structured dialogue process.

Inverse pointers enable traversal of the object graph in a "bottom-up" manner; i.e., from leaf nodes that correspond to sets to internal nodes that correspond to relations and functions. This ability is particularly important since the dialogue begins in the context of objects that correspond to sets and proceeds to contexts represented by objects that correspond to relations and functions. This is in keeping with the intuitive transition of dialogue about simple concepts to interaction about more complex concepts.

While the first three slots represent syntactic inter-dependencies, the fourth slot, **process-relations**, represents domain-specific axioms. It so happens that these axioms about the domain are of a simple structure that facilitates their representation via a slot. Consider the example shown below.

If purchased-at (X, L, T) then stored-at (X, L, T)
or supplied-from (X, L, T)
or ∃P used-in (X, P, L, T)

The axiom is non-horn and states that if a commodity X is purchased at a given location then it is either stored at that location, supplied from that location or used in a production process housed in that location. The process-relations slot represents the list of processes related to the purchase process, enabling the system to bring these related processes to the attention of the user. Finally, the last two slots represent procedural knowledge that implements the logic used in the dialogue and model revision process. Each of these slots have **rule-action** facets. In contrast to the **value** facets used in the first four slots, **rule-action** facets are active facets (much like the if-needed facets in traditional frame-based systems) that encode Prolog procedures. In the example, the slots **to-fill-in** and **if-confirmed** have rule-action facets which represent the procedures **should-we-proceed** and **perform-tasks**. The logic implemented in these facets is described later. Each object in the KB is implemented in Prolog as a set of clauses. A fragment of the purchased-at object used as an example is shown below. The general notation used is

⟨object-name⟩ (⟨slot-name⟩, ⟨facet-name⟩, ⟨value-filler⟩)

Where value-filler is either a list of objects, an object or a Prolog procedure. Thus the purchased-at object is represented as shown below.

purchased-at (related-objects, value, [raw-material, purchase-location, time])
purchased-at (to-fill-in, rule-action, should-we-proceed)

The next section describes the control logic used to manage the generation of dialogue.

3.3.1 Dialogue generation

The primary responsibility of the dialogue generation module is to interactively aid the user in defining the logic model of the problem. This is done by generating hypotheses (dialogue) in the context of situations, entities and relationships that characterize PDI planning. The traversal of the object graph to generate dialogue is performed in a bottom-up manner and characterized by two important steps:

(a) Queries are generated initially in the context of the leaf nodes (i.e. the sets) of the object graph. These queries are aimed at identifying the various types of entities in a particular planning problem and ascertaining the existence of relationships between these types of entities. They are referred to as **askable** queries since the information they obtain from the user is not inferable. An example is shown below.

What are the different types of product produced in the system?
|: steel
Please supply the elements of the set "steel"
|: **[stainless-steel, tensile-steel]**

The first query requests the specification of different types of products to which the user identified steel as the only type. The next query required the user to enumerate the elements of the set steel. User responses are translated into PM sentences. The sentences asserted in response to this interaction are shown below.

subtype (steel, product)
ins-of (steel, [stainless-steel, tensile-steel])

(b) Responses to the askable queries form the kernel of the evolving PM specification of the problem. Domain-specific axioms (such as those represented in the **process-relations** slot) and other rules encoded as procedures are used to hypothesize situations implied by the evolving PM specification. Hypothesis that are confirmed by the user result in additions to the PM specification. For instance, assume that the user already indicated that coal is purchased at coal mines. The domain-specific axiom represented in the process-relations slot of the purchased-at object is used to hypothize the set of processes related to the purchase process. The user is required to confirm the existence of one or more of these related processes. The axiom and associated dialogue are shown below.

if purchased-at (X, L, T) then stored-at (X, L, T)
    or supplied-from (X, L, T)
    or $\exists$P used-in (X, P, L, T)

The axiom states that if a commodity is purchased at a location, it is either stored or supplied from that location or used in production at the same location. This axiom results in a series of queries to the user.

is coal stored at the coal mines? (Y/N)
is coal supplied-from the coal mines? (Y/N)
is coal used in production at the coal mines? (Y/N)

The illustrated use of domain axioms to guide user interaction is a novel feature of PDM and a measure of the power to be gained from a domain-specific approach. Furthermore, the requirement that the user identify at least one related process as relevant prevents several simple infeasibilities that arise in problem specifications due to errors of omission.

The "bottom up" traversal of the object graph has been implemented using an agenda scheme (Lenat, 1976).

Agenda-based Control: An agenda-based control strategy employs a queue to order the tasks at hand. In our context, the flow of dialogue is initiated and controlled by the addition of objects in the object graph to the queue which might then be sampled under a variety of queuing disciplines.

A significant advantage of the agenda scheme is the ability to tune the order in which objects are sampled thereby effecting control over the flow of dialogue. The interpreter is implemented as a simple recursive procedure in Prolog as shown below.

interpret ([]).
interpret ([H|T]):- process-frame (H, T, Current),
        interpret (Current).

The first clause represents the base case of the recursion and indicates that the interpreter halts when the agenda is empty. The second clause implements a FIFO (First In First Out) policy and considers the first object in the agenda using the procedure process-frame. This procedure activates the procedures in the **to-fill-in** and **if-confirmed** slots of the object under consideration. These procedures decide on dialogue generation and upon completion queue in objects in their appropriate inverse slots into the agenda thus ensuring the flow of dialogue. Changes to the agenda status are determined and the procedure recurses on a new binding of the agenda status.

In the context of our object graph, dialogue is initially generated in the leaf nodes. Upon completion, interior nodes that are part of inverse slots of the leaf node are added to the agenda resulting in the continued generation of dialogue among interior nodes. Dialogue generation halts when the agenda is empty.

Dialogue Generation: An important feature of the dialogue generation process is the need to generate dialogue in vocabulary familiar to the user. We have adopted a simple strategy to effect this feature.

Dialogue is generated by procedures attached to the **to-fill-in** and the **if-confirmed** slots of an object. These procedures contain inference rules and templates of text. An example of a rule used to generate dialogue in the context of the purchased-at object is shown below.

If X is a type of raw-material and
If Y is a type of purchase-location
If Z is a type of time-period
Then ascertain the existence of a relation between
    X, Y, and Z

The variables X, Y etc. are bound to user-supplied predicates that describe objects and processes specific to the problem at hand. These variables are combined with a template of text to generate dialogue using vocabulary previously supplied by the user. An example template is shown below.

is ?X purchased-at ?Y in Z?

The ?X denotes variables that are to be bound. Templates that have instantiated variables result in text. Thus ?X being bound to coal and ?Y to coal-mines and ?Z to weeks results in the dialogue shown below.

/* Comments are enclosed within these symbols
    */
is coal purchased-at coal-mines in weeks? (yes/no)
|: yes
Please supply a unique name to this relation
|: coal-purchase-plan
/* The PM sentence corresponding to this answer -
    is */
/* type (coal-purchase-plan, [coal, coal-mines,
    weeks]) */

The first line of the dialogue queries the existence of a relation between coal and coal-mines which were user-supplied descriptions of objects and locations in his particular problem. Having ascertained the existence of the relation, the user is required to supply a name for the relationship and tuples that represent instances of the relation. As the dialogue proceeds, such interaction results in sentences in PM being asserted. These type of questions are generated for each combination of objects that satisfy the dialogue generation rules.

A useful feature of the dialogue system is the ability to save the state of the agenda and object graph midway through problem description. While saving the state of the queue suffices to save the state of the agenda, the state of the object graph is saved using a system of markings. Each object

which has been investigated (i.e. dialogue generation having resulted in the addition of PM sentences) is marked. This allows the interpreter to skip over marked objects when user interaction is continued at a later time to prevent the redundant generation of dialogue. The important advantage of being able to save the state of the agenda and the object graph is the ability to work with the PDM system as and when desired.

The algorithm used to control the flow of dialogue is presented below.

ALG Process:
Do while agenda is not empty;
choose object from agenda
if object is marked /* if 1 */
then queue objects in the inverse-relation slot based on problem
context to the agenda and delete object from agenda /* end if 1 */
if object is unmarked /* if 2 */
then
    if objects in its related-objects slot are marked
        /* if 3 */
    then invoke perform-task and
        if new PM sentences are added /* if 4 */
        then mark object and queue in objects in
            inverse-relation slot
        else queue in objects in inverse-relation slot
            and
        delete object from agenda /* end if 4 */
    else delete frame from agenda /* end if 2, 3 */
End Do While;

Limitations: While the dialogue system amply demonstrates the functionality to be gained from a knowledge-based tool, a state of the art graphics/icon driven system would be far more user-friendly.

3.3.2. Model revision

Model specifications are constantly revised as assumptions that underlie problem specifications change. These changes in assumptions about the problem being modeled typically result in additions and/or deletions of sets, relations and functions or in additions and deletions of their respective elements. This alteration of an existing problem specification has been termed model revision.

Since elements that make up the problem specification are tightly inter-related, a change in one part tends to affect other parts. This implies the need to control and manage the process of propagating local changes throughout a problem specification. Propagation of changes requires the explicit representation of inter-dependencies between problem elements. The object graph (i.e. the KB) in PDM supports model revision since it encodes the syntactic inter-dependencies between elements that make up the problem specification. It is used in conjunction with the agenda-based scheme described in the previous section to effect propagation of local changes. Consider a fragment of a production planning problem in PM. The sentences have been labelled for ease of reference.

sent1: subtype (steel, product)
sent2: subtype (open-hearth, production-process)
sent3: subtype (oxygen, raw-material)
sent4: subtype (oxy-used-in-open-hearth, used-in)
sent5: type (oxy-used-in-open-hearth, [oxygen, open-hearth, mill, year])

The PM specification describes the usage of oxygen in the open-hearth process used in steel-production. Now if the open-hearth process declared in sent2 were to be removed from the problem specification, the sentences labelled sent4 and sent5 should also be deleted since they are directly or indirectly related to the deleted object constant. Since each user-supplied object constant is related to a object constant of the closed vocabulary (i.e. an object in the object graph), propagation of deletions is implemented using a selective traversal of the object graph.

This traversal begins by accessing the object in the graph related to the user-supplied predicate being deleted. In the example since open-hearth, the predicate being deleted is a production-process, an object in the object graph, the production-process object is accessed and all the objects in its **inverse-relation** slot are queued into the agenda. These objects correspond to object constants of the closed vocabulary that are directly dependent on the production-process object. The interpreter examines those objects that are marked (recall that marked objects correspond to object constants of the closed vocabulary that are part of the current PM specification) and deletes all PM sentences which contain a marked object. To ensure continued propagation, objects in its (the object under consideration by the interpreter)

inverse-relations slots are also added to the agenda. Processing halts when the agenda is empty.

The principal advantage of this approach is its focus of attention on only that part of the problem specification that needs to be changed. This is an important factor in the context of large specifications where a brute force search for sentences that need to be deleted may be infeasible.

In addition to this ability to propagate deletions, PDM also supports the addition of new sets and relations. When new sets or relations are added, there is a need to focus the users attention on the ramifications of the addition. For example, if a new type of product is added, new relationships have to be defined with existing production processes and other relevant objects involved in processes such as sales or storage. Once again the object graph and the agenda scheme are employed. When a user-supplied set or relation is added to an existing specification, the object of the closed vocabulary that it is related to (an object in the object graph) is queued into the agenda. The generation of dialogue is similar to that described previously with one major difference. Before any dialogue is generated in the context of any object in the object graph, a comparison is made between situations that are hypothesized and those that already exist in the PM specification. This prevents the redundant generation of dialogue. Once again due to the explicit representation of dependencies in the object graph, the process is focussed with only the minimal number of queries being generated.

This ability to revise model specifications is an important feature in PDM due to the flexibility offered to the user. Additionally, it also supports structural revision of the LP model since structurally revised PM specifications yield structurally revised LP model schema. This is particularly important since currently available LP modeling systems do not support this feature

4. Model construction

Linear Programming (LP) models are algebraic models. The construction of an algebraic model from a qualitative model requires the representation and application of model building knowledge.

This, in PDM, has been effected using a small set of domain-independent modeling principles such as material balance and resource utilization. The principal insight used in model construction derives from the observation that all the measurement functions [4] used in the qualitative model to represent numeric attributes are directly transformable to variables and parameters of the algebraic model. The model building rules are strictly concerned with determining the functional form of the mathematical relationships that relate these variables and parameters.

Model building rules such as the material balance rule shown below represent generic types of mathematical relationships. These generic relationships are encoded in terms of domain-independent abstractions referred to as **canonical objects**.

If [X] is a list of inputs to a system and
If [Y] is a list of outputs to a system
Then the sum of the set of inputs $\geq$ sum of the
    set of outputs

Model building requires these rules to be applied to a PM specification. However, the lack of a common vocabulary presents a problem, i.e., model building rules are stated in terms of canonical objects while PM specifications are stated in terms of problem-specific vocabulary. This has been resolved by adopting a simple two step procedure. First all problem specific objects, processes and attributes that make up the PM specification are transformed into canonical objects. Rules used for this task are referred to as **transformation rules**. The canonical objects so generated are combined using the model building rules into algebraic functions and constraints that make up the schema of the LP model.

While the foregoing presented the synopsis of the logic used in model construction, the implementation in PDM takes account of certain other problems. Specifically, model building in PDM proceeds at two distinct levels: the construction level and the meta construction level. The application of transformation rules and model building rules take place at the construction level. However, these tasks at the construction level are controlled using meta-rules that encode knowledge about the order or sequencing of rule application.

---

[4] Examples of measurement functions are production-level, utilization-rate etc.

Meta-rules are essential to ensure correctness in model building and serve to improve the efficiency of the model building process. The following illustrates with a simple example, the knowledge representation and model building strategy employed in each of these levels.

Example

Consider a simplified steel production process which uses various types of coal to produce several types of steel. Assume that the production of each unit of steel utilizes a fixed amount of coal. Let its value be given by the parameter, coal-util-rate. Coal is supplied via purchase and let the variable coal-purchase-level represent the amount of coal purchased. Finally let the steel production level be measured by the variable steel-production level.

Given this fragment of simple problem, the capacity constraint for coal that we seek to generate is modeled using material balance resulting in the capacity constraint shown below.

sum(S) sum(P) (coal-util-rate (C, P, L, T) *
    steel-production-level (S, P, L, T)) $\leq$
    coal-purchase-level (C, L, T)

The letters S, C, P, L and T correspond to indices for the sets steel, coal, production process, location and time-period.

The equivalent qualitative model of the problem in PM is shown below.

subtype (coal, raw-material)
subtype (steel, product)
subtype (coal-usage, used-in)
type (coal-usage, [coal, steel-production-process, mill, years])
ftype (coal-util-rate, [coal, steel-production-process, mill, years), [real-number])
fsubtype (coal-util-rate, utilization-rate)
ftype (steel-production-level, [steel, steel-production-process, mill, years), [real-number])
fsubtype (steel-production-level, activity-level)

The differences in the representation of the problem in PM and quantitatively as an algebraic model are significant. The PM representation simply declares the type of steel, coal and the production process and declares the relations and functions that characterize the problem. On the other hand, the algebraic constraint represents a mathematical relationship between numeric variables and parameters. The following briefly demon-

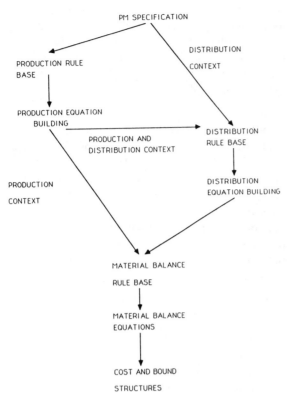

PM SPECIFICATION

PRODUCTION RULE
BASE

DISTRIBUTION
CONTEXT

PRODUCTION EQUATION
BUILDING

PRODUCTION AND
DISTRIBUTION CONTEXT

DISTRIBUTION
RULE BASE

PRODUCTION
CONTEXT

DISTRIBUTION
EQUATION BUILDING

MATERIAL BALANCE

RULE BASE

MATERIAL BALANCE
EQUATIONS

COST AND BOUND

STRUCTURES

Fig. 4. Meta rules.

strates the steps used to construct the material balance constraint from the PM specification.

First since the context of the problem is production planning, a meta-rule at the meta construction level is used to suggest the application of a "transformation-in-form" rule denoted fig. 4 as the production rule base.

The "transformation in form" rule is based on a generic resource utilization process and relates the utilization-rate of a resource commodity that is input to a production process to the production level of the commodity produced as output of the same production process. The rule [5] is shown below.

If utilization-rate (X, R, RU, P, L, T) and activity-level (PL, RU, P, L, T)
    and index (X, IR) and index (PL, IPL) and index (P, IP) and
    index (R, Iru) and subtype (Dom, utilized-at) and
    type (Dom, [R, L, T))

[5] The collection of model building rules may be found in Appendix A (available from the author).

then gensym (RUL, utilization-level) and
    fsubtype (RUL, process-level) and fdomain
        (RUL, Dom) and
    RUL := sum(Iru) sum(IP) (X : IR * Pl : IPL)

The rule constructs the function RUL from canonical objects that are instances of the utilization-rate and activity-level objects. The application of this domain-independent rule to a PM specification requires the application of transformation rules to the PM specification. The collection of transformation rules associated with model building rules is referred to as a rule base or rule set.

The exact details of the transformation rule application are detailed and space limitations prevent a full-fledged description. The reader is referred to Krishnan (1988) and Krishnan (1987) for an indepth discussion of transformation rules. The idea behind transformation rules is simple. Essentially these rules encode knowledge about the relationships between the domain-specific processes that underlie the problem specification in PM and the generic processes that underlie the model construction rules. They yield instances of canonical objects as output. Thus, in the context of our example, the transformation rules recognize the steel-production-process as a process that utilizes coal as a resource to produce steel. After a series of transformations this leads to the generation of steel-production-level as an activity-level object and the coal-util-rate as an utilization-rate object. They are shown below.

steel-production-level
        canonical-object-type:
            value : activity-level
        context:
            value : [s, p, l, t]

coal-util-rate
        canonical-object-type:
            value : utilization-rate
        context:
            value : [c, p, l, t]

An important feature of these canonical objects are their context slots that represent index information. The assignment of indices to the elements of a PM specification is performed by index assignment procedures that are also activated by meta rules. Essentially, the strategy used in index assignment is as follows. Each set is assigned a unique symbol as index. These indices may either be supplied by users or provided by the system. Indices of named relations and functions are derived from index information associated with the sets that define their domain. An example is shown below.

if type (N-pred, [A1, ..., An]) and index (A1, IA1) and

  and ... and index (An, IAn)
then index (N-pred, [IA1, IA2, ..., IAn])

Thus type and ftype declarations in PM prove useful in index assignment. Indices set the context of an object and are used to determine if two or more objects can be combined by a given model building rule. The objects steel-production-level and coal-utilization-rate are combined using the transformation-in-form rule introduced previously to yield a new canonical object which encodes the left hand side (LHS) of the constraint we are in the process of constructing. The function built using the "transformation-in-form" rule and the canonical object that encodes it are shown below.

coal-utilization-level (c, l, t) = sum(s) sum(p)
    (coal-util-rate (c, p, l, t) *
    steel-production-level (s, p, l, t))

coal-utilization-level
    canonical-object-type:
        value: activity-level
    context:
        value: [c, l, t]
    function:
        value: [[sum, [s, p]], [coal-rate, [c, p, l, t]],
        [*], [production-level, [s, p, l, t]]]

The object is similar to the objects introduced earlier with one major exception. It has a function slot which encodes the LHS of the constraint under construction.

Upon completion of the model building rule application, control transfers once again back to the meta-level which suggests the application of the material balance rule. Once again the transformation rules associated with material balance are applied to the PM specification to yield coal-utilization-level, the canonical object described above, as an output object and the coal-purchase-level as an input object. The coal-purchase-level object is

shown below.

coal-purchase-level
    canonical-object-type:
        value : output
    context:
        value: [c, l, t]

These objects are combined using the material balance rule since they represent inputs and outputs of the commodity coal to a system (the indices in the objects are used to ensure similarity in contexts) into the capacity constraint being constructed. This yields the constraint for coal shown below.

coal-utilization-level (c, m, t) ≤ coal-purchase-level
    (c, m, t)

The constraint is similar to the one derived earlier except that the LHS in the constructed constraint is itself a function that was defined earlier.

Three concluding remarks are in order. First, meta-rules were used to sequence the application of the model building rules and their associated rule sets as a function of the problem context, i.e., since the context was production planning, only the resource utilization and material balance rules and their associated transformation rules were activated. This results in significant gains in efficiency since rule sets tend to be large and transformation to yield canonical objects involves significant amount of chaining. Second, the construction process used is "bottom up". That is constraints are built from left hand sides (LHS) and right hand sides (RHS) using the material balance rule. The LHS and the RHS themselves may be functions constructed through previous rule applications. This is illustrated in our example where the LHS was a resource utilization function built from primitive canonical objects using the "transformation-in-form" rule. The generic "bottom-up" procedure used in constraint building is depicted in Fig. 5.

An important implication of this "bottom up" approach to model building is the need to sequence the application of the model building rules since the input [6] of one rule is dependent on the

---

[6] In the example, the material balance rule used the coal-utilization object that was the output of the "transformation-in-form" rule as an input in constraint construction.

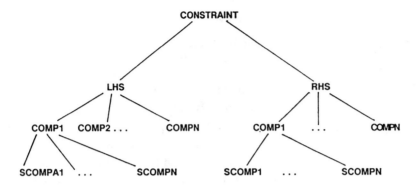

$$\textbf{SUM (i) (rate (i, j)} \quad * \quad \textbf{level (i))} \le \textbf{CAP (j)}$$

Fig. 5. Model construction strategy.

output of another to ensure correctness. Thus meta rules serve to ensure correctness of model building and to increase the efficiency by only invoking relevant rule sets. Meta rules thus serve an important role in that they explicitly represent "model construction" know how. In being the sole repository of such knowledge they support the alteration and manipulation of it in the event of change.

An important aspect of the model building strategy that we have not discussed as a result of space limitations is the role of transformation rules. Transformation rules are used to transform elements of the PM specification to canonical objects. This process is straightforward or complex depending on the availability of a rule/rules specific to the situation being modeled by the PM specification. If directly applicable rules exist, the transformation process is straightforward. However, in the absence of directly applicable rule sets, PM problem specifications are augmented with additional variables and decomposed into situations for which directly applicable rule sets are available. A common example of this case include transhipment processes which are augmented with additional variables into transportation processes and material balance processes for which directly applicable rules exist. This process of diagnosing situations that need augmentation and decomposing them into situations that are transformable into canonical objects is an important non-trivial feature of transformation rules. The interested reader is referred to Krishnan (1987, 1988) for a

detailed description of the model construction process.

5. Conclusions

The main contribution of this paper has been the description of two key modules in the PDM system with an emphasis of the structure and content of the knowledge employed to effect user-interaction, model revision and automatic model construction. The novel features in PDM that were detailed included a description of the close interaction between the object-oriented system employed in the front end and the logic-based language PM used in problem representation, the use of domain-specific axioms to guide user inter-action, and the application of domain-independent model building rules to simulate a "first principles" approach to automated model construction.

There are two principal limitations in PDM. First, the user interaction system is textual and cumbersome and a graphics based tool would greatly help the type of non-expert users that PDM hopes to support. Another limitation is the restriction to linear models and the PDI planning domain. An useful extension would be a domain-independent logic modeling language that would be used to specify mathematical and qualitative models within an uniform framework. Research is underway on all these issues.

References

[1] Binbasioglu, M. and Jarke, M. (1986), Domain specific tools for knowledge based model building, Decision Support Systems, 2, 1, pp. 213–223.

[2] Bu-Halaiga, M., and Jain, H. (1988), An Interactive Plan Based Procedure for Model Integration in DSS, Proceedings of the Twenty First Hawaii Conference on the System Sciences, IEEE Press.

[3] Geoffrion, A.M. (1987), Introduction to Structured Modeling, Management Science, 33, 5, pp. 547–588.

[4] Krishnan, R. (1987), Knowledge Based Aids for Model Construction, Unpublished PhD Thesis, University of Texas, Austin, TX 78712.

[5] Krishnan, R. (1988), Automated Model Construction: A Logic Based Approach, Annals of Operations Research, Special Issue on Linkages between AI and OR, 21, pp. 195–226.

[6] Lenat, D. (1976), AM: An AI Approach to Discovery in Mathematics as Heuristic Search, Rept-STAN-CS-80-814, Stanford University, CA.

[7] Ma, P., Murphy, F., Stohr, E. (1986), The Science and Art of Formulating Linear Programs, to appear in IMA Journal of Mathematics In Management.

[8] Murphy, F., Stohr, E. (1986), An Intelligent System for Formulating Linear Programs, Decision Support Systems, 2, 1.

[9] W.A. Muhanna and Pick, R. (1988), Composite Models in SYMMS, Proceedings of the Twenty First Hawaii Conference on the System Sciences, IEEE Press.

An active modeling system for econometric analysis

Daniel R. Dolk

Naval Postgraduate School, Monterey, CA 93943, USA

Donald J. Kridel

Southwestern Bell Corporation, St. Louis, MO 63101, USA

This paper examines the feasibility of developing an "artificially intelligent econometrician" as an active decision support system (ADSS) in the sense articulated by [Manheim, 1988]. We review the system components of an ADSS and then relate them to a modeling system for econometric analysis that we have implemented. We present the query language of the PERM (Progressive EconometRic Modeling) system and offer an extension to the language based on process-oriented constructs for model integration. The query language and its extension correspond to the ADSS's user-directed and computer-directed process managers, respectively. Schemas representing statistical strategies are stored as processes in the extended language and serve as the econometric knowledge base. We suggest an approach to building an inference processor for this system based on experiments to record user query protocols and relate them to the schemas in the knowledge base. The connection between user processes and schemas is implemented by demon constructs in the extended language. Finally, we examine the extent to which our proposed system constitutes an ADSS.

Keywords: Active DSS, Econometric modeling, Model control language, Schema, Process manager, Inference processor, Demon.

Daniel R. Dolk is Associate Professor of Information Systems at the Naval Postgraduate School in Monterey, CA. He has published several papers on model management and the use of dictionary systems for managing information resources. His current research interests focus on model integration and the development of integrated modeling environments, including "active" systems which support both dynamic and static mathematical models. He is a member of ACM, TIMS, and the IEEE Computer Society and an Associate Editor for *ORSA Journal on Computing, Information Systems Research*, and the *Journal of Database Administration*.

1. Introduction

Manheim [1988] introduces the concept of an "active" DSS wherein the computer and user work as partners in the problem-solving process. The active DSS (ADSS) is particularly interesting because it relies more on ideas from cognitive science than organizational behavior [Keen and Scott Morton, 1978] or system design [Sprague and Carlson, 1982]. Manheim presents a number of research issues including the feasibility, design, and utility of an ADSS which we intend to examine as the basis for developing an intelligent modeling system for econometric analysis.

Remus and Kottemann [1986] provide a convincing argument for statistical analysis as a fertile domain for expert systems applications. Their "artificially intelligent statistician" (AIS) augments the cognitive limitations of decision-makers by identifying and executing sound statistical strategies which the user may not otherwise be aware of, and thus unwittingly violate. Our experience with a conventional modeling system we've developed for econometric forecasting in the telecommunications industry reinforces the desirability of this kind of support for econometric analysis. In econometrics there is a plethora of continually evolving estimation techniques, only a fraction of which the average user can be expected to know. On the other hand, as the discipline grows, so does the body of knowledge concerning acceptable strategies for employing these techniques.

Our objective in this paper is to lay the groundwork for an "artificially intelligent econometrician" based on Manheim's concept of an active DSS (ADSS). We start by reviewing the concepts

Donald J. Kridel is Director, Strategic Marketing at Southwestern Bell Corporation in St. Louis, Missouri. He has published papers on diffusion models and applying discrete choice techniques to new service prediction problems. His research interests focus on applied econometrics, telecommunications demand analysis, and active or expert decision support systems for econometric modeling.

and architectural components of an ADSS in Section 2. In subsequent sections, we develop constructs for each of the various components. These constructs comprise a mixture of the concrete and the abstract, starting in Section 3 with a specific example of a model manipulation language for econometric analysis which we've developed for the PERM (Progressive Econometric Modeling) system. In Section 4, we present an extension to this language which serves as a model integration control language for synchronizing processes [Kottemann and Dolk, 1988]. We discuss the difficulties inherent in econometric modeling and suggest the control language as a vehicle for capturing proper modeling strategies. The model manipulation language and its extension correspond to Manheim's user-directed and computer-directed process managers, respectively. Finally, we suggest an approach for developing an inference processor to associate user protocols with stored strategy schemas.

The primary contribution of this paper is the specification of components of a model manipulation language for econometric analysis which not only extend the features of conventional modeling systems but also provide a possible migration path to more powerful ADSS.

2. Active decision support systems

Manheim presents the notion of an active DSS as "a DSS which can usefully do more than what its users explicitly direct it to do", but which requires a "system design based on an explicit model of human problem-working processes" [Manheim, 1988]. The ADSS concept differs from conventional DSS approaches in that it is learning-based and therefore more in the context of cognitive science rather than system design [Sprague and Carlson, 1982] or organizational behavior [Keen and Scott Morton, 1978].

The system architecture for an ADSS consists of three main components: process managers, history processor, and display interfaces. Since DSS's ostensibly support the process of decision-making (or problem-working), process managers are fundamental components of the architecture. Specifically, there are two kinds of process managers: user-directed (UDPM) and computer-directed (CDPM). The UDPM activates resident

processes in response to commands issued directly by the user (e.g., a query processor to do data retrieval, or matrix manipulation routines to perform an ordinary least squares estimation). The CDPM, on the other hand, activates processes in response to commands issued by the history processor as it attempts to provide active support. Thus, the CDPM may invoke a particular, predefined regression estimation decision tree once it determines that the user really wants to perform this kind of analysis.

The history processor consists of two parts: a history recorder which simply journals user inputs and the resultant outputs in a history record, and a history inference processor (HIP) which attempts to identify or build a model of the user's image of the problem from the history record.

Finally there are display interfaces which allow the user to activate the UDPM, and which filter the various outputs of the system.

The system is structured as shown in fig. 1 and works roughly as follows:

(1) The user initiates action via some kind of command medium (a language, menu selection, mouse, etc.).

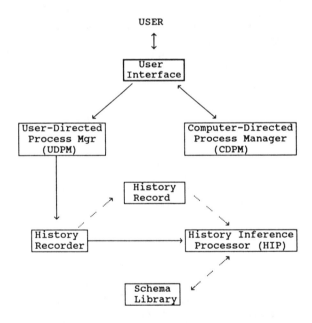

(Note: Dotted lines indicate data flow; Solid lines indicate process flow.)

Fig. 1. ADSS Design Architecture.

(2) The UDPM activates one or more processes (e.g., regression routine) to satisfy the action command.

(3) The history recorder logs the command and resultant output in the history record.

(4) The inference processor scans the history record and attempts to create a model of the user problem-working process either deductively by pattern-matching with a library of existing model templates (schemas), or inductively by some form of dynamic pattern recognition.

(5) Once the inference processor identifies a model, it passes control to the CDPM which invokes the processes associated with the model. If no model can be identified, control is returned to the user along with the user-directed process output.

(6) The CDPM returns the user-directed and computer-directed process output to the user after executing its requisite processes.

The key ingredient in this scenario is the history inference processor which is based on a model of human problem-working processes. Manheim suggests a general processing model which is reminiscent of neural networks. The model consists of a hierarchical network of schemas which form concepts. Schemas can be classified as template schemas which are similar to frames, procedural schemas which provide action sequences similar to plans, and mixed schemas which are combinations of the two. Problem-working consists of activation of schemas, under the direction of some higher level control logic, itself a schema.

The challenging part of an ADSS is building a computer model which emulates the above model. This involves the following steps:

(1) Construction of a schematic network from an evolving library of schemas. This involves the continual modification and addition of schemas as well as changes to the connectivity of the schemas.

(2) Operation of the schematic network to formulate hypotheses about the user, the problem, and the relevant problem-working processes.

(3) Testing of the hypotheses through the equivalent of simulation modeling.

The construction and evolution of a schema library is critical to the successful implementation of an ADSS. This can be built from a number of sources:

(1) Protocol analysis which tries to identify actual thought processes empirically.

(2) Predefined schemas derived from conventional wisdom or heuristics in much the same way expert system knowledge bases are created today.

(3) Pattern recognition, or script recognition, derived from a dynamic analysis of the history record.

The implementation of an ADSS raises many practical questions which are not addressed in Manheim's original proposal (see Manheim [1989] for a treatment of these issues). In many respects, an ADSS has more in common with the neural network approach to cognitive science [Rumelhart and McLelland, 1986] than with standard expert, or decision support, system technology. There are places, however, where current DSS design architecture can be adapted to begin investigating ADSS. In the remaining sections, we attempt to build a bridge to an ADSS for econometric modeling that works from the architecture of an existing conventional modeling system.

3. PERM: A modeling system for econometric analysis

Our objective is to build an active modeling system which provides some intelligent support to the modeler. Specifically we are interested in helping modelers use econometric estimation techniques properly. Another way of looking at this is that we are attempting to build an expert system which simulates the knowledge of an expert in econometrics. Our approach is to use the concepts of an ADSS as a way to build this system. As a result, we use the terms "active modeling system", "expert system", and "ADSS" interchangeably throughout the remaining discussion. Further, we use the term "conventional" in juxtaposition with "active" to denote systems which don't provide intelligent support. We begin by describing a conventional modeling system based on the econometric modeling life cycle.

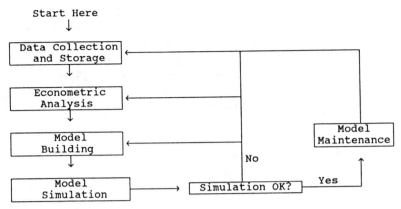

Fig. 2. Life Cycle of Econometric Modeling Process.

3.1. Econometric modeling life cycle

A simple econometric modeling life cycle for forecasting models is shown in fig. 2.

For many econometric applications significant economic theorizing may well precede the "empirical" steps outlined in fig. 2. Furthermore, depending on the "type" of econometric analysis to be performed, this life cycle may be further simplified, e.g., if the aim of the econometric exercise is to estimate elasticities of demand, then the life cycle is restricted to the data collection and econometric analysis phases.

Data collection, storage and manipulation is the most basic of tasks and logically precedes any empirical analysis. Collection and storage require little in the way of clarifying comments. Data manipulation, however, can be an important element in the life cycle. Since economic theory provides little guidance with respect to the selection of "functional form", many alternative specifications will typically be tested, e.g., does SALES depend on INCOME, the square of INCOME, or the log of INCOME. These specification searches require that alternative forms of the data-series be easily calculated and retrieved. Updating and scaling of data-series is necessary as well.

Econometric analysis is comprised of a wide variety of separately identifiable tasks and techniques. The primary goal of this stage of the life cycle is parameter estimation. The different techniques that facilitate coefficient estimation will be described in more detail in the next section. Prior to estimation some preliminary data analysis should be performed. This data analysis will typically include checking the distributional properties of variables and systematically checking for obvious outliers in the data. Statistical as well as informal testing should also be employed at this stage of the life cycle; for example, verifying that coefficient estimates are statistically significant and that these parameter estimates are broadly consistent with existing experience. Lastly, some form of residual analysis or diagnostics should be performed.

Model building in its simplest form is nothing more than "saving" coefficient estimates in a form that allows simulation for forecasting or what-if sensitivity analysis. For more complicated simultaneous models, there may be model-closing identities, adjustment constants, or other complicating factors.

Model simulation is the process of solving the model for specific purposes, e.g., forecasting. The particular solution process will depend on the desired application. For example, forecasting may require different solution techniques than model testing.

The testing phase of the simulation process is also application dependent. While this will almost certainly include some informal comparison of actual and predicted values, there may also be comparisons with other models, evaluation of forecasts in different economic circumstances (boom vs. bust), and impact multiplier calculations. Which of these are performed and how the results are weighted in the evaluation process will depend on the end-user application.

As more data or experience become available, all previous steps will be repeated in the model maintenance phase. For example, as new data become available, the data-series will require updating, regressions will be re-estimated to include the additional data, the model equations will be changed to reflect the revised coefficient estimates from the new regression equations, and new model simulations and testing will be performed.

3.2. A conventional modeling system for econometric analysis

An active system for econometric modeling must support the life cycle phases described above. We describe a conventional modeling system for econometric analysis called the Progressive EconometRic Modeling system (PERM) [PERM, 1983] which supports these activities, and then show in subsequent sections how this system can be extended to provide active support.

PERM is a system developed by one of the authors and currently used by several telecommunications corporations for econometric estimation, simulation, and forecasting. PERM supports the entire econometric modeling life cycle shown in fig. 2 by providing the following functional capabilities:

(1) data management: a full complement of data storage, modification, and retrieval commands;
(2) statistical estimation: an ample suite of econometric techniques including discrete choice, maximum likelihood estimation, and pooling;
(3) simultaneous equation model-building: regres-

```
The general structure of PERM commands is given below
(Brackets, { }, denote optionality and | means "or"):

    COMMAND {VARLIST | #EQUATION-ID} {FOR CONDITIONALS}
```

COMMAND   An 8 character or less verb specifying which operation is to be performed; see description of available commands in Figure 4-2;

VARLIST   Variable list specifying names of data-series to be retrieved; series name is 15 characters or less beginning with a letter and may contain any character other than & @ $ ' # " , ; < > or blank;

A lag or lead may be specified with a data-series name by specifying the lag (negative integer) or lead in parentheses after the name, e.g., PINC(-2) refers to the data-series PINC lagged two periods; Polynomial distributed lags may be used in regression commands with the syntax:
<degree, length of lag, constraint>

EQUATION-ID   A number specifying an equation's id.

Data-series names and equation-id's are mutually exclusive in the sense that one or the other may appear in a particular command (depending upon the command), but never both.

FOR   Specified only if data selection conditionals are to be used;

CONDITIONALS   Standard boolean conditions with the following operators available: EQ, NE, LT, LE, GT, GE, and BETWEEN...AND

The words OPTIONS, RANGE, OUTPUT, and INPUT have special significance when used in conditionals and are reserved.

OPTIONS EQ 'option1'{/'option2'/....} allows the user to invoke command-specific options.

RANGE BETWEEN yyyypp1 AND yyyypp2 specifies a data range for retrieval (yyyy=year and pp=period).

OUTPUT | INPUT EQ 'filename' designates I/O files.

Fig. 3. Syntax for PERM Action Language.

```
Command       Description

                         DATA MANAGEMENT COMMANDS

DEL........ Delete Data
DIR........ Databank Directory
READ....... Read Data
SCALE...... Scale Data
TRANS...... Create Transformed Variable
UP......... Update Data Values
USE........ Access Databank (Read/Write)

                      STATISTICAL ESTIMATION COMMANDS

ANAL....... Analyze Data
BOXCOX..... Box-Cox Specification Search
DIAGNOSE... Regression Diagnostics
HECKIT..... Heckit Estimation
LOGIT...... Logit Estimation
MLE........ Maximum Likelihood Estimation
OLS........ Ordinary Least Squares Regression
POOL....... Pooled Cross-section Time-series Regression
PROBIT..... Probit Estimation
RCR........ Random Coefficient Regression
RIDGE...... Ridge Regression
ROBUST..... Robust Regression
SUR........ Seemingly Unrelated Regression
TOBIT...... Tobit Estimation
VCR........ Variance Components Regression
WLS........ Weighted Least Squares Regression
2SLS....... Two Stage Least Squares
3SLS....... Three Stage Least Squares

                         MODEL BUILDING COMMANDS

EDTEQ...... Edit Equation
ENTEQ...... Enter Equation
SVEQ....... Save Regression as Model Equation

                        MODEL SIMULATION COMMANDS

GO......... Perform Simulation
LOAD....... Load Simulation
WHATIF..... Change Exogenous Values in Simulation

                        MODEL MAINTENANCE COMMANDS

AUP........ Automatic Update Propagation
REESTEQ.... Reestimate Regression Equations in Model
```

Fig. 4. Sample of PERM Commands.

sions can be saved as equations in simulation models;

(4) model simulation: models formed in the previous step can be solved and "what-if"s performed to provide econometric forecasts;

(5) model maintenance: data-series which are logically linked will be automatically updated by updating the base data-series, and models can be completely reestimated via a single command.

The PERM Action Language (PAL) provides the interface with the user. PAL is similar to the SQL database language except the user need not be concerned about which tables contain which data. All data-series are stored as vectors and users refer to these data-series directly by name. Fig. 3 provides the basic syntax for PAL. A typical command might be:

OLS DEMAND PRICE INCOME POPULATION FOR STRIKE EQ 0 AND OPTIONS EQ 'LOG'

which says "Perform an ordinary least squares regression with all data-series in logarithms (OPTIONS EQ 'LOG') on the dependent variable DEMAND as a function of PRICE, INCOME, and POPULATION for those observations when there was no strike (STRIKE EQ 0)."

PAL provides other important enhancements to SQL. Whereas SQL is primarily used for data retrieval, PAL has a large set of commands which not only retrieve data but operate upon it as well (fig. 4).

PAL is structured so that every command corresponds to a process, thus when the user specifies 2SLS, PERM invokes a statistical routine which performs two-stage least squares. PAL is therefore equivalent to the user-directed process manager (UDPM) of the ADSS. Further, the commands and resulting output can easily be journaled in a history record as they are issued. This provides a basis for investigating modeling protocol given some knowledge of the problem the modeler is trying to solve. For example, if we saw the following consecutive entries in the history record (parenthetical remarks would not appear in the history):

OLS varlist   (Linear form)
OLS varlist FOR OPTIONS = 'LOG' (Log form)
OLS varlist FOR OPTIONS = 'LLHS' (Log-Linear form)
OLS varlist FOR OPTIONS = 'LRHS' (Linear-Log form)

we would be inclined to suspect the modeler was trying to determine the proper functional form of the regression.

PERM provides powerful features for building and simulating econometric models, but it does not constitute an active modeling system. This requires the addition of intelligent support to facilitate the modeling process.

4. A model control language for representing modeling strategies

Most modeling systems provide access to data and analytic techniques, but little, if any, guidance on how to apply those techniques correctly. An "intelligent" modeling system should be able to support model formulation and evaluation in a way that extends the capabilities of beginning and experienced modelers alike [Murphy and Stohr, 1985]. This is especially true for statistics and econometrics where guidance in the proper use of various estimation techniques may avoid common mistakes and subsequently improve the quality of resultant models.

4.1. Estimation techniques

The list of estimation techniques available to the applied econometrician is growing rapidly. Least squares techniques have always been the cornerstone of applied econometrics. Ordinary least squares (OLS), with the option of autocorrelation and heteroscedasticity corrections, is the most widely used technique. These as well as other error term violations have tended to shift the emphasis from OLS to generalized least squares (GLS). Having the ability to efficiently perform GLS allows the analyst much greater flexibility; for example, the pooling of time-series and cross-sectional data in either the least squares dummy variable (LSDV) method or Zellner's seemingly unrelated regression (SUR). These generalized abilities have led to other difficult estimation issues, however. The applied econometrician may well be faced with the following kinds of questions: what are the appropriate restrictions when pooling time-series and cross-section data (e.g., LSDV, SUR, or in-between), which error term assumptions are violated, and what is the appropriate functional form.

In addition to the more common least squares methods, the efficiency gains in computing have made maximum likelihood (ML) techniques feasible for applied econometrics. While the discrete choice methods like logit and probit are the most frequently used ML methods, there are several others techniques that commonly utilize ML in their solution, e.g., tobit, heckit, and some random coefficient methods [Judge et al., 1980]. The biggest and most powerful advance, however, is the application of general purpose ML routines developed for unconstrained nonlinear optimization problems. These routines allow the analyst to specify any likelihood function and then maximize it to obtain coefficient estimates. While most of these general purpose ML implementations are still crude in the sense that they require significant user expertise (e.g. derivatives of the likelihood function must be supplied), availability of ML techniques has significantly advanced the state-of-the-art of applied econometrics.

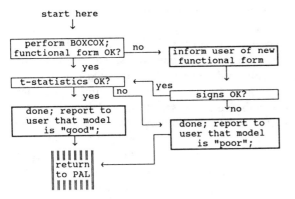

Fig. 5. Decision Tree for Functional Form Selection.

4.2. Modeling strategies as decision trees

We begin by assuming that the user has estimated a regression model; this model is assumed to contain the appropriate independent variables and to have coefficient estimates with the theoretically correct signs. For the moment, we further assume that the regression technique is OLS and the standard regression assumptions are met, e.g., the error term has zero mean, constant variance across observations, and is not correlated with itself across observations (time).

In this case (fig. 5), we wish to choose the correct functional form and insure that all coefficient estimates are statistically significant. The Box–Cox specification search is used to find the appropriate functional form. By comparing the signs of the coefficients with the original estimates and performing simple t-tests, we verify that the coefficient estimates have the correct signs and are statistically significant. The results of these "tests" are then reported to the user.

For the next example shown in fig. 6, we choose the simple textbook problem of testing for auto-

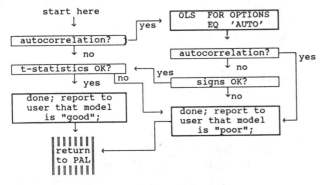

Fig. 6. Decision Tree for Autocorrelation Testing.

correlation, e.g., the error term is not independent across time-series observations. Since correcting for autocorrelation typically reduces the size of the t-statistics, we will once again test for statistical significance of the estimated parameter estimates. Using a Durbin–Watson (DW) test to determine if autocorrelation is a problem, we simply re-estimate the equation invoking an autocorrelation correction option if the DW test is failed. If the correction is employed, we test for correct signs and t-statistics and report the results to the user. Notice that it would be straightforward to expand the "model is poor" message to detail the model failings by indicating, e.g., that the model has wrong signs or statistically insignificant coefficient estimates. As before, we have assumed that the user has selected the appropriate design matrix, coefficient signs are correct, and the regression technique is OLS.

In comparison to these textbook or hypothetical examples, real world problems become increasingly complex. For example, simply combining the two examples into one, where the analyst is attempting to determine functional form when autocorrelation may be present, more than triples the number of tests to be performed [see Dolk and Kridel, 1989].

Straightforward generalizations are easily implemented, however. For example, if a lagged dependent variable is included in the regression as an independent variable, the Durbin H test can easily be substituted for the Durbin–Watson test. In addition reasonability checks can also be included. For example, the system could test if the estimated coefficients or implied elasticities were within some reasonability region. This region could be rather crude for general use or have a "finer" testing region for specific problems.

Understanding the impact of relaxing error assumptions is critical in comprehending the complicated nature of applied econometric analysis and the burden this implies for the analyst. An example will help clarify this point. The Box–Cox specification search is very sensitive to the underlying error assumptions. If the error term is not well-behaved, then direct application of the Box–Cox procedure will often lead to the selection of "incorrect" functional forms. As a result, not only does allowing violations of the standard error term assumptions require additional testing facilities, but it requires the ability to select functional form and correct for these violations simultaneously. Unless the analyst is aware of the implications of violations of the standard assumptions on all potential regression techniques, errors in estimation will certainly occur. While multiple violations of the standard assumptions pose no problem theoretically, when multiple violations are allowed, the complexity of the decision trees and testing processes become quite burdensome. Of course, this is exactly the reason why intelligent modeling is useful to the analyst.

Additional decision trees have been developed to assist the user in performing regression diagnostics [Belsley, Kuh and Welsch, 1980] and assessing the quality of forecasting models. The forecasting template checks the performance of the model in different periods (booms, busts) and compares implicit multipliers to reasonability standards as well as more common performance tests (root mean square error).

One of the challenges in building an ADSS is to identify local command patterns, or sequences, and match them with global modeling strategy sequences such as the decision trees identified above. One way of representing modeling strategy sequences explicitly is in the form of processes rendered in an appropriate model control language.

4.3. PERM control language (PCL)

Kottemann and Dolk [1988] identify requirements for a model integration control language (MICL) which allows processes to communicate with one another, and subsequently facilitates the specification of solution procedures for integrated models. The MICL supports variable correspondence, sequentiality, and dynamic synchronization among processes by providing structured programming constructs, message passing protocols, and variable monitoring (demons).

An MICL is a necessary component of a model manipulation language for an active modeling system because it serves as the medium in which schemas of statistical analysis strategy are encapsulated and subsequently activated. To demonstrate this point, we sketch a simplified PERM Control Language and show how it can be used to capture the modeling strategies outlined above. We emphasize that PERM does not currently support a PCL, although a prototype is under development.

The PCL must provide three capabilities: structured programming constructs, message passing protocols, and demons. The first two features can be accommodated by providing a simple language shell with sequence, selection, and iteration constructs in which ordinary PAL commands are embedded, plus a set of reserved words that serve effectively as arguments which can be passed among processes. The PAL commands activate various processes, usually statistical estimation techniques, which return a set of parameters such as the R-squared statistic, t-statistics, regression coefficients, and standard errors. These parameters are then used to determine whether acceptable statistical criteria have been met, and in this way, an overall model building strategy can be developed.

PCL supports standard programming language constructs of sequence, IF-THEN-ELSE selection, and REPEAT UNTIL iteration, as well as assignment statements, and input/output statements (fig. 7). Any acceptable PAL command is also acceptable in PCL. Additionally, there is a list of reserved variable names which serve as the output variables from any PAL statistical command. For example, BETA(INCOME) refers to the regression coefficient for the independent variable INCOME. Each of the reserved words can be indexed by a regression identifier so that parameters can be compared between regressions. If no regression identifier is specified, then the default is the current regression (i.e., the last regression executed). The four basic data types in PCL are MATRIX, VECTOR, SCALAR, and STRING with STRING being the default.

In addition to the structured programming constructs and reserved words, it is necessary to provide some facility for demons, or dynamic triggers, to detect the conditions under which the PCL processes are to be activated. The general structure of a demon is:

Demon: WHEN ⟨Condition(s) are detected⟩
        THEN ⟨Activate PCL Command(s)
             and/or Process(es)⟩
End-Demon

Demons will normally appear as headers to PCL processes so that it is readily apparent when the processes will be invoked. Implementation issues

94

Programming Constructs

```
REPEAT UNTIL              ASSIGNMENT STATEMENTS
  statement(s)              variable = expression
END REPEAT
                          ARITHMETIC & BOOLEAN
                            OPERATORS
IF boolean(s)               +, -, *, /, **, >, <, >=,
THEN statement(s)           <=, ><, EXP, LOG, SUM,
{ELSE statement(s)}         PI, SIGN, etc, etc.
ENDIF
                          MATRIX OPERATORS
INPUT/OUTPUT                +, -, *, INV, ' (trans-
  INFORM(string)            pose)
  ACCEPT(string)
```

Data Types

```
MATRIX     Ordinary matrix,   eg: INDEP_VAR[100,7]
SMATRIX    Symmetric matrix,  eg: VAR_COV[7,7]
VECTOR     Ordinary vector,   eg: DEP_VAR[100]
SCALAR     Ordinary scalar,   eg: R**2
STRING     String of chars,   eg: 'LOG'
```

Reserved Words

```
BETA(var,regr)   Coefficient of independent variable "var"
                   and regression "regr".
ELAST(var,regr)  Elasticity for independent variable "var"
                   and regression "regr".
T(var,regr)      T-statistic for independent variable "var"
                   and regression "regr".
FUNCTFORM(regr)  Functional form for regression "regr"
                   = 'LIN' for linear
                   = 'LOG' for logarithm
                   = 'LLHS' for log-linear
                   = 'LRHS' for linear-log
RSQ(regr)        R**2 of regression "regr"
DW(regr)         Durbin-Watson of regression "regr"
F(regr)          F-statistic of regression "regr"
VARLIST[regr]    Variable list for regression "regr"
RHO[regr]        Estimated rho(s) for regression "regr"
```

Fig. 7. Partial Specification of PCL Syntax.

```
PROCESS SELECT_FUNCT_FORM
DEMON
  WHEN HIST_REC.PREV_COMMAND EQ "OLS"
  AND HIST_REC.CURRENT_COMMAND EQ "OLS FOR OPTIONS EQ 'LOG' "
  ACTIVATE
END DEMON
*    Save functional form from current regression
FF0=FUNCTFORM
*    Invoke PAL command for Box-Cox specification search
BOXCOX varlist
IF FUNCTFORM >< FF0 THEN
  INFORM "FUNCTFORM is the better functional form"
ENDIF
*    Perform t-tests on estimated coefficients
IF T(varlist) < t_cv  THEN
  INFORM "Warning: Model is poor; BETA(var(s))
                    statistically insignificant"
ELSE
  INFORM "Model is acceptable"
  RETURN
ENDIF
```

Fig. 8. PCL Process for Functional Form Selection.

arise with respect to demons in the PERM system but before addressing these problems, it is useful to see what a PCL process looks like.

4.4. Schemas as PCL processes of modeling strategies

The notion of schema is central to the ADSS. Our view is that schemas for econometric modeling are PCL processes which encapsulate statistical strategy for specific situations. To demonstrate what we mean, we will render the decision trees in Section 4.2 as PCL processes.

As before we assume the user-specified regression is "current", that the coefficient signs are correct, and that the regression technique is OLS. Fig. 8 displays the PCL process for the example presented in fig. 5. It should be noted that to perform the t-tests in the second IF, a table lookup for the critical value of the t-statistic (t_cv) is required.

The PCL template for the second decision tree discussed above is presented in fig. 9 (once again we maintain the same assumptions described in fig. 6). The information supplied to the user at each step could also include modeling suggestions. For example, if the model failed the second autocorrelation test, the system could suggest that the autocorrelation problem may be due to misspecifi-

cation and suggest that the user consider adding additional independent variables to the regression. As noted in the previous example, all statistical and reasonability checks require table lookups.

A number of comments are germane at this point. First, the PCL serves as the Computer-Directed Process Manager (CDPM) of the ADSS. Once the ADSS recognizes that the user input pattern fits into one of the schemas, or modeling strategies, in the schema library, then it will invoke the appropriate PCL process(es). Thus the ADSS is augmenting the user-directed command by overlaying a more comprehensive modeling strategy.

Second, demons are critical to the ADSS since they are the mechanism whereby user command sequences in the history record are "recognized" as part of a more wide reaching strategy schema. The method of embedding these demons in the PERM system presents a challenge, however, since each demon must effectively be implemented by some kind of suspend-resume mechanism explicitly programmed in the Fortran source code, a task for which Fortran is not well-suited. For example, in order for the ADSS to recognize the two consecutive commands

OLS varlist {FOR Conditionals}
OLS varlist FOR OPTIONS EQ 'LOG'

```
PROCESS AUTO_TEST
DEMON
   WHEN HIST_REC.PREV_COMMAND EQ "OLS"
   AND DATA-SERIES >< CRS
   ACTIVATE
END DEMON
*    Save BETA from current regression
BETA0(varlist) = BETA(varlist)
*    Durbin-Watson test for autocorrelation
IF DW > dw_cv THEN
*    Invoke PAL command for autocorrelation correction
   OLS FOR OPTIONS EQ 'AUTO'
   IF DW > dw_cv THEN
     INFORM "Warning: Model is poor; ... autocorrelation"
     RETURN
   ENDIF
   IF SIGN(BETA(varlist)) >< SIGN(BETA0(varlist)) THEN
     INFORM "Warning: Model is poor; Incorrect signs "
     RETURN
   ENDIF
ELSE
   IF T(varlist)) < t_cv THEN
     INFORM "Warning: Model is poor; Insignificant ..."
     RETURN
   ENDIF
   INFORM "Model is OK; estimated rho is 'RHO(regr)' "
ENDIF
RETURN
```
Fig. 9. PCL Process for Autocorrelation Correction.

{AND Conditionals}

as an attempt to establish functional form, it must interrupt the program at some point (probably immediately after each command is issued) to perform the pattern checking. There is now no way for the PERM system to do this automatically from only a PCL demon declaration. The situation is further complicated because a user-directed process may be interrupted in a way that requires complex process synchronization as well. For example if an ordinary least squares regression is interrupted in midstream to check for collinearity, it may be necessary to synchronize various stages of the collinearity process with stages of the OLS process. Thus, in the general case, each demon specified in PERM must be implemented by explicitly inserting traps in the appropriate places in the code. This is unacceptably cumbersome, thus some compromises must be made, such as testing for demons only at a few, prespecified points.

Third, PCL provides a tractable medium in which experts can build predefined model strategy schemas and thus develop a more comprehensive schema library. The PCL processes themselves form a knowledge base of econometric modeling strategy.

5. History inference processor

The most difficult problems in an ADSS arise in the history inference processor (HIP). Recall that the HIP is responsible for building a computer model which emulates the user's problem-working process. This requires formulating and testing hypotheses about the user, the problem, and relevant problem-working processes. These processes are represented as a network of schemas which are developed from protocol analysis, expert definition, or dynamic pattern recognition.

In the case of an artificially intelligent econometrician, this requires matching strings of user commands with statistical strategies contained in the schema library. Our initial approach to developing a HIP is as follows:

(1) Build a library of PCL process schemas developed by experts in the area of econometric analysis. These schemas will reflect expert knowledge of various statistical strategies as shown in Sections 4.2 and 4.3.

(2) Conduct a number of experiments with modelers to identify patterns of command sequences which are likely to appear in the particular problem situations represented by the schemas. This can be done currently by examining a PERM history record for a session to see what PAL commands were issued.

(3) Insert a demon in PERM which, after every user-directed command is issued, examines the history record and tries to match the current command sequence with one of those derived from the second step. When a match is found, the relevant PCL process is activated to supersede the current user command.

We see several research issues which are relevant to this effort. One is the determination of what aspects of statistical strategy we can reasonably expect to capture. Oldford and Peters [1986] present an ordering of statistical strategies from low-level (e.g., collinearity diagnosis) to high-level (overall model analysis and design), and suggest that there is a limit to the level at which a DSS can usefully support statistical strategy. In particular, this level is a function of how context-dependent the problem is. This is the familiar domain problem which characterizes all expert system applications. Since we are working from the bottom up with respect to this ordering, one of the things we hope to discover is where that practical limit occurs for econometrics.

Another research issue is deciding how intrusive an ADSS should be. Such a system could potentially dominate the "dialog" with a user, continually activating "helpful" schemas which may become annoying after awhile, not to mention expensive. On the other hand, a system which provides support with little, or no, dialog may take on a mystical quality which could undermine its eventual utility. The question of how much support to provide is also a function of user sophistication; naive econometricians will need more help than the seasoned veterans who write the schemas, for example.

The approach outlined above comprises a simplified version of an inference processor, yet could nevertheless provide powerful support in formulating econometric models. Whether this approach constitutes an ADSS is another issue, however. One feature it currently lacks is the ability to identify patterns and create new schemas dynamically. This would require more powerful pattern recognition heuristics as well as some form of automatic code generation capability to transform new patterns into PCL processes.

A fully active system may very well require a radical departure from conventional expert system technology. Research in neural networks is one promising alternative that supports many of the requirements of an ADSS. With neural networks, knowledge is not encoded as rules but rather as patterns of connectivity between nodes. Further, these patterns evolve from usage and experience rather than having to be hard-wired by a programmer or knowledge engineer. Thus, processes yield the data structures (rules) dynamically as opposed to current expert systems where the data structures are required a priori for reasoning to take place. Another appealing feature of neural nets is that some kinds of learning take place quite naturally, thus under the right conditions, it is possible to "train" a net so that an input pattern will result in a specified output pattern [Rumelhart and McLelland, 1986].

The kind of behavior exhibited by neural networks is directly in line with the precepts of ADSS. However, one problem with using neural networks for applications of the kind we have described is that their focus is at a very microscopic level. Much work needs to be done with respect to combining and layering these networks in order to address more macroscopic problems. Although it is not clear at this time how one would incorporate this research into DSS technology, we plan to investigate whether any of the adaptive pattern recognition mechanisms inherent in neural networks can be adapted for use in the HIP.

6. Conclusions

We have marshaled ideas from model management, econometrics, and conventional expert systems to consider the feasibility of a developing an active DSS that would serve as an "artificially intelligent econometrician". We have presented a model manipulation language for econometric analysis which is a slight modification of SQL and which can serve as the user-directed process manager in an ADSS. We then discussed an extension to this language which allows demon descriptions and provides structured programming constructs. This model control language serves as the basis for representing statistical strategy schemas and as a computer-directed process manager in an ADSS. Finally, we outlined an approach to building an inference processor which attempts to recognize model manipulation command sequences as a subset of a more comprehensive strategy schema. Once pattern recognition occurs, one or more schemas is activated to support sound econometric analysis.

We have not answered conclusively whether an ADSS for econometric analysis is feasible. It seems to us that one can go only so far using conventional rule-based expert systems technology, however. More innovative approaches like neural networks may be required to realize a fully active system. Nevertheless, we believe that the system we have described shows the promise of ADSS concepts for implementing intelligent modeling systems.

References

Belsley, D., Kuh, E. and Welsch, R., Regression Diagnostics, Wiley, 1980.

Dolk, D.R. and Kridel, D.J., Toward a Symbiotic Expert System for Econometric Modeling, Proceedings of the 22n HICSS, Volume III, IEEE Computer Society, 1989, pp. 3–13.

Judge, G., Griffiths, W., Hill, R., and Lee, T. The Theory and Practice of Econometrics, Wiley, 1980.

Keen, P.G.W. and Scott Morton, M., Decision Support Systems: An Organizational Perspective. Addison-Wesley, 1978.

Kottemann, J.E. and Dolk, D.R., Process-oriented model integration. Proceedings of the 21st HICSS, Vol. III, IEEE Computer Society, 1988, 396–402.

Manheim, M., An architecture for active DSS. Proceedings of the 21st HICSS, Vol. III, IEEE Computer Society, 1988, 356–365.

Manheim, M., Issues in Design of a Symbiotic DSS. Proceedings of the 22nd HICSS, Vol. III, IEEE Computer Society, 1989, 14–23.

Murphy, F.M. and Stohr, E.A., An intelligent system for formulating linear programs. Decision Support Systems, 2, 1985, 39–47.

Oldford, R.R. and Peters, S.C., Implementation and study of statistical strategy. In Artificial Intelligence and Statistics, W.A. Gale, ed., Addison-Wesley, 1986.

Remus, W. and Kottemann, J.E., Toward intelligent decision support systems: An artificially intelligent statistician. Management Information Systems Quarterly, December 1986.

Rumelhart D.E. and McLelland, J.L., Parallel Distributed Processing, Volume 1. MIT Press, 1986.

Sprague, R. and Carlson, E., Building Effective Decision Support Systems. Prentice-Hall, 1982.

User's Manual for PERM, Software Model Management Systems, 15230 Oak Hills Drive, Salinas, CA 93907, C1983.

Only Diamonds are Forever: Caching Knowledge for Episodic Classification Problems

Gregg Elofson and Benn Konsynski

* In a recent Harvard case study[1], a major software vendor planned to ease the workload on its customer service representatives with the introduction of expert system technology. The vendor received over 330,000 calls annually, and wished to create an on-line service that allowed customers to get software support. The plan included having customers interact with an expert system instead of the service representative. The system would have required the customer to report the nature of the problem (eg. I've got an abend); ask questions of the customer that would have been asked by the service representative (eg. Was it a System abend? A user abend? Was there a console message? none of the above?); and provide, when possible, a classification/solution to the problem. If the expert system could not provide an answer, then the service representative would take over.

Besides differentiating themselves from their competitors, the firm believed that the expert system would help reduce the service representative's work-load and encourage them to remain at their jobs longer (their average length of job service was 20 months and the cost of retraining was viewed as significant). Thus, the plan found encouragement from many individuals within the company. Unfortunately, the endeavor ultimately failed because of the large knowledge acquisition effort required to bring the project on-line, along with resistance on the part of the service representatives to spend additional time helping to build the system.

Reprinted from the *Proceedings of the 23rd Annual Hawaii International Conference on System Sciences*, 1990, pages 281-288.

** To supply the strategic planning function with information regarding threats and opportunities to the organization, area specialists and intelligence analysts combine their efforts in monitoring and searching the environment external to their enterprise[2]. Area specialists are experts in some aspect of the external environment such as political events, regulatory measures, competitor financial status, etc., and decide on monitoring sets of qualitiative indicators that might provide insight into various threats and opportunities to the organization. Once the indicators are chosen, the area specialists request estimates from the intelligence analysts of the indicators' values. The intelligence analyst has the role of locating and forwarding information that will shed light on the disposition of the indicators in question.

On a continuous basis, the area specialist generates a list of information requirements and sends them via electronic-mail to the intelligence analyst. Once the sought after information is made available to the area specialist, inferences and classifications over the data's content are made. For example, the area specialist may look for patterns over variables such as bidding behavior, R & D expenditures or hiring, new manufacturing methods, suppliers, etc.. The area specialist may use his expertise to infer that a very low bid on the competitors part may indicate several conditions: 1) the competitor's backlog is very low, or 2) the competitor has made a leap in manufacturing methods and can reasonably meet their bid, or 3) the competitor has made a gross error in judgement, or 4) the competitor is using a new supplier that can provide materials at a much lower cost. The area specialist would use the other variables to decide which of these explanations is most likely. If R & D hiring has recently increased, and the competitor has invested in a new manufacturing site, it may be that technological innovation is the best explanation for the very low bid. Conversely, if it is known that R & D expenditures have recently been cut and that there has been a hiring freeze, then the area specialist will likely infer that either the competitor's backlog is low or there was a gross error in judgement.

Here, not only is pattern classification knowledge useful along with knowledge of what indicators are needed. Not only is it important to provide an assessment of information once the right questions have been asked, but also necessary is to know just what those "right questions" are. Additionally, as in the case of the customer service representatives, the area specialists are rarely available for knowledge engineering interviews. Consequently, the problems that they are responsible for classifying tend to change over time as the goals of the organization also change. For these two reasons, an expert system solution is not a feasible approach[3].

*** Digital Synthetic Aperature Radar (SAR) imagery is being produced in ever-increasing quantities. One of its uses is as a relatively low cost intelligence platform to track the activities and locations of military targets. Looking similar to a star map, low resolution SAR imagery is "read" by image analysts as they comb through a given area in search of tactical deployments. An example of a typical pattern found in SAR imagery is a SAM (surface to air missile) site. In SAR imagery a SAM site often appears to have a "five-on-a-die" pattern. Another typical series of returns is the tank company - appearing as a line of "stars" with one slightly out of line (usually the commander). As one might expect, the force deployments change with time and terrain. So, new configurations must be classified by an image analyst with some regularity. Any computer based system that could assist the image analyst in reducing the amount of imagery that he must process would contribute positively to total throughput[4].

Image analysts are in short supply. This scarcity of expertise, coupled with the changing nature of the problems to be classified, additions of new weaponry and force deployment, marks similarities between the SAR image exploitation problem, the monitoring problem, and the software service problem.

Episodic Classification Problems

These problems have been evaluated from an expert system point of view. In each case, expert system technolgy was found to be an innapropriate solution.Typically, expert or knowledge based systems used on classification problems enjoy the luxury of several characteristics:

1. The problem is recurrent for the foreseable future
2. An expert is available to help populate the knowledge base
3. The goal of the process is to find correct answers

However, in many operational environment problems exist that, while requiring knowledge intensive solutions, do not have these characteristics. Instead, they have the following characteristics:

1. The problem is recurrent for a limited period of time
2. An expert will not be available to populate the knowledge base
3. Knowing the correct questions to ask, in addition to finding correct answers, is very useful

The customer service representative will answer questions about software problems, and those problems will last until the next release. The area specialist will scan for particular threats and opportunities until the next strategy meeting, when the firm's change in direction will redefine what constitutes a threat or opportunity. The image analyst will identify particular force deployments, until new ones are created to suit changing terrain and tactics.

Also, the customer service representatives remain in their positions for a short period of time, and are typically overburdened to the point of being unavailable for knowledge engineering sessions. Area specialists fall into the same category. For example, specialists in identifying political conditions in foreign countries are in short supply - when their expertise is applied to underwriting policies for the insurance industry, policies stop being created the moment that the individual is away. Too, the number of image analysts available to interpret SAR imagery is small with respect to the demands placed on them - making them inaccessible for knowledge acquisition activities.

With respect to the time limitations faced by these experts, small gains can provide a significant advantage. For instance, simply asking a series of routine questions of an individual needing software support can offer meaningful advantages for the service representitives, giving them additional time to concentrate on more challenging and unique problems. So too, with the area specialists: much time can be spent in the activites of recalling their monitoring strategies for a particular threat or opportunitiy and asking for that information from an information analyst. Again, with the image analyst, much of their time is spent in combing through an image, simply locating potentially meaningful clusters, and this is before any classification is made about their content.

These problems, with their characteristics differing from those traditionally amenable to an expert system approach, we call episodic classification problems (ECP's). They are transient, emerging and receding in importance over time. They appear in envoronments where knowledge intensive attention is highly scarce. And the opportunity cost in searching for confirming and clarifying data is high.

Currently, both the diachronic and synchronic characteristics of an expert system architecture, its product and process attributes, make it difficult to use for solving ECP's. The lengthy time requirements of knowledge acquisition, the changing nature of high priority problems, and the monolithic structure of traditional knowledge bases makes the expert systems architecture an unfeasible design alternative.

To overcome the problems in the expert systems approach, the system in question must be able to assimilate the expert's knowledge, organizing it by classes or categories. Also, the necessary system must have the ability to deliver the expert's knowledge to others in a usable form. The system must unobtrusively learn the concepts that the expert uses in solving ECP's, and make those concepts available to others in the organization.

We propose a method of solving ECP's called knowledge caching. Central to the concept of knowledge caching is the intelligent agent. Here, the intelligent agent acts as *apprentice* to an expert. The apprentice's orientation is problem specific. For example, when scanning an organization's environment for threats and opportunities, one apprentice would be concerned only with political violence problems while another would be concerned only with new technology threats.

The functional behavior of an apprentice can be described by an organization doing a particular monitoring activity. For example, when an organization monitors the political climate of a foreign country, the attributes an area specialist considers include the following: pro-regime and anti-regime sense of relative deprivation; pro-regime and anti-regime belief in violence; coercive force available to both pro-regime and anti-regime actors; and institutional support for both pro-regime and anti-regime actors[5]. In seeking attributes for these values, the area specialist initiates a request for information by passing a structured message to a particular apprentice - in fact, creating a new apprentice. The message would state the following:

a) attributes for which the area specialist requires values and the name of the apprentice - which corresponds to the threat or opportunity being monitored

b) an explanation or elucidation of the attributes to better clarify the nature of each attribute being requested

c) scaling information specifying the values which are acceptable as answers to the attribute request.

This structured message, the questions about the attribute values together with the explanations and scaling information, is "hand-carried" by the Apprentice to the intelligence analyst. To each of the attribute questions the intelligence analyst responds with a value corresponding to one of the scaled values provided by the Apprentice. Additionally, the intelligence analyst may provide a written explanation of why he chose a particular scaled value.

Once this is done, the Apprentice carries its newfound information back to the area specialist. And, upon returning to the area specialist with its new information, the Apprentice shows the specialist the answers to the specified questions and asks (in effect), "What does it mean?" To this, the area specialist may ask for an explanation of one of the intelligence analyst's answers, or give the Apprentice an assessment, a classification, of the information provided. With the answer, the Apprentice forms an initial concept, a concept which is represented as a collection of attribute-value pairs and a classification.

The next time the area specialist needs information about the same threat or opportunity, restating the questions, explanations, and scaling information is unnecessary. The area specialist need only send the Apprentice to do its work- it already has the questions and other requisite information. From that point, the Apprentice proceeds to the intelligence analyst, as before, and asks the same questions and receives a new set of answers. With these new answers the Apprentice returns to the area specialist, and, if the Apprentice has a concept that matches the answers provided by the intelligence analyst, it reports its classification to the specialist. Otherwise, it again asks the area specialist, "What does it mean?" And the specialist provides another classification which the Apprentice uses to augment its concepts and make further generalizations.

What is taking place is that the Apprentice is gathering information from the intelligence analyst and knowledge from the area specialist. The Apprentice asks questions and receives answers from the intelligence analyst, and in doing so, gathers information. When the Apprentice asks the area specialist what a particular set of attribute-value pairs means, and receives a classification with which to form a concept, the Apprentice is gathering knowledge from the area specialist. Also, the the apprentice is classifying information supplied by the intelligence analyst. That is, when information supplied by the intelligence analyst matches one of the concepts held by the apprentice, the information is given the concept's classification.

Increasing Span of Attention

An apprentice caches the knowledge an expert uses in solving problems. In doing so, the apprentice helps to solve an ECP by increasing the expert's span of attention. That is, the expert that re-apportions his knowledge to an apprentice is better able to attend to more challenging problems. For example, when the goals and objectives of the organization are first communicated to the environmental scanning group, a lot of time is spent identifying just what to look for, where to look for it, and how to look for it. In other words, decisions are made as to what the possible threats and opportunties might be, and how best to monitor for them. Environmental scanners refer to this kind of work as "creative work." As time passes, and their tasks become more structured, an increasing amount of time is spent doing those tasks that have been structured, which become redundant, and less time is available for the generation of new ideas to the problem of identifying threats and opportunities.

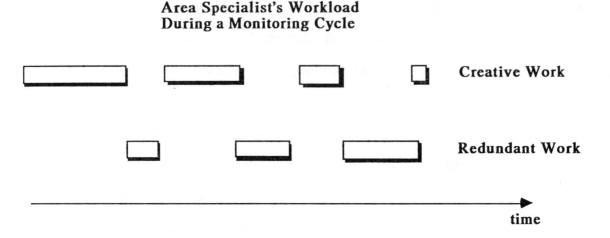

**Area Specialist's Workload
During a Monitoring Cycle**

Creative Work

Redundant Work

time

Figure 1. Change in Work over Time

In figure 1 above, the proportional change from creative to redundant work is illustrated. As time passes for the area specialist, the creative work process becomes more infrequent as the amount of redundant work increases. Both tasks are necessary to the proper fulfillment of the environmental scanning group's responsibilities. And, while the area specialist is viewed as having a fixed span of attention, little can be done to increase the amount of time available for creative work. The problems aren't around long enough, and the expert's time is too scarce, to build an expert system. But, caching the expert's knowledge increases his span of attention through the delegation of redundant tasks. Knowledge caching allows the execution of the redundant tasks by an apprentice, and gives the area specialist the opportunity to continually augment his search for new and unexplored sources of intelligence.

Figure 2 illustrates the way in which an area specialist can delegate redundant work to an apprentice. During this sequence of events, the intelligence analyst will often be asked to pursue other data requests by other area specialists. The initial request takes some time to expedite and other requests, perhaps of a higher priority, present themselves to the intelligence analyst in the course of expediting the original request. Consequently, several hours can elapse between the time of the initial request and the response to that request. The area specialist too has other tasks to perform in the interum of waiting for the answer to his first data request. Other threats and opportunties to the organization must be scanned for; hence, other data requests must be made. When the area specialist does receive an answer to his initial request for data, he must reorient himself to the goals of the scanning. What was being searched for must be recalled. The strategy for deciding how to procede must also be recalled. What the data means must be decided, and what to ask next must also be decided. If the required information is only part of a line of questions that have already been asked and answered, the previous information regarding the classification must also be recalled and integrated into the final classification.

	Intelligence Analyst	Area Specialist
t1		Identify threat or opportunity to scan for
t2		Choose attribute values to search for
t3	←	Send attribute-value request to information specialist
t4	Decide/Recall where to search for attribute-value	
t5	Interruption of high priority request	
t6	Expedite high priority request	
t7	Recall progress/state of attribute-value search	
t8	Return attribute-value found to information specialist →	
t9		Recall what threat or opportunity to look for
t10		Evaluate attribute-value found
t11		Recall attribute-values already found
t12		Recall attribute-values to search for
t13		Choose attribute-value to search for and goto (t3) or Recall what attribute-values mean as a pattern

Figure 2 - Tasks Performed by Area Specialists and Intelligence Analysts

The shaded parts of the figure depict those activities that an apprentice can assume after an initial inquiry is made by the area specialist. Based on the threat or opportunity to be investigated, a chosen apprentice will already have the correct data values to search for and conduct a question-answer session with the analyst. It will attempt to evaluate all attributes found and continue searching until it has either made a classification or exhausted its problem solving knowledge. If the latter occurs, the chosen apprentice returns to the area specialist with the attribute-values and asks for a classification. In all cases the apprentice can immediately take over the query responsibilities of the specialist, and over time it can handle greater portions of the classification reponsibilities.

Agent Architecture

An Apprentice is made up of three layers (figure 3), which together perform the tasks of: 1) gathering, classifying, and distributing the information needed to classify the ECP, and 2) gathering, classifying and distributing the knowledge used by experts in diagnosing the ECP. The three layers are the concept formation layer, the knowledge source layer, and the blackboard layer, (A prototype of the apprentice has been developed on a MAC II using Allegro Common Lisp).

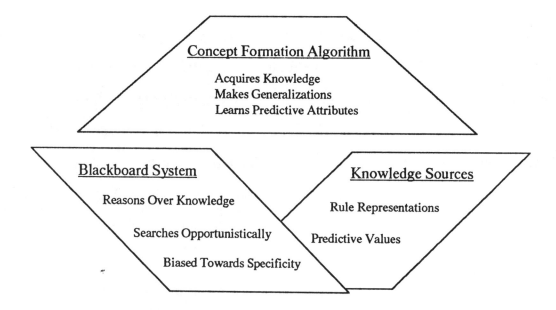

Fig. 3. Apprentice Architecture

The concept formation layer's central responsibility involves the gathering of groups of attribute-value pairs to form generalizations based on regularities in those groups. The knowledge source layer receives knowledge from the output of the concept formation layer. That is, the tree generated by the concept formation layer is parsed to yield a distinct set of concepts which become the knowledge sources for the Apprentice. The blackboard layer acts as the inference engine for the Apprentice, using the search information provided by the knowledge sources to intelligently query the data source for specific values of chosen attributes.

The Concept Formation Layer

The algorithm chosen for the concept formation layer was Unimem[6]. Unimem is an incremental conceptual clustering algorithm that creates a hierarchy of feature-vectors from inputs of labelled sets of attribute-value pairs. Thus, with each new piece of data, Unimem updates its hierarchy.

The classifications of the feature-vectors are identified by either a single label or a disjunction of labels. Within the hierarchy created by Unimem, those feature-vectors close to the root are more general (having fewer attribute-value pairs and more labels) than those near the leaves. Also, the arcs pointing to the nodes in Unimem's hierarchy have predicative attribute-values associated with them. These predictive attribute-values provide heuristic search information to the blackboard, as the node pointed to incorporates the predictive attribute-value pair while the other nodes probably do not.

Unimem gathers its new inputs of classified attribute-value pairs from the data source (this could be SAR image metrics, intelligence analyst's answers, or software user responses). The classification of this information, the judgement call made by the expert about the returned information, becomes the label of the attribute-value data.

Knowledge Source Layer

The knowledge source level is the result of parsing the hierarchy formed by Unimem. The result is a number of hypotheses that correspond to each of the hierarchy's nodes, together with the arc-labels pointing to them. Thus, a given hypothesis will contain information about both its predictive and predictable attribute-values, as well as the classification given to it. The actual representation would appear as follows:

(((a red)(c very-fast)) ((b medium-weight)(d expensive)) (Ferrari Testarossa))

Here, from left to right, there are three groups in this hypothesis: predictive values, predictable values, and classification label. In this example, if the object in question is red and very fast, it is likely that it is also medium-weight and expensive - more particularly a Ferrari Testarossa. The values "red" and "very-fast" are the predictive values - their presence suggests the presence of the predictable values "medium-weight" and "expensive." Using this hypothesis, if all four attribute-value pairs are matched, then the conclusion is that the object is a Ferrari Testarossa.

The Hybrid Blackboard Layer

While a blackboard is used for the purpose of exhibiting global data to the various knowledge sources, neither multiple levels nor links are employed. The knowledge sources correspond directly to the concepts developed by the concept formation level of the apprentice. And, using the predictive information provided by the concept formation level, along with the varying degrees of specificity of the knowledge sources (the more attribute-value pairs that describe the concept, the more specific it is), the control or search method is opportunistic.

Together, these three layers effect the required functionality of the Apprentice. The concept formation layer is put to use when the Apprentice "asks" the expert for a classification of attribute value pairs. The classification given is used, along with the attribute-values provided by the idata source, to augment the concepts via the learning algorithm. The output of Unimem is put into the knowledge sources, which are used by the blackboard to conduct a search of the data source. Thus, different parts of the apprentice's architecture are used according to the individual with which the apprentice is interacting. The blackboard and knowledge sources are used with the data source, and the concept formation layer is used with the area specialist.

Case Study

To illustrate the functional characteristics of an apprentice in a real world application, an archival case study[7] was performed concerning a multi-national corporation[8] monitoring the political climate of Poland in the summer of 1980[9]. Here, an "area specialist" monitored the political climate of Poland in the summer of 1980 while an Apprentice captured knowledge about how to act in the absence of that same "area specialist."

The reasons why an organization might take an interest in Poland during the summer of 1980 could be large in number. In this instance, a hypothetical company is posited, Machine Corp., and one of its concerns is in negotiating and winning a contract with the Buhmar Company, Poland's largest manufacturer of tractors. The negotiation is over a contract of several million dollars to supply parts for Buhmar's new line of back-hoe's. While the value of this particular contract is significant to Machine Corp., also valuable is the possibility of future contracts with Buhmar. The negotiations are expected to take at least several weeks. Machine Corp. began serious talks with Buhmar in the first week of July, 1980, and formal negotiations began during the last week of July.

Machine Corp.'s position in the negotiations is simple - it believes that longer negotiations are to its advantage. Because its inventory of parts required by the contract in question is very low, lengthening negotiations will allow it to create the necessary inventory without going to over-time for its workers or paying premium prices to suppliers. Conversely, Buhmar wishes the negotiations to move along swiftly, as their production quotas have been falling off. Also, they prefer working with an American supplier at this time because many of the necessary licenses are easy to acquire as a result of their long-standing relationship with International Harvester. (They began joint production with IH as early as 1971.)

Knowing that Poland's economy has been having difficulty, and also knowing that such difficulties sometimes result in worker unrest, is the reason for Machine Corp. monitoring the political climate in Poland. For, if riots should break out on a large scale- and be met with predictably harsh suppression - the Carter administration would most likely levy trade sanctions against Poland. And, these trade sanctions very often take the initial form of restricting licensing of exports to Poland. The gist of this is that Machine Corp. wishes to buy as much time as possible in negotiations, but they do not wish to be without a contract and licenses in the event of Polish political turmoil and the resulting licensing restrictions. Hence, if it looks as though turmoil is about to break out, Machine Corp. wants to close the deal as quickly as possible.

The actual area specialist used was a composite of attributes, values, and rules employed by political analysts in identifying the likelihood of political turmoil. A well known approach to analyzing the political climate of a country was developed by Gurr[10]. His model takes into account a number of qualitative indicators to assess the well-being of a country's political health or the likelihood of an outbreak of political violence. These attributes were used in illustrating how an area specialist would seek and classify information about Poland. They are explained in table 1 below:

Pro-Regime Relative Deprivation - a measure of the extent to which members characterized as pro-regime feel frustrated regarding their economic condition and general welfare.

Anti-Regime Relative Deprivation - a measure of the extent to which members characterized as anti-regime feel frustrated regarding their economic condition and general welfare.

Pro-Regime Belief in Violence - a measure of the extent to which members characterized as pro-regime believe that, given the practical opportunities and limitations of the current political situation, violence is justified on either pragmatic grounds, or on moral, doctrinal, and historical grounds.

Anti-Regime Belief in Violence - a measure of the extent to which members characterized as anti-regime believe that, given the practical opportunities and limitations of the current political situation, violence is justified on either pragmatic grounds, or on moral, doctrinal, and historical grounds.

Coercive Support for Pro-Regime - a measure of the extent to which pro-regime members are supported, in terms of equipment, training, size, strategic location, and loyalty of armed manpower from within and without the country.

Coercive Support for Anti-Regime - a measure of the extent to which anti-regime members are supported, in terms of equipment, training, size, strategic location, and loyalty of armed manpower from within and without the country.

Institutional Support for Pro-Regime - a measure of the extent to which pro-regime members are supported, in terms of organizational cohesion and the size and geographic location of their resources, as well as psychological, economic, and political support short of coercive force, in achieving their objectives.

Institutional Support for Anti-Regime - a measure of the extent to which anti-regime members are supported, in terms of organizational cohesion and the size and geographic location of their resources, as well as psychological, economic, and political support short of coercive force, in achieving their objectives.

Success of Anti-Regime Movements Outside of Country - a measure of the extent to which anti-regime members outside of the country have succeeded in achieving their own political objectives.

Table 1. Attributes used for identifying political turmoil

With these variables, the area specialist in the case study projected the likelihood and type of violence that might have occurred in Poland. The events that are relevant to this case study take place in a short period of time - 2 months. The "high points" of this period of time are chronicled in table 2 below[11]:

July 1: The Central Committee announces a large hike in meat prices

July 2: The first strike breaks out in the Ursus plant near Warsaw. The strike was for higher wages to cover the increased meat prices.

July 9: Central Committee First Secretary Gierek makes public statement that no broader wage increases will be allowed, but workers continue striking.

July 16: Strikes Spread to nearby Lublin

July 27: Gierek goes on holiday to Moscow, and doesn't return until August 14.

August 15: Telephone lines to Gdansk are cut.

August 16: Representative from 21 enterprises convene in Gdansk to form the interfactory strike committee (MKS), a group formed to coordinate strike action, promote solidarity, and begin broadening demands to include political concessions.

August 18: the MKS continues to grow, while Gierek makes a television speech that no political concessions will be made with the strikers.

August 19: Dissidents are arrested on a widespread basis.

August 23: Barcikowski, Deputy Prime Minister, begins talks with the MKS on national television.

August 24: Four top Central Committee members are relieved of their posts.

August 30: The Gdansk agreement is signed, guaranteeing the right to strike and self-governing trade unions.

Table 2. Highlights of Polish conflict in the summer of 1980

These "high points," together with information concerning general trends and conditions in

Poland, make up the substance of the case study that follows. And a series of data capturing steps

occur, where the area specialist asks for information on a periodic basis.

Beginning on July 7, the area specialist creates an apprentice and sends it to the intelligence analyst

who answers its questions and returns it. With the July 7 information, the area specialist makes a

classification of the attribute-values he receives. On July 21, after 2 weeks, the area specialist

again sends the apprentice to do its job, and classify the attribute-values upon its return. Because the July 21 attribute-values held the potential for escalating violence, the area specialist sends the apprentice again after 9 days instead of 2 weeks. Now he finds that his suspicions were correct, and that the situation in Poland had become somewhat more volatile - but not alarmingly so. Thus, he sends the apprentice again, one week later, and finds that the situation has met no dramatic change. Another week passes and he sends the apprentice again. It is now August 16 and the area specialist finds that the Central committee has chosen a destabilizing course of action - cutting telephone lines into Gdansk. Now, the possibility for violence is strong, and the specialist alerts the CEO's office of Machine Corp. to this effect. They consider the situation - whether to come to a quick conclusion to their negotiations or to wait. And, because the administration's political rhetoric on the subject remains entirely "low-keyed," they decide to wait. Now the area specialist increases the frequency of his monitoring, sending the apprentice out again after 5 days, and finds that tensions in Poland still remain very high. The CEO's office is alerted to this state of affairs. Three days later the area specialist sends out the Apprentice again. Now, tensions have somewhat subsided, but the possibility of political violence is still present.

Applying the variables from table 1 to the events in table 2, the apprentice generated the knowledge base shown in figure 4 below (as of August 23). There are three possible classifications of the likelihood of political turmoil in this knowledge base thus far: Somewhat likely, Likely, and Highly Likely. The attribute values in the top layer of the tree are the predictive values used by the blackboard in selecting a search strategy. The values in the middle layer of the tree are the predictable values that follow from the occurrence of the predictive values. If all values match the available information, then the appropriate classification at the bottom of the tree is chosen.

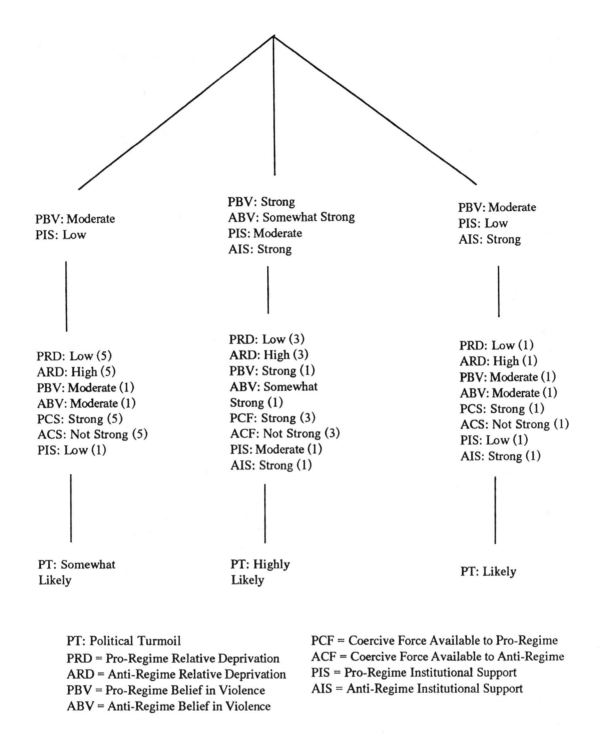

PBV: Moderate
PIS: Low

PBV: Strong
ABV: Somewhat Strong
PIS: Moderate
AIS: Strong

PBV: Moderate
PIS: Low
AIS: Strong

PRD: Low (5)
ARD: High (5)
PBV: Moderate (1)
ABV: Moderate (1)
PCS: Strong (5)
ACS: Not Strong (5)
PIS: Low (1)

PRD: Low (3)
ARD: High (3)
PBV: Strong (1)
ABV: Somewhat
Strong (1)
PCF: Strong (3)
ACF: Not Strong (3)
PIS: Moderate (1)
AIS: Strong (1)

PRD: Low (1)
ARD: High (1)
PBV: Moderate (1)
ABV: Moderate (1)
PCS: Strong (1)
ACS: Not Strong (1)
PIS: Low (1)
AIS: Strong (1)

PT: Somewhat
Likely

PT: Highly
Likely

PT: Likely

PT: Political Turmoil
PRD = Pro-Regime Relative Deprivation
ARD = Anti-Regime Relative Deprivation
PBV = Pro-Regime Belief in Violence
ABV = Anti-Regime Belief in Violence

PCF = Coercive Force Available to Pro-Regime
ACF = Coercive Force Available to Anti-Regime
PIS = Pro-Regime Institutional Support
AIS = Anti-Regime Institutional Support

Figure 4. Knowledge Base of an Apprentice

Using this knowledge base, the apprentice was allowed to do its own analysis of the events up to and

including August 24th (the assumption being that the "area specialist" had taken a vacation). In this case,

Pro-Regime Relative Deprivation	Low	The pro-regime party has enjoyed special privileges for some time
Anti-Regime Relative Deprivation	High	The economic conditions of the workers have not improved, but declined over the past decade
Pro-Regime Belief in Violence	Moderate	Gierek agreed to unions holding secret elections on the 25th - indicating continued efforts at cooperation
Anti-Regime Belief In Violence	Moderate	Continued success of MKS in getting secret elections will further convince strikers of soundness of organized approach
Pro-Regime Coercive Force Available	Strong	The Polish Army and Police are supportive of the party and the Central Committee
Anti-Regime Coercive Force Available	Not Strong	The Polish workers are not armed and little armed support for them exists outside of their country
Pro-Regime Institional Support	Low	Gierek's concessions to the unions will only futher polarize the already divided party and Central Committee
Anti-Regime Institutional Support	Strong	Achievement of political gains in terms of secret elections will further strengthen the resolve of the strikers

Table 3. Attributes, Values, and Explanations for Political Events on August 24

when it was the apprentice's "turn" to classify the political information (see table 3), the apprentice noted

that the information fit two classifications - "PT: Somewhat Likely" and "PT: Likely." Had the area specialist been present, undoubtedly only one classification would have been provided. This fact supports what we would intuitively believe of an apprentice; that is, after existing for only six weeks and having seven learning experiences, it is not going to be as good at classifications as an established expert. Nevertheless, the apprentice was able to provide a useful indication of what the pattern of qualitative political data meant. The strategy of an Apprentice is conservative. It identifies only what it has already observed or some subset of what it has already observed. If it is confronted with a pattern completely unlike anything it has come across before, it defers judgement and asks for a classification.

This case illustrates how an apprentice can be successfully used to capture knowledge about "real-world" information and established methods of classifying that information. At any time during the period discussed above, the other area specialists of this hypothetical organization also had access to the apprentice monitoring political violence in Poland. For example, during the Solidarity movement the stock market fell over a period of time while the price of gold rose. Investment personnel may have chosen to use the apprentice as one of the inputs to their investment decisions - and they could continue using it in the originating area specialist's absence. Finally, had the area specialist responsible for the creation of the political violence apprentice left the firm, instead of taking a vacation, his replacement would have had an immediate starting point, using the apprentice, from which to continue his predecessor's work.

Conclusion

Not all knowledge intensive problems are amenable to expert system solutions. Episodic Classification Problems - temporary in nature, very scarce in available expertise, benefiting even from appropriate query generation - fall into this category. We have introduced an approach for solving these kinds of problems that centers on caching knowledge. The application that has been discussed was in the area of environmental scanning. But we believe that relatively simple modifications to the basic architecture introduced would also result in positive results where other ECP's are encountered.

Conceptually, we have encouraged the notion of increasing a decision-maker's span of attention through the re-apportionment of routine cognitive responsibilities to intelligent agents. Implicit in this concept is the idea that small wins can be had by relaxing the typical constraints that are brought to a problem-solving endeavor. That is, complete solutions are usually sought for software support, environmental scanning, or SAR image interpretation. The problem solver wants a final answer. By relaxing this constraint, by looking for utility in partial solutions, small but important gains can be had. And this is the motivation for caching knowledge.

End Notes

[1] Porter, L., "McDonald and Denny, Inc.: The Keeps Project," *Harvard Case Series*, No. 9-187-001, 1986.

[2] Ansoff, H.I., "Managing Strategic Surprise by Response to Weak Signals." *California Management Review,* Winter, 1975, Vol. 18, No. 2.

[3] Elofson, G.S. and Konsynski, B.R., "Supporting Knowledge Sharing in Environmental Scanning Units," *Proceeding of the 23rd Hawaii International Conference on Systems Sciences,* January 1990.

[4] SAR Tactical Interpretation and Reporting System (STIRS), Final Design Study, Science Applications International, Contract No. DACA76-84-C-0001.

[5] Heuer, Richard J., Jr., *Quantitative Approaches to Political Intelligence: The CIA Experience,* Westview Press, Boulder, Colo., 1978.

[6] Lebowitz, M., "Generalization from Natural Language Text," *Cognitive Science,* 7, 1983, 1-40.

[7] From a methodological view-point, archival case studies have been performed and accepted for some time. For example, Rosner (Rosner, M., M., Administrative Controls and Innovation, *Behavior Science,* vol 13, 1968) used hospital records to evaluate the hospital's willingness to innovate. And some classic studies of organizational behavior have depended heavily on records (eg. Selznik, P., *TVA and the Grass Roots,* Berkeley: University of California Press, 1949).

[8] As early as 1973 nearly half of the U.S. based multinational corporations were regularly monitoring the political climate of foreign countries as part of their day-to-day operations [Zink, D., *The Political Risks for Multinational Enterprises in Developing Countries,* Praeger Publishers, New York, 1973).

[9] Weydenthal, J., *The Polish Drama: 1980-82,* Lexington Books, Lexington, Mass, 1983.

[10] Gurr, T., R., "The Conditions of Civil Violence; First Tests of a Causal Model," Princeton University, Center of International Studies, Research Monograph no. 28, 1967.

[11] It should be noted that this information was widely available during this time period. For example, from July to November the New York Times printed a front page story on Poland every 2.5 days.

The Impact of Parallel and Neural Computing on Managerial Decision Making

Robert Trippi
Sigma Research Associates
La Jolla, California

and

Efraim Turban
California State University, Long Beach
Long Beach, California

Abstract

Parallel processing has moved in recent years from a largely theoretical issue to the commercial arena. This paper discusses parallel, multiple-CPU architectures, including neural computers, and assesses their potential contribution to managerial decision making.

1. Introduction

During the last three decades there has been considerable progress in the use of computers and quantitative analysis to support managerial decision making. However, despite the vast amount of technical and theoretical work, the rate of practical application remains fairly low. At least two factors might account for this.

First, many real life problems, especially those within the purview of top management, are too complex for formulation as mathematical models. Input data might be fuzzy, trends might be unextrapolable from past experience, or important factors might be difficult or impossible to quantify. Second, notwithstanding the progress in hardware and software, we are approaching the physical limits of current semiconductor technology for Von Neumann sequential processing machines. Marginally greater computational speeds can be achieved only through use of increasingly expensive semiconductor technologies.

The solution to the computational problem might be provided by parallel processing, namely, using many low-cost processors operating simultaneously. Research papers specializing in many aspects of parallel processing are appearing regularly, and many low to high-end hardware and software products are available for system developers [25]. It has been estimated that the market for all types of parallel processing products will increase from $600 million in 1986 to $8.6 billion in 1992 [29].

The general advantages of using parallel computation are:

- Faster execution of large scale problems using existing or slightly modified algorithms.

- Ability to solve complex problems which are currently unsolvable (or take too long to solve) by existing computing tools.

- Development of new algorithms which specifically match parallel computing hardware and software capabilities, and which result in faster computations and/or the ability to solve those problems which are not presently amenable to conventional computational approaches.

Reprinted from the *Journal of Management Information Systems*, Vol. 6, No. 3, Winter 1989/1990, pages 85-98. Copyright © 1990 by M.E. Sharpe, Inc. Reprinted with permission.

The purpose of this paper is to assess the potential impact of parallel processing technology and its derivatives on managerial decision making. This assessment can provide guidelines for further research in this area, as well as point out potential applications. The two most likely contributions to managerial decision making are the possibility of a quantum increase in productivity, and the ability to approach certain types of problems from an entirely different direction. Two types of parallel processing are discussed in this paper: coarse-grain and neural. Coarse-grain parallel computers offer the greatest promise for productivity improvements, while neurocomputers implement a completely different form of computation, which shows promise for being more effective than conventional computation for certain types of problems.

2. Parallel processing architectures

In order to be effective, any parallel processing hardware must be complemented by software designed to exploit parallelization opportunities. For some types of applications, it might be sufficient for parallel-oriented software to be at a level other than that of the application software. Concurrency of some computational steps might be achievable at the compiler, system software, microcode, or hardware logic level. Other applications might demand that mapping to the architecture takes place at the source code level — as, for example, when a uniquely parallel optimization algorithm is programmed in a high level language.

Hardware parallelism can be achieved in several ways. The five most common approaches are 1) vector processing, 2) array processing, 3) very long instruction word CPU's, 4) coarse-grained multiple-CPU machines, and 5) fine-grained multiple-CPU machines (neurocomputers). The first three have a relatively limited repertoire of capabilities, and are not even considered true parallel architectures by some writers (for example, Frenzel [15]). The most relevant to problems of managerial decision making are the latter two. These are also the most dependent on the use of parallel oriented application software to exploit the hardware capabilities.

3. Granularity and complexity of processing

The coarse-grained architectures employ a relatively small number (up to a few thousand) of the more powerful CPU's. The fine grained structures, in contrast, employ up to several millions of much simpler processors. Applications to be run on multiple-CPU architectures virtually always demand parallel-oriented software at least at the compiler level, and in many instances also at the source code level.

Parallel processing architectures can be distinguished by the complexity of the computation done by each processing element, and by the complexity of the communication among the elements. The processors of coarse-grain machines are, in general, capable of the same types of highly complex processing tasks as a single-CPU machine; that is, those with many algorithmic steps between the input and output. However, the communication network is relatively simple — in most cases just a common memory that can be written to and read by all processors. Most fine-grain architectures, in contrast, embody processors capable of only very simple, and in the case of neural computers, identical processing tasks [2]. The complexity of fine-grain architectures is manifested in the communication links among processors. For example, the neural networks created by connecting many processing elements of a neurocomputer are often quite hugh, with thousands or hundreds of thousands of individual inter-processor data transfer links. Their computation is often said to be non-algorithmic, although a relatively simple form of algorithmic processing does take place at the processing element level.

4. Coarse-grained technology

An example of a coarse-grained processing element is the INMOS transputer. The transputer family employs 32-bit reduced-instruction-set computer chips which include high-speed serial I/O capability, on-chip memory, and, optionally, a floating point processing unit. These can be linked in a network, with a great deal of flexibility in its topology. Communication is point-to-point, avoiding possible contention problems of a common bus. Each processor operates in a sequential mode similar to traditional Von Neumann machines, but there is simultaneous processing of different parts of the same problem.

Because of the high degree of integration of logic, memory, and I/O in the transputer, and its ability to communicate with others without use of a common bus, the Transputer is often considered to be in a class by itself. More conventional examples of coarse-grained machines are Sequent Computer System's Symmetry system, which employs a cluster of thirty 80386 chips, and the Intel IPSC with 32 proprietary microprocessors. The former has the raw processing power of an IBM 3090 mainframe, at about five per cent of the cost, while the latter reportedly can perform at 100 megaflops (millions of floating point operations per second), which is in the same league as a Cray X-MP/12 costing over ten million dollars. The success of coarse-grained computers in improving computational performance depends on the ability of the software to detect data dependency structures suitable for parallelization (for example, see Wolfe and Banerjee [36] and Shasha and Goodman [28]). Coarse-grained machines typically have a limited potential for inter-processor communication, which encompasses the mode, quantity, and timing of data transfers from one processor to another. Inter-processor communication demands on a coarse-grained machine are likely to vary considerably for different types of problems. A listing of representative commercially available coarse-grained parallel computers appears in Davis [10].

The number of processors required by a parallel algorithm in relation to its input is one measure of the complexity of the hardware required. Coarse-grain parallel algorithms can generally make effective use of up to a certain number, N, processors, which generally depends on the number of inputs. However, performance gains might diminish markedly or disappear altogether with additional processors, as all or nearly all parallelization opportunities become exploited. In some applications close to a linear reduction in computation time can be achieved provided the number of processors made available does not exceed a certain critical value of N for the particular problem size.

Another performance limit on coarse-grained machines is set by Amdahl's law, which is based on the percentage of the nonparallelizable work plus overhead and communication. This law states that the parallel speedup factor (as a percentage) relative to the speed of a single processor performing a task, is bounded from above by $100/((100-p)+p/N)$, where p is the percentage of total work that can be done in parallel and N is the number of processors. The practical speedup limit was thought to be about 200 times. However, researchers at Sandia Laboratories were recently reported to have solved classic engineering problems with 1,024 processors more than 1,000 times faster than with a single processor (for details see Waldrop [34]).

5. Coarse-grained applications in mathematical modeling

Several types of modeling methodologies are expected to be significantly impacted by advances in coarse-grain technology. Large-scale problems such as those below, in which the inherent algorithmic structure lends itself to parallel computation, are good candidates:

Mathematical programming

Many important mathematical programming problems have large but sparse constraint coefficient matrices. These are amenable to a variety of decomposition methods which result in a series of sub-problems which might be solved in parallel at each iteration (for example, see Dantzig [9]). The solution of the symmetric linear complementarity problem implied by LP primal-dual feasibility has been the subject of parallel computing approaches as well (for example, see Mangasarian and De Leone [22], Pang and Yang [24], Phillips and Rosen [26]). Auction algorithms, which have been applied to network flow, assignment, and certain other matching problems, lend themselves naturally to parallel processing. This is especially so in those cases in which bidding and assignment might be carried out asynchronously, that is, with bids comprising whatever prices are currently available (for example, see Bertsekas [5] and his references).

Dynamic programming

A dynamic programming problem structure lends itself naturally to CG processing. These problems become very difficult to solve when the number of feasible state-decision combinations exceeds a few hundred thousand, which can easily occur with multidimensional state and decision variables of realistic coarseness. Since the order of computation of the partial returns for the state-decision combinations within the same stage is immaterial, such computations might be performed in parallel. When this is accomplished (in parallel) at one stage, processing can begin on the next stage.

Markov processes

Descriptive Markov chain applications and Markovian decision problems might realize productivity benefits from parallel processing in a similar way as dynamic programming. For systems which are governed by a transition matrix, the equilibrium probability vector, plus possibly other statistics such as mean passage and recurrence times, might be computed for each state in parallel. For the Markovian decision problem (state-stage transition function incorporating probabilities), parallel computation is possible because there is no sequentiality requirement for computing partial returns of state-decision combinations.

Branch-and-bound problems

In one parallel approach to branch-and-bound problems, individual processors are assigned to search specific areas of the tree (particular disjoint sets of values of the variables) more-or-less independently. After every iteration, each processor need only check its current upper and lower bounds, which are used in "pruning" the tree, against a temporary overall problem's upper and lower bounds. If either of the processor's current bounds are superior they simply replace those of the overall problem, and vice-versa. However, anomalous behavior of parallelized branch-and-bound algorithms has been reported by several researchers. Under certain search strategies additional processors might actually result in an increase in processing time (for details see Kindervater and Lenstra [21] and their references).

Heuristic programming

Many heuristics have a high degree of inherent parallelism. For example, it has long been known that good solutions to the traveling salesman problem, which seeks a least-cost cyclical permutation, can be obtained by employing the simple rule: "next visit the closest unvisited city". With N processors, an N city problem can be solved by testing all possible starting cities simultaneously. Many heuristic procedures for solving problems involving permutations are sensitive to either first variable fixed or initial feasible solution, and are thus easily parallelizable (for example, see [32]).

Simulation, modeling, and expert systems languages

Future generations of popular simulation languages such as SIMSCRIPT and GPSS will probably recognize and exploit parallel structure in problems, assigning sub-systems of the overall simulation model to individual processors. This is essentially an issue of software design similar to that of compilers for high-level procedural languages. Current language standardization efforts are proceeding with parallel architectures in mind. Expert system languages and development tools, such as "shells," also have the potential to exploit parallel architectures (for example, see Deering [11]).

6. The neural processing element paradigm

The neural computer employs a radically different form of computation from the conventional, algorithmic processing mode of single-CPU and coarse-grain parallel processing computers. In the usual neural computer model, the processors can each perform only an identical, very simple type of processing task. Each processor typically has its own relatively small local storage area for use in performing this task. An individual processor is referred to as a processing element, "PE," or "neurode".

There are a variety of different, proprietary hardware and software configurations, including inexpensive neurocomputer software emulation packages, such as NeuralWare's NeuralWorks products (see [1]). In most, processing is largely limited to elementary operations of computing weights (also called local energy levels) and combining them with those developed by the other processing elements. Each neurode has multiple inputs and one output determined by transfer function coefficients and weights (connection strengths) applied to the inputs. Neurodes combine inputs and weights by taking the dot-product of the two (weighted sum of inputs), and then pass the results through a transfer or activation function to produce the output.

Neurocomputers might be implemented, at least in theory, with electro-optical or optically bi-stable devices as well as electronic devices. It is important to recognize, however, that currently available neurocomputers are actually software emulators of the multiple-neurode model, implemented using rather conventional computer hardware. Most neural network hardware products on the market are really floating-point accelerator boards with large memories for storing problem-generated matrices and vectors, and which interface with the vendor's proprietary network emulation software. When performed by many simulated neurodes at once, the dot-product operation, which is at the core of the input-output transfer function, becomes a matrix multiplication (Conner [8]). Hence the desirability of accelerator boards when dealing with large neural networks. At this time (December, 1988) there are no hardware neurocomputer chips on the market.

The speed of a neurocomputer is given in interconnects per second (ips), which is a measure of the number of transfers of an output of one neurode to the input of another within one second. The more interconnections, the faster the neurode-level processing must be to maintain a given ips level. Therefore, a network configuration whose processing elements have a greater average input vector size will run slower on the same system than one with a small average input vector size. Neurocomputers can be very fast due to the simplicity of the processing tasks that take place at the neurode level. The future availability of hardware-implemented neurode arrays will obviously permit a manyfold increase in the processing speed of virtually every neural computer application.

Despite certain limitations on the complexity of processing, a variety of important decision problems, including large-scale and/or complex combinatorial and other optimization problems, problems requiring inference from incomplete information, and problems of pattern recognition and classification, might be effectively approached using neurocomputers. These are discussed next.

7. Neurocomputer solution of difficult optimization problems

In their pioneering paper, Hopfield and Tank [19] reported the development of optimal and nearly optimal solutions to traveling salesman problems using two networks. The first network produces a high energy value if an infeasible tour is generated. The second network's energy value is an increasing function of the length of the tour, without respect to its feasibility. The second network has a slower time constant than the first. Therefore, if an infeasible tour is in the process of being generated (for example, if not every city is being visited), the large energy increase in the first network can be rapidly applied to the second network, thus steering the system back to the region of feasible solutions.

The two-network system by itself yields locally optimum solutions only. However, through a technique called simulated annealing, that is, adding "noise" to the outputs of the processing elements, globally optimal solutions can often be attained or approximated. This is somewhat analogous to perturbation of a locally optimal solution in a conventional algorithm to seek out other local optima, except that it is done dynamically by the neurocomputer as the network converges on a stable solution. The neurocomputer at each iteration will update the values of all variables simultaneously rather than sequentially (for example, see Szu [30]). Simulated annealing mitigates against convergence on local optima, since local extreme points tend to be obscured by noise more easily than the global optimum, thus preventing the system from getting "stuck" at a local optimum.

There remains considerable skepticism about whether the Hopfield-Tank network performs well (that is, yields both feasible and good tours) when scaled upward to larger problems (for example, see Wilson and Pawley [35] and Hegde, Sweet, and Levy [18]). However, more effective energy functions, yielding improved results, have also been reported (for example, see Van den Bout and Miller [33] and Brandt, Wang, Laub, and Mitra [6]).

The neurocomputer approach has been applied to the solution of several other combinatorial problems, including more general types of integer programs. This line of research could result in significant breakthroughs in mathematical programming, as processing time is in effect divorced from problem size in the neural processing approach. In contrast to conventional methods (partial enumeration, heuristic, etc.), the number of iterations to reach a stable solution for a given problem structure does not necessarily increase with the number of variables. Reported results related to the effectiveness of neurocomputers for the solution of optimization problems is mixed but on the whole promising. Tank and Hopfield [31] and others have solved assignment problems using neural networks, and energy functions for graph partitioning and other types of NP-complete combinatorial problems have been proposed (for example, see Ramanujam and Sadayappan [27]). In such problems, an optimal solution cannot be guaranteed to be found by one run of any algorithm which must terminate within a number of steps bounded by a polynomial function of the number of constraints and variables. A brief discussion of the time complexity concept appears in the Appendix. Another interesting potential application is that of job-shop scheduling, which has been examined by Foo and Takefuji [13], [14]. Their network model, as most others, does not guarantee an optimal solution. The effectiveness of neural network optimization can thus only be in a relative sense — in comparison with computation times and accuracy of other heuristic and exact methods such as branch-and-bound.

8. Simulation

Neurocomputers have the potential to revolutionize the design and execution of complex simulation models of managerial and/or economic phenomena involving numerous, highly diffused elements. For example, micro-simulation of consumer behavior requires a relatively large sample of the population to be modeled to arrive at meaningful results. Each element in the sample is vector-valued, reflecting relevant economic and demographic characteristics of individuals and their historical choice preferences. The processing is relatively simple, although time-consuming when done serially. Appropriately configured neurocomputers would permit massive model databases to be accessed and predictive results for market researchers to be obtained almost instantly.

Other types of managerial and economic simulations which could benefit from neurocomputers include those involving assets traded on commodity and financial markets. There is a significant current need for research in institutional factors and policies affecting market stability which could be facilitated by highly detailed operational models of markets implemented on neurocomputers. Networks could be designed to permit random pairing or to force Walrasian (one price for all buyers and sellers) market clearing, with results being useful for regulatory and economic prediction purposes. Similarly, simulation of complex manufacturing and distribution systems could be enhanced with neurocomputers.

9. Expert systems

Considerable attention has been given lately to the potential use of neural computing in AI work in general and in ES in particular. Several characteristics of conventional AI search lend themselves to integration with neural computing. They are: use of pattern matching, use of heuristics, considerable amount of search that can be done in parallel (for example, when a depth first search is conducted), and incomplete or fuzzy information. Neural network subsystems can help with complex pattern matching, incomplete information, and extremely large numbers of transactions.

The neural computing approach solves a major problem in ES construction, namely, facilitating the knowledge acquisition process by eliminating the need for an expert. In place of the expert's elicited knowledge, the neural network uses a training set of cases. Most proposed neural network-based expert systems have been designed around a pattern classification learning paradigm. After the network is trained with the training sample, another set of cases is used to validate its performance. Unlike rule induction in conventional expert systems, a trained neural network might stabilize on decision criteria which have little apparent relevance to the problem, and which might even conflict with conventional theory, but which nevertheless produce good results.

Success in training neural networks to make decisions using historical data in areas such as mortgage insurance underwriting and credit approval has been reported by Nestor, Inc. [7]. In field tests, their system produces predictive risk assessments on mortgage insurance applications, based on the experience of the company's underwriters. Applications are rated with greater speed and accuracy than could be done with a conventionally implemented ES.

AVCO Corp., for example, has compared the performance of a neural network credit scoring system with its conventional statistical one. The trained neural network, without increasing the default rate, was able to increase lending volume by 25 per cent, obviously a great benefit to the firm as well as to its prospective customers. In addition, it was found that out of the 96 individual score items, only 46 were needed for making satisfactory assessments of risk. This is typical of the way that neural networks can discriminate significant from insignificant and redundant factors when used for prediction.

Risk assessment is an example of a generalization problem. These differ from recognition problems, to which neural networks have been most frequently applied. In the former case, the network is expected to correctly predict an output from an input which is not contained in the set of examples that it was trained with. Dutta and Shekhar [12] have successfully applied neural network technology to the generalization problem of rating bonds. Their network was able to categorize bonds with a total squared error of an order of magnitude smaller than the most competitive conventional approach (multiple regression). Standard AI approaches (for example, rule-based systems) are difficult to apply successfully to this particular problem since the domain lacks a well defined model or theory.

A potential problem with neural network implemented expert systems is the difficulty of making the network "relearn" when the input-desired result relationship changes. Thousands of cases might be poorly handled before the network's weights readjust sufficiently to compensate for an external change which might have taken place.

10. Adaptive learning

Most neural approaches attempt to implement some form of learning in setting interconnect weight coefficients (for an overview, see McClelland and Rumelhart [23]). The simplest rule, for example, is the Hebb rule, which strengthens the interconnect weight w_{ij} incrementally whenever processing element i receives an input from processing element j. This can be done with a product form such as $w_{ij} = kx_i w_{ij}$, where k is a constant which determines the learning rate. A more sophisticated method is the Delta rule, which is a sort of gradient-descent algorithm that adjusts the interconnect weights based on local improvement. There are about a half-dozen commonly used learning rules. The goal of learning is usually one of the following [4]:

> *Associating patterns.* When input-output pairs are repeatedly presented during training, the network will learn to output one of the elements of the pair when presented with the other.

> *Replicating patterns.* A set of patterns is presented during training. The network will learn to complete any pattern that is later presented with some features missing.

> *Classifying patterns.* The network is presented during training with a predetermined set of classes to which each pattern belongs. When a similar pattern is encountered in the future, the network should correctly classify it.

> *Recognizing patterns.* In this case there is no training. The system develops its own set of classes which best classifies the input patterns. This is analogous to statistical techniques such as cluster and discriminant analysis.

Learning is an important component of the decision-making process, especially in the early phases of modeling which are concerned with problem definition and data collection. Relationships among the input and output variables to a system might not be clear at that stage. Neural networks can deduce relationships in the absence of expert knowledge, even when those relationships are "fuzzy". They are well-suited to making "good" classifications, generalizations, or decisions, in those cases where less than 100 percent accuracy can be tolerated, and they are not limited by a particular type of separation function, such as linear or polynomial. When used for data reduction, for example, a completely certain solution, or sometimes even repeatability with the same input data, is not guaranteed. Even in optimization, as discussed earlier, most neural computer approaches cannot guarantee the best solution.

11. Other potential neural network applications

Problems of a mass assignment nature, such as those associated with waybill processing, vehicle selection and routing, and airline fare determination (pricing) systems, are potential candidates for the application of neurocomputer technology. For example, Behavheuristics Inc. has developed a successful neural-network based airline-seat capacity management system called the Airline Marketing Tactician, which solves the problem of allocation of seats in different fare classes to maximize revenue.

Closely related are physical location problems, such as site analysis, franchise assignment, and other applications that can be approached through discretization of density functions of the appropriate economic, demographic, or physical data on a cartesian map. At least one fast food company is exploring the use of a neural network model for restaurant location.

An immediate potential application of neurocomputers is in the area of mass scoring operations of various types; for example, as discussed earlier for credit applications. Mass scoring is often needed in connection with new product, consumer response, and warrantee analysis, and insurance policy applications. Some of these applications might not be related directly to decision models, but might be related indirectly (for example, providing input data). TRW, for example, is evaluating neural network scoring technology in connection with its credit reporting system.

In the manufacturing sphere, inexpensive visual inspection and nondestructive testing systems are being developed which capitalize on the neurocomputer's success at pattern recognition. For example, HNC Corp. has already developed a prototype visual inspection system for a bottler.

Neurocomputers are also being applied experimentally (with differing degrees of success) to other types of visual pattern-classification problems. Such problems require the computer to most closely match a visual or other pattern to one of possibly many templates that it has been previously exposed to. These include recognition of military vehicles, facial identification in law enforcement, and recognition of handwriting and vocal signatures. Generally a complex goodness-of-fit criterion function is implicitly minimized by the network in template fitting. Single or multiple solutions (with ex-post probabilities) might result. It is possible for the templates themselves to be incomplete or fuzzy. In the latter case the elemental features might possibly belong to more than one template in the template set.

12. Problem formulation and knowledge processing

In addition to speed, neural computing possesses several other properties that make it very attractive for managerial decision making. Three of the most important applications are sensor processing, knowledge processing, and adaptive control.

a. *Sensor processing*. This includes pattern recognition and pattern preprocessing transformation operations. The potential uses are in robotics (error recovery), time-series analysis (by comparing spectra with stored examples), continuous speech recognition, and problem identification in situations that involve fuzzy diagnosis.

b. *Knowledge processing*. This capability provides the following abilities:

Autonomous acquisition of knowledge from data;

incrementally mapping relational data into an existing knowledge base (via a fuzzy cognitive map); and

carrying out logical hypothesis testing using nondeterministic, not highly quantitative knowledge, where contradictions and errors might exist in the raw data.

c. *Adaptive control.* In this application, control of some operation (for example, a robot's arm, or a continuous production process) is determined not by a control formula, but by what the network has "learned" of the behavior of the system under different input data regimes. (see Hecht-Nielson [17] for details)

13. Summary and conclusions

The real promise of parallel computation for managerial problem solving is not just in doing the same things in a different way, but in routinely solving problems which were heretofore virtually intractable (for example, combinatorial problems), or where the solution was not economically justifiable because of the large computational effort or the amount of time necessary to reach a solution. Multidimensional dynamic problems appear to be amenable to efficient solution using coarse-grained parallel machines. Many applications which were previously impractical for real-time computation now seem potentially viable (Hornstein [20]). Also, the technology should assist in formulation and solution of problems which require extensive symbolic manipulation but are poor candidates for existing AI technology (that is, problems that require "deep" modeling).

Neurocomputers, in particular, enable approaching certain problems from an entirely different perspective, one which is learning-based. This technology has the potential to automate aspects of problem solving that involve learning. It is also well suited to formulation and solution of problems with fuzzy, inexact or incomplete information (for example, making inferences with missing facts). Neurocomputer-based natural language decision support system interfaces are likely to emerge. Such an enhancement could increase significantly the use of computerized modeling tools by managers.

Two major technical obstacles to be overcome for meaningful commercial assimilation of both coarse and fine grain technologies appear to be the proliferation of competing architectures and the shortage of software standards. Application software, and in some cases development tools, are also relatively scarce. Investment in application software for neural network products of uncertain longevity is a risky business at best. When application generators become more readily available this situation will rapidly improve. Finally, the exploitation of these technologies for improved managerial decision making will require in some cases a fresh approach to modeling, an approach which will consider the utilization of the capabilities of the technologies in the most efficient manner.

Appendix — Measurement of time complexity

The most easily solved problems are those in which the time complexity function $g(n)$ is polynomial (rather than exponential). A function $f(n)$, which might represent the time or number of steps required to solve a problem of size n, is said to belong to the set $O(g)$ if there exists a finite constant c such that $|f(n)| \leq c \cdot |g(n)|$ for all integer values of $n \geq 0$. In other words, the "worst case," rate of increase in computation time with respect to n is that of g (when computation time increases at the identical rate as g, the notation $\theta(g)$ is used, and when the rate is bounded from below by that of g, the notation $\Omega(g)$ is used). The most easily solved problems are those in which time complexity is a polynomial (rather than exponential) function. However, even within the polynomial set there is a particularly difficult class of problems called nondeterministic polynomial time (NP). These problems can only be solved in a time which is guaranteed to be bounded from above by a polynomial on some, but not necessarily all, executions on a nondeterministic Turing machine (one with the ability to make randomly generated "guesses" at solutions on each run). The most difficult of these are known as NP-complete (see Baase [3] for a formal mathematical treatment of problem complexity). Many decision problems are NP-complete, including the traveling salesman problem, the knapsack problem, and job scheduling with penalties.

References

[1] Aguiar, Saul, "The NeuralWorks Professional," PC AI, Vol. 2, No. 1, 1988, pp. 56-58.

[2] Almasi, G.S. and Gottlieb, A., *Highly Parallel Computing*, Benjamin/Cummings, Redwood City, 1989.

[3] Baase, S., *Computer Algorithms*, Addison-Wesley, New York, 1988.

[4] Bayle, Aime, "Learning in Neural Networks," PC AI, Vol. 2, No. 4 (November-December 1988), pp. 40-48.

[5] Bertsekas, D., "The Auction Algorithm: A Distributed Relaxation Method for the Assignment Problem," in *Annals of Operations Research: Parallel Optimization on Novel Computer Architectures*, Vol. 14, P. L. Hammer, Editor, 1988. pp. 105-120.

[6] Brandt, R., Wang, Y., Laub, A., and Mitra, S.,"Alternative Networks for Solving the Traveling Salesman Problem and the List-Matching Problem," *Proceedings of the IEEE International Conference on Neural Networks*, July, 1988, pp. II-333-340.

[7] Collins, E., Ghosh, S. and Scofield, C., "An Application of a Multiple Neural Network Learning System to Emulation of Mortgage Underwriting Judgments," *Proceedings of the IEEE International Conference on Neural Networks*, July, 1988, pp. II-459-466.

[8] Conner, D., "Data Transformation Explains the Basics of Neural Networks," *EDN*, Vol. 33, No. 10, May 12, 1988.

[9] Dantzig, G.B., "Planning Under Uncertainty Using Parallel Computing," in *Annals of Operations Research: Parallel Optimization on Novel Computer Architectures*, Vol. 14, 1988, pp. 1-16.

[10] Davis, Dwight, "Parallel Computers Diverge," *High Technology*, February, 1987.

[11] Deering, M., "Architectures for AI," *Byte*, Vol. 10, No. 5, April 1985, pp. 192-206.

[12] Dutta, S. and Shekhar, S., "Bond Rating: A Non-Conservative Application of Neural Networks," *Proceedings of the IEEE International Conference on Neural Networks*, July, 1988, pp. II-443-450

[13] Foo, Y. and Takefuji, Y., "Integer Linear Programming Neural Networks for Job-Shop Scheduling," *Proceedings of the IEEE International Conference on Neural Networks*, July, 1988, pp. II-341-348.

[14] Foo, Y. and Takefuji, Y., "Stochastic Neural Networks for Solving Job-Shop Scheduling," *Proceedings of the IEEE International Conference on Neural Networks*, July, 1988, pp. II-275-290.

[15] Frenzel, L. E., *Crash Course in AI and ES*, Howard W. Sams, 1988, Chapter 11.

[16] Hecht-Nielson, R., "Neurocomputing: Picking the Human Brain," IEEE Spectrum, March, 1988, pp. 36-41.

[17] Hecht-Nielson, R., "Neurocomputer Applications," *National Computer Conference Proceedings*, 1987, pp. 239-244.

[18] Hedge, S., Sweet, J, and Levy, W., "Determination of Parameters in a Hopfield/Tank Computational Network," *Proceedings of the IEEE International Conference on Neural Networks*, July, 1988, pp. II-291-II-298

[19] Hopfield, J. and Tank, D., "Neural Computation of Decisions in Optimization Problems," *Biological Cybernetics*, Vol. 52, July 1985.

[20] Hornstein, J.V., "Parallel Processing Attacks Real-Time World," *Mini-Micro Systems*, December 1986, pp. 65-77.

[21] Kindevater, G. and Lenstra, J., "Parallel Computing in Combinatorial Optimization," *Annals of Operations Research: Parallel Optimization on Novel Computer Architectures*, Vol. 14, 1988, pp. 245-290.

[22] Mangasarian, O. and De Leone, R., "Parallel Gradient Projection Successive Overrelaxation for Symmetric Linear Complementary Problems and Linear Programs," *Annals of Operations Research: Parallel Optimization on Novel Computer Architectures*, Vol. 14, 1988, pp. 41-60.

[23] McClelland J.L. and Rumelhart, D.E., *Parallel Distributed Processing*, 1986, Chapters 2, 8, 11, and 17.

[24] Pang, J. and Yang, J., "Two-Stage Parallel Iterative Methods for the Symmetric Linear Complementarity Problem," *Annals of Operations Research: Parallel Optimization on Novel Computer Architectures*, Vol. 14, 1988, pp. 61-76.

[25] Perrot, R. H., *Parallel Programming*, Addison-Wesley, New York, 1987.

[26] Phillips, A. and Rosen, J., "A Parallel Algorithm for Solving the Linear Complementarity Problem," *Annals of Operations Research: Parallel Optimization on Novel Computer Architectures*, Vol. 14, 1988, pp. 77-104.

[27] Ramanujam, J. and Sadayappan, P., "Optimization by Neural Networks," *Proceedings of the IEEE International Conference on Neural Networks*, July, 1988, pp. II-325-332.

[28] Shasha, D. and Goodman, N., "Concurrent Search Structure Algorithms", *ACM Transactions on Database Systems*, Vol. 13, No. 1, March 1988.

[29] Stubbs, George, "Future of Supercomputers Lies in Parallel Processing," *EDN*, March 18, 1987. pp. 291-92.

[30] Szu, H. "Fast Simulated Annealing," *AIP Conference Proceedings on Neural Networks for Computing*, 1986, pp. 420-425.

[31] Tank, D.W. and Hopfield, J.J., "Collective Computation in Neuronlike Circuits," *Scientific American*, Vol. 257, No. 6, 1987, pp. 104-114.

[32] Trippi, R., "Strategies for Solving Economic Problems Involving Permutations," *Decision Sciences*, Vol. 6, No. 4, October, 1975.

[33] Van den Bout, D.E. and Miller, T.K., "A Traveling Salesman Objective Function that Works," *Proceedings of the IEEE International Conference on Neural Networks*, July, 1988, pp. II-299-303.

[34] Waldrop, M., "Hypercube Breaks a Programming Barrier," *Science*, Vol. 240, April 15, 1988.

[35] Wilson, G.V. and Pawley, G. S. "On the Stability of the Travelling Salesman Problem Algorithm of Hopfield and Tank," *Biological Cybernetics*, Vol. 58, 1988, pp. 63-70.

[36] Wolfe, M. and Banerjee, U., "Data Dependence and Its Application to Parallel Processing," *International Journal of Parallel Programming*, Vol. 16, No. 2, 1987.

Exploring Active Decision Support: The JANUS Project

Sridhar A. Raghavan
Donald R. Chand

CIS Department,
Bentley College, Waltham, MA.

Abstract

This paper describes our research approach for developing active decision support systems. We provide a detailed discussion of our research framework, methodology, and system architecture for developing advanced forms of process support and intellectual support. We present the details of the JANUS system, our research prototype, where we have implemented our ideas. We discuss the contributions of the JANUS work and summarize our experiences and plans for the future.

1. Purpose and Organization

This paper has two objectives: Presenting our research ideas and approaches for developing active decision support systems; and describing our research prototype called JANUS that implements our ideas.

The rest of the paper is organized into five sections. Section 2 provides an introduction to the concept of active decision support and reviews the key works from the literature. Section 3 describes our research framework for exploring active decision support ideas. Section 4 is devoted to the detail description of the JANUS system. The system is described in terms of the goals and objectives, functional features, design overview, and a sample session. In Section 5, we establish the unique contributions of the JANUS project by establishing its relationships with relevant prior work. We also reflect on the outcomes of the JANUS project, provide a list of the key research problems that have emerged, and discuss our plans for future work. The final section summarizes the key aspects of the paper.

2. Active Decision Support

2.1 Introduction

The concept of active decision support systems represents a variation and refinement of the fundamental DSS philosophy[Gory71]. Whereas the DSS philosophy merely calls for enhancing human decision making through computer-based tools, the active decision support concept advocates developing advanced forms of decision support where the underlying tools actively participate in the decision making process.

The notion of active participation in decision making can represent a broad range of ideas such as: monitoring the decision making processes of the user and detecting inconsistencies and problems; automatically scheduling and carrying out the necessary activities by understanding the intent and the context of the decision maker; alerting the decision maker to the aspects of the problem and problem-solving processes he may be unconsciously ignoring; carrying on conversations with the decision maker that can lead to proper formulation of decision problems; stimulating creative ideas; serving as a sounding board for ideas; and criticizing decision maker's actions and decisions from various perspectives.

Active decision support ideas stand in striking contrast to the approaches underlying the conventional DSSs. The latter are largely passive partners in decision making. They are passive in the sense that they merely place a set of useful facilities at the disposal of a decision maker. They expect that the decision maker will somehow exploit these facilities effectively during decision making. They are not capable of taking initiatives - they can only respond to users requests. In summary, they provide a weak form of support that does not exploit the full potential of a computer-based system.

2.2 Underlying premises

The key premises underlying the active decision support research can be summarized as follows:

. Decision support systems are essentially man-machine systems for improving decision making[Raghavan87a]. Since man and machine have distinguishing characteristics and skills, a potentially promising synergy exists between them. This synergy can be realized by properly distributing the roles, skills, and responsibilities between the man and the machine within the man-machine setup[Woods86].

. It is possible for the machine component to play active roles during decision making without violating the fundamental support philosophy of decision support systems.

. It is necessary to incorporate active roles in the machine component for fully exploiting the potential power of a computer.

. AI/Expert systems technology can provide the necessary implementation techniques for implementing active support ideas.

Reprinted from the *Proceedings of the 22nd Annual Hawaii International Conference on System Sciences*, 1989, pages 33-45. Copyright © 1989 by the Institute of Electrical and Electronics Engineers, Inc. All rights reserved.

2.3 A Review of the Key Ideas

Research in active DSSs is carried out under a variety of labels such as intelligent decision support systems[Hollangel86], symbiotic DSS[Manaheim88], and joint man-machine cognition[Woods86, Raghavan87a]. Currently there are four broad threads of ideas in this area: idea stimulation, autonomous processes, expert systems, and active elicitation and structuring.

2.3.1 Idea Stimulation

Idea stimulation is widely recognized as a very important form of providing active decision support[Young82, Manaheim88, Krcmar86, Neirenberg87, Raghavan87a]. There are at least two systems that illustrate this approach[Kracmar86, Neirenberg87]. Later we will also discuss how this approach is pursued in our JANUS system.

[Krcmar86] have developed a DSS that can help users identify new ways to exploit information technology as a competitive weapon. They use questions as triggers for stimulating new ideas. They generate the trigger questions by using a theoretical model that is widely used for studying information technology and its impacts.

The underlying model provides primitive variables for characterizing information technology, impacts, and their inter-relationships. Each relationship in this model represents a potentially new idea for exploiting information technology as a competitive weapon. This provides a basis for stimulating new ideas - facilitating the user to think about the potential relationships between the variables in the model. The system accomplishes this by systematically instantiating the model variables, and posing questions about the possible relationships. Since the number of questions at any point in time can be combinatorially explosive, the system uses contextual information for pruning down the irrelevant ones. The authors do not provide any system performance measures.

Whereas Krcmar uses a problem-specific model for idea stimulation, [Neirenberg87] employs a set of domain independent modules for stimulating ideas. Their system, named Idea Generator, is essentially a decision structuring tool. The underlying technique uses simple primitives such as problem, goal, actions, and strengths of relationships for structuring a decision problem. The system uses idea generation modules for helping the user identify novel actions.

Each module in the system is based on a specific scheme for generating novel actions. Some of the schemes used by the modules are:

. Think of similar situations.
. Think of metaphors for the situation.
. Think from other perspectives - that is think of how other people may solve the problem.
. Focus on goals one at a time and then collectively.

. Reverse your goals and actions.
. Focus on the people who will be affected by your actions.

The user can collect the ideas that are generated into a temporary workspace. The system provides facilities for grouping, pruning, and synthesizing these ideas. Authors claim that the system has been used in several simple business problems and has proved to be quite effective.

2.3.2 Autonomous Processes

Here the active support is implemented as a set of daemons or agents that watch over the decision making process of the user and trigger appropriate responses autonomously. In [Raghavan84] we proposed several initial ideas in this direction: observing decision maker's activities and scheduling the necessary related tasks; keeping track of the pending tasks and ensuring that they are completed; eliciting and enforcing constraints; forcing a divergent process if the user is judged to be prematurely converging; and forcing a convergent process if user is deemed to be getting disorganized with too many tasks and thoughts.

Recently, Manaheim[Manaheim88] has proposed a general architecture for active DSSs based on autonomous processes. The key aspect of his architecture is the existence of two kinds of processes in the system: user directed, and system directed. User directed processes correspond to tasks in conventional passive DSS. The system directed processes, on the other hand, are processes that are autonomously initiated by the system while playing its role as an independent and active agent in the decision making process.

The ability of the system to play active roles in this architecture rests on the following critical factors: having a good understanding of the decision making processes of the user; having a normative criteria for judging the decision making process; and having strategies for improving the process. Once these requirements are met, the system can closely monitor the decision making process of the user and intervene when necessary to criticize and offer suggestions. It can raise pointed questions and force the user to think of other alternatives and to provide rationale and justifications for his actions. It can also anticipate users needs and schedule processes in advance.

Since Manaheim's architecture rests on having an explicit model of decision making process (he uses the term problem-working process), much of his work [Manaheim87] focusses on developing the necessary theoretical bases. At present there are no prototype systems to demonstrate his ideas.

2.3.3 Expert Systems as Active DSSs

One could argue that every expert system is an active DSS because it can be used merely for getting advice rather than for decisions. However, they make very poor DSSs when used in this fashion as their design makes them suitable only for playing a decision making/recommendation role. But, it is possible to develop expert systems to function effectively as active DSSs. The key is to develop them as critiquing agents[Miller84, Mili88] rather than as expert decision makers.

[Miller84] provides a comprehensive description of the ATTENDING system, a critiquing expert system for the medical domain. Here the system becomes active only after the user has a tentative decision. The system interacts with the user and gathers the details of the problem, his decision, rationale and justifications. This dialog process itself can be very insightful to the decision maker, as he is forced to communicate and justify his decision to the system. After the details are collected, the system reconstructs a plausible decision making process using its knowledge base and internal models, and identifies potential problems and possible improvements.

A closely related approach is to capture the generic reasoning processes of different problem-solving perspectives for the purposes of critiquing. For example, a decision maker can greatly benefit by getting his decision analyzed from the marketing perspective, finance perspective, legal perspective and so on. AI systems such as PARRY[Colby75] and POLITICS[Carbonnel80] have demonstrated the feasibilities of these approaches. It may be possible to extend this approach for playing other kinds of generic roles such as devil's advocate, adversarial, conservative, and aggressive personalities.

Another popular approach for active support is to use embedded intelligent agents in the decision support system for purposes such as: automatic selection and construction of models, explaining the results of model runs, recognizing patterns in data, and making complex retrievals and inferences. Though these can be argued as valid active support ideas, they are less interesting from our perspective and therefore not discussed further.

2.3.4. Active Problem Elicitation and Structuring

Here the system is based on a structuring technique that is suitable for the problems of interest. For example, goal-oriented structuring, analytical hierarchy structuring etc. Since structuring techniques are normative models of decision making, they immediately provide: a basis for active problem elicitation, a basis for making recommendations, criteria for judging the decision making process, and a framework for incorporating idea stimulation and other machine-based personalities. Thus this approach makes it easier to implement many of Manaheim's ideas by avoiding the problem of understanding the unconstrained decision making process of the user, a critical requirement of his architecture.

The key role of the system that is based on this approach is helping the users to organize and structure their own knowledge and expertise effectively for solving problems. The GODESS system[Pearl84] is an excellent example of such a system. The acronym GODESS stands for goal-oriented decision structuring system. Goal-oriented structuring is an adaptation of means-ends analysis, a technique that is widely used in AI planning systems. Here a problem is structured in terms of goals, actions, preconditions, states, factors, and strengths of relationship between these components.

GODESS can play both support and decision-making roles. In the support role, the system carries on an active dialog with the user and formulates the decision problem in terms of the primitives of the goal-oriented structuring technique. Since the system is domain-independent, its only knowledge is that of the structuring technique. It relies on the decision maker to be very knowledgeable about the problem and supply the problem-specific knowledge.

GODESS structures the details of the problem, as they unfold, around an And-Or tree. This tree is used throughout the dialog process for meaningfully communicating with the user, making decisions about how the focus should shift between various parts of the problem, and determining what aspects of the problem need further elaboration. At the end of problem information gathering, the system processes the information accumulated in the And-Or tree to make recommendations.

The GODESS work adds several key ideas for developing active decision support: active problem elicitation and decision structuring; domain independent decision support; exploiting users' knowledge of the decision problem; and adapting AI problem-solving techniques for decision structuring. Though the system does not use any specialized domain knowledge, its architectural framework does not preclude the incorporation of knowledge bases.

2.4. Summary

We discussed four broad themes of ideas for developing active decision support: idea stimulation, autonomous processes, expert critiquing systems, and active elicitation and structuring techniques. Though we described them as disjoint ideas, they are closely related to each other and can be easily combined together.

3. Our Research Framework

3.1 Overall Context and Goals

The overall context of our research is developing decision support environments where man and machine can engage in an effective partnership during decision making. We visualize these environments as integrated set of tools and facilities that operationalize the various alternative strategies for decision support.

We recognize three major strategies for developing decision support: resource support, process support, and intellectual support. In the resource support approach the focus is on providing the resources that are necessary for decision making. In the process support approach the focus is on addressing the generic needs of decision making processes. In the intellectual support approach the thrust is to enhance the creativity of the decision maker. The operational level goals of these approaches are summarized in Tables 1, 2, and 3.

In our research we concentrate on process support and intellectual support approaches. Our goal is to resolve the conceptual and implementation problems underlying these approaches. We do not address active support as an explicit goal, as it is a recurring theme throughout our research.

3.2 Methodology

The key intellectual problem in our research is bridging the gap between the conceptual ideas and implementation techniques. There are uncertainties associated with both the ends. We cannot be certain that our ideas represent valid abstractions, are at the right level, and carry enough content and direction for developing implementations. We are also not certain that our ideas can be implemented using the available implementation techniques. This is akin to situations that normally occur in the artificial intelligence(AI) research. Therefore, we use the exploratory systems development paradigm of research that is generally used in AI for tackling such problems. The paradigm is founded on the following premise - implementing ideas on a machine makes exacting demands on rigorousness, conceptual clarity, and resolution of details; therefore getting a working implementation is a very valuable research process and a good test of the ideas.

In this paradigm, the research process proceeds as follows. The researcher begins by developing an exploratory prototype. He then uses this prototype as the experimental vehicle/environment for refining and overcoming the problems associated with his ideas and implementation techniques. He evolves the prototype continuously as he recognizes and resolves the problems. When the research is completed, the prototype represents a clear expression of both the problems and solutions to the problems. The prototype plays a critical role in the research process as well as becomes a significant output of the research.

Within this overall paradigm, we use the following step-by-step approach:

Pick a good structuring technique. Use it as the basis for the steps that follow.

Data
. Models
  . Statistical models
  . OR/MS, optimization models
  . Other Quantitative models
  . Qualitative and Symbolic models
  . Causal models
. Knowledge bases
  . Domain specific
  . General heuristics
. Machine-based experts
. Expert consultants

Table 1: Useful Resources for Decision Making

. Supporting the planning, organizing, and the execution of complex and inter-related tasks that constitute decision-making
. Supporting flexible process sequences during decision making
. Supporting interruption and resumption
. Simulating decisions and studying their potential consequences
. Supporting multiple worlds/contexts for exploring potential scenarios
. Providing various schemes for choice reduction
. Maintaining the details about intermediate decisions and their inter-relationships

Table 2. Aspects of Process Support Approach

. Active elicitation and structuring of problems
. Surfacing the assumptions, justifications and contingencies
. Stimulating creative ideas, learning, and discovery
. Suggesting alternatives and improvements
. Critiquing decision makers' processes, judgments, and decisions
. Overcoming decision makers tunnel vision, fixations, and biases
. Promoting convergent and divergent thinking
. Employing machine-based personalities for analyzing problems from diverse perspectives
. The machine playing various kinds of sounding board roles. For example: playing a devil's advocate

Table 3. Aspects of Intellectual Support Approach

- Develop a machine representation for organizing the problem details.

- Enhance the representation for primitives such as assumptions, justifications, and contingencies.
- Develop elicitation strategies

- Implement the process support mechanisms

- Identify criteria and strategies for improving the decision making process

- Incorporate machine personalities that can stimulate thinking and enhance the problem solving process

- Develop knowledge-bases needed for the machine personalities. Develop modules for what-if, sensitivity, and contingency analyses.

3.3 Conceptual Architecture

The conceptual architecture we use for our exploration is shown in Figure 1. We recognize four major functional components: Representation, Elicitation, Analysis, and User interface. Representation provides the schemes for representing information internally, and mechanisms for retrieval and inferencing. It also provides the base for organizing and utilizing domain-specific and generalized knowledge bases. Analysis block provides for internal consistency checks, constraint satisfaction, triggers and daemons, sensitivity analysis, scenario analysis, and decision simulation.

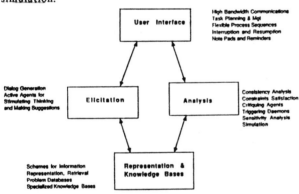

Figure 1. Conceptual Architecture

Elicitation carries dialog generation strategies, and active agents for critiquing, stimulating ideas, and playing partnerships roles. User interface provides high bandwidth communication, process support mechanisms for: mixed-mode initiative i.e the ability to shift control between the system and the user freely, flexible process sequences, interruption and resumptions.

The structuring methodology underlying the system is the conceptual glue that unifies the architectural components of the system. It provides the primitives and vocabulary for thinking about and articulating domain problems, graphical primitives for man-machine communication, rules for internal consistency, methods for analysis, and bases for making recommendations.

4. The Description of the JANUS System

4.1 An Overview of the Functional Features

JANUS is an experimental research prototype we have developed for exploring our research ideas. The system (~8000 lines) is implemented in C-Prolog under VAX/Ultrix. The system uses Saaty's analytical hierarchical process as the underlying decision structuring methodology.

The primitives of the analytical hierarchical process are Goals, Factors, Subfactors, and Judgments. Figure 2 illustrates the relationships between these primitives through a simple decision problem. In the JANUS system we have added three additional primitives-Notes, Justifications and Contingencies. Note is an

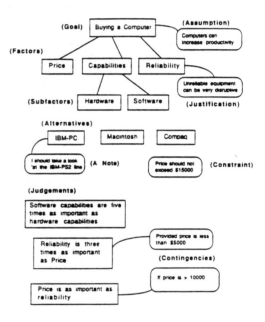

Figure 2. The JANUS Structuring Primitives

arbitrary piece of text or annotation that can be attached to any element of the representation. The justification primitive is used for capturing the assumptions and premises underlying the elements of a decision problem. The contingency primitive is used for capturing the relationships between the elements of the problem and the exogenous variables.

The following is the summary of the major functional features/capabilities implemented by the system:

Elicitation

. Active elicitation and structuring of the details of a decision problem i.e goals, factors, alternatives, and judgments.

. In addition to the essential details, the system is also capable of eliciting and capturing the assumptions, justifications and contingencies behind users statements.

. A keyword facility automatically extracts key words from the input text, and organizes the text for flexible retrieval.

. The system provides a notepad facility for creating and retrieving notes. The notes are arbitrary pieces of text that can be attached to any element of the problem. They can be used in a variety of ways. For example, leaving reminders to oneself; jotting down important ideas for later use etc.

. A constraint/contingency entry and checking facility for imposing constraints and contingencies on judgments made by the decision maker.

Process Support

. The system supports dual initiative. That is, the overall decision making process can be controlled either by the user or by the system. The control can be freely switched between them at any point in time.

. The system supports flexible process sequences. That is, the decision structuring process is not constrained to follow any predetermined order. Though the underlying structuring strategy has a top-down orientation, the system permits a high degree of flexibility regarding the order in which the details are collected. For example, the user can describe factors before alternatives and vice versa. He can also defer answering questions if he feels a need to do so. The system will keep track of the resulting loose ends and raise questions at the appropriate later times.

. The system supports interruptions and resumptions
. by providing mechanisms for saving and restoring problem contexts. This mechanism is also used for by the system for accumulating its data base of solved problems.

. Users can customize the various aspects of the structuring process through the user programmability feature.

Decision Recommendation & Analysis

. The system can make decision recommendations by performing the calculations defined by the analytical hierarchy process.

. While describing/explaining its recommendations, the system can integrate the relevant notes, assumptions, justifications and contingencies.

. The user can perform what-if analyses by changing the values of the judgments and contingency variables.

Mind Expansion

. The system provides intellectual support through a "mind expansion module". The module supports four different personalities/roles: Spock, Bozo, Mom, and Aesop. Spock emulates logical thinking. Bozo emulates lateral thinking. Mom emulates a personality that is obsessed with justifications and counter arguments. Aesop is a story teller.

Knowledge Base

. The system provides facilities for developing a database of solved problems for use by the mind-expansion module for suggesting new ideas to the user. The problems are organized and indexed using the primitives of the structuring model and key words.

. The knowledge base of the mind-expansion personalities are represented in a declarative form using templates. This facilitates the ease of evolving and enhancing the knowledge bases.

Customization

. A keyword facility for defining keywords and complex relationships among keywords such as syntactical synonyms, semantic synonyms, antonyms, and hierarchies.

. The system provides appropriate entry and exit points for the user to define daemons and insert code segments for customizing the various aspects of the structuring process.

4.2 Design Overview

4.2.1 Architecture

The architecture of the system is shown in Figure 3. At the overall level the modules in the system are: user-interface, scheduler, action-cluster, and representations manager. The user interface module is responsible for low-level system-user interactions. It gathers user inputs and displays messages.
The scheduler module controls the overall operation of the system. It consists of an agenda structure, a scheduling logic, and a work data base. The agenda structure is used for keeping track of the pending tasks. Modules in the system invoke each other by placing task requests in the agenda. Any task that

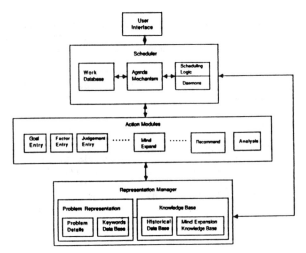

Figure 3. The Architecture of the JANUS System

can occur in the system has a priority level and a generic task description. The priority levels are assigned (at the design time) to reflect the natural order in which the problem elicitation should proceed. The scheduling logic determines how the tasks are selected for execution. The default selection criteria uses only priority levels. However, the scheduler is capable of using any other criteria specified through the customizing code.

The scheduler also carries daemons (there are none at present) which watch over the representation, the agenda, and the works data base. When a daemon fires, it becomes a task in the agenda and gets selected as per the normal scheme of things.

The work data base within the scheduler is used for various purposes: storing secondary details of tasks (only primary details are stored on the agenda), maintaining the overall system context information, and as a message exchange area by the modules of the system.

The action-cluster carries all the worker-modules of the system. As a general rule, there is one worker module for each major activity in the system. A partial list of the worker modules are: goal-entry, factor-entry, alternative-entry, judgement-entry, mind_expander, problem_analysis, constraints-entry, and notepad-entry. The scheduling modules invokes the appropriate worker module when a task needs to be completed. Usually worker modules schedule tasks for other modules when they complete. For example, the last step in the goal_entry processing is scheduling tasks for factor_entry, and alternatives entry.

The representation manager is responsible for providing a higher level interface that shields the low level implementation details of the representation from other modules. It maintains the decision problem information, keywords data base, and mind expansion knowledge bases. The keywords data base maintains

the keyword taxonomies, syntactical synonyms and semantical synonyms, and links to the textual information contained in the problem structure and knowledge bases. The mind expansion knowledge base maintains a library of reference problems, text templates, stories for the aesop module, and specialized rules for matching and retrieval.

4.2.2 System Operation

The basic execution cycle of the system is as follows. The scheduler picks up a task from the agenda and invokes the appropriate worker module. The worker modules gets the details of the task from agenda and the work data base. Typically it accesses the representation to retrieve the relevant details of the problem. It may then schedule a task for the user interface to collect some input from the user. As a last step in its processing, it may reschedule itself for processing the user input.

The user interface module is then invoked. It interacts with the user and places the users input in the work data base and relinquishes control back to the scheduler. Now the earlier worker module gets reinvoked for processing of the user input. This time the module may schedule appropriate tasks for other modules before completing.

This basic cycle repeats. During this cycle, the user may force his initiative any time the user interface is waiting for his input. By issuing a command he can request any task of his choice to be performed. The command translates into a high priority task on the agenda and gets scheduled next. When the task all its related tasks are completed, the control returns back to the system automatically.

If the user requests mind expansion functions, then the underlying personalities are invoked in sequence. The personalities engage in an appropriate conversation to stimulate the user. They use the overall context information from the scheduler, the problem details that has been gathered till that point in time, and their own internal context to guide their conversation. For example, if the user is working on factors for a personal computer purchasing problem, the mind expander may show him the factors that were associated with an equipment selection decision that was made in the past.

Whenever the user inputs text say for a goal, or factor, first the representation is updated. Then the keywords in the text are automatically extracted and retrieval links are established for promoting flexible retrieval. The system provides various alternative ways to extract a piece of text: using the conceptual primitives like goal, factor etc.; by traversing the problem graph, for example, getting to the factors from the goal; by using the keyword mechanism- either by direct match or by matching through synonyms, antonyms, closeness measures etc. These flexible retrieval mechanisms provides the base for the operation of the mind expansion personalities.

4.2.3 Knowledge Representation

The basic structures in the knowledge base are: trees for storing problem information and key word taxonomies; lists for pointers from keywords to the various conceptual entities; templates and rules for text generation; and production rules for specifying situation-action pairs. The standard prolog primitives of relations, lists and rules are used for implementing these structures.

Since the overall control structure of the system, i.e. the scheduling operations, are data-driven, we have implemented a simple forward-chaining interpreter on top of the backward-chaining scheme of the prolog engine.

4.2.4 Mind expansion Module

The system supports four distinct mind-expansion personalities: Spock, Bozo, Mom, and Aesop. Each personality pursues a characteristic strategy for helping the decision maker.

Spock emulates logical thinking. It uses the keywords associated with the current problem context to retrieve similar problems from its data base to trigger ideas. Its slogan is "If problem A is similar to problem B then the knowledge of goals, factors, and alternatives of the problem A can be useful for solving problem B".

For example, if the user is working on the problem "Buying a Boat", Spock may suggest that Cost, Loan Rate, Resale value as relevant factors by extracting them from the problem of "Buying a Car".

Bozo emulates lateral thinking. It forces the user to develop alternative problem formulations by tracing the goals-means hierarchy, by thinking about incorrect and infeasible formulations and how they may be made feasible. Its uses several slogans: "A goal is a means to a higher level goal", "Any problem A is contained in some other problem B; therefore solving problem B solves problem A", "A good way to come up with novel alternatives is to think of non-alternatives and think clearly why they do not work and how they can be made to work", and "Think of at least N alternatives before making a choice", "Think of what alternatives some person X would come up with".

Thus Bozo will raise questions such as: Well are there alternatives which you would definitely not consider ? Why ? Under what conditions will they work ? Under what conditions will this alternative not work ? If Car is to Transportation, What is X(his problem) is to _____ ?

Mom emulates a personality that is obsessed with justifications and counter arguments. Its slogans are: "My son has not thought about all possible cases. I have to raise counter examples", "He is making assumptions", and "His justifications could be wrong". So it poses potential alternatives and makes the user think about why they should be rejected or accepted. It also forces the user to justify his factors, alternatives and judgments.

Thus in the context of "Buying a Computer" problem, Mom may use the keywords taxonomy to find out that words such as calculator, Macintosh, VAX are related to computer, and raise questions such as "How about Macintosh ?", "Why do you think service is important than price ?" etc.

Aesop is a story teller. It presents the user with short parables that have general morals for problem-solving. The intent is to help the user overcome his fixations and tunnel visions. For example, it may present the story of Newton making the egg stand on its ends by placing it on a ring to warn the user that he may be unduly constraining himself.

The user can invoke these personalities any time during elicitation. The mind expansion module attempts to use the available contextual information to generate appropriate idea stimulating responses. The system remembers the phrases it has used before and avoids repeating them during a given problem.

4.3 Sample Session

The following is an edited excerpt from a sample session with the system. To keep the illustration short, we focus mostly on the interaction with between the user and the mind expansion module.

Legend: > - janus system messages
[- our annotations
rest are texts typed by the user.

> Welcome to JANUS system
>
> What is your goal? (return = abort, help=help)

I want to buy a computer.

> Give factors for: "I want to buy a computer".

Cost

> Adding factors to: "I want to buy a computer".
> 1. Cost
>

Availability of programs.

> Adding factors to: "I want to buy a computer".
> 1. Cost
> 2. Availability of programs
>

? [User is invoking idea stimulation]

> I have problem information for the following:
> It may aid you in identifying more factors:
>
>   1. buy
>
> Indicate the item of interest

1

> I have factors and alternatives for:
>
> 1. I want to buy a boat.
> 2. I want to buy a house.
>
> It seems logical that one of them may help
> you find a factor. Indicate the item of
> interest.

2

> For the goal: "I want to buy a house."
>
> I have the following factors:
> 1: Cost
> 2: Location
> 3. Interest rate
>
> And I have the following alternatives:
>
> 1: Condo
> 2: Farmhouse
> 3: Split
>
> Would you like to see more? (Yes/No)

no

> Adding factors to: "I want to buy a computer".
> 1. Cost
> 2. Availability of programs
>

Reliability of the machine

> Adding factors to: "I want to buy a computer".
> 1. Cost
> 2. Availability of programs
> 3. Reliability of the machine
>

<cr>

> Will you want to add some more factors to this goal
> later ?
> (Yes/No):

yes [System will come back to ask for more later]

> Enter alternative for "I want to buy a computer"

IBM PC

> Enter Alternatives for "I want to buy a computer" :
> 1: IBM PC
>

? [User is invoking idea stimulation]

> I have factors and alternatives for:
>
> 1. I want to compete with IBM
> 2. I want to get a job with IBM
> 3. I want to become an IBM OEM
>
> Indicate the item of iterest.

1

> The factors for "I want to compete with IBM" are:
>
>   .. Money
>   .. Market Share
>   .. Product
>
> The alternatives are:
>
>   ..Merger with Apple
>   ..Increase R&D Budget
>   ..Hire marketing consultant
>
> Would you like to see more?

No

> Enter Alternatives for "I want to buy a computer"
>1: IBM PC
>

Apple

> Current Alternatives for "I want to buy a computer"
> 1: IBM PC
> 2: Apple

? [User is invoking idea stimulation]

> Are there any alternatives that you would >
definitely not consider?
>

Compaq

> Why ?

Because my ex-wife's ......

> I would say that "I want to buy a computer" is >
really not your goal. Is there a higher goal that >
you are trying to achieve?
>

I want to be more productive.

> Consider "I want to be more productive"
> Why have you not included this as a factor ?

```
> Enter Alternatives for "I want to buy a computer":
> 1: IBM PC
> 2: Apple
> 3: Leading Edge

? [User is invoking idea stimulation]

> Why is "IBM" such a good alternative?

Because IBM has good service.

> How come "MAC" is not an alternative?

Never heard of it.

> What's so great about "Leading Edge" ?

Shutup

> I'm only trying to help. No need to be rude.
> ....
```

5. Discussion

5.1 The Project Goals and Outcome

The objectives for this project were: Exploring process support and intellectual support; developing a good understanding of the underlying conceptual and implementation problems; developing strategies for resolving these problems; and developing a research prototype that can be used for on-going research exploration. The project has succeeded well on all these counts.

We have been able to translate much of our process support and intellectual support ideas into working features of the JANUS system. Specifically, we have successfully implemented the following features: active elicitation, capturing contingencies and justifications, the system keeping track of pending tasks, flexible process sequences, mixed-mode initiative, and idea stimulation through machine-based personalities. Though the current implementations of these features are rudimentary in nature, they provide a good starting point for further exploration.

We have not a conducted a formal evaluation of the performance and effectiveness of the system. But, our preliminary and informal evaluations are very reassuring. We have verified that the system makes correct decision recommendations as per the analytical hierarchy model. We have received good feedbacks from friendly-users who have used the system for simple decision problems. Their experiences indicate that the features of the system are well-founded and effective.

The system has several limitations that are customary of prototype systems. The user interface is very basic and crude. The problem can be traced to two sources. First, the use of main-frame environment - notorious for their user interfaces. Second, since developing good user interfaces would have diverted our limited resources from other aspects we were exploring, we did not give it a high priority. We are currently remedying the interface problems by porting the system to run under Arity Prolog on IBM-AT compatibles and to take advantage of the extensive user interface capabilities available in that environment.

The knowledge base and keywords data base of the system are at present very small. This greatly limits the performance of the mind-expansion personalities. Our plan was to evolve/expand the underlying knowledge bases slowly over time. But we are recognizing the need to start with a sizeable knowledge base and keywords data base in the system. Therefore we have started a mini-project for populating the knowledge base with: representative decision problems; adages and stories related to problem solving; a library of probing questions for stimulating lateral thinking and problem reformulations; and adding a keywords dictionary.

On the whole, the project has been a rich learning experience in terms of understanding the underlying conceptual and implementation problems. We will talk more about these in Section 5.3. For now, our experiences so far has been very encouraging. We seem to have made the right decisions regarding the architecture and the choice of Prolog as the implementation langauge. The system has taken shape as an easily-extensible system, and promises to be a good research vehicle for our further exploration.

5.2 Relating to Prior Work

The JANUS work integrates and extends several current approaches to active support. [Krcmar87] and [Neirenberg87] explore the use of questions as mechanisms for stimulating ideas. In [Krcmar87], questions are generated using a model of the competitive analysis problem. The advantage of this approach is the specificity of the questions. However, the system may bias the user to think within the framework of the model. Further, the system becomes problem-dependent. On the other hand, [Neirenberg87] uses generic questions that are independent of the problem domain. While this can promote divergent thinking, it lacks the specificity enjoyed by Krcmar's approach.

In JANUS we have tried to get the best of both these worlds. We use a generic structuring technique to guide problem-solving. Therefore the system can be effective for a wide range of problems that can benefit from the underlying structuring strategy. The questions we raise originate from this model. Therefore they can be focussed and efficient. At the same time, since the model is generic, the questions can apply to a variety of situations. Further, our mind expansion facilities try to use the problem context information to generate questions and locating analogous situations. Our architecture supports a knowledge base that can be loaded with information specific to the kinds of problems expected to be solved using the system.

Some of the features in JANUS are essentially operationalizations of the conceptual ideas outlined by Manaheim[Manaheim88]. In JANUS, the user is not constrained to execute his tasks in any predetermined chronological order. As the user performs tasks, the system sort of watches over his activities and schedules related tasks which have to be completed. The system periodically reminds the user of tasks that are pending and need to be completed. These are operationalizations of the system-directed processes ideas of Manaheim. The system also has daemons which can enforce constraints and consistencies. At a later date, we hope to use the daemons to change the system mode dynamically to force the user to think divergently or convergently[Raghavan84] as needed.

A critical requirement of Manaheim's architecture is to have a good understanding of the users decision making processes. Given that decision making is an extremely complex process, we believe that it may be extremely difficult, if not impossible, to meet this requirement. We feel that the most productive approach is to use a good generic structuring technique, and implement it with appropriate process support mechanisms so that user is free to carry his processes in a flexible and more or less unconstrained manner. We have illustrated this approach through the JANUS system.

Though JANUS is similar to GODESS in the sense that both are essentially generic structuring systems, they are considerably different from each other in terms of the support they provide to a decision maker. JANUS goes far beyond GODESS because it not only provides structuring support like GODESS, but also provides process support mechanisms and mind-expansion personalities. The popular approach for enhancing the performance of a generic structuring system is to incorporate domain-specific knowledge. In JANUS we have shown other alternate approaches for enhancing the support capabilities of a generic structuring system.

At present, our mind expansion personalities are not critiquing agents, or expert personalities in the sense of our discussions in "employing expert systems as active DSS" (Section 2.3.3). But JANUS provides the overall architectural framework for productively exploring these ideas. A project is underway to implement mind-expansion personalities along the lines of PARRY[Colby75] and POLITICS[Carbonnel80].

In summary, the JANUS work shows how the various active support approaches can be integrated and extended. The work is significant from many perspectives: exploration of process support mechanisms and mind expansion facilities; exploration of active support in a generic fashion; and the methodological thrust - the use of bottom-up strategy for developing conceptual and implementation ideas in parallel.

5.3 Future Work

During the course of the project, we have acquired valuable insights into the problems that underlie the development of man-machine joint cognition systems. We have developed a long-list of research problems that need to be investigated. These will be the focus of our on-going research. Since the list is rather long, we will discuss only some of the key problems.

The mind-expansion personalities in the current system are based on simple and intuitive models. As a result, their capabilities are quite limited. They can only 'speak'; cannot 'listen'. That is, they are not capable of understanding and utilizing the responses of the user, and integrating them in their on-going dialogs. Further, as their reasoning capabilities are superficial they are not capable of making use of all the available information in the problem context. We have already initiated a project[Raghavan87e] to develop personalities that are based on formal models of inquiry and role playing, and employ expert critiquing techniques.

As the decision problem becomes large, the number of pending tasks tend to explode. We are becoming aware that our present mechanisms for task selection and scheduling are inadequate to deal with this problem. We need better approaches and criteria for deciding what part of the problem should receive attention at a given point in time, and when and how the focus should be switched.

At present, we have taken a very simple approach to interruption and resumption. The system is capable of restoring its context, and starting from where it left off. But the system provides no help to the user to regain his mental context when he resumes after interruption. In this regard, we need good mechanisms for summarizing, and explaining what has transcribed over time during a decision making process.

The philosophy and pragmatics of man-machine joint cognition dictate that knowledge and expertise will be distributed in the man-machine setup. As a consequence, the system has to acquire the necessary problem-specific and background knowledge from the user. The primary mechanism for the system to fulfil this goal is to pose questions to the user. We are discovering that this can trigger endless series of questions and can be a severe distraction from the central purpose of dialog between the user and the system. To address this problem we need systematic and effective approaches for: pruning down the questions; distributing/inserting the questions during the course of the dialog; motivating the user to cooperate with the system for satisfying the system's needs; and determining what knowledge the system should begin with, and how it should acquire additional knowledge over time.

We are also recognizing the need for the elicitation process to be 'interesting', and 'natural' to be effective. These are unique problems of intellectual support systems. Whereas in traditional systems the consistency and predictability of the interface is a key requirement, in intellectual support systems they can be very ineffective. An intellectual support system cannot be effective if it repeats the same phrases and uses the same examples. It needs to exhibit interesting variations, have elements of surprise and unpredictability. These require the system to carry a rich knowledge base of phrases and examples, and carry on conversations in a manner that reduces monotony, and avoids repetitions.

We are also recognizing that a user may not relate to the system's use of the structuring primitives such as 'goals', 'factors', 'judgments' etc. Therefore we need to make extensive use of analogies to establish common basis for communication. We have done some initial exploration of this idea in the DRONA system[Raghavan87b].

Thus we have identified a whole set of detailed conceptual and implementation problems. These will be the focus of our on-going research. However, in the immediate future our focus will be mostly on exploring the concept of machine-based personalities in more depth.

6. Summary and Conclusions

We set out with the two goals: describing our on-going research efforts in building advanced decision support systems that can engage in an active partnership with a decision maker during decision making; and describing the JANUS system and project in detail. We have accomplished both these goals.

We started with an overview of the current approaches and themes for pursuing active support. We followed this with a detailed discussion of our research framework, methodology, and architecture for developing advanced forms of process support and intellectual support. We then presented our JANUS system to show how we are implementing and evolving our ideas. We established the unique contributions of the JANUS work by relating it to the relevant prior works. We reflected on what we have learnt through our research, and presented a list of key problems that need to be addressed in the future.

We conclude this paper by summarizing the key ideas of our work:

. Developing and implementing the process support and intellectual support approaches
. Developing a domain-independent approach to active support

. Integrating and extending the available approaches to active support, and
. Emphasizing the use of AI research paradigms in DSS research.

REFERENCES

[Carbonnel80] Carbonnell, J.G. Jr., "POLITICS: An experimenting subjective understanding and integrated reasoning", in Inside Computer Understanding: Five programs plus miniatures, R.C. Schank & Reisbeck (eds.), Erlbaum, Hillsdale, N.J., 1980.

[Colby75] Colby K., Artificial Paranoia, PergammonPress. New York, 1975.

[Gory71] Gory, G.A., Scott Morton, M.S. "A Framework for Management Information Systems", Sloan Management Review, Vol. 13, No. 1, pp55-70, Fall 1971.

[Krcmar87] Krcmar, H., Asthana, A., "Identifying Competitive Information Systems: A symbiotic approach" in the Proceedings of the twentieth Annual Hawaii International Conference on Systems Sciences, 1987, pp 765-773.

[Manaheim87] Manheim, M.L., Isenberg, D., "A Theoretical Model of Human Problem-Solving and Its Use for Designing Decision-Support Systems", The Proceedings HICSS-87, IEEE Computer Society, 1987, pp 614-627.

[Manaheim88] Manaheim, M.L., "An Architecture for Active DSS", Proceedings of HICSS-21, IEEE Computer Society, 1988, pp 381-386.

[Miller84] Miller, P., "ATTENDING: A Critiquing Approach to Expert Computer Advice", Pitman Publishing Program, Boston, 1984.

[Mili88] Mili, F., "A Framework for a Decision Critic and Advisor" 21st HICSS Conference, January 1988, Vol III, pp 381-386, IEEE Computer Society Press.

[Nierenbe87] Nierenberg, G.I., "The Idea Generator" (A Software Product), Experience in Software Inc., Berkley, CA, 1987.

[Pearl82] Pearl et al, "GODESS: A goal directed decision structuring system", IEEE Transactions on Pattern Analysis and Machine Intelligence, 1982, PAMI-4, 250-262.

[Raghavan84] Raghavan, S.A., "A Decision Support System based on Generic Support Concepts and their Application to Decision-Making Processes",

Unpublished Doctoral Dissertation, Information Systems Department, Georgia State University, June 1984.

[Raghavan86]   Raghavan, S.A., et al., "TOS: A Unix Thoughts Organizing System", MSE Project Course Report, Wang Institute of Graduate Studies, Spring 1986.

[Raghavan87a]   Raghavan, S.A., Chand, D.R., "Decision Support Systems and Expert Systems", in the Proceedings of Fifth Generation Computing Systems Symposium, Madras, February 24-27, 1987.

[Raghavan87b]   Raghavan, S.A., et al., "DRONA: A Decision Structuring System", MSE Project Course Report, Wang Institute of Graduate Studies, Spring 1987.

[Raghavan87c]   Raghavan, S.A., et al., "JANUS: A Decision Structuring System", MSE Project Course Report, Wang Institute of Graduate Studies, Spring 1987.

[Raghavan87d]   Raghavan, S.A., Chand, D.R., "Towards Decision Support Environment: The Thoughts Organizing Project", in DSS-87 Transactions, June 1987, pp. 83-86.

[Raghavan87e]   Raghavan, S.A., Chand D.R., "CASE: Towards Man-Machine Partnership in Software Engineering", in the Proceedings of the First International Symposium on Computer-Aided Software Engineering, May 1987.

[Raghavan88]   Raghavan, S.A., Chand D.R., "Intellectual Support in CASE Environments", in the Proceedings of the Second International Symposium on Computer-Aided Software Engineering, July 1988.

[Woods86]   Woods, D.D., "Cognitive Technologies: The design of joint human-machine cognitive systems", AI Magazine, Vol 6. No. 4, Winter 1986, pp 86-92.

[Young82]   Young, L.F., "Computer Support for Creative Decision-Making: Right Brained DSS", in "Processes and Tools for Decision Support", edited by H.G.Sol, North-Holland, 1982, pp.47-64.

Computer-Based Critics

Gerhard Fischer and Thomas Mastaglio

Department of Computer Science and Institute of Cognitive Science
University of Colorado, Boulder

ABSTRACT

The computer-based critic is a paradigm for intelligent human-computer communication that overcomes some limitations of other approaches such as tutoring and advising. Critics are much more user-centered and support users working on their own activities. They provide information only when it is relevant. They allow users to do what they want and interrupt only when users' plans, actions, or products are considered significantly inferior. They are applicable to tasks in which users have some basic competence because users must be able to generate a plan, action, or product by themselves. They are most useful when no unique best solution exists in a domain and trade-offs have to be carefully balanced. Critics need to be knowledge-based. They must incorporate knowledge about the application domain, support explanation, model individual users, and provide innovative user interfaces. Over the last few years we have implemented a number of critics in different domains, including programming and design. The rationale, design, and evaluation of these systems is described as a starting point for a general framework for computer-based critics.

INTRODUCTION

Our goal is to establish the conceptual foundations for using the computational power that is or will be available on computer systems. We believe that artificial intelligence technologies can improve productivity by addressing, rather than ignoring, human needs and potential. In the spirit of Einstein's remark *"My pencil is cleverer than I"*, we are building systems that *augment human intelligence* -- in other words, we are building "systems for experts, not expert systems." Winograd and Flores [28] argue that the development of *tools for conversation*, the computer serving as a structured dynamic medium for conversation in systematic domains, is a more realistic and relevant way of exploiting information and communication technologies than is the most widely perceived goal of artificial intelligence, *"to understand and to build autonomous, intelligent, thinking machines"* [25].

We have used "intelligent support systems" as a generic name for systems that augment human capabilities. High functionality computer systems, such as UNIX or LISP machines which contain tens of thousands of objects and tools, have been the major application domain of our intelligent support systems. Our goal is to make usable the total space of functionality that computational environments have rather than diluting it or orienting the user toward only a subset of the system's capabilities. Intelligent support systems should facilitate access, application of knowledge, and learning. We have constructed a number of different intelligent support systems: documentation systems [14], active and passive help systems [12], design environments [11], and critics [7, 13], which we focus on in this paper. All of these systems have two things in common: they are knowledge-based and they use innovative techniques in human-computer communication.

In this paper we describe computer-based critics and articulate some of the general principles learned from our system-building experience. We propose a general framework for critics, present specific requirements, and describe two prototypical critic systems: LISP-CRITIC, which criticizes LISP programs, and CRACK, a system that assists the user in designing a kitchen. Then we illustrate the generalized main components of our critic systems and discusses their evaluation. We conclude with some plans for future work.

A Characterization of the Critic Paradigm

The computer-based critic is a useful and attractive approach for applying techniques from both human-computer communication and artificial intelligence research. Computer-based critics allow the potential of humans and computers to combine in a symbiotic system, that is, a successful combination of human skills and computing power to carry out a task that cannot be done either by the human or by the computer alone. Underlying symbiotic systems is acknowledgment of the fact that most knowledge-based systems are intended to assist human endeavor and that only a few are intended to be autonomous agents. Therefore, a subsystem supporting human-computer interaction is an absolute necessity. By using the capabilities of a knowledge-based architecture and innovative approaches to human-computer communication, critics allow users to remain in control and to solve problems they themselves want to work on, and yet critics support learning opportunities as well.

Intelligent Support Systems

Empirical investigations [6, 12] have shown that habitually only a small fraction of the functionality of complex systems such as UNIX, EMACS and LISP is used. Consequently it is of little use to equip modern computer systems with more and more computational power and functionality, unless we can help the user take advantage of them. The "intelligence" of a complex computer system must therefore be made to contribute to its ease of use and to provide effective communication, just as truly intelligent and knowledgeable human communicators, such as good teachers, use a substantial part of their knowledge to explain their expertise to others.

It is not sufficient for intelligent support systems just to solve a problem or provide information. The user must be able to understand the systems and and question their advice. One of our assumptions is that learners and practitioners will not ask a computer program for advice if they have no way of examining the program's expertise. Users must be able to access the system's knowledge base and reasoning processes. Domain knowledge has to be explainable.

Cooperative Problem Solving in Critic Systems

One model frequently used in human-computer systems (e.g., MYCIN [3]) is the *consultation model*. From an engineering point of view, it has the advantage of being clear and simple:

Reprinted from the *Proceedings of the 22nd Annual Hawaii International Conference on System Sciences*, 1989, pages 427–436.

the program controls the dialogue, much as a human consultant does, by asking for specific items of data about the problem at hand. It precludes the user volunteering what he or she might think is relevant data. The program is viewed as an "all-knowing expert", and the user is left in the undesirable position of asking a machine for help.

The critiquing model supports cooperative problem solving. When a novice and an expert communicate, much more goes on than just the request for factual information. Novices may not be able to articulate their questions without the help of the expert, the advice given by the expert may not be understood, and the novice may request an explanation; each communication partner may hypothesize that the other has misunderstood, or the expert may give unsolicited advice, a phenomena we have explored in our work on *active help systems* [12]. Our systems should capture the essence of this human-to-human process. Critics are designed to incorporate as much of this process as possible.

Individualizing Computer Systems

User-centered learning. User-centered learning allows individuals to follow different learning paths. Forcing the same intellectual style on every individual is possibly much more damaging than forcing right-handedness upon a left-hander. To support user-centered learning processes, computational environments have to adapt to individual needs and learning styles. Giving users control over their learning and work requires them to initiate actions and set their own goals. Critics require individualized knowledge structures to support differential descriptions. They can use them to present explanations which represent new concepts in relation to knowledge previously held by specific users.

Incremental learning. Not even experts can completely master complex, high-functionality computer systems. Support for incremental learning is required. Incremental learning eliminates suboptimal behavior (thereby increasing efficiency), enlarges possibilities (thereby increasing functionality), supports learning on demand by presentation of new information when it is relevant, uses models of the user to make systems more responsive to the needs of individuals, and tailors explanations to the user's conceptualization of the task.

Learning on Demand. The major justification for learning on demand is that education is a distributed, lifelong process of learning material as it is needed. Learning on demand has been successful in human societies when learners can afford the luxury of a personal coach or critic. Aided by a human coach or critic, learners can articulate their problems in an infinite variety of ways. Computer-based support systems should be designed to conform to this metaphor.

On a broad scale, learning on demand is neither practical nor economical without computers. Learning on demand should include "learning to learn," providing the user with skills and showing the user how to locate and utilize information resources. It should not be restricted just to learning procedures but should help to restructure the user's conceptual model of the domain. It should not only provide access to factual information but also assist the user in understanding when that knowledge can be applied.

Learning on demand is a guided discovery approach to learning. It is initiated when the user wants to do something, not learn about everything. Learning on demand affords the following:

- It is easier to understand the uses for the knowledge being learned;
- Learning occurs because knowledge is actively used rather than passively perceived;

- At least one condition under which knowledge can be applied is learned;
- It can make a crucial difference in motivating learning.

Learning on demand can be differentiated according to whether the user or the system initiates the demand.

- *Demands Originating with the User.* The demand to learn more can originate with the user. It can be triggered by a discrepancy between an intended product and the actual product produced. Experimentation with a system may turn up interesting phenomena that users find worth exploring further. The user's mental model can serve as a driving force towards learning more. Users "feel" that there must be a better way of doing things. Adequate tools to support learning on demand are crucially important in making users willing to embark on an effort to increase their knowledge.

- *Suggestions from the Coach or the Critic.* The demand to learn cannot originate with users when they are unaware that additional functionality exists. The system has to take the initiative, but to avoid the problem that the system becomes too intrusive, a metric is necessary for judging the adequacy of a user's action. Interrupting too often can destroy motivation, but too few interruptions results in learning experiences being missed. Except for narrow problem domains (e.g., simple games [4]), optimal behavior cannot be uniquely defined. Therefore, the underlying metric should not be a fixed entity but a structure that users can inspect and modify, increasing the user's control over interaction with the system. Adequate communication structures must exist to make this a manageable task.

Tutoring episodes can play an important role in learning on demand. They can expose the user to certain tasks. The critic can offer to act as a tutor -- the crucial difference from the normal tutoring approach is that tutoring is initiated by the user and occurs in the context of the user's work.

Related Work

The critic paradigm is similar to the critiquing approach used in research efforts on medical systems [18, 19, 16, 22]. The critiquing approach uses domain knowledge to help physicians perform diagnoses or develop patient treatment plans. Techniques from expert systems research were modified after researchers recognized the need to assist physicians directly in their work, leaving them in control rather than attempting to replace them with an autonomous system. In contrast, our research and system development efforts have a human-computer interaction perspective. We ask how knowledge-based approaches can improve collaboration between a computer and a user.

REQUIREMENTS FOR CRITIC SYSTEMS

Design requirements for computer-based critics should be based on empirical studies. As we have studied human critics, it became obvious that knowledge is the most important feature of a good critic.

Empirical Studies

Cognitive scientists have studied human-to-human dyadic relationships. These studies emphasized psychological [5] and linguistic [15] aspects of dyadic human cooperative efforts. Our own empirical work investigated why users work suboptimally, failing to take advantage of available system functionality. We observed the following problems:

1. Users do not know about the existence of tools and are not able to ask for them; passive help systems are of little use in such situations.

2. Users do not know how to access tools; retrievability is a big problem in information-rich societies and in complex, high-functionality systems.

3. Users do not know when to use these tools; they do not know the applicability conditions under which a piece of knowledge can be used successfully.

4. Users do not understand the results that tools produce; finding the information is in many cases not the end but the beginning of difficulties.

5. Users cannot combine, adapt, and modify a tool to their specific needs; reuse and redesign [8] have to be supported.

A consequence of these problems is that many systems are underused. We are strongly convinced that we need is not more information but new ways to structure and present it.

In other empirical studies we investigated how a model of the expertise of another user is acquired by a domain expert. This study was based on think-aloud protocols from experts [10]. A questionnaire showed that expertise is, not consistent for a class of users. The results indicated that systems must model the individual's knowledge in terms of underlying domain concepts because simple classification approaches are inadequate.

The design of our critic systems has been influenced by these empirical studies. Our approach is based on two assumptions: that cooperative work is a powerful approach to both improving problem solving and learning, and that users need to be encouraged to explore.

Knowledge-Based Architectures

Knowledge-based systems are one promising approach to equipping machines with some human communication capabilities. Based on an analysis of human communication, we developed the model shown in Figure 1, and we have tried to instantiate this general architecture in a variety of systems.

The system architecture in Figure 1 contains two major improvements over traditional approaches:

- The **explicit** communication channel is widened (incorporating the use of windows, menus, pointing devices, etc.).

- Information can be exchanged over the **implicit** communication channel -- a prerequisite is shared knowledge structures.

There are four domains of knowledge shown in Figure 1:

1. *Knowledge about the problem domain:* Intelligent behavior builds upon in depth knowledge about specific domains. This knowledge constrains the possible actions and describes reasonable goals and operations. Most computer users are not interested in computers per se but want to use them to solve problems and accomplish tasks. To shape the computer into a truly usable and useful medium for them, we

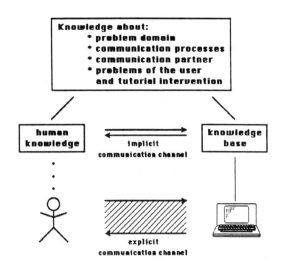

Figure 1: Architecture for Knowledge-Based Human-Computer Communication

have to make it invisible and let them work *directly* on their problems and their tasks; we must support human problem-domain communication [11].

2. *Knowledge about communication processes:* Information structures that control communication should be made explicit.

3. *Knowledge about the communication partner:* The user of a system does not exist; there are many different kinds of users, and the requirements of an individual user change with experience. Systems will be unable to interact with users intelligently unless they have some means of finding out what the user really knows; they must be able to infer the state of the user's knowledge.

4. *Knowledge about the most common problems users have in using a system and about instructional strategies:* This knowledge is required if someone wants to be a good coach or teacher and not only an expert; a user support system should know when to interrupt a user. It must incorporate instructional strategies based on pedagogical theories, exploiting the knowledge contained in the system's model of the user.

Domain Knowledge

Expertise cannot exist without domain knowledge. The actual representation chosen for domain knowledge is not critical; rule-based systems, object hierarchies and frames are all appropriate. We have used rule-based systems because they support the incremental accumulation of domain knowledge. It remains to be seen how adequate our representation will be for some of the extensions we are currently pursuing.

Domain knowledge must be acquired; associated with that requirement are all the traditional issues of knowledge acquisition in knowledge-based systems. It may be that the critic methodology is an opportunity for using the content of previously developed knowledge bases, particularly those that are a part of expert systems that have not found acceptance as stand-alone systems.

Models of the User

To support incremental learning and learning on demand, systems should possess knowledge about a specific user, information about the user's conceptual understanding, the set of tasks for which the user uses the system, the user's way of accomplishing domain-specific tasks, pieces of advice given and whether they were remembered and accepted , and the situations in which the user asked for help.

In short each user must be treated as an individual. Computer systems based on a static model of users are often too rigid and limited to meet the demands of a diverse user community. There is no such thing as "the" user of a system: there are many different kinds of users and the requirements of an individual user change with experience. Robust and dynamic user models are a desirable design goal for computer-based critics.

Explanations

Explanation is critical for cooperative systems. It is a more difficult problem in critic systems than in tutoring systems because problems being addressed are arbitrary; that is the problem space is large, and the choice of which problem to solve is not controlled by the system.

Users learn best when they are situated in the context of their work and are able to receive explanations from an expert who can clear up misconceptions and clarify understanding. This helps the user to restructure his or her knowledge [21]. Learning is habitually supported with tutoring but a more likely situation, and one similar to that which evokes human-to-human interaction, is to provide for learning with a good explanation capability [27]. Good tutors (and critics) explain things by using concepts that a student already understands [26].

That explanations must be tailored to the user implies that the system must capture and represent the set of concepts each individual knows in a user model. The system then has to formulate (or select) explanations appropriate to the knowledge level and experience of each individual.

PROTOTYPICAL SYSTEMS

We have developed computer-based critics for several domains and have emphasized different issues, for example level of analysis, narrowly bounded versus open problem spaces and active versus passive approaches. We expect that by a careful analysis and detailed comparison of these system-building efforts, we will develop general principles for designing critics and other intelligent support system. In this section, we briefly describe two systems: LISP-CRITIC, a system that critiques LISP code and CRACK that assists kitchen designers (for a detailed descriptions see [7, 13]).

The LISP-CRITIC. The LISP-CRITIC, a passive critic for *FranzLisp* (see Figure 2), suggests improvements to program code. The critic works in one of two modes. Improvements can make the code either more *cognitively* efficient (i.e., more readable and concise) or more *machine* efficient (i.e., smaller and faster). Users can choose the kind of suggestions in which they are interested. LISP-CRITIC is more than a tutoring environment; it differs from LISP TUTOR [1] in that it augments the user's working environment by providing an available expert to assist him or her in producing a better program. In a session with LISP-CRITIC, as opposed to a structured tutoring episode, the user maintains control of both problem selection and the user-

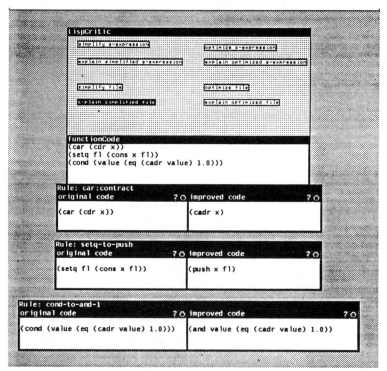

This figure shows the LISP-CRITIC running on a bit graph terminal in a UNIX environment. The user can initiate an action by clicking a button. The FUNCTIONCODE pane displays the text of the program that LISP-CRITIC is working on. The other three windows show suggested transformations. The "?" in the title line of the windows is a button for obtaining an explanation.

Figure 2: The LISP-CRITIC

Replace a Copying Function with a Destructive Function

```
(rule append/.1-new.cons.cells-to-nconc/.1...       ;;; the name of the rule
  (?foo:{append append1}                            ;;; the original code
    (restrict ?expr                                 ;;; condition
       (cons-cell-generating-expr expr))            ;;; (rule can only be applied
                                                    ;;; if "?expr" generates
                                                    ;;; cons cells)
     ?b)
  ==>
  ((compute-it:                                      ;;; the replacement
    (cdr (assq (get-binding foo)
              '((append . nconc)
                (append1 . nconc1))))))
   ?expr ?b)
  safe (machine))                                    ;;; rule category
```

Example (see Figure 5):

```
(append (explode word) chars)
==>
(nconc (explode word) chars)
```

Figure 3: Example of a Rule in the LISP-CRITIC

---

computer interaction. In addition to improving the user's work, a by-product of this interaction is that the user learns more about LISP as a domain in the context of his or her work.

The system can be used by two different user groups. One group consists of intermediate users who want to learn how to produce better LISP code. We have tested the usefulness of LISP-CRITIC for this purpose by gathering statistical data on the programs written by students in an introductory LISP course. The other group consists of experienced users who want to have their code "straightened out." Instead of refining their code by hand (which in principle these users can do), they use LISP-CRITIC to help them carefully reconsider the code they have written. The system has proven especially useful with code that is under development, continuously being changed and modified.

LISP-CRITIC is able to criticize a user's code in the following ways:

- replace compound calls of LISP functions by simple calls to more powerful functions:
  `(not (evenp a))` may be replaced by
  `(oddp a)`;

- suggest the use of macros:
  `(setq a (cons b a))` may be replaced by
  `(push b a)`;

- find and eliminate 'dead' code:
  as in `(cond (...) (t ...) (dead code))`;

- find alternative forms of conditional or arithmetic expressions that are simpler or faster;

- replace copying (garbage generating) function with a destructive function:
  `(append (explode word) chars)`
  may be replaced by
  `(nconc (explode word) chars)`;
  see Figures 3 and 5;

- specialized functions:
  replace `equal` by `eq` - use integer instead of floating point arithmetic wherever possible;

- evaluate or partially evaluate expressions:
  `(sum a 3 b 4)` may be simplified to
  `(sum a b 7)`.

The Architecture of the LISP-CRITIC

The structure of the overall system is given in Figure 4. The user's code is simplified and analyzed according to the transformation rules, and protocol files are produced. They contain information (see Figure 2) that is used to generate explanations. The user model (for a more detailed discussion see [9]) obtains information from the rules that have fired, from the statistical analyzer, and from specialized knowledge acquisition rules which look for cues indicating that a specific concept of LISP is either known or not known by the user. In return, the user model determines which rules should fire and what explanations should be generated.

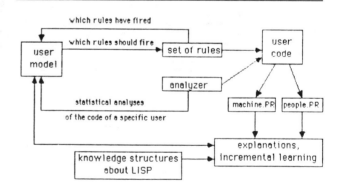

Figure 4: The Architecture of the LISP-CRITIC

```
(setq result                                    (setq result
    (append (explode word) chars))    ==>          (nconc (explode word) chars))
```

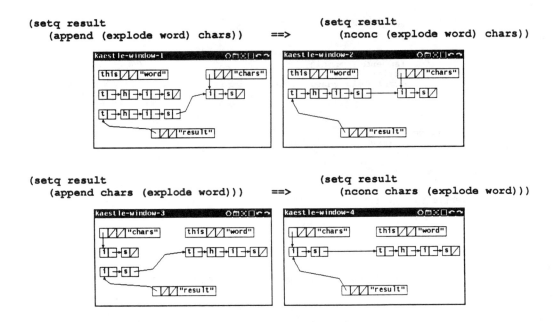

```
(setq result                                    (setq result
    (append chars (explode word)))    ==>          (nconc chars (explode word)))
```

In the environment shown in the individual screen images, the variable `word` is bound to the value `this` and the variable `chars` is bound to the list `(i s)`.

Figure 5: Illustration of the Validity of a Rule Using *Kaestle*

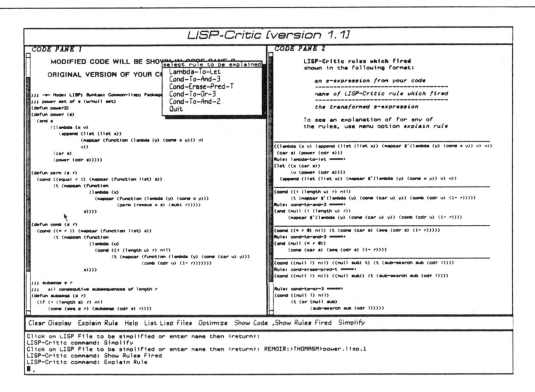

The interface shows the user working on a LISP-CRITIC code file. The user has seen the recommendations of LISP-CRITIC, has asked for a display of the rules which were applied and is about to request explanation of a particular rule.

Figure 6: The LISP-CRITIC Interface on the Symbolics Computer

152

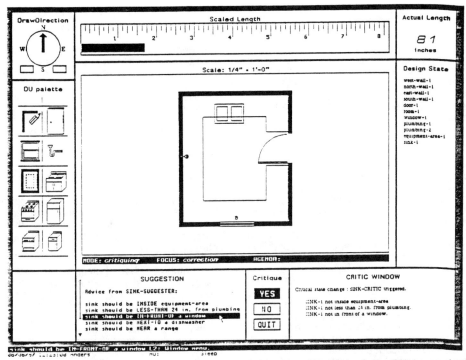

CRACK's user interface is based on the metaphor of an "architect's workbench". Design units (DU's) are selected from the DU Palette, and their architectural symnbol moved within the work area (the center window). The user manipulates DU's by clicking on their name in the Design State window. The user can question suggestions and criticism by clicking on the text. Critiquing can be turned on and off.

Figure 7: Suggestions from the SINK-CRITIC

Support for Understanding the Criticism

Our experience with LISP-CRITIC in our LISP courses has been that the criticism given is often not understood. Therefore we use additional system components to illustrate and explain the LISP-CRITIC's advice. KAESTLE, a visualization tool that is part of our software oscilloscope [2], allows us to illustrate the functioning and validity of certain rules. In Figure 5, we use *Kaestle* to show why the transformation

```
(append (explode word) chars) ==>
(nconc (explode word) chars)
```

is safe (because `explode` is a cons-generating function; see Figure 3), whereas the transformation

```
(append chars (explode word)) ==>
(nconc chars (explode word))
```

is unsafe (because the destructive change of the value of the first argument by `nconc` may cause undesirable side effects.)

Present Research System Environment

LISP-CRITIC has been ported to other computing environments, most recently to the Symbolics 3600 (see Figure 6). Future research will use the Symbolics as a prototyping environment with COMMON LISP as the target domain. We emphasize issues in human computer interaction: usability, explanation, and user modelling.

CRACK

CRACK (see Figure 7) is a critic system that supports users designing kitchens. It provides a set of domain-specific building blocks and knows how to combine these building blocks into useful designs. It uses this knowledge "to look over the shoulder" of a user carrying out a specific design. If CRACK discovers a shortcoming in users' designs, it offers criticism, suggestions, and explanations. It assists users improve their designs through a cooperative problem solving process. CRACK is not an expert system; it does not dominate the design process by generating new designs from high-level goals or resolving design conflicts automatically. The users controls the behavior of the system at all times (e.g., the critiquing can be turned on and off), and if users disagree with CRACK, they can modify its knowledge base.

CRACK aids users in designing the layout of a kitchen floor plan while seated at a graphics workstation (see Figure 7). The system is actually a collection of critics, each of which is an expert on a specific design unit (DU). These critics serve a dual purpose: they monitor what the user is doing and interject their critique when appropriate, and they can provide a suggestion if asked. Users can also ask for an explanation of either a criticism or a suggestion. These explanations are "hard-wired" into the system.

Most of the knowledge contained in the critics was obtained from protocol studies, a questionnaire, and traditional kitchen design books. We found that the system needed a method for overriding these sources of knowledge when user preferences conflicted with them. CRACK allows users to modify a critic in order to better fit it to their preferences.

COMPONENTS OF OUR CRITIC SYSTEMS

Domain Knowledge

We represent domain knowledge in rule based formats. In the case of LISP-CRITIC, these rules are expressed in LISP in a format developed for this application. CRACK uses the ART expert system shell environment and its underlying rule based architecture for knowledge representation. Example rules for the LISP-CRITIC system are shown in Figure 3.

Model of the User

As discussed previously, computer-based critics must contain a user model in order to reach their full potential. Our work with CRACK indicated that it is possible to develop a usable system without an underlying user modelling component. Also, LISP-CRITIC in its initial form did not attempt to create individual user models and appeared to function at a satisfactory level. However, for these systems to be truly integrated into an individual's personal working environment, they must adjust to the knowledge level and preferences of the individual user.

Representing the User Model. Our first attempts in LISP-CRITIC to model the user were classification approaches. We categorized an individual by his or her expertise, inferred by observation of programming habits. This approach turned out to be inadequate and caused us to reflect on expertise in the domain of LISP. Knowledge needs to be represented in the user model as a collection of concepts that each individual knows. It cannot be assumed that a whole class of users know the same set of concepts just because they have the same background or experience. A survey of experienced LISP programmers in our department confirmed this intuition. Our test of expertise was the programmer's understanding of generalized variables in COMMON LISP [24] and preference for using and teaching the "setq" and "setf" special forms. We discovered a significant variability not only in preference but also in their understanding of the concept. These experiences have led us to represent each user as a collection of concepts that he or she knows or doesn't know about LISP along with an associated confidence factor.

Acquisition of the User Model. The problem of knowledge acquisition for the user model in LISP-CRITIC will be solved primarily by examining code written by the user. Techniques described in [7] have been developed to extend the system beyond recognizing pieces of code that can be improved to recognizing the use of both constructs and concepts that LISP-CRITIC thinks are preferable. A module statistically analyzes the code for average function length and depth of nesting. This analysis gives a measure of readability and allows the system to infer a crude approximation of the user's expertise.

Explicit acquisition of user knowledge has not been attempted for the LISP-CRITIC itself; however, we experimented with this approach when we attempted to build an initial model of the user for a tutoring system for a personal workstation environment. This approach appeared to work well in a limited domain, but it is severely limited in its ability to acquire an accurate initial model of the user's knowledge of a domain as complex as LISP.

Implicit acquisition of user knowledge will have to be supported in order to make our system robust. Our approach to implicit knowledge acquisition involves a hierarchy of levels:

1. CUES - low-level primitives evidenced by the use of particular syntax or constructs;

2. CHUNKS - the representation of LISP concepts in the user model;

3. STEREOTYPES - groups of the chunks used for inferring additional data in the user model.

The primary source for cues is LISP-CRITIC rules that fire when a pattern is found in the user's code. Collections of rules that have fired imply that the programmer knows a particular concept (possesses a chunk), and furthermore that the system believes this with a certain level of confidence. Similarly, collections of chunks trigger a stereotype [23]. Chunks in that stereotype in addition to the set that triggered the stereotype can now be indirectly inferred and added to the user model.

Explanations

Critics must be able to explain their actions in terms of knowledge about the underlying domain. Our first approach to these explanations was to select appropriate textual explanations from prestored information -- canned text. This approach was not entirely satisfactory because advice was often not understood and textual descriptions alone made the concepts hard to visualize.

We believe that human's efficient visual processing capabilities must be utilized fully. Traditional displays have been one-dimensional, with a single frame on the screen filled with lines of text. New technologies offer ways to exploit human visual perception with multiple window displays, color, graphics, and icons. Figure 5 shows one of our visualization tools that illustrates the rationale for a complicated rule in the LISP-CRITIC.

EVALUATION

Research on intelligent support systems must move beyond "arm-chair design". These systems are so complex that building them is not good enough. We have to test our implementations in real-world domains, those in which people actually use the computer as a medium for their work.

Evaluation Techniques

We have tested our critics systems with real users over extended periods of time. Various evaluation methods (e.g., think-aloud protocols [17] and questionnaires) showed that a strictly quantitative evaluation is not feasible because many important factors are only qualitative.

Results of Evaluation

The results of our evaluations of LISP-CRITIC showed its strengths and weaknesses.

Some of the strengths of LISP-CRITIC are:

- It supports users in doing their own tasks and it supports intermediate users, not just beginners;

- It enhances incremental learning;

- It fosters reusability by pointing out operations that exist in the system;

- It can be applied to every program (in the worst case nothing is found to critique;)

- It is not just a toy system because users have used it in the context of their everyday work;

- Using it does not require users to provide information in addition to the code.

Some of the weaknesses of LISP-CRITIC are:

- It use only low-level transformations (i.e., it operates primarily at the level of s-expressions;)

- It has absolutely no understanding of the user's problem; this limits analysis because LISP-CRITIC cannot distinguish between constructs the user does not know and those not required to solve this problem.

- The rules are not tied to higher-level concepts;

- The explanations should be generated more dynamically [20].

In our evaluation of CRACK, which has been an operational system almost a year, we accumulated feedback about its strengths and shortcomings. One of our colleagues who is not a professional kitchen designer, remodeled his kitchen. He considered CRACK a valuable tool. The criticism generated by the system during his design process illustrated several design concepts of which he was not aware. In addition to generating a specific design for his kitchen, our colleague increased his knowledge about kitchen design.

The system was also used by a design methodologist who considered the cooperative, user-dominated approach of CRACK its most important feature. He felt that this set CRACK apart from expert system oriented design tools that users have little control of and that often reduce users to spectators of the system's operations. We have deliberately avoided equipping the current version of CRACK with its own design capabilities. Too much assistance and too many automatic procedures can reduce the users' motivation by not providing sufficient challenge. In contrast to most current CAD systems, which are merely drafting tools rather than design tools, CRACK has some "understanding" of the design space. This knowledge allows the system to critique a design during the design process -- a capability absent in CAD systems.

Our evaluations also confirmed that the critic paradigm, although attractive and useful in many situations, does have limitations. It is not an expert system capable of generating, on its own, a complete and correct solution to every problem. Nor is it a better tutoring approach but merely one that is appropriate under certain circumstances. A totally naive user should still be exposed to initial instruction in a domain to prevent floundering and frustration. We do feel, however, that the critiquing approach uses techniques that approximate human-to-human cooperation in day-to-day work settings.

FUTURE RESEARCH AND CONCLUSIONS

The deficiencies we uncovered in our evaluation work are the basis for our future research agenda.

Structured Representation of Domain Knowledge

The results of our initial efforts indicated the need for representing domain knowledge in a form which can be used in the critiquing process itself, for explaining criticism, and for representing the user's knowledge state. Rules alone are inadequate. We are investigating the decomposition of LISP as a domain into concepts, called "chunks" in our user model. The user model is a collection of chunks which the system inferred a user does or does not know along with an associated degree of confidence in that inference. Rules will continue to be the applicative form of our LISP knowledge in the critiquing process. They will be catalogued and organized by our taxonomy of concepts, and used to guide explanation.

Beyond Canned Explanations

Explanations of LISP-CRITIC's "behavior" have been canned text pegged to the user's knowledge level (novice, intermediate, or expert). We are investigating approaches for generating explanations on the fly using the domain knowledge structure and the user model, thereby integrating the "explainable experts systems" approach [20].

Differential Descriptions

Another approach which depends heavily on the user model and on maintaining a record of context for the user's work is the use of differential explanations. Descriptions of concepts new to a particular user will be generated by relating them to concepts already known; the latter are contained in the user model.

Cooperative Problem Solving Systems

The long-term goal of this effort is to develop the full potential of the critic paradigm and to make it a prototype for designing cooperative problem solving systems. We would like to endow our critic systems with various techniques of deliberation that would allow users to choose a critic approach that fits their style of working and learning.

Conclusions

Computer-based critics incorporate many powerful ideas from human-computer communications and artificial intelligence into a system that makes use of the best aspects of human and computational cognition. They have the potential to provide a symbiotic relationship between a user and a knowledge-based system. This environment can support cooperative work between these two agents while helping the user learn in the context of his or her own work.

Implementation of this concept will require that computer-based critics contain domain knowledge represented in a form that is applicable both to problem solving and to explanations. An explanation component will use that knowledge base and an inferred user model to generate contextual explanations. The system will share its knowledge with the user while building up a dynamic user model.

We have developed several critic systems that incorporate some of these ideas and have formulated a plan to extend at least one of these system, the LISP-CRITIC. The successes and failures of this research will help us define the characteristics and design considerations for critic systems as well as gauge their potential. These results should be applicable to the entire class of cooperative problem solving systems.

Acknowledgment

Many people have contributed to the development of LISP-CRITIC over the last few years. The authors would like to thank especially Heinz-Dieter Boecker, who developed many of the original ideas; Andreas Lemke, who contributed to the general framework; Helga Nieper-Lemke, who developed KAESTLE; and Anders Morch who is the author of CRACK. We also thank John Reiman, Paul Johl, and Patrick Lynn for recent work on LISP-CRITIC user modelling and explanations components, Hal Eden for porting the system to the Symbolics environment. The research is partially supported by a grant from the Colorado Institute of Artificial Intelligence, *The CIAI is sponsored in part by the Colorado Advanced Technology Institute (CATI), an agency of the State of Colorado. CATI promotes advanced technology education and research at universities in Colorado for the purpose of economic development.*

References

1. J.R. Anderson, B.J. Reiser. "The LISP Tutor". *BYTE 10*, 4 (April 1985), 159-175.

2. H.-D. Boecker, G. Fischer, H. Nieper. The Enhancement of Understanding Through Visual Representations. Human Factors in Computing Systems, CHI'86 Conference Proceedings (Boston, MA), ACM, New York, April, 1986, pp. 44-50.

3. B.G. Buchanan, E.H. Shortliffe. Human Engineering of Medical Expert Systems. In *Rule-Based Expert Systems: The MYCIN Experiments of the Stanford Heuristic Programming Project*, Addison-Wesley Publishing Company, Reading, MA, 1984, Chap. 32, pp. 599-612.

4. R.R. Burton, J.S. Brown. An Investigation of Computer Coaching for Informal Learning Activities. In *Intelligent Tutoring Systems*, D.H. Sleeman, J.S. Brown, Eds., Academic Press, London - New York, 1982, ch. 4, pp. 79-98.

5. D.F. Dansereau. Cooperative Learning Strategies. In *Learning and Study Strategies: Issues in Assessment, Instruction and Evaluation*, Academic Press, New York, 1988, Chap. 7, pp. 103-120.

6. S.W. Draper. The Nature of Expertise in UNIX. Proceedings of INTERACT'84, IFIP Conference on Human-Computer Interaction, Amsterdam, September, 1984, pp. 182-186.

7. G. Fischer. A Critic for LISP. Proceedings of the 10th International Joint Conference on Artificial Intelligence (Milan, Italy), Los Altos, CA, August, 1987, pp. 177-184.

8. G. Fischer. "Cognitive View of Reuse and Redesign". *IEEE Software, Special Issue on Reusability 4*, 4 (July 1987), 60-72.

9. G. Fischer. Enhancing Incremental Learning Processes with Knowledge-Based Systems. In *Learning Issues for Intelligent Tutoring Systems*, Springer-Verlag, New York, 1988, Chap. 7, pp. 138-163.

10. G. Fischer, P. Johl, T. Mastaglio, J. Rieman. A Study of Expert Inferences of Novice Programmer Knowledge from Their Programs. in preparation, Department of Computer Science, University of Colorado, 1988.

11. G. Fischer, A.C. Lemke. "Construction Kits and Design Environments: Steps Toward Human Problem-Domain Communication". *Human-Computer Interaction 3*, 3 (1988), 179-222.

12. G. Fischer, A.C. Lemke, T. Schwab. Knowledge-Based Help Systems. Human Factors in Computing Systems, CHI'85 Conference Proceedings (San Francisco, CA), ACM, New York, April, 1985, pp. 161-167.

13. G. Fischer, A. Morch. CRACK: A Critiquing Approach to Cooperative Kitchen Design. Proceedings of the International Conference on Intelligent Tutoring Systems (Montreal, Canada), June, 1988, pp. 176-185.

14. G. Fischer, M. Schneider. Knowledge-Based Communication Processes in Software Engineering. Proceedings of the 7th International Conference on Software Engineering (Orlando, FL), IEEE Computer Society, Los Angeles, CA, March, 1984, pp. 358-368.

15. B. Fox, L. Karen. Collaborative Cognition. Proceedings of the Tenth Annual Conference of the Cognitive Science Society, Cognitive Science Society, 1988.

16. C. Langlotz, E. Shortliffe. "Adapting a Consultation System to Critique User Plans". *International Journal of Man-Machine Studies 19* (1983), 479-496.

17. C.H. Lewis. Using the 'Thinking-Aloud' Method in Cognitive Interface Design. RC 9265, IBM, Yorktown Heights, NY 1982.

18. P. Miller. *A Critiquing Approach to Expert Computer Advice: ATTENDING*. Pittman, London - Boston, 1984.

19. P. Miller. *Expert Critiquing Systems: Practice-Based Medical Consultation by Computer*. Springer-Verlag, New York - Berlin, 1986.

20. R. Neches, W.R. Swartout, J.D. Moore. "Enhanced Maintenance and Explanation of Expert Systems Through Explicit Models of Their Development". *IEEE Transactions on Software Engineering SE-11*, 11 (November 1985), 1337-1351.

21. J. Psotka, L.D. Massey, S. Mutter. Intelligent Instructional Design. In *Intelligent Tutoring Systems: Lessons Learned*, Lawrence Erlbaum Associates, Hillsdale,NJ , 1988, pp. 113-118.

22. P.L. Reichertz, D.A.B. Lindberg (Ed.). *A Computational Model of Reasoning from the Clinical Literature*. Springer-Verlag, New York, 1987.

23. E. Rich. "Users are Individuals: Individualizing User Models". *International Journal of Man-Machine Studies 18* (1983), 199-214.

24. G.L. Steele. *Common LISP: The Language*. Digital Press, Burlington, MA, 1984.

25. M.J. Stefik. "The Next Knowledge Medium". *AI Magazine 7*, 1 (Spring 1986), 34-46.

26. K. VanLehn. Student Modeling. In M. Polson, J. Richardson, Ed., *Foundations of Intelligent Tutoring Systems*, Lawrence Erlbaum Associates, Hillsdale,NJ , 1988, pp. 55-78.

27. E. Wenger. *Artificial Intelligence and Tutoring Systems*. Morgan Kaufmann Publishers, Los Altos, CA, 1987.

28. T. Winograd, F. Flores. *Understanding Computers and Cognition: A New Foundation for Design*. Ablex Publishing Corporation, Norwood, NJ, 1986.

CHAPTER 3
ORGANIZATIONAL ISSUES
IN DSS DEVELOPMENT

Vogel, et al.

Sviokla

McIntyre and Higgins

Chen and Nunamaker, Jr.

An, Hunt, and Sanders

Electronic Meeting System Experience at IBM

DOUGLAS R. VOGEL, JAY F. NUNAMAKER, JR.,
WILLIAM BENJAMIN MARTZ, JR., RONALD GROHOWSKI,
and CHRISTOPHER McGOFF

DOUGLAS R. VOGEL is Assistant Professor of MIS, College of Business and Public Administration, University of Arizona, Tucson. He has been involved with computers and computer systems in various capacities for over 20 years. He received his M.S. in Computer Science from UCLA, and his Ph.D. in MIS from the University of Minnesota, where he was also research coordinator for the MIS Research Center. His current research interests bridge the business and academic communities in addressing questions of the impact of management information systems on aspects of interpersonal communication, group decision making, and organizational productivity.

JAY F. NUNAMAKER, JR., is Head of the Department of MIS and is Professor of MIS and Computer Science at the University of Arizona. He received his Ph.D. from Case Institute of Technology in systems engineering and operations research. He was Associate Professor of Computer Science and Industrial Administration at Purdue University. He joined the faculty at the University of Arizona in 1974 to develop the MIS program. He has authored numerous papers on group decision support systems, the automation of software construction, performance evaluation of computer systems, decision support systems for systems analysis and design, and has lectured throughout Europe, Russia, Asia, and South America. He is Chairman of the Association for Computing Machinery Curriculum Committee on Information Systems.

WILLIAM BENJAMIN MARTZ, JR., received his B.B.A. from the College of William and Mary, and his M.S. and Ph.D. in MIS from the University of Arizona. His experience covers the design and coding of software for work groups, the facilitation of work groups at Arizona's facilities, and the coordination of the implementation of the work group software at IBM. His current interests include group decision support systems, electronic business planning tools, and small group theory in an electronic environment.

RONALD GROHOWSKI is the Director of MIS and Telecommunications at the IBM Systems Integration Division in Bethesda, Maryland. He has a B.S. in Mathematics from Wilkes College and an M.S. in Operations Research from Union College in New York. He is responsible for tactical and strategic planning, business control guidance, data processing equipment planning and acquisition, and telecommunications/net-

An earlier version of this paper was originally published in the *Proceedings, Twenty-second Hawaii International Conference on System Sciences*. IEEE Computer Society Press, 1989.

working activities. He is also responsible for the direction of over 1,000 IS professionals and over 1,000 MIPS for 16,000 employees.

CHRISTOPHER MCGOFF is an IBM Program Manager at the IBM Systems Integration Division in Bethesda, Maryland. He received his B.S. degree from the University of Scranton and has done postgraduate studies in Ergonomics/Human Factors at Texas Tech University. As a program manager, he is involved in decision center information systems strategy and computer-supported cooperative work. The systems integration division supports a population of 19,300 professionals with 10 3090s, 26 308xs, 19 4381s, that provide 14 MVS systems and 19 VM systems.

ABSTRACT: Electronic meeting systems (EMS) have been introduced inside IBM in a cooperative effort between IBM and the University of Arizona to address the demands of an increasingly competitive and turbulent business environment. This paper presents and integrates the results of two field studies intended to evaluate the implications of electronic meeting system use at IBM. The first study focused on session process and outcome effectiveness, efficiency, and user satisfaction at a single IBM site. The second study collected data on EMS tool use and facilitation approach within sessions at four IBM sites. The two studies are complementary in reflecting the impact of computer-based support on group process and outcome. Effectiveness, efficiency, and user satisfaction are generally enhanced independent of type of activity supported or perspective, e.g., participant, facilitator, or session initiator. Facilitation training is a critical requirement for successful integration and application of electronic meeting system software and procedures in the group processes this paper addresses.

KEY WORDS AND PHRASES: Electronic meetings, decision rooms, group decision processes, facilitation of electronic meetings.

Introduction

TODAY'S ORGANIZATIONS FACE A FUTURE OF INCREASING TURBULENCE and international competitiveness. Rapid adaptation to change is paramount. Managers and executives spend over half of their time in meetings addressing these and other important organizational issues. Ironically, while we have provided considerable computer-based support for individuals and the organization as a whole, we have historically provided virtually no such support for meetings. This situation is now beginning to change. Electronic meeting systems (EMS), defined by Dennis et al. [3] as "an information technology-based environment that supports meetings," have been introduced inside IBM in a cooperative effort between IBM and the University of Arizona. The systems are being used on a daily basis and support groups addressing a wide variety of activities such as planning, problem solving (reacting), and to enhance general group communication. By nature, these tasks tend to be complex due to the number of variables affecting the outcome. Stakeholder groups are large and have different perspectives.

The purpose of this paper is to present and integrate the results of two field studies intended to evaluate the implications of electronic meeting system use at IBM. The first study focused on session process and outcome effectiveness, efficiency, and user satisfaction at a single IBM site. The second study collected data on EMS tool use

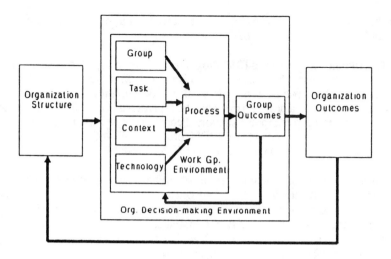

Figure 1. GDSS Research Model

within sessions at four IBM sites. Data were collected on the impact of facilitation training as a function of tool use. In both studies, realism was emphasized to assure that the results were indeed representative of natural use of these systems on a daily basis by IBM groups with a vested interest in the session outcomes. Data were collected using a combination of historical information, log files of system use, questionnaires, and follow-up interviews.

Background

THE RESEARCH MODEL USED IN CONJUNCTION WITH THIS RESEARCH is illustrated in Figure 1. The model was based on extensive experience coupled with a review of relevant literature. The variables in the model are representative of those variables studied most often in past Group Decision Support System and computer-mediated communication research. Readers are directed to Nunamaker, Applegate, and Konsynski [7] and Dennis et al. [3] for additional background on the research model.

As shown in Figure 1, the model addresses issues related to individual, group, project, and organizational levels of analysis that we feel are particularly relevant to Group Support System design and implementation. At the center of the model, the characteristics of the group, task, context, and technology are represented as influencing process and, together with that process, establishing the group work environment. The environment, in turn, drives group outcomes, which then provide feedback within the organization's decision-making environment. A group's characteristics include its size and the composite of experience, cohesiveness, motivation, hierarchical mix, and history that constitutes group member attitudes and involvement. Task characteristics include task type, complexity, degree of rationality, and clarity. Context characteris-

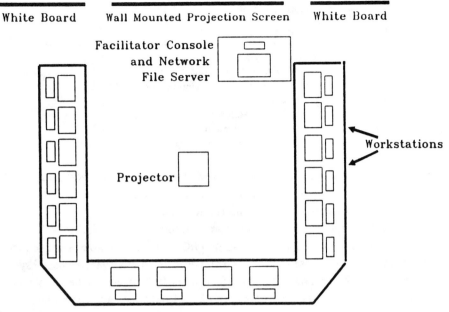

White Board   Wall Mounted Projection Screen   White Board

Facilitator Console
and Network
File Server

Workstations

Projector

Figure 2.

tics include aspects of the organizational environment such as incentives, reward system, and organizational culture. Technology characteristics include hardware, software, and setting configuration. Process includes aspects of the procedures, anonymity, level of participation, facilitation, and interaction of group members that influence group outcomes such as satisfaction, quality of outcomes, time required to reach resolution, consensus, and decision confidence. This model provided the framework for Group Support System implementation and evaluation at an IBM installation. The study addressed the research question of how well an operational Group Support System functions in a real-world, organizational setting.

Implementation Chronology

Following visits by IBM corporate personnel to University of Arizona facilities that included "hands-on" use of the work group support tools to address a corporate planning activity, company representatives decided to install similar facilities within the corporation for operational use on a daily basis. The site selected for the initial test installation was an IBM laboratory and manufacturing facility with approximately 6,000 personnel, located in upstate New York. A conference room was remodeled to house the Group Support System. The corporate site facility is illustrated in Figure 2.

The facility (approximately 900 square feet) required enhanced electrical service, air conditioning, and substitution of incandescent lighting for fluorescent. In the room, a U-shaped table is equipped with microcomputers connected via a local area network (LAN). One microcomputer is designated as a server with the remainder as workstations. An additional microcomputer attached to a large screen projection system is

Table 1   Chronology of Phase 1 Implementation Activities

date	activity
4/87	initial site visit
5/87	facility construction consultation
5/87	prototype installation in temporary facility
9.87	formal group support system installation
9/87	facilitation training
12/87	operational evaluation

also on the network to permit display of work done at individual workstations or of aggregated information from the total group. An adjacent small room is designated for "backroom" functions such as printing out session results.

The Phase 1 software implementation process, initiated in the Spring of 1987 with a site visit, was concluded in December of 1987 with a corporate evaluative report. Data collection using Phase 1 software commenced in January 1988. A Phase 2 system implementation process was initiated in September 1988 extending the initial tool set in Phase 1. Table 1 presents a summary of Phase 1 implementation activities.

Close communication and cooperation between IBM and the University of Arizona ensured that the implementation proceeded smoothly and established a strong foundation for extended facility use and evaluative efforts. The transfer of technology from an academic research environment to a corporate mainstream application was a new experience for both the University of Arizona and IBM groups involved in this implementation. Prior University of Arizona experience had been based on six academic implementations.

Facility Use

Problem-solving groups from throughout the site were encouraged to use the facility. Groups most often heard of the facility through word-of-mouth from other groups. Groups ranged from the facility executive management to line organizations. Representatives of several hierarchical levels were often included in the same group. Some groups were ongoing entities (e.g., business organization) while others were newly established (e.g., ad hoc or task forces). Group size ranged from four to ten members with an average size of eight. Larger groups tended to be new ones having been assigned a particular task and representing a wide variety of functional areas. Group members typically had detailed knowledge of one aspect of the problem area and general knowledge of the problem domain. As such, the knowledge domains of group members were distinct yet overlapping relative to the question at hand.

Tasks addressed by the groups were for the most part of a planning and problem-solving nature, e.g., strategic planning process problems, factors contributing to cost overruns, and functional area data processing needs. Some were cross organizational involving many functional areas; others represented many management/employee layers within a particular functional area. The groups participating in sessions brought with them myriad problem domains, e.g., requirements analysis, strategic planning, and resource allocation. The majority of tasks were complex to the extent that they required creativity and had no known "right" answer, particularly for the larger groups of size eight to ten. Groups also tended to address tasks that were oriented toward evaluating a set of issues. A pre-planning meeting was held before each group session to align the best use of the tools with the task to be undertaken.

The Phase 1 technology provided consisted of four linked software tools:

An *Electronic Brainstorming* tool supported idea generation, allowing group members to enter simultaneously and anonymously and share comments on a specific question.

An *Issue Analyzer* tool helped group members identify and consolidate key focus items resulting from idea generation. Support was also provided for integrating external information to support identified focus items.

A *Voting* tool provided a variety of prioritizing methods including Likert scales, rank ordering, and multiple choice. All group members cast private ballots. Accumulated results were displayed at which time action items and an agenda for a future session, if appropriate, were identified.

A *Policy Formation* tool support group in developing a policy statement or mission through iteration and group consensus. Members contribute sample text, which is then edited through group discussion and returned to participants for further refinement. The process continues until consensus is reached.

The Phase 2 technology provides ten additional tools to enhance Phase 1 functionality. Phase 2 tools consist of:

An *Idea Organizer* tool supports the Nominal Group Technique in which group members have an opportunity to independently develop a list of issues followed by "round robin" sharing with other members culminating with discussion and prioritization.

An *Alternative Evaluator* tool provides multi-criteria decision-making support. A set of alternatives can be examined under flexibly weighted criteria to evaluate decision scenarios and tradeoffs. Results are displayed in a variety of graphical and tabular formats.

A *Questionnaire* tool provides support for researchers, group leaders, and the facilitator in designing an on-line questionnaire as well as summarizing participant responses. The questionnaire is a dynamic in the sense that additional questions can be triggered based on selected response values.

A *Topic Commenter* tool supports idea solicitation and provision of additional details in conjunction with a list of topics. Participants enter, exchange, and review information on self-selected topics. Each topic may be subdivided as required to solicit more focused comment.

A *Stakeholder Identification and Assumption Surfacing* tool is used to evaluate systematically the implications of a proposed policy or plan. Stakeholders and their assumptions are identified, scaled, and presented to the group graphically for discussion and analysis.

A *File Reader* tool provides participants immediate read-only access to previously stored material at any point in a group session—even during the use of another tool. Users may browse stored material and return to interactive participation at their own discretion.

A *Group Dictionary* enables a group to define formally a word or phrase to focus their own thoughts or provide reference for future group work. The process is interactive and iterative, if appropriate, to encourage members to participate in arriving at definition consensus.

An *Enterprise Analyzer* tool provides support for capturing characteristics of an organization, including data sets, information systems, and structure, to provide a foundation for impact analysis as well as general processes and the relationships among those processes.

A *Semantic Graphics Browser* provides a graphic browsing system for reviewing related stored information, e.g., from the Enterprise Analyzer. Users can move through a "world space" and "zoom in" on specific areas of interest for more detail in graphic and text formats.

A *Session Manager* tool provides support for pre-session planning and agenda generation as well as in-session and after-session follow-up support. The Session Manager additionally facilitates integration information across sessions and between groups.

Data Collection

A particularly important aspect of the installation and use of the Group Support System at the IBM site was collection of evaluative data from a broad range of end users addressing a variety of tasks. Data collection was accomplished by combining information contained in system log files with that collected from on-line pre- and post-session questionnaires filled out by group members, facilitators, and follow-up interviews with managers and participants on aspects of process and three key objectives: outcome effectiveness, efficiency, and user satisfaction. Session log file, questionnaire, and interview details are provided in the following sections for each study. Additional evaluative measures included the time required for completing the project, number of meetings required, the length of individual meetings, and the number of people in the group meetings as well as cost measures that were separated as administrative and man-hour costs. Actual man-hour data were aligned with anticipated time estimates based on leader experience and historical precedence.

Study Number 1 Results

THE MAJOR THRUST OF THIS RESEARCH WAS TO ASSESS THE USE of an operational Group Support System in an organizational setting. An important facet of this study was to go beyond user acceptance to ascertain reaction to the Group Support System

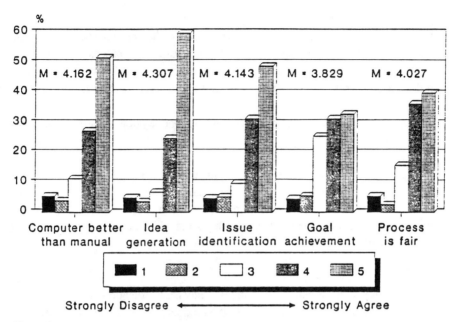

Figure 3. Agreement about System Effectiveness
Percentage of Responses ($n = 551$)

process and outcome in terms of effectiveness, efficiency, and user satisfaction. Initial test data were collected in December 1987. Data collection commenced in January 1988 in conjunction with the pilot testing of the data collection process, the focus of this study, representing the beginning of a multi-year study. This section will report the summarized results from sessions using the Group Support System.

Effectiveness

For purposes of this study, Group Support System effectiveness was comprised of two components: quality of session process and quality of outcome. One measure of the quality of session process is the degree to which the participants took part in the process and contributed to its outcome. The quality of outcome is a measure of the degree to which the system provided the product that the session initiator desired. A further indication of outcome quality comes from follow-up on how the results from the system actually were used.

The quality of session process was measured through the use of log files, through which it is possible to learn the evenness of participation among the participants, and of information gathered from the participant post-session questionnaires, and follow-up interview forms. Analysis of log file data revealed that, compared with traditional group dynamics, Group Support System use tends to equalize participation [4]. Results were independent of participant typing skills and familiarity with micro-computer technology. As an additional indication of Group Support System process effectiveness, participants were asked to express their agreement with a number of statements about the system, using a five-point Likert scale. Figure 3 presents participant responses.

These responses indicate a strong agreement among the participants that the system did provide process effectiveness. Further, those who had used the automated system before consistently had a higher mean score on questions of process effectiveness ($p < .0001$). These responses indicate a significant increase in belief in the effectiveness of the Group Support System process for those who had used the system before over those who had not.

Effectiveness of the output of the Group Support System was addressed in the follow-up interviews with managers who were also participants. The managers consistently noted that the session results were used and useful. Follow-up in the form of feedback, additional meetings, and implementation of suggestions was commonplace, as were presentations to higher management levels. In some cases, ideas were combined from a number of sessions involving both a single group as well as groups from various corporate areas to achieve a higher level of integration and comprehension. Plans were developed and decisions made.

Efficiency

The efficiency of the system as used in this study is an indication of the relative costs and benefits to the organization compared with doing the same function manually. It was not possible to run parallel sessions with control groups to measure efficiency directly. However, prior to use of the facility and without knowledge of automated support capabilities, each group leader was required to recommend and document a feasible project schedule for the accomplishment of his or her group's objectives, based on previous experience with similar projects. These schedules defined historical parameters for the projects and a baseline for comparison with the efficiency of the automated support. The plan provided by the group leader was then translated into an outline for use of the automated support tools.

After completion of the project, expectations before use of the tools were compared with what actually occurred. Further, the output from the sessions was independently evaluated by a knowledgeable third party to gain a measure of what it would take to arrive at the same level of accomplishment using traditional manual processes. Overall, there is reason to believe that the results gave at least a reasonable approximation of the estimated parameters, based on the experience of the group initiators, the "owners" of the sessions.

As illustrated in Figure 4, man-hours were saved in every case recorded, with an average per session saving of 51.15 percent. Percentages have been used to compensate for varying project lengths. A matched-pairs t-test was significant at a level $p = .0001$.

The data align with that recorded in the pilot test that preceded formal data collection. In the pilot test of 11 groups, an average man-hour savings of 61 percent was reported in conjunction with a 92 percent average calendar time reduction in time required to complete a project. Results from subsequent data collection in the Washington, D.C. metropolitan area reflected average man-hour savings of 55.6 percent. These results strongly confirm the robust nature of man-hour savings because the second site is primarily administratively oriented, as opposed to the laboratory and

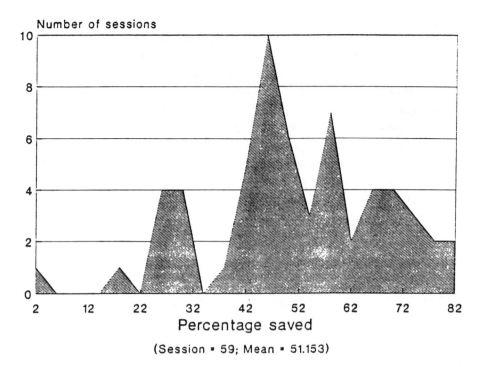

Figure 4. Group Support System Efficiency

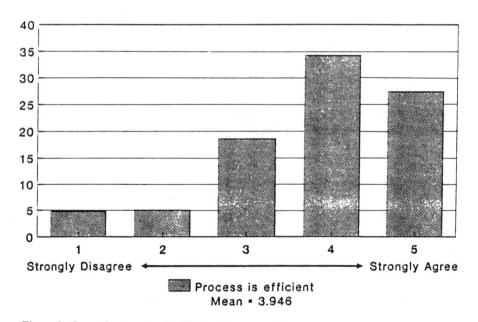

Figure 5. Group Support System Efficiency
Percentage of Responses (*n* = 387)

manufacturing orientation of the initial site. The time savings reported are independent of particular site characteristics on a group level of analysis.

High levels of performance in terms of man-hour savings were strongly correlated with the degree to which the group's task was stated clearly and concisely ($p = .004$). Larger groups (i.e., eight to ten) tended slightly to outperform smaller groups relative to expectations. Man-hour savings were independent of the individual knowledge completeness of group members, ongoing nature of the group, degree to which cooperation was required, and composition relative to number of management levels or different departments represented. However, more formal, more recently established, and less cohesive groups tended to achieve higher levels of man-hour savings relative to expectations from similar groups that met without benefit of automated support. These groups also tended to be larger.

Participants were also asked, first in post-session questionnaires and later in follow-up interviews, to provide data on system efficiency. In the post-session questionnaire, one of the questions asked the participants to indicate their level of agreement with a statement about system efficiency. Results are indicated in Figure 5. Seventy-two percent of the participants regarded the process to be efficient.

User Satisfaction

User satisfaction was evaluated in three ways. First, utilization rates of the Group Support System were maintained as an indication of general user acceptance and satisfaction. Second, the post-session questionnaire provided self reports of user satisfaction. Finally, interviews with 17 users of the automated system were conducted to obtain a broader range of personal impressions. Each of these measures will be reviewed in turn.

One of the strongest measures of this criterion is the utilization rate of the system. Since it was opened in October 1987, the room has been fully utilized, according to the records of those responsible for facilitating sessions. Currently, there is a three week waiting period for use of the room. In fact, the inability to get into the room as soon as desired has been mentioned by some users as a problem with using the system. A further measure of the acceptance of the system by the organization has been the decision to install automated group rooms at additional company sites. Thus, user acceptance, which can be considered a measure of satisfaction, has been demonstrated.

The post-session questionnaire provided self reports of user satisfaction. Two questions were specifically directed at this area of interest. The first addressed satisfaction with the computer-aided process. The second addressed satisfaction with the group's problem-solving process. The results are presented in Figure 6.

Discussion

In this first study, we gathered data on Group Support System process and outcome effectiveness, efficiency, and user satisfaction under varying group, task, and context characteristics. The most striking conclusion is the overall positive nature of the results

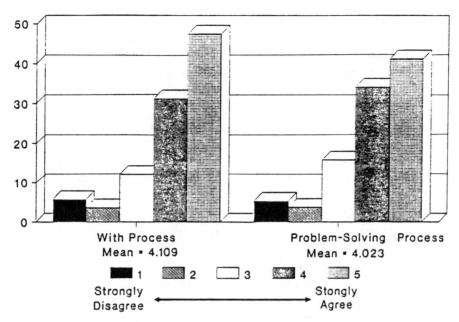

Figure 6. Levels of Agreement on User Satisfaction
Percentage of Responses ($n = 387$)

independent of these characteristics. Interestingly, results were independent of typing and micro-computer skills as well as of the number of sessions (both manual and automated) in which users had participated. Thus the findings seem reasonably robust within the site studied. User acceptance of the system at an organizational level has also been demonstrated by the corporate decision to install this system at additional sites. However, questions of the generalizability of these results across sites as well as the significance of enhanced facilitation training were beyond the scope of this initial study and thus provided the motivation for a second field study.

Study Number 2 Results

RESULTS FROM THE INITIAL STUDY JUSTIFIED THE BROADENING and intensifying of the analysis of electronic meeting systems. Rooms were constructed at three additional sites in three states across two different divisions in a effort to maximize study generalizability. The second study was designed, developed, and implemented by IBM exclusively. This served several purposes. First, the independent nature of the study served to remove any possibility that University of Arizona researcher involvement with study processes might have inadvertently confounded study results. Second, the study provided an opportunity to examine the implications of the use of Electronic Meeting Systems from a different research perspective and thus facilitate contrast and comparison of study results. Third, the second study served to extend the study of Group Support Systems in important dimensions beyond the scope of the first study.

In addition to verifying the positive impact of the electronic meeting systems on group dynamics compared to groups using no electronic support reported in study 1, the second study collected information on activities *within* sessions as well as the sessions as a whole at four IBM sites. Thus the second study significantly extended the first study focus on overall session process and outcome effectiveness, efficiency, and user satisfaction at a single IBM site. Activities addressed in the second study included idea generation, focus item analysis (focus item identification and consolidation), and voting. Data were collected using questionnaires before, during (for each activity), and after each session. Further, groups using the electronic meeting system were supported with two facilitation approaches. The first facilitation approach focused on how the tools would be used when the training was technically oriented. The second facilitation approach focused on use of performance aids for users and facilitators as well as training in group leadership skills in addition to incorporating all of the training associated with the first facilitation approach. In the second approach, facilitators were also trained in group facilitation techniques and how to ask and answer questions in front of groups.

The second study collected data as a function of each activity on participant as well as facilitator perceptions of the degree of non-task related interaction and satisfaction with the process and work product. Participant data were also collected on willingness to participate again as a function of each activity supported. The participants were also asked to rate their level of knowledge about the topic and level of skill for each activity. Overall session perceptions were captured from participant, facilitator, and session initiator with respect to work product quality and resultant satisfaction.

The following sections will address aspects of effectiveness, efficiency, and user satisfaction based on the data collected with particular focus on comparison of sessions supported by minimally trained facilitators versus those supported by specially trained facilitators.

Effectiveness

The facilitator and participants as well as the session initiator were asked for their perception of the quality of the work product at the conclusion of each session. The results are illustrated in Figure 7.

Participants, facilitators, and initiators alike rated the quality of the work product as high based on a 7-point scale. Differences in facilitator and initiator perceptions are not statistically significant as a function of facilitation approach. An additional measure of session effectiveness is willingness to participate in future similar sessions. Although overall results were positive (based on a 7-point scale), willingness to participate in future sessions varied considerably as a function of the facilitation approach, as illustrated in Figure 8. Participants were more willing to participate in activities involving electronic support for focus item analysis, albeit without statistical significance, when facilitators had received enhanced training. For both brainstorming ($p = .023$) and voting ($p = .019$), group members were more willing to participate in the future after participating in sessions for which facilitators had received only basic technical training.

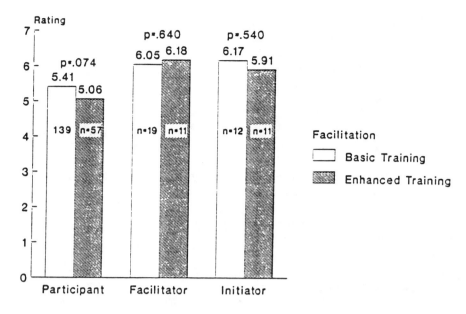

Figure 7. Quality of Session Work Product

Efficiency

The degree of non-task interaction is one measure of process efficiency. Non-task interaction in this case refers to the degree to which participants and facilitators perceived that the session stayed focused on the task at hand in electronically supported meetings compared with typical unsupported group meetings. Non-task interaction was evaluated by both session participants and facilitators as a function of use of each tool as illustrated in Figure 9.

In *all* cases, use of the automated support was concluded to result in less non-task interaction compared to typical group meetings. Participants and facilitators differed in their perception of degree of non-task interaction for brainstorming as a function of facilitation support, but were in agreement with respect to focus item analysis. No data were collected on facilitator perceptions of non-task interaction for voting. Facilitators who had received enhanced training judged the non-task interaction to be less for both brainstorming ($p = .094$) and focus item analysis ($p = .057$). Participants concurred with facilitators on non-task interaction for focus item analysis. Participants, however, felt that there was significantly less non-task interaction ($p = .030$) when facilitators had received no enhanced training for electronic brainstorming. The differences illustrated as a function of type of activity reflect participant response to facilitation instructions and the integrated nature of the tools. For example, participants specifically instructed during brainstorming not to criticize might tend to generate additional extraneous ideas and non-task related comments. However, lack of consistent instruction through scripts on focus item analysis (which by nature has

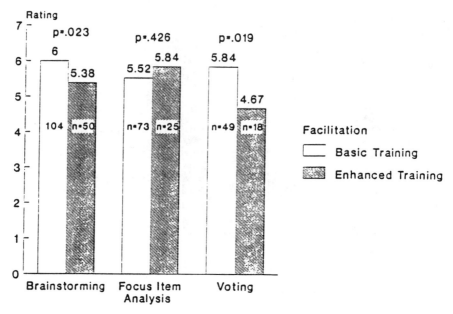

Figure 8. Willingness to Participate in Future Sessions

a higher component of participant face-to-face discussion) might result in confusion leading to heightened non-task interaction.

User Satisfaction

Satisfaction was measured in terms of session facilitator, and participant satisfaction with the group's work product based subdivided within the session as a function of each activity, i.e., brainstorming, focus item identification, and voting as illustrated in Figure 10. Although the results are not statistically significant, those facilitators who had received enhanced training perceived a generally higher level of satisfaction independent of type of activity than their technically trained counterparts.

Participants were also queried relative to their satisfaction with the computer-supported process. The results are illustrated in Figure 11. Brainstorming received slightly higher ratings than focus item analysis. The focus item identification process has a much higher degree of face-to-face discussion relative to the electronic brainstorming and voting, in addition to being a cognitively complex process, comparatively speaking. Only those results for voting were statistically significant relative to facilitation approach ($p = .005$).

Discussion

The results from this second study, like those of the first, were very supportive relative to the effectiveness, efficiency, and user satisfaction associated with the use of EMS.

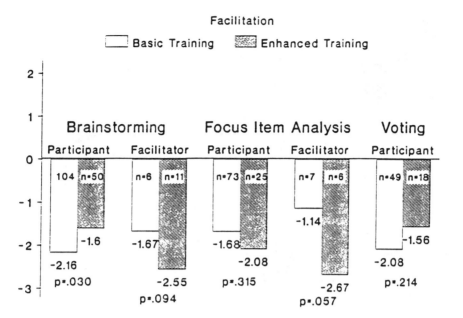

Figure 9. Degree of Non-task Interaction

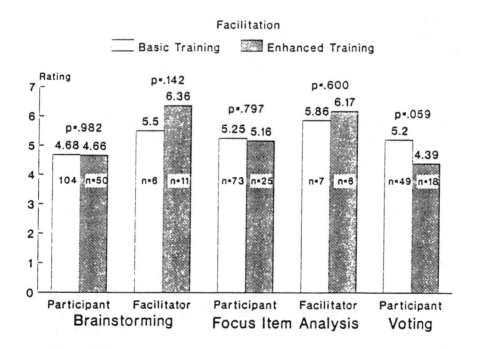

Figure 10. Satisfaction with Group Work Product

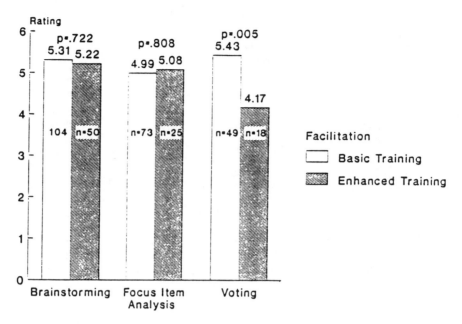

Figure 11. Participant Satisfaction with Process

Perceptions of the quality of the work product and willingness to participate in future sessions were consistently high, accompanied by a consistently low perceived level of non-task interaction. Overall, there was a high level of satisfaction with the group's work product and process accompanying the high sense of product quality and less than typical non-task interaction by participants, facilitators, and initiators alike. In other words, virtually everyone involved was generally pleased with the use of the EMS and the quality of the product in an atmosphere of enhanced efficiency.

Some interesting differences did occur, however, based on facilitator and participant perceptions of results as a function of facilitation approach. In general, those facilitators receiving special training judged their sessions to have achieved a higher quality work-group product and were more satisfied with the work-group product; they recognized decreased non-task interaction resulting from each activity than did their technically trained counterparts. The participants, however, were generally unable to distinguish differences as a function of facilitation approach, but did react positively to trained facilitation for focus item analysis in terms of willingness to participate in future sessions and satisfaction with the work-group product and process. Session initiators concurred with participants regarding quality of the work product and satisfaction with the session.

The importance of facilitation training extending beyond basic technical training should not be underestimated. A common trait of inexperienced facilitators, for example, is to talk too much. Enhanced training is essential to develop and internalize sound facilitation techniques. Over time, characteristics of good facilitation will increasingly be embedded in EMS software as developers exhibit sensitivity to the expanded nature of facilitation and experiences from the field. Technical facilitator training needs will decrease dramatically. What will always remain, however, is the need for facilitators to be sensitive to group dynamics and to exhibit flexibility within a general shell or structure in order to best meet the needs of a particular group. Successful facilitators manage (rather than dictate) cadence and content in blending extended facilitation training with tool experience, recognizing the interaction between the tools and facilitation in an atmosphere of sensitivity to differences in group characteristics.

The challenge we face is to integrate lessons learned and successfully applied through experience prior to the availability of EMS with an appreciation of the opportunities inherent in the additional degrees of freedom present through extended functionality of computer-based support. The effective blending of robust aspects of facilitation in traditional face-to-face environments with the multi-channel efficiencies achievable through computer-based support is paramount. This becomes particularly apparent in cognitively complex tasks involving idea organization and consensus formulation involving a combination of face-to-face discussion, computer support, and sound facilitation skills. Ultimately, a combination of familiarity with the computer tools coupled with specially developed guidelines and training incorporating sensitivity to varying group characteristics will, in all probability, lead to more effective facilitation.

Conclusion

THIS PAPER PRESENTED AND INTEGRATED THE RESULTS OF TWO FIELD STUDIES intended to evaluate the implications of EMS use at IBM. The second study went considerably beyond the first in studying EMS implications at the tool level as well as the session level and addressing differences as a function of facilitation approach. The two studies are complementary in reflecting the positive impact of computer-based support on group process and outcome. Effectiveness, efficiency, and user satisfaction are generally enhanced independent of type of activity supported or perspective, e.g., participant, facilitator, or session initiator. IBM's decision to develop additional sites underscores user and corporate acceptance and satisfaction with electronic meeting systems. Much, however, remains to be learned. Additional research is warranted to expand field observations and integrate aspects of field and experimental research in order to achieve a more comprehensive understanding of the implications for organizations of the adoption of EMS.

REFERENCES

1. Applegate, L. Idea Management in Organization Planning. Unpublished doctoral dissertation, University of Arizona, 1986.
2. DeSanctis, G., and Gallupe, B. A foundation for the study of group decision support systems. *Management Science*, 33(5), May 1987, 589–609.
3. Dennis, A.; George, J.; Jessup, L.; Nunamaker, J.; and Vogel, D. Information technology to support electronic meetings. *MIS Quarterly*, December 1988.

4. Heminger, A. Group Decision Support System Assessment in a Field Setting. Unpublished doctoral dissertation, University of Arizona, 1988.

5. Huber, G. Issues in the design of group decision support systems. *MIS Quarterly*, September 1984.

6. Martz, B. Information systems infrastructure for manufacturing planning systems. University of Arizona Working Paper, 1988.

7. Nunamaker, J.; Applegate, L.; and Konsynski, B. Computer-aided deliberation: model management and group decision support. *Journal of Operations Research*, November/December 1988.

8. Nunamaker, J.; Vogel, D.; and Konsynski, B. Interaction of task and technology to support large groups. *Decision Support Systems*, June 1989.

9. Vogel, D.; Nunamaker, J.; Applegate, L.; and Konsynski, B. Group decision support systems: determinants of success. *Proceedings of the 7th International Conference on Decision Support Systems*, June 8–11, 1987.

Expert Systems and Their Impact on the Firm: The Effects of PlanPower Use on the Information Processing Capacity of the Financial Collaborative

JOHN J. SVIOKLA

JOHN J. SVIOKLA is Assistant Professor of Business Administration at the Harvard Business School. He received his B.A. from Harvard College, and his M.B.A. and D.B.A. from Harvard University. His research focuses on the impacts of computer-based decision aids. More specifically, he has examined the identification, design, implementation, and effects of the use of knowledge-based systems and decision support systems within business organizations. He is also working on an interfunctional research project that examines how information systems influence the coordination of activities across functional boundaries.

ABSTRACT: Expert Systems (ESs) have the potential to make a competitive difference in industry, academia, and government, yet there is little knowledge of how to manage these complex software tools. New activity in the field is booming, as a result of civilian and government programs that are investing more time and money in ES development. Early initiatives, aided by improvements in computer hardware and software, have successfully created ESs to rival human experts within some narrow problem domains.

The study is guided by the notions of organizational programs as defined by March and Simon [3], and the information-processing capacity of the firm as defined by Galbraith [1, 2] to organize, describe, and compare the effects of ES use across the site.

It was clearly shown that, within the definition, the information-processing capacity of the PlanPower site did increase from pre-ES to post-ES. The interesting implication of the increased information processing capacity was that the firm (The Financial Collaborative) seemed to gobble up the capacity and create new issues and concerns. Instead of the task becoming more certain and more simple, as one might expect with increased information-processing capacity, the task mutated and the firm began to operate with a higher need for information-processing capacity.

The ES seemed to increase the effectiveness and efficiency of the user firm. The price of the benefits was an increased rigidity in the task. In considering ESs, a manager should be concerned not only with the ES itself, but with the process by which the ES is adapted, and the overall process of creating and using the ES. In addition, the manager needs to consider the effects of the ES on the uncertainty associated with the task and should consciously manage that uncertainty to foster the level of adaptation necessary to keep the ES alive and viable in the organization.

This paper was originally published in the *Proceedings, Twenty-second Hawaii International Conference on System Sciences*. IEEE Computer Society Press, 1989.

KEY WORDS AND PHRASES: Expert systems, expert systems in financial planning organizational impacts.

Introduction

THE FINANCIAL COLLABORATIVE (TFC) IS A SMALL, EXPERTISE-INTENSIVE and relationship-oriented financial planning firm whose aim is to serve individuals with incomes of six figures or more who also have a net worth of over $1,000,000. In late 1985, TFC's immediate needs centered on increasing its ability to write financial plans and to service clients better. TFC looked to PlanPower for help. PlanPower is an expert system designed to help financial planners create more accurate and comprehensive financial plans in less time.

In this article, the term "expert systems" means software systems that address ill-structured problems, that is, those problems for which no exhaustive or optimal solution can be delivered successfully. Moreover, these systems mimic the problem-solving behavior of the expert.

The Company Setting

PLANPOWER WAS CREATED AND IS MARKETED BY Applied Expert Systems of Cambridge, Massachusetts (APEX). The Financial Collaborative (TFC) uses PlanPower regularly to help provide its clients with financial planning services and products.

There had been a close relationship between APEX and TFC—a connection largely forged by Jim Joslin. Joslin was one of five cofounders of TFC in 1980 and, in 1983, was a cofounder of APEX. He was one of the core experts consulted in the development of the PlanPower concept and knowledge base. APEX looked to TFC as an example of a firm that created excellent plans. Many of the planning assumptions and much of the planning philosophy in PlanPower were similar to TFC's approach. The earliest beta-site for the software and its first successful implementation was also at TFC. In order to understand how and why PlanPower is used at TFC, it is helpful to know the goals, organization, and business of both firms.

APEX

APEX WAS FOUNDED TO APPLY AI TECHNIQUES TO BUSINESS OPPORTUNITIES in the financial services industry. Dr. Fred Luconi, a Ph.D. from the Massachusetts Institute of Technology in computer science and one of the company's founders, brought fifteen years experience with INDEX systems—a provider of information systems consulting and decision support software—to the new company. Other people involved in the company included Dr. Randy Davis, a professor at MIT's Sloan School of Management, and Richard Karash, a cofounder of another software company called Management Decision Systems, which had successfully created and marketed decision support software.

Since its founding, APEX has offered financial planning products and services, including a personal computer-based financial planning aid. From 1984 to 1986 the company has grown from a core group of 20 people to a staff of over 70. Many of the new employees have been hired to support the roll out of PlanPower—its first expert-system-based product.

APEX is unwilling to present specific financial results to the public, but did divulge that a number of institutional investors are backing the company, including Travelers Insurance, Chemical Bank, Beneficial Corporation, and TRW Information Systems Group. In June 1986, APEX received an additional $8 million of financing, which raised estimates of total capital invested in the company to between $15 and $25 million.[1] Much of the money was spent on PlanPower development costs.

The Financial Collaborative—The User Firm

The Financial Collaborative (TFC), the user of PlanPower, aims at serving individuals with incomes of six figures or more whose net worth is well over $1,000,000. The company prides itself on being a premier financial planning firm—one of New England's best. Located in an elegant office townhouse on Union Wharf overlooking Boston Harbor, the Collaborative evinces an air of "new-tech rich" where personal computers and mahogany desks blend in an elegant ambiance. The office helps communicate TFC's philosophy of quality, professionalism, and managed growth to its wealthy clientele.

The firm was incorporated in 1980. Fred Pryor, TFC's president, related its strategy:

> The Financial Collaborative was founded on one concept—quality. We aim to become the "trusted financial adviser" of individuals with high net worth and income—preferably $2,000,000 or above in net worth and $300,000 plus in income. We have other clients, but we perform best for a person with complex finances.

To achieve this end, TFC was founded by a team of five financial experts with experience in each of the important areas of financial planning. Fred Pryor was experienced in estates, trusts, and administration; Jim Joslin had over twenty years experience as a portfolio manager and investment adviser; Warner Henderson was an insurance agent with more than ten years experience in insurance, investments, and tax shelters; Steven O'Neill possessed an extensive background in personal estate planning and real estate; and Gordon Snyder was a tax attorney.

The five principals each owned twenty percent of the firm. They wanted to grow TFC's client base to between 110 and 140 individuals with high net worth. Ultimately, each principal hoped to be able to receive about $100,000–150,000 in compensation from TFC yearly.

In terms of reputation, the founders of TFC wanted to be known as one of the premier planning firms in the Northeast. Pryor expounded on their strategy:

> Our marketing is "word of mouth." It may cause us to grow slower, but we think it allows us to grow better. An advertisement in a magazine is not going

to attract the person we want into the type of relationship we prefer. A recommendation from a satisfied customer is our best advertisement.

Since 1980, TFC's client base has grown to 83 clients; the average net worth was $2.5 million. By 1985, TFC had net income of $320,000—two-thirds from fees, one-third from commissions.

The Issue—Financial Planning

PLANPOWER IS AN EXPERT SYSTEM DESIGNED TO HELP FINANCIAL PLANNERS create more accurate and comprehensive financial plans in less time. Broadly defined, personal financial planning is the creation of a systematic set of monetary objectives and action plans for an individual or a family. There are many components in a comprehensive financial plan. Ideally, it begins with an analysis of the client's financial and estate goals. These goals are tempered by the person's or the family's income and net worth. The analysis includes many considerations:

> tax planning
> investment advice
> education planning
> retirement planning
> estate planning
> insurance planning
> legal planning—wills, trusts, etc.

Interest in the planning field had increased dramatically during the 1980s. From 1980 to 1986, the membership of the Institute of Certified Financial Planners, a trade organization, grew from 1,108 to 17,637.[2] Deregulation of the financial markets, along with a growing consumer awareness of financial concerns, fueled expansion. A study conducted by SRI International, a research firm based in Menlo Park, California, estimated that by 1990 twelve million people in the United States would be wealthy enough to warrant financial planning. Further, SRI estimated that over 25,000 professional financial planners would be needed to service that market.[3] APEX hoped to address this high level of perceived market demand with PlanPower.

For many people, a well-executed financial plan can make a significant difference in their long-term net worth by lowering taxes, marshaling expenses, and providing sound investment advice. To date, there is no consensus on financial planning. Philosophies, techniques, and content vary widely.

Financial planners routinely make judgments regarding the likely return and risk of different investment vehicles—in effect, predicting the future. A financial planner weaves a fabric of recommendations that makes up a plan which takes into account the issues listed above (e.g., tax planning, investment advice, insurance needs, etc.) and their financial ramifications. There are additional, subjective complexities in creating a comprehensive financial game plan. Even if there were an accepted model for all financial planning, individual differences and preferences could still alter the plan. For example, many TFC clients owned their primary residences outright—with no mortgage remaining. It often made sense for such a client to borrow money against the unencumbered house. This common practice not only sheltered income from taxes because the borrower could deduct the interest on the home loan, but also provided investable capital. However, many clients would "not borrow one dime" against their houses for investment purposes regardless of the strength of the logic behind the financial arguments. Many strong, emotional, non-economic considerations can permeate the planning of an estate.

TFC Organizational Structure

BY 1985 AND PRIOR TO THE INSTALLMENT OF PLANPOWER, there were eleven people in TFC: five professionals, four paraplanners, one data administrator, and a secretary. As president, Pryor was responsible for day-to-day management of the firm. He and Warner Henderson were the most active in TFC. The other three principals spent two or more days a week in residence, but they also pursued outside interests. Mary Zelek, Trish Brajer, Jean Williams, and Marilyn Edgerton, were all "paraplanners," which meant that they worked to support one of the five principals in managing and servicing his clients. Zelek worked with Pryor, Brajer with Joslin, Williams with Henderson, and Edgerton with O'Neill.

Connie Wyllie was receptionist and secretary. Willow Reilly was data administrator; she was responsible for keeping client files up to date. For example, every time a client filled out his or her tax return, he or she would send a copy to TFC; this was used by Reilly to update the client's file. Often she found errors made by the client's accountant. Making the client aware of such errors impressed the client with TFC's thoroughness.

The organization was especially well staffed relative to the size of its client base. As Gordon Snyder noted:

> Compared to other planning firms, we are "top heavy." I know one guy who calls himself a financial planner and has over 700 clients—all on his own. We have much more talent coming to bear on each client and we perform more comprehensive service.

TFC's Processes

At TFC there are five important, interrelated business tasks: (1) transactions, (2) review of existing clients, (3) product review and inventory, (4) creation of plans for new clients, and (5) presentation of plans to clients. The principals had hoped that the PlanPower system could help with the first four processes, but especially with the fourth task—creation of plans for new clients. These organizational programs [3, p. 141] were analyzed for pre-PlanPower and post-PlanPower patterns.

New Clients and Planning

Planning for a new client usually began with the client sitting down and discussing his or her planning needs with one of TFC's principals. Then the client filled out a two-page data form that gave some basic family facts, financial goals, and other pertinent information.

After this initial contact, Pryor and Henderson met to determine the fee and the "fit." There is an art to determining which clients would be "a good fit," that is, which clients would be willing to give accurate, timely data and would seriously consider TFC's recommendations. TFC did turn some clients over to other planning firms because of "poor fit."

Once Pryor and Henderson "accepted" the client, they decided which of the five TFC principals should become the senior person responsible—the "client administrator." The client administrator was to stay informed about all client activity and shepherd the client through TFC's planning process to assure good service. If the client signed on, he or she paid 1/2 the fee up front, with 1/2 to be paid at delivery of the final plan.

Many different inputs went into the creation of a financial plan: client data, expert opinion, planning, and research. Data accuracy was critical to the entire process. Some clients gave data promptly, but for many it was the most grueling part of the entire planning process. Mary Zelek recounted an extreme case: "When I asked one of our clients to provide the data for the plan, he gave me three phone numbers—one for his attorney, one for his banker, and one for his accountant. That one took a lot of digging."

Getting client data was one of the worst bottlenecks in the planning process. Many aspects of the data collection required an understanding of planning. For example, the client might give the paraplanners a series of financial documents full of jargon and complexities that were only decipherable by a knowledgeable reader.

When sufficient data to obtain a reasonably complete picture of a person's financial situation were collected, the client administrator, the paraplanners, and Willow and Connie, put together a 1 to 2 page Client Profile. This included a balance sheet containing all assets and liabilities, funds flow statement, and a synopsis of the client's goals and personal issues—the building blocks for a plan.

Systems at The Financial Collaborative

Henderson had taken the lead in developing personal computer-based systems for the preparation of plans, creation of exhibits, and client tracking. There were three primary systems in his design. One helped in the management of text documents. The second was a group of Lotus 1-2-3 templates for financial planning, product tracking, and client fee estimation. The third was a set of small database files used for tracking client status.

Every time a bit of data was changed or a Lotus template altered, it was recorded and dated using logging procedures set up by Henderson. He also kept revising the "basic" 1-2-3 templates to reflect changes in assumptions the firm used in planning, or changes in tax laws, etc. Almost all of the financial exhibits clients received in their plans were generated by Henderson's 1-2-3 models.

TFC's philosophy of integrated financial planning was embodied in the firm's organization and processes. Every Wednesday, all five principals gathered around an oblong conference table to convene the "Wednesday Meeting," as it was known at TFC. At this meeting, they designed and reviewed the cases for the day. They worked on one, and, occasionally, two new plans, along with existing client reviews, product reviews, and general business. Stephen O'Neill noted the importance of the Wednesday meetings to the firm:

> Our distinctive competence is that every client is reviewed by the entire team of experts at our Wednesday meetings. The knowledge that comes to bear at the time on that person's financial affairs is as good as, or better than, any other planning firm.

It was at the Wednesday meeting that the interconnection among planners occurred. Input by each planner was provided—a team effort. The Wednesday meeting also served as an efficient use of the principals' time because all could examine and interact on the plan together and quickly. Also, the Wednesday meeting allowed firm members to share new planning information and keep in regular contact.

There were some guiding principles the planners used for each client: asset diversification, risk tolerance, and life-cycle phase. The asset diversification model was based on the notion that wealthy individuals should diversify their holdings in countercyclical investments—thus reducing investment risk. The categories in TFC's model were: fixed income (bonds); American (American equities); international (international equities); natural resources (oil, agriculture, etc.); real estate; and tangibles (gold, stamps, antiques, etc.).

At the Wednesday meeting all planners would review the 1 to 2 page Client Profile and suggest changes in light of the guiding principles and the client's specific needs. The first meeting mapped broad changes to be tested and researched. Subsequent meetings traced specific actions and products. Three to five iterations through the Wednesday meeting were typical for a new Client Plan.

Client needs varied. Some had very simple financial situations in which the primary issues and actions were almost self-evident. Others had finances with many interrelated and complex issues. It was the latter type the principals enjoyed most. As Gordon recounted: "When we get working on a tough case everyone is interested—the planning most enjoyable. The challenge of a new and different financial problem is fun."

The paraplanners took notes on the planners' suggestions and followed them through by gathering new data, running the numbers, and making sure all recommendations tied together. Sometimes it meant going back to the client or designing new solutions. Mary Zelek noted: "I love figuring out how to do a complex financial plan. To develop the numbers, do the analysis, and design the solution—that's challenging."

When the plan had progressed through the Wednesday meeting enough times, the written plan was begun. Often the report could be as long as 100 pages, covering a wide range of client issues. The text usually served two purposes: it explained basic concepts of asset diversification, life-cycle, risk, etc., and it gave a precise accounting of the individual's financial situation, TFC's recommendations, and rationale.

From the founding of the firm until September 1985, the plan writing had been done by one person—Pam Patton. Patton had been skillful in assembling the plan parts into a coherent whole. Her prose was concise, her style businesslike. Often she had been the contact point for the client and her dual role as plan writer and client contact person had kept her on top of the issues and the plan current.

When Patton had the report completed, all the principals presented the plan to the client. Generally, Pryor began the presentation and was followed by the other four principals, each explaining his own area of expertise. The presentation usually took four to five hours in all.

It was a challenge to keep the plan current. Often, clients made changes between the date they gave their data to TFC and the date of the presentation. Changes caused TFC to make adjustments up to the last minute to reflect the client's current status. In extreme cases, one of the paraplanners might be modifying and proofing text and exhibits outside the presentation room during a presentation. Henderson's Lotus 1-2-3 spreadsheets were instrumental in allowing rapid update of a client's exhibits and text.

By early 1985, two things had changed. First, the volume of clients had been straining Patton's capacity to generate plans. Then Patton left the firm in July 1985 to pursue other interests. Since Patton's departure, TFC had shifted to generating "miniplans" around specific issues. Client presentations were targeted on specific topics and only 30 to 60 minutes long. TFC scheduled three to five presentations for each client to deliver the entire plan.

The Immediate Need for PlanPower at TFC—Plan Writing

The principals at TFC had hoped that PlanPower would help them in all parts of the planning process. Most pressing in late 1985 was their need for a plan writer. They felt that the miniplans had been effective, but they wanted to get back to complete plans and single presentations.

By Henderson and Pryor's approximations, their planning capacity had remained approximately the same without Patton. At any given time, TFC had three to five new client plans "in the works" with a seven to ten client backlog. Each year, they added ten to fifteen new clients, and their renewal rate on existing clients was about 95 percent. Pryor estimated that they created between twelve and fifteen new plans per year. The average fee per client for the initial plan was approximately $6,000–$8,000 with wide variation ($500–$25,000). The retainer fee was customarily 50 percent of the initial plan cost—renewed or revised yearly.

The PlanPower Solution

TFC TOOK DELIVERY OF THE PLANPOWER SYSTEM during the last week of November 1985 and began using it immediately. When PlanPower came to TFC, Warner Henderson worked closely with Willow Reilly and Connie Wyllie to learn the system and its strengths and limitations. Henderson expressed his feelings in November 1985:

I think PlanPower will allow better planning meetings. Now the meeting begins with data. After PlanPower, the meetings will begin with the PlanPower plan as the base line—an improvement. Yet, we will need to invest a considerable amount of time and effort with the system before we can tell if it's a success for us.

Because there were no standards in financial planning, the APEX system "took a stand" on the "correct approach" to the task. The core philosophy of the system was similar to that of TFC—that is, asset diversification and the investment pattern that the asset-diversification model implied was the driving force behind the logic of the system.

PlanPower provided coverage of all the areas involved in the creation of a financial plan: estate planning, insurance, tax advice, etc. It was broad and detailed in its knowledge but, in any one area, it was not as knowledgeable as an expert in that area. Overall, it performed well for most planning situations it was expected to encounter. Yet, because there were no standards in the field, nor were there any figures on the number of people who had "standard" financial issues, the specific applicability of the PlanPower system to all the possible types of planning situations was unknown.

There were three basic components to PlanPower: the knowledge representation system, the expert framework, and the computed text. In the knowledge framework, information was represented in terms of objects and their financial characteristics, e.g., bonds, stocks, employment criteria, and descriptions of family members. The system contained over 200 classes of objects and accessed nearly 2,000 characteristics associated with the objects. The multiple attributes allowed the system to take many factors into account when choosing tools to meet a particular financial objective.

In the expert framework, the rules of analysis—which had been gathered from a panel of experts—were encoded to analyze and manipulate the data objects and make trade-offs to create solutions. As a product release stated: "The APEX framework does real planning, not just diagnosis. It simulates and tests its recommendations in a consistent and integrated way, i.e., it will model all the buy-and-sell transactions required to implement its recommendations."[4]

The third component, computed text, generated prose that was "ready to be viewed by the client."

The PlanPower software ran on a Xerox 1186 workstation, a computer specially built to run LISP, a language common to expert systems software. Physically, the Xerox 1186 had a large screen with very high resolution. Many "windows" could be opened to view different client data or perform different tasks on the client's data simultaneously.

The Xerox 1186 did have the capability to run IBM personal computer software, but there was no compatibility between PlanPower data and any other data. For example, one could run Lotus 1-2-3 on the 1186, but PlanPower could not read the data residing in existing Lotus 1-2-3 spreadsheets.

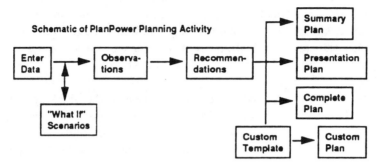

Figure 1.

Using PlanPower

Financial planning using PlanPower began with entering the data into the system. Depending on the level of detail, this process could take from 30 minutes to 3 hours per client. There were many default values, and few required data, so even a complex plan could be sketched quickly for a preliminary analysis.

After data entry, one could ask for the "observations," a process that usually took ten to twenty minutes. In this analysis, the system provided observations on the client's position, such as, "Mr. Mulcahey's leverage is low, with a debt to equity ratio of 1.0 to 1.1." There were no recommendations in this "pre-planning scenario," as it was called.

Next, the user could ask for recommendations. This process could take anywhere from ten minutes to an hour or more, depending on the complexity of the plan. In this stage, the system went through a person's entire financial situation and generated a series of specific recommendations—known as the "after-plan scenario." The observations and recommendations, or "obs and recs," provided an overview of what the plan would look like and where the recommendations came from.

Often, after the obs and recs had been created, some experimentation was done with the plan. The planner could go in and simulate client transactions, such as buying stock or selling land. This would create a new pre-plan case from which new obs and recs could be generated.

Four types of documents could be made from the after-plan scenario:[5] summary, presentation, complete, and custom. (See Figure 1 for a diagram of the basic plans available.)

The summary plan, which provided a brief overview of the summary exhibits and text, was intended for use by the planner. Its wording and appearance were not designed for client viewing. The presentation plan, as its name indicated, was designed to be used as the basis for a client presentation. The complete plan, which has 40 to 100 or more pages of text, graphics, and tables integrated together, was the most complete standard plan.

If the TFC planners desired, they could create a custom plan by assembling the plan components into a "template," as it was called. In a template, a planner chose the exhibits, text, and charts to include. However, the time and effort to create such a template was warranted only if it could be used for a number of clients. Otherwise, it was easier to make changes to the text in a word processor that was also integrated as part of PlanPower.

Any of the four documents could be edited in the PlanPower word processor. This method was often faster than making changes and rerunning a plan. However, care had to be taken to check the consistency of the plan, because when a number or recommendation was changed in the word processor, the implications of that change were not reflected in the other planning exhibits or recommendations. These other changes had to be made by hand.

The user had considerable flexibility in inputting assumptions about the economy, the planning parameters, and the client. The assumed inflation rate and the yield on different investment categories were two of the many assumptions that could be specified by the user. There were also a number of "influence points" where the planner could "turn off" or "turn on" certain recommendations by entering the appropriate data. A simple example was client preferences: Every investment category had a data item that recorded the client's "preference" toward the investment. More specifically, each investment had a rating of "APPROVED" or "DISAPPROVED." If the planner marked oil and gas tax shelters DISAPPROVED for a particular client, then the plan would never recommend that type of investment for that client. After using PlanPower for a number of plans, a planner could learn the interactions of the influence points and their effects on recommendations.

TFC did not have access to view or change the rules of thumb the system used. If the user wanted to change the recommendations of the system, he or she would have to work within the available variables.

PlanPower

THE FINANCIAL COLLABORATIVE RECEIVED PLANPOWER on Friday, November 22, 1985 and began using the system on Monday, November 25, 1985. Of TFC's five major tasks—transactions, review of existing clients, product review and inventory, creation of plans for new clients, and presentation of plans to clients—the fourth task, new client planning, was most influenced by the use of PlanPower. The first three seemed largely unchanged by use of the ES.

At the highest level of analysis, the new-client planning organizational process map had five steps (see Figure 2). Within the large and complex organizational program depicted in Figure 2, the last three steps—plan design, plan writing, and presentation—seemed most affected by the use of PlanPower. Consequently, the discussion that follows centers on the last three phases of the TFC new-client planning process before and after PlanPower use.

Pre-PlanPower Plan Design

Plan designing at TFC took place during the Wednesday meetings. This weekly

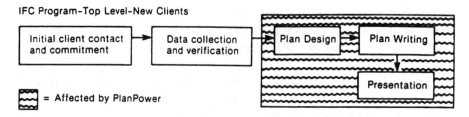

IFC Program-Top Level-New Clients

Initial client contact and commitment → Data collection and verification → Plan Design ⇒ Plan Writing → Presentation

= Affected by PlanPower

Figure 2.

gathering was the planning pulse of the firm and was orchestrated to bring together different expert views of the client's financial situation. From a business perspective, it was the combination and active involvement of the different specialists that differentiated TFC from a mediocre planning firm. TFC management felt that the integrated, informed talents of the five individuals at the table on Wednesday was the primary reason TFC could charge $2,000–$30,000 per plan and still have satisfied customers.

Each plan passed through the Wednesday meeting repeatedly. The first meeting for a new client began with a crisp 1 to 2 page brief on the client's finances, goals, and issues. Initial plan design came quickly as the experts identified major gaps in the client's financial fabric.

In between Wednesday meetings, the paraplanners would run the numbers and check the specific implications of the broad investment strategies. As the plan iterated through the process, the initial strategy became progressively refined and detailed. Usually, after three to four iterations, a plan was ready to be written. However, there were delays. Some clients stopped in mid-planning, others put the whole process on hold, and still others were just reluctant to obtain the needed data. Consequently, elapsed time ranged between five and seven weeks or more before the planner was ready to begin writing the plan.

Pre-PlanPower Plan Writing and Presentation

Writing of the miniplans occurred on an ad hoc basis. After the client's finances had been through the Wednesday meeting a few times, the important client issues were identified and a presentation document was drafted to address the immediate problems. Usually only 2 to 15 pages in length (1 to 5 pages of text and 1 to 10 of exhibits), the miniplans were written by the paraplanner, the principal involved with the client, and the specialist in the area.

Presentation of the miniplans was also ad hoc. Fred Pryor estimated that a client could have anywhere from 3 to 6 miniplan presentations given to him or her depending on the size and severity of the issues. Each time, the planners attempted to tie the miniplan recommendations into an overall picture for the client. Henderson and Gordon Snyder (the principal with a specialty in tax law) noted that this issue-oriented planning allowed for fast closure on specific concerns. However, they, like Pryor, expressed consternation over the miniplan approach because the presenters had to repeatedly re-educate the client by sketching out the overall plan in order to provide context for the current miniplan issue. They hoped PlanPower would help them return to full plans.

Post-PlanPower Plan Design

PlanPower was inserted into the TFC process flow right after data collection and right before plan design. Soon after the introduction of PlanPower, the nature of the Wednesday meeting changed. This occurred in two stages. In the first stage, a new client's financial picture was introduced to the Wednesday group by means of the observations and recommendations document from PlanPower. The major difference between the 1 to 2 page brief and the PlanPower document was that the latter contained specific solutions generated by the ES for every planning issue. The meeting thus began with a set of recommendations in addition to the complete client data.

The arrangement and nature of the PlanPower recommendations were unfamiliar to Pryor, Snyder, and O'Neill. Because Warner Henderson and Jim Joslin were the principals of the firm most familiar with the logic of the system, they played a central role in introducing and describing the PlanPower plan. When one of the planners or paraplanners asked why a particular recommendation was given by PlanPower, Warner or Jim would explain the logic behind the recommendation. If necessary, Warner would call APEX after the meeting and report back to the group with further explanations later in the week.

The meeting focus shifted from one where the principals made suggestions to one where the principals asked questions about why PlanPower suggested a particular solution. In effect, the process had changed from one of design to one of critique. In addition, Warner and Jim educated the planners to the reasoning behind the recommendations.

After PlanPower's preliminary use in the plan design step, it became apparent that there was a problem. The process of reviewing the PlanPower plan did not "feel right" to the principals at TFC. As Warner Henderson said:

> When we put the PlanPower observations and recommendations first, people turned off their creativity. All the suggestions were already made, at least in basic format, and people generally added to the recommendations, or quietly assented. They did not really "get into" the planning unless Plan-Power made a mistake or did not have logic to address a particular problem. When solving a new problem, the old spark returned. We got involved!

Even though there was no direct evidence that plan quality had been eroded, Henderson was concerned about the long-term effects of a loss of interest in the planning meeting:

> The issue of people "turning off" is important for us. Consequently, we decided to put the PlanPower recommendations at the end of the planning meet-

ing—an additional planner if you will. That seemed to work much better, with PlanPower providing a checklist and reminding us of the basics.

In the second stage of PlanPower use, the PlanPower exhibits and observations were used as input to the process, but the recommendations were moved to the end of the meeting. This shift in the use of planning input reflected Fred and Warner's careful attention to detail. The atmosphere of the meetings was a crucial mechanism to help keep the planners active and involved in the design process, which was a critical success factor for their business. By moving the recommendations to the end of the meeting, Fred and Warner reestablished the design focus of the Wednesday meeting.

PlanPower Usage

After the arrival of PlanPower, Warner Henderson immediately began putting client data through the system so that a summary PlanPower plan could be run and used as input for the first Wednesday meeting on new clients. In effect, PlanPower output became the major input to the plan design stage—supplanting the 1 to 2 page client brief.

In the past, the plan design process was the same for all clients. With PlanPower, the process became differentiated. As of July 1986, there had been ten plans put through PlanPower. From the descriptions in the interviews regarding these ten efforts, three distinct types of process flow emerged:

1. ES only
2. modified ES
3. by hand

In "ES only," the data were put into the system and the ES created the entire plan. Of the first ten plans, two were ES only—presented to the client with only minor changes. At the other extreme, there were some clients suited for the "by hand" process. Since the installation of the system, only one case had been done entirely without PlanPower. It was a relatively simple case, and it was decided that it was more efficient to design the plan the old way because it was not worth the time to enter the data into the ES.

The ES-modified route presented some interesting challenges because the Plan-Power logic was not accessible to the user. Often the planners would have a particular set of recommendations in mind for a client. PlanPower might generate a plan with some slightly different recommendations. There were two ways that the planners modified the output. First, if the changes were minor, it was sometimes possible to change the output in the PlanPower word processor. This method became cumbersome if there were many changes, because all the numbers and recommendations in the PlanPower plan were interrelated. Consequently, one could only go so far before the data and facts were so disrupted that it was easier to start fresh than to continue "repairing" the current attempt.

The second way to modify the plan was to try to determine the logic behind the recommendations and change the input to influence the output. Early in TFC's use of

PlanPower, the planners had a particularly challenging experience trying to enter stock options into the planning system because PlanPower did not have the ability to model that particular asset. Consequently, Warner, Mary, and Connie experimented on and off, for two days, until the trio successfully manipulated the cash flows, the dates, and investment classifications in such a way that PlanPower correctly recognized the options, and calculated their tax implications. The effort to create "hybrid input" took perseverance and many, many calls to APEX.

When a plan came out of PlanPower that made recommendations which were not what the planners wanted or were incorrect from the planners' point of view, it might take significant digging, both on the phone with APEX and by trial and error, to discover ways to fix it. Because the actual written plan PlanPower created was such an integral part of the planning process, TFC often took the time to create hybrid input so that the plan could be presented as a whole with the correct recommendations. This hybrid system—part ES, part by hand—seemed to be the most time-consuming and frustrating activity of all.

Planning Capacity—Before and After PlanPower

THE LAST ISSUE TO BE EXAMINED IN LIGHT OF PLANPOWER use is the capacity of the TFC organization to plan. All in all, capacity of the TFC system increased. Before PlanPower, the amount of planning activity flowing through the firm varied widely, with the majority of activity falling around tax time when clients came for help and just before year-end when clients scrambled to make amends. On a yearly basis, the firm accepted about 10 to 15 new clients per year. The fall-off rate was approximately 5 to 7 percent. The existing client base was approximately 80–85 and, given its rate of growth and fall-off, net growth was approximately 10 clients per year.

After PlanPower, it was too early to see the effects on the client-base additions, because it would take years to discover trends in the number of clients added. The strongest concrete indicator of increased capacity was the reduced cycle time of the plans through the process. Fred Pryor, TFC president, estimated that the time needed to create a plan shortened from 4 to 5 weeks to 3 to 4 weeks with the use of PlanPower. In reviewing archival data, Pryor's impression was supported. In fact, the effect seemed to be much more pronounced than he estimated.

Pryor kept a record of important dates and fee information on every client the firm ever had. According to this data, the average time between the collection of client information and the delivery of the final plan—here called the cycle time—was 15 weeks. For the four cases after PlanPower, it had shrunk to only 9 weeks.

The difference is even more striking when one remembers that pre-PlanPower data are based on almost five years of data, whereas the post-PlanPower data are based on a period from November 1985 to May 1986. The latter period data were collected during TFC's two busy times of the year—end of year and tax time. During these periods, the planners have many non-plan-writing demands on their time, such as giving advice to clients on specific transactions. The shortening of the cycle time may be even more pronounced over the entire year.

The large difference between the archival numbers and Pryor's estimate can probably be attributed to the fact that Pryor was only referring to the active planning time and did not include the extra time needed to schedule the presentation meeting. Most of TFC's clients were wealthy, busy people and delays in scheduling meetings were common. Hence the discrepancy between the recorded dates and Pryor's recollection seems reasonable. Even if the decrease is only one week per plan, it would allow the planners to generate at least one or two more plans per year—given a 10 to 15 week cycle time.

Another indicator of increased capacity was that Pryor, Henderson, and the other principals at TFC were thinking of providing more service to the existing client base. Service might take the form of more types of product offerings or more planning by using PlanPower for annual or biannual plans. In July 1986, alternatives were in review. Before PlanPower was installed, the principals had felt that the organization was "at capacity." Only after the system was up and running did they think of creating new revenue sources.

Post-PlanPower Information-processing Capacity

GALBRAITH [1, 2] DEFINES THE INFORMATION-PROCESSING CAPACITY of an organization to be the diversity of the outputs, the number of different input resources, and the level of task performance. For example, an organization with a high diversity of outputs, a high level of task performance, and a large number of inputs has a high level of information-processing capacity. The determination of the information-processing capacity of The Financial Collaborative consisted of evaluation of the three components that make up information-processing capacity. In the current discussion, inputs includes the people (division of labor), data, and systems used in the execution of the task. Outputs are those things resulting from the task that help others do their work—a definition consistent with Galbraith. Task performance is a subjective, overall assessment—made by this researcher—of the effectiveness and efficiency of the task organization. This assessment takes into account all available objective measures of performance combined with the subjective assessments of the employees and the managers using and managing the ES.

PlanPower at The Financial Collaborative (TFC), shows an increase on all three information-processing capacity components. Table 1 provides a tabulation of the inputs, outputs, and task performance components for the pre- and post-PlanPower financial planning process at TFC.

Inputs

After the use of PlanPower, the inputs to the planning process at TFC were greater. For example, the client data file was the central repository of information. The core of the client data file was the data booklet, which was given to the client at the start of the planning process. The data booklet to be used as input for the PlanPower process was more detailed, almost twice the length of the previous data-gathering document (35+ pages versus 20+ pages).

Table 1

before PlanPower	after PlanPower
inputs—increased	
experts consulted	= experts consulted
✓ trade publications/guides	= trade publications/guides
✓ principals	= principals
✓ Warner's 1-2-3 templates	= Warner's 1-2-3 templates
✓ client data	+ client data—more detail
	++ PlanPower
	++ APEX staff's advice
outputs—increased	
✓ investments	= investments
✓ transaction advice	= transaction advice
✓ money management	= money management
✓ miniplans	++ full, integrated plan with more exhibits
	++ advice to APEX on PlanPower
level of task performance—increased	
✓ expect draft plan after a few weeks	+ expect draft plan after a few days
✓ highest quality possible	+ highest quality possible
✓ 4–5 weeks after client date received to make plan (Pryor's estimate), 15 weeks archival data	++ 3–4 weeks after client data received make plan (Pryor's estimate), 9 weeks archival data

* The designations before each item on the list are indicators of the direction and strength of the change in that category. For example, = is the same, ++ is strongly increased, - is decreased, etc.

Because the client data booklet for the PlanPower system was still undergoing minor revisions at the time of this study, TFC did not give it to its clients. However, after PlanPower had been introduced at TFC, Connie Wyllie began to use the data booklet as a guide for the data input and as the main document for client data. Wyllie and Henderson both said that the PlanPower data booklet was more thorough and, when completed, would allow for faster planning.

As Connie Wyllie said:

> The PlanPower data booklet is excellent for gathering all the relevant data. If we can get clients to fill that out correctly, then planning should be a breeze.

Warner Henderson commented:

> Once the bugs get ironed out of the PlanPower booklet, the system would be a big help. If we can get our entire client base up and on the system and keep them up to date, it would give us the ability to do any sort of interim planning we wanted to do. We might decide to do a plan each year for a cli-

ent, or for some clients, when a major issue or change came up, such as a divorce, death, etc., we could run an entirely new plan on the spot.

Another change in the input to the planning process was the use of dual-data entry system at TFC. Because the PlanPower system was new and more cumbersome and time-consuming to use for small calculations than the 1-2-3 templates Warner Henderson created, all client data was put into both systems. This double-data input allowed TFC personnel to verify the numbers by comparing two sets of data. Furthermore, all the exhibits created by PlanPower were created from the same database of numbers and all the different exhibits from net worth through expense projections matched to the dollar. Before PlanPower, when creating exhibits using Henderson's 1-2-3 templates, each template required its own data entry. The exhibits were not integrated nor drawing from a common database, as they did in PlanPower. Consequently it was more possible for the numbers in Henderson's exhibits to vary from one to another than it was with PlanPower. In this instance, the database required by the ES PlanPower caused more inputs to the data part of the planning process.

Another change in the input to the process brought about by PlanPower was the use of the PlanPower observations and recommendations as an input to the planning process. This short document (usually 5 to 20 pages) was viewed as the input from the "sixth planner."

Consultation with the APEX product support and design group was an almost continual dialogue, and certainly a new input to the process. Henderson, Wyllie, and Zelek all stated that, when they were planning with the system, it was not uncommon to call APEX daily or more often. Most often, the planners called asking about the logic behind an observation or recommendation. This information was particularly important in making the PlanPower plan understandable to the TFC principals.

Other major inputs to the planning process, such as outside experts consulted and the participation of the principals, did not seem to change. Every member of TFC noted no major additions or deletions in these two inputs to the planning process. Overall, there was an increase in the inputs to the planning process at TFC.

Outputs

The outputs from the planning process have also increased since the before-planning stage. First, the firm switched from presenting a series of miniplans to the client to a fully integrated, single plan. Before PlanPower's introduction, the company was delivering "miniplans" to its clients in which issues were addressed on a one-by-one basis. They felt unable to create complete plans for clients without a replacement for their plan writer, Pam Patton. After PlanPower, the firm returned to generating entire plans that were at least as comprehensive as TFC's previous "full plans." The post-PlanPower plans began with the PlanPower output as the base upon which exhibits and other material were added, resulting in a longer, more detailed document.

Another increase in the output was the generation of more plans. Once the data were entered for a particular client, it was possible to generate any one of four standard outputs: observations and recommendations (used as an input to the planning process—described above), the summary plan, the presentation plan, and the full plan.

In practice, the planners used the summary plan and the full plan for internal review. In their presentation to the client, they used the presentation plan output and gave the client a copy of the full plan. As of July 1986, the different plans and their content were just beginning to be explored with regard to their marketing possibilities. For example, it was thought that it might be worthwhile to use the summary plan for interim mailouts of planning service—a once-a-year summary of financial position and issues. An effort was also made to customize the full plan to TFC's desires. The number of outputs—in terms of plans and their applications—had gone up—overall an increase in outputs.

Task Performance

Task performance also increased from pre- to post-PlanPower. One important change was that the cycle time was lower. As noted above, Pryor felt that the savings were one week per plan. Archival data showed that the benefit in turnaround might be even greater—on the order of four weeks per plan. The discrepancy might be due to the fact that Pryor was referring only to planning time, while the archival data included the time needed to schedule a presentation. Nevertheless, Pryor's estimation and the archival data pointed to the same conclusion—shorter cycle time.

The principals at TFC felt that PlanPower was helping them to do their job better. Henderson and Pryor both said that the PlanPower system was an integral part of TFC's ability to provide better service in less time to the client. The decrease in cycle time and the ability to provide closure was especially important to TFC because, in planning, the principals felt that the faster one could follow up on client planning issues and bring a client through the entire planning process, the easier it would be to get the client to act on the planning recommendations.

By July 1986, the managers of TFC felt that their experience with the system was only the beginning. They felt that many new possibilities would arise after all clients were on the system. The ability to promise and deliver interim plans and do replanning with relatively little effort enticed them.

This is not to say that the principals of the firm did not have any reservations. They were worried about the amount of investment in time and effort they were making in the system and they knew that an overall assessment of the efficacy of their effort would not be known with certainty until a few years had passed. However, their interim report on the system and its effect on task performance was definitely positive—task performance had increased.

Changes in the Programs at TFC

OVERALL, THE MAJOR BENEFIT OF USING PLANPOWER was a return to full plan writing without having to hire an additional plan writer. The cycle time had shortened and the quality of data entry and review had also improved because client data was put

Table 2

before PlanPower	after PlanPower

*plan design:
  1–2 pages
  design all one way
	*plan design:
	  obs and recs as input
	  three-way planning

*plan writing:
  miniplans
	*plan writing:
	  full plans

*cycle time: 15 weeks	*cycle time: 9 weeks

into both the 1-2-3 templates and the PlanPower system. The cost of the better data was the double data entry on all the numbers associated with a plan (see Table 2).

All in all, the principals felt that PlanPower was a success in the short term. However, they were unsure of its long-term benefits. PlanPower would be a success if the learning and effort that had been put into the PlanPower introduction could be leveraged across their existing client base by allowing them to provide more products and services more profitably. If the fundamental plan they offered continues to need significant customization or shoehorning into the system, its future and value were not good. The principals estimated that it would take one to two years of use before they knew the consequences of their PlanPower experiment.

NOTES

1. APEX Gets $8 Million in Additional Financing. *Mass High Tech*. June 9-22, 1986, 13.
2. Financial Planning. *Wall Street Journal*, Special Section, 12/2/85, p. 4D.
3. PlanPower Press Kit.
4. PlanPower Press Kit, Technical Overview, 7-7-7.
5. The documents mentioned here are the most commonly used in creating a new plan. There were many other document options.

REFERENCES

1. Galbraith, J. *Designing Complex Organization*. Reading, MA: Addison-Wesley, 1973.
2. Galbraith, J. *Organization Design*. Reading, MA: Addison-Wesley, 1977.
3. March, J. G., and Simon, H. A. *Organizations*. New York: Wiley, 1958.

Embedding Stakeholder Analysis in Object Oriented Organizational Modeling

Scott C. McIntyre and Lexis F. Higgins

College of Business and Administration
University of Colorado at Colorado Springs
Colorado Springs, CO 80933-7150

Abstract

This paper described techniques used by the authors to introduce stakeholder analysis into an object oriented organizational model. Knowledge based representations of stakeholders' positions are used to assess their impact on stimulated decision scenarios. The architecture of an object/rule oriented stakeholder tool is described, as well as its interfaces with an object oriented environment for organizational modeling. The process used by the authors for eliciting positions and modeling their impact on the organization is also described.

Introduction

In a previous paper [8] the authors described an object oriented environment used for organizational modeling. The paper described three advantages afforded by the object paradigm for producing organizational models: (1) objected oriented programming (OOP) can contribute to the formation of accurate models of the target organization: (2) OOP can aid the process of model building, allowing incremental model refinement according to the current state of knowledge about the target organization; and (3) OOP can enhance construction of not only passive/descriptive, data-oriented models, but also active models which can be used to simulate target organization activities.

When OOP is used for analysis and design of organizational systems, "what if" scenarios can be modeled by adding, deleting, or changing model features, and then simulating organizational response to the changes. This paper describes the use of this ability for stakeholder analysis, that is, the impact on organizational decisions of positions taken by various participants in the modeled organization ("stakeholders"). A position is a statement of belief which is asserted by a stakeholder and which has some impact in a decision environment.

To summarize the process, positions are elicited from stakeholders and included in the object oriented model. Sets of positions are applied in simulated decision processes to assess their impact. The architecture and use of the Stakeholder Analysis tool is described, as well as its interface with the object oriented environment for organizational modeling described in [8].

Modeling stakeholders as objects

According to Mason and Mitroff, "Stakeholders are all those claimants within and without an organization who have a vested interest in decisions faced by the organization... A business firm might be conceived of as the embodiment of a series of transactions among all of its constituent purposeful entities, that is, its stakeholders. The final outcome of an organization's plan will be the collective result of the effects of the individual actions taken by its stakeholders" [7, p. 43].

Object oriented organizational models describe the organization's entities, relationships between entities, and activities which involve entities. In order to introduce the stakeholder concept into these models, a person or group modeled as an entity must be able to express a vested interest which relates to a decision. That vested interest must itself be modeled in such a way that its potential impact can be assessed.

197

Figure 1 is a simplification of the object class hierarchy used by the authors to represent the organization. It was described in detail in [8] and is loosely based upon IBM's Business Systems Planning methodology [6]. The organization is represented as including personnel entities (whether specifically by individual or generally by job title), business functions, information, information systems and projects. Data, relationships, and activities associated with a specific organization are modeled when these class objects are instantiated.

Not all personnel entities are stakeholders. In the class hierarchy, "positions" are taken by an entity in order to express (in Mason and Mitroff's terms) a vested interest relating to some issue. The entity becomes a stakeholder by taking such a position. By thus representing a stakeholder, the larger context of a stakeholder's relationships with other facets of the modeled organization is maintained.

According to Toulmin, arguments used to advance vested interest might be understood as movements from accepted data through a warrant, to a claim [10]. In Mason and Mitroff's scheme, data are "accepted" and "factual." For example, "The firm sold 43,000 units last year." Warrants are inferential statements that act as a bridge between data and a claim. Warrants can be represented in the familiar form of a rule: ("If some data D is true, then some claim C is true.") For example, "If the firm sold 43,000 units last year, then our profit margin was 11 percent." The certainty that a claim is true can also be expressed in probabilistic terms, from absolutely false to absolutely true [7, pp. 213-215].

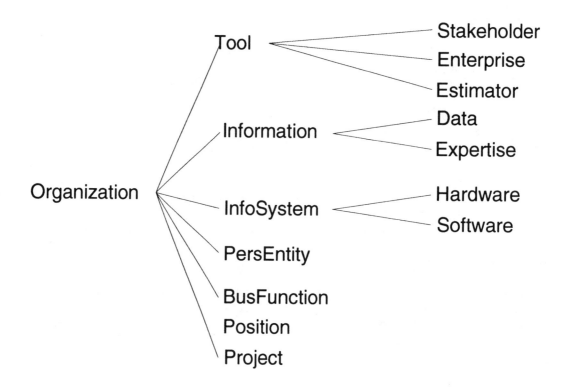

Figure 1. Organizational object class hierarchy

In the environment built by the authors, stakeholders' positions take two forms, assertions and rules. These correspond to the data and warrants described above, with one minor exception. Whereas "data" was considered to be factual, our "assertions" might be the option of the stakeholder. Figure 2 demonstrates the "position" class object. A position is "owned-by" one or more organizational entities. Its "type" is either assertion or rule. Its "value" contains the text of the assertion or rule. It also has "documentation." Positions are completely integrated in the object environment; that is, within its value, a position might reference other objects or initiate messaging.

Assertions are represented as value-attribute pairs. The example in Figure 2 is that the budget for an expert systems development project must not exceed one hundred thousand dollars.

Rules are expressed in IF-THEN format. In the example, the position is advanced that if a knowledge engineer with very high experience is assigned to the expert system development project, the development time can be reduced by twenty percent.

In conclusion, the stakeholder role of a personnel entity enhances the model of an active person within an organization. As Figure 3 demonstrates, it is now possible to describe a given entity with appropriate data and relate him/her to business functions, information, and information systems. The entity performs appropriate modeled functions via object oriented methods and messaging. An entity becomes a stakeholder by owning one or more positions. In the figure, John Smith is the manager of Advanced Technologies Development. He performs Advanced Product Estimating, among other functions. He has access to the Historical Cost data base and uses the Estimator to perform cost estimating. Among his numerous positions is that if an experienced expert system developer is assigned to the task at hand, development time will be reduced by fifteen percent over the average. The model of John Smith exists within a much larger "world model," and his relationships to that world are explicitly present in the object oriented model.

Position $BH13	
Owned_By	$rickstrum
Type	Assertion
Value	(Budget_ES_Devel 100000)
Doc	Equals new development dollars for '89

Position $RS9	
Owned_By	$bobhubler
Type	Rule
Value	If (KE_exper VHI Then (Develtim * 0.8)
Doc	Equals new development dollars for '89

Figure 2. Position object examples

Embedded stakeholder analysis

In [8] the authors advanced arguments that OOP not only produced useful models (for example, organizational models), but that model creation and manipulation processes are enhanced by OOP (for example, in the processes of information systems analysis and design). In the same vein, once stakeholders' positions are modeled, what does one do with them? This section discusses object oriented stakeholder analysis via the Stakeholder Analysis tool (Stake). The process used by the authors for identifying stakeholders' positions is overviewed. The Stake tool's architecture are described.

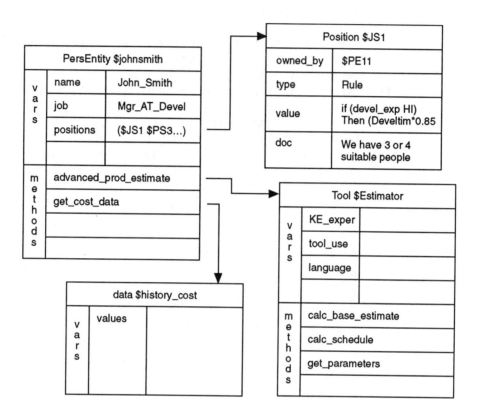

Figure 3. Integration of stakeholders into model

To summarize this section, the Stake tool receives the positions of one or many stakeholders and performs inferencing. Results of the inferencing have been used by the authors to support organizational decision processes.

Throughout this section a case of recent use of the Stake tool in a large telecommunications firm (called Telecom for the purpose of this paper) is used illustratively. The foundation of the case is as follows. Telecom has multiple subsidiaries linked by complex voice and data network architectures. Besides the services it provides to external customers, Telecom provides an internal network communications center (NCC) to handle problems with internally used computer and network equipment. The analysis in the NCC have highly complex and diverse knowledge: it takes approximately 18 months to absorb enough information to become "average" at their jobs. Each analyst handles approximately 100 calls per day of varying degrees of complexity. The decision supported by the use of Stake was whether Telecom should support the analysts with a "help desk" expert system.

Identifying and representing positions

From knowledge engineering literature (for example see [4]) and from the authors' experience, it is clear that eliciting stakeholders' positions is not simply a matter of asking. Based upon knowledge engineering techniques and information elicitation techniques from Group Decision Support Systems (GDSS) research (see for example, [1], [3], [5], [9]), the authors combined structured brainstorming and structured interviewing to capture stakeholder positions.

"Structured brainstorming" techniques and their electronic counterparts underlie information elicitation processes in most group decision environments. In a typical structures brainstorming session, a group of decision makers who have been guaranteed anonymity are asked a question, and their responses recorded. In each successive round, a participant is presented with the original question and a set of previous answers. The participant responds to the question and the previous answers.

The authors use this technique in a two stage process. Given the decision that has to be made, structured brainstorming is used to identify the major types of decision parameters. In the case, the structured brainstorming question that was asked of Telecom in the first state was, "Given that the decision is whether or not to build an expert system to aid the NCC service desk, what are the major parameters of that decision?" Example results from the case are "projected benefits of the system," "impact on each subsidiary of Telecom," and "functionality of the system."

In a second stage of structured brainstorming, each major decision parameter identified in the first stage becomes a question. Table 1 lists partial results obtained by asking the questions, "What are the potential benefits of the proposed expert system?" and "What functionality is required of the proposed expert system?"

Structured interviews are undertaken after the second brainstorming stage in order to elicit stakeholder positions. Before developing structured interviews, the authors depended solely upon knowledge engineering techniques with individual decision makers in order to elicit positions. The authors have found that a much more comprehensive list of decision parameters is elicited by using the brainstorming techniques initially, and then addressing the resultant list with individuals. This process gives stakeholders the opportunity to take positions on others' ideas as well as their own.

Individuals are presented with the detailed list of parameters and asked whether or not they have positions to take on any of them or on others not yet identified. Table 2 is an illustrative list of positions taken by two stakeholders in the Telecom case. Assertions and rules are gleaned from the text of the interviews, formally defined, and stored as positions in the object oriented model described in the previous section.

Use of the stake tool

The Stake Tool is itself coded as a set of objects within the modeled world. Therefore it is not only available to the user, but also to entities in the modeled world via messaging. Figure 4 demonstrates the architecture of Stake.

Stakeholders' positions are "activated" so that they might be processed by the Stake tool. Activation is accomplished by pointers to position objects in the Position Storage. Via the pointer, access to all knowledge about the position is maintained, for example the text of the position and position ownership. Positions to be stored are specified on any of three levels: all positions of one or more stakeholders, positions of one or more stakeholders have to do with a given decision criteria (for example, higher analyst productivity), or positions of one or more stakeholders having to do with a given object (for example, budget).

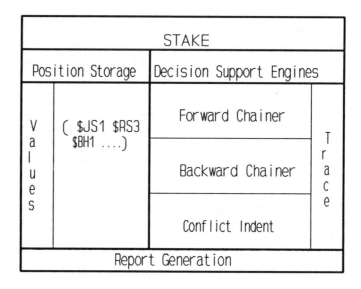

Figure 4. Stake architecture

Table 1. Partial results of the second stage of structured brainstorming in the Telecom case

Question: What are the potential benefits of the proposed expert system?

- higher analyst productivity
- hire less people
- analyst's job more formally defined
- new analysts become effective more quickly
- expertise of all analysts is combined synergistically
- training new analysts more easily accomplished
- structured decision path that reflects customer concerns
- solutions proposed in order of likelihood
- reduce number of calls taken by analysts
- stable interface between analyst and customer

Question: What functionality is required of the proposed expert system?

- standalone on PC for prototype
- integrated with other analyst tools after prototype
- tier one intelligence (easy calls handled)
- tier two intelligence (more difficult calls handled)
- ease of maintenance
- add intelligence incrementally
- audio text front end
- automatically initiate trouble ticket
- partially populate trouble ticket
- interface with historical data bases (input and output)
- touch tone recognition front end

Table 2. Illustrative positions

Stakeholder: Manager of NCC Operations

■   productivity of all analysts must increase 15 percent next year
■   IF we can define the analyst's job more formally THEN we should institute an
■   analyst training program
■   standalone PC system is not acceptable after 1-1-89

Stakeholder: NCC Analyst

■   IF the expert system can combine analyst expertise THEN the effectiveness of a
■   given analyst will increase
■   standalone PC system will increase analyst productivity by 10 percent

Positions are activated in order to make them available to the Decision Support Engines. These Engines consist of inference engines (backward and forward chaining), a conflict identification engine, and a decision trace engine. All reporting is done via the Report Generator, a command driven, and therefore programmable, facility. Users and entity objects can request that specific information be provided in specific formats as a result of running the Decision Support Engines.

Once positions have been loaded into the Position Storage, the Decision Support Engines are applied in much the same manner as in a conventional expert system. That is, assertions are treated as facts and IF-THEN structures as rules. The use of forward chaining, backward chaining, conflict identification and tracing to support decision making is the subject of the remainder of this section.

Stakeholder analysis with the decision engines

Once an object oriented model of an organization has been constructed and the stakeholders modeled within it, stakeholder analysis can be facilitated. The object oriented decision simulation is not completely automated; for that reason the Stake tool is used more as a decision support than an expert system. The authors have used the Stake tool in the following ways: the potential impact on decisions of one or groups of stakeholder's positions are assessed; decision paths are traced; potential conflicts are identified between stakeholders' positions; the need for information and gaps in reasoning are identified; groups of stakeholders who might cooperate in decisions are identified.

Including and Withholding Stakeholders. As described in [8], a decision process is modeled as interactions between objects. In the Telecom case, a brief outline of the decision to build the expert system is that if the benefits are perceived to equal or exceed the cost, the system will be built. Benefits are defined variously according to different stakeholders, and each defines the relationship differently between the various types of benefits and costs.

Via the Stake tool the authors explored the impact of including the withholding a given stakeholder or groups of stakeholders in the decision environment. Stakeholders' positions to be included were loaded into the Position Storage, and the forward chaining and trace Decision Support Engines were employed. This also permits what Mason and Mitroff called "chains of argument" to be identified [7, p. 218].

Applying only selection positions has permitted the following kinds of questions to be addressed: What would happen if the NCC analysts' criteria (i.e. the expert system users' criteria) were considered above all others? What if the head of operations imposed his perspective? What would happen if those stakeholders who demand a conservative budget were considered above those who were more liberal?

What impact would be felt upon the design decisions of emphasizing the Human Factors group's positions?

Inclusion or exclusion of various perspectives not only permits an interesting exercise in decision analysis, but fuels discussions of the roles various stakeholders play in a complex decision. In the author's experience, this exercise has been valuable to force decision makers to examine the impacts on the whole decision of its various components. This has helped overcome vague conclusions based too heavily upon "gut level feelings" or power plays. In an early phase of the Telecom expert system decision, the Vice President in charge of Operations vacillated between building the system "because he trusted the developers," and not building it "because the budget resources might be hard to identify." The use of Stake demonstrated the need for a far more complex decision process.

An example of an argument chain established with the forward chainer follows. One stakeholder reasoned that if the audio text front end to the expert system were used, it would answer 30 percent of the calls currently answered by the analysts. Another reasoned that if the number of calls could be reduced by over 20 percent, the analysts would be able to formalize their jobs, since they would have time for self study. A third reasoned that a more formalized definition of the analysts' job would enable developers to proceed to a more complex knowledge base (the tier two level) for the expert system. When these were formally represented as positions and applied to the forward chainer, the chain or argument became evident. This was captured by the trace engine, which sits in the background and records/reports each conclusion reached by any of the other Decision Support Engines.

Conflict Identification. An important step in any decision process is recognizing conflicts. Conflicts make important contributions to policy decisions and are common when stakeholders have different perspectives. Conflict recognition often becomes lost in complexity and emotion. While the very process of modeling stakeholders' positions helps to identify conflicts, modeling can itself be so lengthy and complex that conflicts are lost.

The conflict identification engine identifies conflicts in three ways. The first is simple contradiction. For example, the Vice President of Operations established a position that the budget for the first prototype of the expert system must not exceed $40,000. The developers estimated that it would costs $50,000. This contradiction was identified by a simple comparison between the two positions: (proposed_budget_prototype 40000) belonging to VP_Ops, and (proposed_budget_prototype 50000) belonging to Chief_Developer.

A second level of contradiction is established when two rules with the same antecedents conclude two different consequences. This is a gross test which does not necessarily establish a conflict, but points out that one might exist. If it does exist, the nature of the conflict might be too subtle for even sophisticated automated detection. For example, a part of the Telecom decision was who to use in the development. One supervisor expressed the position that if the developer experience were very high then the time to develop the project would increase dramatically. Her manager took the position that development time would decrease somewhat. When the conflict was identified and discussion took place, it turned out that the manager was making what he felt to be a logical and general assumption. The supervisor had a specific developer in mind, the only one she regarded as having "very high" development experience. She felt this developer was already significantly committed and, with the small amount of time he had available, would slow down development time over a less committed developer.

A third level of conflict analysis seeks to establish possible causes of the conflict. This has been used to date in a specific, well structured decision process and the authors are researching extensions. In the Telecom organization, budget decisions are made according to a specific process. One component of this involves resource estimation using a combination of function point analysis and the type of algorithmic cost analysis described by Boehm in [2]. There are over twenty components of the algorithm Telecom uses. When different stakeholders' positions are applied, different assumptions are often made with regard to resource types and availability, resulting in different estimates. A conflict identification engine developed for this decision recognizes different values for partial and complete estimates and works back through the decision path (the estimate algorithm and function point analysis), identifying different assumptions stakeholders have made for various components of the resource decision.

Information and Reasoning Gaps. Through use of the trace and backward chaining decision engines, support is given for identifying gaps in information and reasoning and for identifying groups of stakeholders who might cooperate in decisions. To initiate this process, a decision goal is established. The backward chaining decision engine searches stakeholders' positions in order to establish potential proof paths for the goal. Rule oriented proofs continue in a similar way to a backward chaining expert system. When the backward chainer reaches a gap in information, that is, when it cannot backward chain based upon current information, it stops and identifies what it needs to know. The trace engine keeps track of which stakeholders' positions have been used for a given decision path, thus establishing potential areas of cooperation for decision making.

This process was used in Telecom for two types of decision making. The more straightforward involved highly specified rules and facts and was used, for example, in budget decisions. One budget was specified to be the sum of personnel, equipment, and overhead costs. Since numerous positions had been taken by managers, developers, budget officers, etc., it was not difficult to backward chain on a question such as "Is it possible to do the project with an initial budget of $100,000?" Gaps involved specific facts such as "What is the salary cost of a very skilled developer for six months?" and "Can we make the assumption that there exists a vendor on the preferred list with a per station PC cost of under $3000?"

A second type of decision made with backward chaining had rules which were subject to numerous interpretations. In this type the need to interpret rules for backward chaining raised constant questions about rules' specific meanings. For that reason the backward chaining supported for a group decision exercise, engendering valuable discussions with the aim of addressing and then reducing the ambiguity in decision paths. For example, a decision goal involved who should build the expert system. One stakeholder's rule was "IF inside developers do not have the expertise to build the proposed system, THEN hire contract developers." The question of whether to hire contract developers was part of the backward chaining. At that point, discussions developed among the decision makers on what expertise was required to build the system, whether training should be considered to give internal people those skills, what foundational skills were needed in candidates for training, what it would cost to supply those skills, and so on.

Implications

Even though knowledge representation and inferencing techniques common to expert systems development were used in the development of Stake, the implications of this research are for Group Decision Support Systems. Results from constructing and applying stakeholder analysis within object oriented models demonstrate promise for techniques to provide a bridge between idea generation, represented here by the use of structured brainstorming, and closure on decisions. Within the context of organizational decision making, this is not, and the authors believe will never be, a completely automated process.

Use of the Stake tool to date has supported decision makers in the processes associated with formalizing issues, constructing argument models, and simulating the impact on the organization of various perspectives. Further research is needed to assess the impact of the Stake technique within a fully functional Group Decision Support System.

References

[1] Applegate, L.M., Chen, T.T., Nunamaker, J.F., Jr., and Konsynski, B.R., "Knowledge Management in Organizational Planning," *Journal of Management Information Systems*, 3, 4, pp. 20-38, Spring 1987.

[2] Boehm, B.W., *Software Engineering Economics*, Prentice Hall, Englewood Cliffs, NJ, 1981.

[3] Easton, A., *An Experimental Investigation of the Effectiveness of a GDSS for Strategic Planning Impact Analysis*, Unpublished Ph.D. Dissertation, University of Arizona, Might 1988.

[4] Fuglseth, A.M. and Stabell, C.B., "Capture Representation, and Diagnosis of User Information Perception," in *Knowledge Representation for Decision Support Systems*, L.B. Methlie and R.H. Sprague (editors), Elsevier Science Publishers, New York, (p. 191 ff.), 1986.

[5] George, J., Nunamaker, J.F., Jr., and Vogel, D., "Group DSS and Their Implications for Designers and Managers: The Arizona Experience," *Transactions of the 8th International Conference on DSS*, Boston, June 7-8, 1988.

[6] IBM, *Business Systems Planning*, (GE 20-0527-1), 1975.

[7] Mason, R.O. and Mitroff, I.I., *Challenging Strategic Planning Assumptions*, John Wiley and Sons, New York.

[8] McIntyre, S.C. and Higgins, L.F., "Object Oriented Systems Analysis and Design: Methodology and Application," *Journal of Management Information Systems*, 5, 1, pp. 25-35, Summer 1988.

[9] Nunamaker, J.F., Jr., Applegate, L.M., and Konsynski, B.R., "Facilities Group Creativity: Experience with a Group Decision Support System," *Journal of Management Information Systems*, 3, 4, pp. 5-19, Spring 1987.

[10] Toulmin, S.E., *The Uses of Argument*, Cambridge University Press, Cambridge, England, 1958, (quoted in [7] pp. 213, 218).

Integration of Organization and Information Systems Modeling: An Object-Oriented Approach

Minder Chen
Department of Decision Sciences and MIS
George Mason University
Fairfax, VA 22030
Phone: 703-993-1788
BITNET: MCHEN@GMUVAX
INTERNET: MCHEN@GMUVAX.GMU.VAX

Jay F. Nunamaker, Jr.
Department of Management Information Systems
College of Business and Public Administration
University of Arizona
Tucson, AZ 85721
Phone: 602-621-2748
BITNET: NUNAMAKER@ARIZMIS

Abstract

This paper presents an object-oriented approach to integrating organization and information system modeling. Characteristics and applications of object-oriented systems are first reviewed to show the evolution of the application of an object-oriented approach from an implementation and programming level to conceptual modeling of organization and information systems. The need to integrate organization and information systems is then discussed. MetaPlex, a metasystem implemented in Smalltalk language to support high-level object-oriented modeling is described in detail. Case studies defining Critical Success Factors in MetaPlex and creating a Structured Electronic Brainstorming System to support collaborative work are used to demonstrate the use of MetaPlex in integrating organization and information system modeling at both individual and group levels. Directions for future research are also discussed.

1. Introduction

In this paper, the authors will address the issues related to integration of organization and information system modeling as well as the development of automated tools to support object-oriented modeling. The possibility of using the same object-oriented approach in various phases of system development (including organization and information systems) promises a cohesive integration of organization and information systems.

In Section 3, we will first establish arguments for the necessity of integrating organization and information system modeling. The architecture, design, and implementation of an object-oriented metasystem called MetaPlex which supports organization and information system modeling at a very high level are discussed in Section 4 and Section 5. Section 6 presents case studies defining Critical Success Factors in MetaPlex and creating a Structured Electronic Brainstorming System to support collaborative work to demonstrate the use of MetaPlex in integrating organization and information system modeling. The paper is concluded with suggestions for future research.

2. The object-oriented approach and its applications

The term "object-oriented systems" has had different meanings for different people [Stefik and Bobrow, 1985]. However, there is general agreement that an object-oriented system should have certain characteristics. In this section, general characteristics of object-oriented systems are first reviewed and then a discussion of application areas using the object-oriented approach is presented.

2.1 Characteristics of object-oriented systems

Concepts, entities, and things are represented as objects in an object-oriented system. Objects have structures and behaviors. The static structures of an object are described by its private data (that is, instance variables) which store the local status of the object. The dynamic behaviors of an object are simulated by instance methods of the object's class. Computations in an object-oriented system are done by sending messages among objects (that is, indirect procedure calls). Objects interact with each other collaboratively to accomplish required tasks. A message has to be sent to an object in order to access or change its status. This *message passing paradigm* is borrowed from the human communication model [Ingalls, 1981]. Objects can interface with the external world only through a set of predefined message patterns (that is, protocol). In most object-oriented languages, direct access to an object's private data is prohibited. The message passing paradigm facilitates *information hiding*, thereby increasing the modularity, modifiability, expandability, and maintainability of a software system [Klahr, etc., 1986]. Different classes can share the same message pattern to support *polymorphism*. For example, the message *rotate* can be sent to instances of Square and Triangle but these objects will have different implementations of their instance methods for responding to the message *rotate*. A message received will be responded to according to the message receiver's designated method. Polymorphism thus reduces the syntactical complexity of the system and allows the development of more generic codes.

Objects are organized by *class hierarchy* (for example, in Smalltalk, Circle is a subclass of Arc, Arc is a subclass of Path, and Path is a subclass of DisplayObject). An object can inherit structures (instance variables) and behaviors (methods) from its class and superclasses. Subclasses can implement a method having the same message pattern to override the generic behavior defined by their superclasses. The class hierarchy promotes both data and procedure abstraction in a software system, which makes the resulting system more reusable.

2.2 Application areas of the object-oriented approach

The object-oriented approach has been recognized as a unified paradigm in the design and implementation of programming languages, knowledge-based systems, databases, and human interface design [Zaniolo, etc., 1986]. Table 1 shows the progress of an object-oriented approach in various application areas (listed loosely in chronological order according to when the object-oriented approach was first applied):

> *1. Simulation.* The area to which the object-oriented approach was first applied was simulation, as in the Simula language [Dahl and Nygaard, 1966]. Simula is actually a general purpose language which introduces the concepts of inheritance between class and instance and the support of polymorphism. Static structures and dynamic behaviors of entities are simulated by data and procedures encapsulated in objects. Recent simulation languages, such as Ross [McArthur et al., 1986], incorporate more object-oriented features.

> *2. Programming language.* Smalltalk is a purely object-oriented programming language environment [Goldberg, 1983; Goldberg and Robson, 1983]. Everything in Smalltalk is implemented as an object, for example, classes, user interface, control structures, etc. Some object-oriented languages are hybrid, such as C++ [Stroustrup 1986] and Objective-C [Cox, 1986].

3. User interface design and implementation. An object-oriented user interface was first used experimentally in the early 1970s when the Smalltalk system used overlapped windows to view objects, a mouse to manipulate objects directly, and a location-sensitive pop-up menus to select an appropriate operation. In Smalltalk-80, a Model-View-Controller (MVC) paradigm has been used as a framework for user interface development [Krasner and Pope, 1987]. Impulse-88, developed by Smith et al., [1987], provides very high level components to support the design and building of object-oriented user interfaces. The object-oriented approach has also been borrowed and implemented in the operating system in Apple's Lisa and Macintosh. Object-oriented interfaces provide consistent and natural ways for users to interact with a computer system and thus help lower the user's learning curve in adapting to a new system.

Table 1. The application areas of the object-oriented approach

Application Areas	Systems or Literature
Simulation languages	Simula [Dahl and Nygaard, 1966] Ross [McArthur et al., 1986]
Programming languages	Smalltalk [Goldberg and Robson, 1983] C++ [Stroustrup, 1986]
User interface design and implementation	MVC paradigm in Smalltalk [Krasner and Pope, 1987] Impulse 88 [Smith, et al., 1988]
Database systems	Iris [Fishman, et al., 1987] GemStone [Maier and Stein, 1987]
Knowledge base systems	KEE [Kunz, Kehler, and Williams, 1984] NExpert [Neuron Data Inc., 1987]
Graphics and hypermedia systems	MacDraw [Apple Computer Inc., 1984] Intermedia [Yankelovich et al., 1988]
Systems analysis and design methods	OOD [Booch, 1991] OOA & OOD [Coad and Yourdon, 1991, 1991a] OMT [Rumbaugh, et al., 1991]
Organization modeling	Blanning [1987]

4. Graphics. The graphics tool MacDraw [Apple Computer Inc., 1984] is an object-oriented graphics drawing package which runs on Apple Macintosh. All the graphic objects in MacDraw can be manipulated by a common set of operations, such as select, copy, move, and enlarge. The consistency in operations helps users in learning how to use the system. Object-oriented techniques have also been used to implement graphic and hypermedia applications such as Intermedia [Yankelovich et al., 1988] and HyperCard [Goodman, 1987].

5. Database systems. The development of object-oriented database systems are being explored because of the persistent problems in storing large amount of data in an object-oriented system as well as requirements to represent complex objects in CAD/CAM and CASE applications. Iris [Fishman, et al., 1987] and GemStone [Maier and Stone, 1987] are examples of object-oriented database systems.

6. Knowledge base systems. Recent developments in commercial expert system shells also show the artificial intelligence (AI) industry's endorsement of the object-oriented approach to knowledge representation. For example, KEE demonstrates how object-oriented tools can be used for knowledge-based system building. It is a hybrid AI tool which integrates rule-based systems, frame-based systems, graphics, and active values (that is, demons) with an object-oriented kernel [Kunz, Kehler, and Williams, 1984]. NExpert [Neuron Data, 1987] is a high-end hybrid rules and object-based expert system environment with an object-oriented architecture.

7. System analysis and design methods. In an object-oriented system analysis and design method, the decomposition of a system is based on the concept of objects [Booch, 1986]. Object-oriented design combines data structure-oriented, procedure-oriented (that is, data flow-oriented), and architectural design because objects carry the notions of data structures and procedures (that is, methods) while, the same time, message passing among objects defines the interface of the system architecture [Pressman, 1987]. Popular object-oriented analysis/design methods include OOD developed by Booch [1991], OOA and OOD developed by Coad and Yourdon [1991, 1991a], and Object Modeling Technique by Rumbaugh et al. [1991].

8. Organization modeling. The information processing model was developed by Galbraith [1977] as a framework for organization design. Blanning [1987] extended this information processing paradigm by applying an object-oriented approach to the modeling and simulation of an organization. Blanning [1987] also believed that an object-oriented approach could be applied to the analysis of organizations as well as to the design and implementation of systems (for example, information systems, decision support systems) that support those organizations.

Using the object-oriented approach in information system analysis and design, as well as in organization modeling, extends the use of the object-oriented approach to conceptual modeling, which is far beyond the original notion of objects at the implementation and programming levels. This shift in focus demonstrates the generality of the object-oriented approach. However, most of researchers neither addressed the issues of integration of organization and information systems nor demonstrated how tools can be developed to support the modeling process. Booch [1986] also showed concern for the way tools can be used to support object-oriented development and called for further research in this direction.

The popularity of object-oriented systems arises from the belief that the notion of an object reduces the semantic gap between the model and the real world. In this research, the authors address issues related to the integration of organization and information system modeling as well as the development of automated tools based on object-oriented modeling. The possibility of applying the same object-oriented approach in various phases of system development (including organization and information systems) promises a cohesive integration of organization and information systems.

3. The need to integrate organization and information system modeling

Information systems are used to facilitate the decision making and communication processes within an organization and have recently been used by companies as strategic weapons against their competitors [Ives and Learmonth, 1984]. Information systems planning methods such as Critical Success Factors (CSF) [Rockart, 1979] and Business Systems Planning (BSP) [IBM, 1984] have started to address the importance of business objectives to the determination of information system requirements. Both BSP and CSF use interviews to involve managers in the information systems planning process. However, none of these models can adequately represent the couplings between organization and information systems models. Only when the design and development of organization and information systems are tightly connected can managers quickly respond to the changing business environment and take advantage of new IS technologies.

The lack of integrated methods and software tools is one of the major causes of the missing link between organization (that is, business system) and information systems modeling. An integrated environment should allow users to specify the complicated linkages between business systems and information systems so that any changes in the information systems can be reflected in their corresponding business counterparts, and the dynamics of the business environment can be propagated to the supporting information systems.

The quality of any system under development is bounded by the available languages and tools as well as the way people use them [Lyytinen, 1985]. The broad scope and the rich semantics needed to describe organization and information systems exclude the possibility of using traditional database systems, structured methodologies, or simulation languages for support of object-oriented modeling. A metasystem system has the flexibility to allow users to define their own terms to describe a target system [Demetrovics, Knuth, and Rado, 1982; Kottemann and Konsynski, 1984; Sorenson, Tremblay, and McAllister, 1988]. The generic nature of the knowledge representation scheme employed by a metasystem allows users to define customized languages for the specifications of both organization and information systems. The flexibility of a metasystem approach reduces the semantic gap between the specification tools and the application domains, thereby facilitating user learning and acceptance of specification tools that are generated.

The disadvantage of most existing metasystems results comes from their poor interface design. The syntactical complexities of their meta language also make it difficult to define a new language. A successful organization modeling tool must allow managers to use it to model their own business environment. MetaPlex is an object-oriented metasystem developed to demonstrate that such a system can be used in a wide spectrum of application domains and at the same time can be easily learned and used by end users.

4. The knowledge representation and architecture of MetaPlex

The development of MetaPlex was inspired by PSL/PSA, a computer-aided tool for system analysis and documentation [Teichroew and Hershey, 1977]. MetaPlex is an object-oriented metasystem which can generate system specification tools for both information and organization system modeling. Systems generated by MetaPlex are intended to be used by managers and end-users. Representing and manipulating relations and the design of friendly user interface have been the focus of MetaPlex development.

4.1 Knowledge representation in MetaPlex

A system can be defined as a group of related components which interact to achieve a high level objective of the system as a whole. Both organizations and information systems are instances of generic systems. To describe an existing system or to design a new system, system analysts or designers are primarily concerned with system components and relationships among them. Various knowledge representation schemes have been studied to see whether they can be used for system specifications. A rule-based system can be used for capturing the designer's know-how on certain design decisions. A frame-based system can be used to represent general design schemata [Lubars and Harandi, 1986]. However, neither of these can explicitly represent the interrelationships of objects in a system. The knowledge representation scheme used in MetaPlex is based on a three-level abstraction of an object-oriented model: the *axiomatic*, *median*, and *instance* levels [Kottemann and Konsynski, 1984].

As shown in Figure 1, Object Types, Relation Types, and Attribute Types are built-in knowledge representation primitives of MetaPlex at the *axiomatic level*. At the *median level*, a domain specific language can be defined by using Object Types and Relation Types with a set of Attribute Types identified in a domain. An Object Type has its name, a comment, and a set of Attribute Types to characterize it. Relation Types specify the relations among Object Types. An Attribute Type is characterized by a name, a data type, legal values, a default value, and occurrence (for example, #one or #many). The data type can have the following data types: Integer, Real, Boolean, String, and Description. Currently the Description data type can be used to encode unstructured and procedural knowledge in text format. The structural knowledge of the domain in general is thus captured at the median level as a system description language. Prototypical knowledge of a domain captured at the median level will be used to guide users in defining a target system specification at the instance level. At the instance level, a target system is defined by a system description language in terms of objects and relations with attributes.

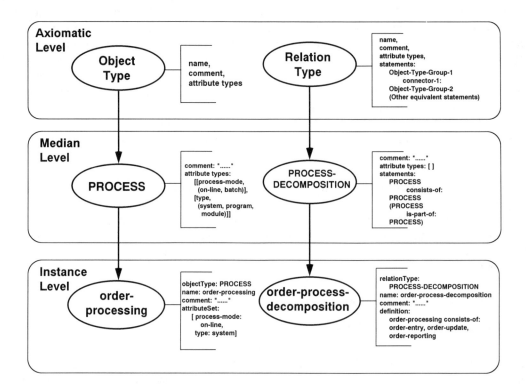

Figure 1. MetaPlex knowledge representation model

4.2 Relations and cross referencing in MetaPlex

In MetaPlex relation types are defined as a *Smalltalk class* so that relation types can have their own attribute types, can be attached with procedures, and can form inheritance hierarchy. Currently, only attribute types can be used to describe a relation. In MetaPlex a relation type is defined as two, or more than two, groups of object types connected by connectors. The internal, graphical, and external language representation of a relation type are depicted in Figure 2.

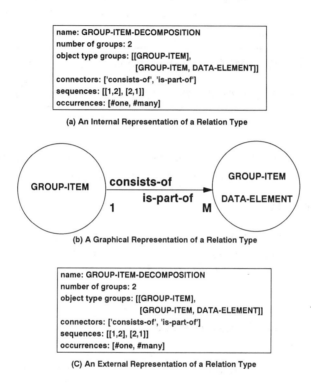

name: GROUP-ITEM-DECOMPOSITION
number of groups: 2
object type groups: [[GROUP-ITEM],
                     [GROUP-ITEM, DATA-ELEMENT]]
connectors: ['consists-of', 'is-part-of']
sequences: [[1,2], [2,1]]
occurrences: [#one, #many]

(a) An Internal Representation of a Relation Type

GROUP-ITEM

consists-of
is-part-of
1   M

GROUP-ITEM
DATA-ELEMENT

(b) A Graphical Representation of a Relation Type

name: GROUP-ITEM-DECOMPOSITION
number of groups: 2
object type groups: [[GROUP-ITEM],
                     [GROUP-ITEM, DATA-ELEMENT]]
connectors: ['consists-of', 'is-part-of']
sequences: [[1,2], [2,1]]
occurrences: [#one, #many]

(C) An External Representation of a Relation Type

Figure 2. The internal, graphical, and external representation of a relation type in MetaPlex

The complementary ways of describing the same relation type which belongs to different object type groups must be specified when language definers define a language. Using the complementary relation types as cross-reference knowledge, the system can automatically cross reference the target system specification. By bringing all relevant information about an object together in one report, the cross reference capability reduces the user's effort in defining a system and facilitates the user's understanding of the target system specification.

4.3 Representing abstraction in MetaPlex

Researchers have identified three major abstraction mechanisms for describing a target system: Classification, Generalization/Specialization, and Aggregation [Gibbs, 1985]. The equivalent representations of these abstraction mechanisms in MetaPlex, discussed below, demonstrate the expressive power of MetaPlex knowledge representation scheme.

1. Classification. The "object type" and "object" in MetaPlex are equivalent to "class" and "instance." The properties and relationships defined for an object type are used to elicit information about objects of this type in a target system. For most applications, two levels of classification are sufficient [Mylopoulos, et al., 1980].

2. Generalization/Specialization. The class hierarchy in an object-oriented system can be represented by an "AKO" relation among object types. For example, we can define "REPORT" is-a-kind-of "DATA", and "MONTHLY REPORT" is-a-kind-of "REPORT". Property inheritance along the class hierarchy can be handled by an inference engine.

3. Aggregation. There are two types of aggregation: Cartesian aggregation and cover aggregation. In MetaPlex, Cartesian aggregation means that an object is an aggregation of its attributes. The cover aggregation can be specified by using a decomposition relation in the following format:

[GROUP-ITEM] consists-of [GROUP-ITEM, DATA-ELEMENT]

[GROUP-ITEM, DATA-ELEMENT] is-part-of [GROUP-ITEM]

Language definers can define a relation type as one-to-one (list structure), one-to-many (tree structure), or many-to-many (network structure). Complicated relations can be easily represented in MetaPlex.

4.4 The architecture of MetaPlex

The design goal for MetaPlex is to develop a simple, but flexible, computer-aided system specification tool that can support and be applied to various domains. The ease of use of MetaPlex is achieved through an interactive menu-driven user interface and a graphic representation of a target system description.

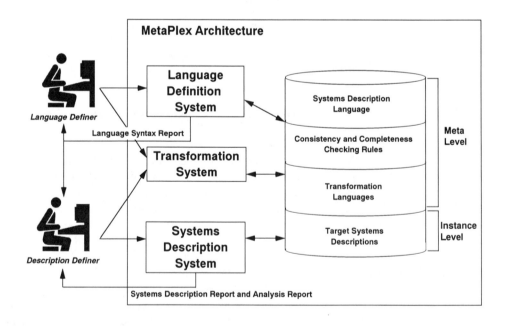

Figure 3. The architecture of MetaPlex

214

While other metasystems use the compilation approach [Yamamoto, 1981; Demetrovics, et al., 1982], MetaPlex uses the interpretation approach for language definition and target system specification. The interpretation approach makes it much easier to develop description languages and to experiment with them. Eventually, users will be able to develop languages of their own without any help from language definers.

The architecture of the MetaPlex System is shown in Figure 3. It has three subsystems: Language Definition System, System Description System, and Transformation System. At the meta level, *language definers* can use the Language Definition System to define system description languages and their consistency and completeness checking rules. Language definers can also use the Transform System to define languages for the transformation of system descriptions from one language to another. Language Syntax Report and Consistency and Completeness Checking Rules Report can be generated by the Language Definition System. These reports also can be used by language definers to check the completeness of the language defined or given to description definers as a user manual of a system description language.

At the instance level, *description definers* can use the System Description System to define a target system description. Report facilities, on-line query functions, and a Structure Browser can be used by description definers during the specification process to verify an existing system description. Consistency and completeness checking rules defined for a system description language can be applied to check the consistency and completeness of its system descriptions. The Consistency Checking Report and the Completeness Checking Report can be generated and used by the description definers. Description definers can also use an appropriate transformation language defined by language definers to convert a system description in one language into a system description in another language. The detailed design of MetaPlex is discussed in Section 5.

In MetaPlex, some functions at the meta level are made available to description definers. For example, description definers can formulate a simple completeness checking rule and check incomplete objects on-line. They can also create a dynamic sublanguage from an existing language and then open an editor to interact with a subset of a system description. Making some meta level functions available to description definers provides them with additional flexibility to fulfill unique requirements of a target system.

5. The design and implementation of MetaPlex

In this section, the design and functionalities of Language Definition System, System Description System, and Language Transformation System are discussed. Implementation issues are also addressed.

5.1 Language definition system

MetaPlex Language Browser is used as a main directory of all the system description languages defined. Language definers can use a Language Editor to define a system description language interactively. A language for a specific domain is defined by identifying a set of Object Types and Relation Types, as well as the Attribute Types associated with them. The Language Syntax Report can be generated from the system. End users can use the Language Syntax Report as a user's manual. Eventually, language definers can "file out" a language definition and then "file in" the language definition in another system. Figure 4 shows both the MetaPlex Language Browser and Language Editor.

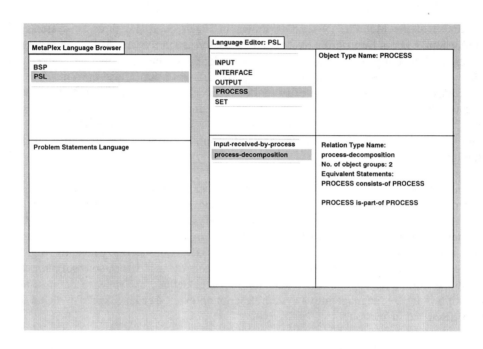

Figure 4. The MetaPlex language browser and language editor

5.2 System description system

MetaPlex can automatically use a defined language to generate a generic environment to be used for specifying target systems. Customized user interface tools can be easily built. As depicted in Figure 5, the generic tools in the Target System Specification System include a Target System Browser and an Attribute Browser. Target System Browser is divided into four panes. The left hand upper pane contains a list of objects which have been defined in the target system. The right hand upper pane displays the comment/definition of the highlighted object. The left hand lower pane shows a list of relations which have been defined in the target system. The right hand lower pane displays the comment/definition of the highlighted relations. The upper pane in the Attribute Browser window presents a scrolling set of attributes of an object or a relation selected from the Target System Editor. Users can switch the contents of the lower pane in the Attribute Browser to display either the definition or the value of the selected attribute. A question mark (?) is concatenated to the end of an attribute name to inform users that the value of the attribute has not yet been defined.

216

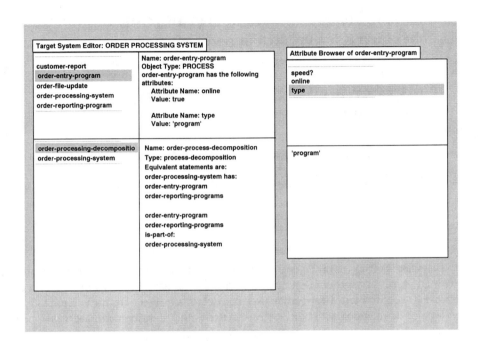

Figure 5. The target system browser and attribute browser

The Formatted System Description Report can be generated from the system with all the relations cross-referenced. Completeness checking rules about a system description can be defined at the language level. An example of a completeness checking rule is shown in Table 2. This rule stated that any DATA STORE in a Data Flow Diagram description which has not generated or received a DATA FLOW is an incomplete object. Users can generate a Completeness Checking Report in a batch mode with all the incomplete objects listed. An on-line completeness checking function is also available. Users can formulate a simple completeness checking rule on-line and let the system find all incomplete objects according to the dynamic formulated rule.

Table 2. A completeness checking rule

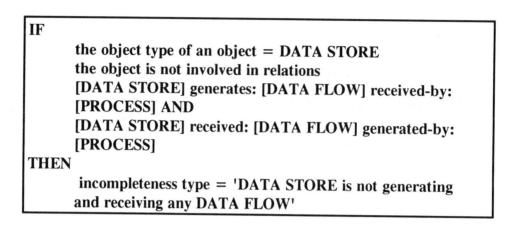

```
IF
       the object type of an object = DATA STORE
       the object is not involved in relations
       [DATA STORE] generates: [DATA FLOW] received-by:
       [PROCESS] AND
       [DATA STORE] received: [DATA FLOW] generated-by:
       [PROCESS]
THEN
       incompleteness type = 'DATA STORE is not generating
       and receiving any DATA FLOW'
```

A Structure Browser, as shown in Figure 6, is designed to enable users to examine the relations associated with an object in a system description. Both tree and network structures of a relation can be examined by using the Structure Browser. A user can select an object from the Structure Browser to examine one type of its relations with other objects. After further development, users will be allowed to create objects and relations in the Structure Browser dynamically.

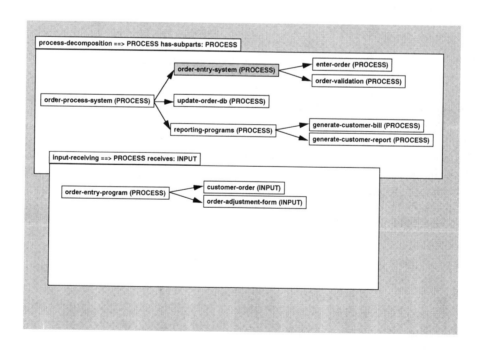

Figure 6. The structure browser for relations in a system description

5.3 Transformation system

Top managers are concerned about organizational goals and objectives, their organization's competitors, and strategic assumptions. Information systems developers are concerned with the detailed information required for the design and implementation of the target systems. In developing a system, its potential users are allowed to use different languages to describe a system from multiple aspects during different phases of the development cycle. Part of the information captured in one phase should be transferable to another phase by using a different language. There are two types of information in a target system description: objects and relations. Since objects and rules are different in their nature, we have decided to use two types of rules to represent the translation of objects and relations: object translation rules and relation translation rules.

Figure 7 shows the design of the Transformation System. Language definers can use the Transformation Language Definition System to define a transformation language between any two existing system description languages (called source language and target language) as long as there is a logical mapping between descriptions in these two languages. The transformation language defined can then be used by the System Description Transformation Language, which can convert objects and relations described in the source language into objects and relations described in the target language. Figure 8 illustrates a Transformation Language Editor in which object translation rules (shown in upper half panes) and relation translation rules (shown in lower half panes) have been defined to translate a BSP system description into a PSL description. If the source of a converted object or a relation is recorded a system description can be traced across various phases of its life cycle by MetaPlex. Traceability is one of the major factors contributing to the successful integrating of organization and information systems because it allows users to trace back from the information systems to the organization systems that they serve.

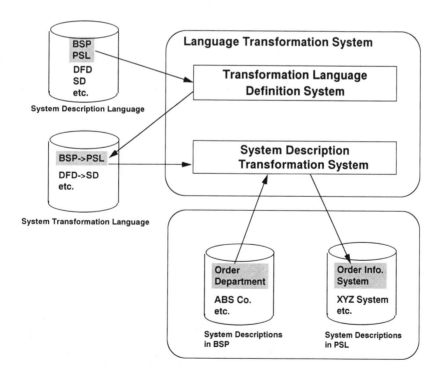

Figure 7. The architecture of the transformation system

219

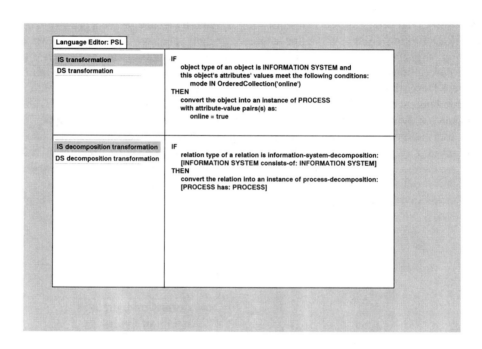

Figure 8. Transformation language editor

5.4 Implementation issues

Object-oriented languages, such as Smalltalk, promote fearless programming [Diederich and Milton, 1987]. Because of its rapid prototyping and highly interactive and graphical interface, Smalltalk was our choice for implementation. An IBM PC/AT version of the Smalltalk-80 language has been used to develop the MetaPlex. Smalltalk allows dynamic binding so that the changes in data structure design are much easier [Goldberg, 1984]. The Smalltalk user interface framework has been used in MetaPlex to provide a consistent user interface at both language definition level and system description level.

6. Case studies using MetaPlex

In this section two cases of using MetaPlex are presented. The first describes use of a tool generated by MetaPlex to support an object-oriented approach to extending Critical Success Factors, an information systems planning method, and thereby integrating organization and information system modeling. In the second case, the authors propose the use of MetaPlex to create a Structured Electronic Brainstorming System (SEBS) for use as a metasystem driven tool for computer-supported collaborative work (CSCW). SEBS can be used as a front-end tool to facilitate the group dynamics in a face-to-face meeting where people from various areas are involved in a system modeling task.

6.1 Defining a system description language for information systems planning: critical success factors

Critical Success Factors is an information systems planning method used to identify the key factors needed by a manager to be successful in the business. The original CSF provided only procedures for conducting the CSF study and focused only on information requirements for an individual manager's decision [Henderson et al., 1984]. Identifying CSF based only on an individual manager's needs made it necessary to make frequent changes in the resulting information systems. The authors have extended the CSF method to allow managers and IS personnel to develop an information system that incorporates the organization's and the perspectives. Object types in the extended CSF method are: CRITICAL SUCCESS FACTOR, MEASURE (to the CSF), REPORT or QUERY (to reflect these measurements), INFORMATION SYSTEM (which generates the reports and queries), BUSINESS GOAL (behind these critical factors), and ORGANIZATION ENTITY (involved). All these object types and the relation types among them have been defined in MetaPlex as a language so that the System Description System in MetaPlex can use that language to guide users when they apply the CSF method.

The CSF method for information systems planning follows a four-step procedure [Martin, 1983]: 1) Identify the critical success factors. Managers as a group are asked to identify the critical factors which will affect the success of their business. 2) Determine the measurements for identified critical success factors. When critical success factors are difficult to quantify, soft measures must be used. 3) Design reports or on-line queries to inform managers of the status of the CSF being measured or changes that have been made. Reports or queries must be generated from an existing or a new information system. The managers who will use these reports or queries are not necessarily the same managers who identify CSF or define the measures for CSF. The original CSF method is designed to be used by individual executive officers to define their own information needs, but the method can be extended for use by a group of managers to determine the information system requirements of an organization as a whole. A group decision support system (GDSS) can be used to support groups who use CSF to define their information needs.

Figure 9 is a representation model (that is, meta-model) for the Critical Success Factors method. This model is a graphical representation of the object types and relation types defined by an extended CSF method. In Figure 9, object types are enclosed in rectangles, relation types among object types are represented by labeled arrow lines to show one direction of the relation types. To simplify the presentation of the model, attribute types that describe object types and relation types are not shown. As illustrated in this figure, the extended CSF method contains object types in both information systems and organization systems domains. It can be used to bridge the gap between information systems planning and business planning. Language definers can extend the language to cover other related object types and relation types in both organization and information systems domains. The MetaPlex System Description System can use the language defined for CSF to generate a tool for description definers to use.

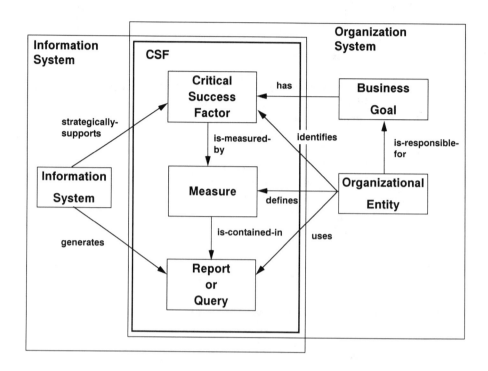

Figure 9. A representation model of critical success factors method

6.2 An example of generating a GDSS tool from MetaPlex: structured electronic brainstorming system

Christakis [1987] noted that "inter-disciplinary teams cannot work productively and efficiently in designing complex systems unless their work is supported and argued by methodologies that have been invented specifically for this task." This concern is especially relevant for large software projects in which members with diverse backgrounds need to work together. A metasystem approach can be used to provide the flexibility to customizing methods for both group deliberation in GDSS and system definition in CASE. GroupSystems [Nunamaker, et al., 1991] is used in the following example to describe how one might use a GDSS as a front-end requirements elicitation tool.

Groups who use GroupSystems in meetings generally use the following process: A meeting agenda is set before the meeting. Meeting participants first use the Electronic Brainstorming (EBS) to generate ideas related to the question posted on a screen at their PC workstations. Ideas created (also called EBS comments) are randomly sent out through a local area network to other participants to stimulate them to generate more ideas. An EBS session usually takes 45 minutes. Following the EBS session, Categorizer (IA) tool is used to identify and consolidate the EBS comments into major issues. A callable voting program can be used to prioritize the consolidated issues. The use of Categorizer usually takes about 60 minutes. Since ideas are entered as free format text, an idea generated by one participant can be interpreted by another outside its original context. Structured Electronic Brainstorming System (SEBS) has been designed to eliminate the possible loss of structures and relations embedded in the original ideas during the group process.

Software development meetings usually are held for specific purposes, such as to define the system objectives, to identify all the required reports and queries, or to determine system functions. These meetings often employ some structured methods, such as Joint Application Design [August, 1991]. Before running an SEBS session, the session leader will work with some key participants to choose or to define a MetaPlex system description language for the meeting discussion. A language for SEBS is defined based on the nature of tasks, the common terminology used in an organization, theories and methods in a specific domain. Once a language for SEBS has been defined, it can be relied upon in place of the facilitation skills required of a session leader for a similar meeting.

The flexibility of the metasystem has expanded GroupSystems into a GDSS generator which can generate customized GDSS environments to support a wide-range of tasks. This extension to GDSS capability, as Huber [1984] suggested, will increase the possibility of successful adoption of a GDSS in an organization. The session leader should define "*the language of business*" to reduce the communication barrier among meeting participants [Martin, 1987]. Since users and managers are allowed to "*speak their own language*," they will be able to participate fully in the discussion.

The language specified by the session leader will be loaded into the SEBS tool to systematically direct the contents and structures of group discussion. Whenever users want to generate a new idea, the SEBS tool asks them to categorize it according to the object types defined in the language. Users can also create relations among ideas, such as specifying "Group Item A can be decomposed into Data Item B, C, and D," "Report E should include Group Item A and F," etc. Detailed attributes about objects and relations, such as "the data format of Data Item is 9(X)," can be collected through the Attribute Browser. Additional advantages of using the SEBS tool are its capability to:

1. Merge the brainstorming and issue identification processes. By merging the original brainstorming and issues analyzing processes SEBS helps to reduce meeting time.
2. Allow users to generate ideas on several related issues at one brainstorming session. Instead of brainstorming on a single question such as, "What are the critical success factors of application ABC?", the system allows users to generate ideas on several categories. An EBS question can be as complex as "What are the Input, Report, and Process in application XYZ?" and "What are the relationships among Input, Process, and Report in application XYZ?"
3. Help users focus on the issues under discussion. Current GroupSystems tools are adequate for exploration type meetings. However, to collect specific information for system development in a meeting, SEBS will be an ideal tool.
4. Facilitate the acquisition of knowledge concerning complex relations. In the current GroupSystems tools, Categorizer supports the identification and consolidation of issues from an EBS file. Relations among issues usually get lost in the consolidation process. SEBS allows participants to enter relations among objects in a structured format to prevent this process loss.
5. Integrate SEBS results into other modeling tools. Information captured has been categorized in a structured format so that SEBS meeting results can be easily transformed and exported to other modeling tools, such as computer-aided software engineering (CASE) tools [Chen and Nunamaker, 1988].
6. Apply completeness and consistency checking on meeting information. Many CASE tools have analysis function to check consistency and completeness of the systems specifications [Chen, Nunamaker, and Weber, 1989]. For example, in PSL/PSA, Problem Statement Analyzer can be used to analyze information in a PSA data base captured through Problem Statement Language [Teichroew and Hershey, 1977]. Similar analysis functions can be applied to meeting information since information is captured

in structured form. The meeting participants will be informed of missing information and of inconsistencies in their argumentation.

The SEBS tool is just one example of using a metasystem to drive a CSCW tool. Currently Topic Commenter in GroupSystems has very limited metasystem features. A facilitator can create a list of topics so that participants can make comments on each topic. Each topic considered in a session is like an object type. The current Topic Commenter does not have the capability to elicit attributes for instances in each topic and does not support the description of relationships. SEBS provides its users with structure and flexibility so that it can be used as a front-end tool to facilitate face-to-face meetings for system modeling involving many participants.

8. Conclusion

The future success of information systems in an organization will depend on how information systems development can be tied in with business systems. In this paper we have presented an object-oriented metasystem approach which allows us to generate a software environment for integrating organization and information system modeling. The relative usability of MetaPlex and other manual and automated tools calls for some empirical studies, through which future research directions will be suggested. The use of MetaPlex to generate GDSS tools as front-ends to collaborative modeling opens up many opportunities for further investigation. The extension this research to integrating systems development and delivery environments is represented in [Chen, Nunamaker, and Weber, 1989]. An approach to integrating various tools in an integrated CASE environment is discussed in [Chen and Norman, 1992].

9. References

Apple Computer Inc., *MacDraw Manual*, 1984.

Applegate, L., Konsynski, B., and Nunamaker, J., "A Group Decision Support System for Idea Generation and Issue Analysis in Organizational Planning," *Proceedings of the Conference on Computer-Supported Cooperative Work*, October, 1986, pp. 16-34.

August, J.H., *Joint Application Design: The Group Session Approach to System Design*, Englewood Cliffs, NJ: Prentice-Hall, Inc. 1991.

Blanning, R.W., "An Object-Oriented Paradigm for Organizational Behavior," *Transaction on DSS-87*, 1987, pp. 87-94.

Booch, G., "Object-Oriented Development," *IEEE Transactions on Software Engineering*, Volume SE-12, Number 2, February 1986, pp. 5-15.

Booch, G., *Object-Oriented Design with Applications*, Redwood City, CA: The Benjamin/Cummings Publishing Company, Inc., 1991.

Chen, M. and Norman, J.R., "A Framework of Integrated CASE," in *IEEE Software*, Vol. 9, No. 2, March 1992, pp. 18-22.

Chen, M., Nunamaker, J.F., and Weber, E.S., "The Use of Integrated Organization and Information Systems Models in Building and Delivering Business Application Systems," *IEEE Transactions on Knowledge and Data Engineering*, Vol. 1, No. 3, 1989, pp. 406-409.

Chen, M., Nunamaker, J.F., and Weber, E. S., "Computer-Aided Software Engineering: Present Status and Future," *Data Base*, Vol. 20, No. 1, Spring 1989, pp. 7-13.

Chen, M. and Nunamaker, J.F., "The Integration of CASE and GDSS: A Metasystem Approach," *The Second International Workshop of Computer-Aided Software Engineering*, July, 1988.

Chikofsky, E.J. and Rubenstein, B.L., "CASE: Reliablity Engineering for Information Systems," *IEEE Software*, March 1988, pp. 11-16.

Coad, P. and Yourdon, E., *Object-Oriented Analysis*, 2nd edition, Englewood Cliffs, NJ: Prentice-Hall, Inc., 1991.

Coad, P. and Yourdon, E., *Object-Oriented Design*, Englewood Cliffs, NJ: Prentice-Hall, Inc., 1991a.

Cox, B.J., *Object-Oriented Programming: An Evolutionary Approach*, Addison-Wesley Publishing Co., Inc., 1986.

Dahl, O. and Nygaard, K., "SIMULA — An Algol-based Simulation Language," *Communications of the ACM*, Sept. 1966, pp. 671-678.

Demetrovics, J., Knuth, E., and Rado, P., "Specification Meta System", *Computer*, May 1982, pp. 29-35.

Diederich J. and Milton, J., "Experimental Prototyping in Smalltalk," *IEEE Software*, May 1987, pp. 82-98.

Fishman, D. H., et al., "Iris: An Object-Oriented Database Management System," *ACM Transactions on Office Information Systems*, January 1987, pp. 48-69.

Galbraith, J.R., *Organization Design*, Addison-Wesley Publishing Co., 1977.

Gibbs, S.J., "Conceptual Modeling and Office Information Systems", in *Office Automation*, edited by Tsichritzis, D., Springer-Verlag, 1985, pp. 193-225.

Goldberg, A., *Smalltalk-80: An Interactive Programming Environment*, Addison-Wesley Publishing Co., 1983.

Goldberg, A. and Robson, D., *Smalltalk-80: The Language and Its Implementation*, Addison-Wesley Publishing Co., 1983.

Goodman, D., *The Completeness HyperCard Handbook*, Bantam Books Inc., 1987.

Henderson, J.C., et al., *A Planning Methodology for Integrating Management Support Systems*, Sloan School of Management, Massachusetts Institute of Technology, CISR WP No. 116, 1984.

Huber, G.P., "Issues in the Design of Group Decision Support Systems," *MIS Quarterly*, September, 1984, pp. 195-204.

IBM, *Business System Planning*, 4th edition, GE20-0527-4, July 1984.

Ingalls, D.H., "Design Principles Behind Smalltalk," *Byte*, August 1981, pp. 286-298.

Ives, B., and Learmonth, G.P., "The Information System as a Competitive Weapon", *Communications of ACM*, Vol. 27, No. 12, Dec. 1984, pp. 1193-1201.

Klahr, P., et al., "TWIRL: Tactical Warfare in Ross Language," in *Expert Systems: Techniques, Tools, and Applications*, edited by Klahr, P. and Waterman, D., Addison-Wesley Publishing Co., 1986, pp. 224-268.

Kottemann, J.E. and Konsynski, B.R., "Dynamic Metasystem for Information System Development", *Proceedings of the 5th International Conference on Information Systems*, pp. 187-204.

Krasner, G.E. and Pope, S.T., "The Smalltalk-80 Model-View-Controller User Interface Paradigm," working paper, ParPlace Systems, September 1987.

Kunz, J.C., Kelhr T.P., and William, M.D., "Applications development Using a Hybrid AI Development System," *AI Magazine*, Fall 1984, pp. 41-54.

Lubars M.D. and Harandi, M.T., "Intelligent Support for Software Specification and Design," *IEEE Expert*, Winter 1986, pp. 33-41.

Lyytinen, K.J., "Implications of Theories of Language for Information Systems," *MIS Quarterly*, Vol. 9, No. 1, March 1985, pp. 61-74.

Maier, D. and Stein, J., "Development and Implementation of an Object-Oriented DBMS," in *Research Directions in Object-Oriented Programming*, edited by Shriver, B. and Wegner, P., The MIT Press, 1987, pp. 355-392.

Martin, J., *Managing the Data-Base Environment*, Prentice-Hall, Inc., 1983.

Martin, J., *Information Engineering Volume 3: Meeting The True Needs of Users More Directly*, Savant Research Studies, January 1987.

McArthur, D.J., et al., "Ross: An Object-Oriented Language for Constructing Simulations," in *Expert Systems: Techniques, Tools, and Applications*, edited by Klahr, P. and Waterman, D.A., Addison-Wesley Publishing Co., 1986, pp. 70-91.

Mylopoulos, J., Berstein, P.A., and Wong, H.K.T., "TAXIS: A Language Facility for Designing Database-Intensive Applications", *ACM TODS*, June 1980, Vol. 5, No. 2, pp. 186-207.

Neuron Data Inc., *NEXPERT OBJECT: An Expert System on VAXStation under VMS*, 1987.

Nunamker, J.F., et al., "Electronic Meeting Systems to Support Group Work," *Communications of the ACM*, Vol. 34, No. 7, July 1991, pp. 40-61.

Pressman, R.S., *Software Engineering: A Practitioner's Approach*, 2nd edition, McGraw-Hill Book Co., 1987.

Rockart, J.F., "Chief Executives Define Their Own Data Needs," *Harvard Business Review*, Vol. 57, No. 2, 1979, pp. 81-93.

Rumbaugh, J., et al., *Object-Oriented Modeling and Design*, Englewood Cliffs, NJ: Prentice-Hall, Inc., 1991.

Smith, R., Barth, P., and Young, R., "A Substrate for Object-Oriented Interface design," in *Research Directions in Object-Oriented Programming*, edited by Shriver, B. and Wegner, P., The MIT Press, 1987, pp. 253-315.

Sorenson, P.G., Tremblay, J.P., and McAllister, A.J., "The Metaview System for Many Specification Environment," *IEEE Software*, March 1988, pp. 30-38.

Stefik, M. and Bobrow, D.G., "Object-Oriented Programming: Themes and Variations," *AI Magazine*, Winter 1985, pp. 40-62.

Stroustrup, B., *The C++ Programming Language*, Addison-Wesley, 1986.

Teichroew, D. and Hershey, E.A., "PSL/PSA: A Computer-Aided Technique for Structured Documentation and Analysis of Information Processing Systems", *IEEE Transactions on Software Engineering*, Vol. SE-3, No. 1, Jan. 1977, pp. 41-48.

Tesler, L., "The Smalltalk Environment," *BYTE*, August 1981, pp. 90-147.

Vogel, D.R., Nunamaker, J.F., Jr., George, J.F., and Dennis, A.R., *Group Decision Support Systems: Evolution and Status at The University of Arizona*, Department of Management Information Systems, University of Arizona, Center for Management of Information Working Paper Series, CMI-WPS-88-02, 1987.

Yankelovich, N., et al., "Intermedia: The Concept and the Construction of a Seamless Information Environment," *Computer*, January 1988, pp. 81-96.

Zaniolo, C., et al., "Object Oriented Database Systems and Knowledge Systems," *Expert Database Systems*, edited by Kerschberg, L., The Benjamin/Cummings Publishing Co., Inc., 1986.

Domain Coverage and Consensus in a
Network of Learning and Problem Solving Systems

Joon M. An, R.G. Hunt, and G.L. Sanders
School of Management, Jacobs Management Center
SUNY at Buffalo, Buffalo, New York 14260

Note: An earlier version of this paper was published in the *Proceedings of the 25th Hawaii International Conference on System Sciences (HICSS)*, January 7-10, 1992.

Abstract

As members of a group begin to interact and solve problems, a group schema evolves. This group cognitive structure is the result of realized consensus about and coverage of the problem domain of the group; and it becomes the mechanism by which the group structures and solves problems. In this paper we describe how a technological agent can be used to control and enhance the evolution of the group schema by creating an environment which facilitates consensus and coverage.

1. Introduction

An organization is viewed here as a network of learning and problem solving systems (LPSS) [31]. The nodes or agents in the LPSS network can be human beings or artificially intelligent computer systems [47]. These agents can act independently, but when acting as a group[1] — a thinking entity — a group cognitive structure emerges with a commensurate organizational psychology. This paper further delineates the psychology of intelligent organizations by describing the group cognitive processes that determine the evolution and structure of group knowledge. We postulate that the performance of the thinking entity can be controlled and enhanced, using a technological agent, so as to control the evolution of the group cognitive structure. This conceptual analysis of group cognitive structure leads to important implications for the designers of intelligent organizations.

2. Organizational knowledge

The concept of knowledge is elusive, but nevertheless central to the development of a network of learning and problem solving systems. It has been variously defined:

in terms of information [14];

as information that has been interpreted, categorized, applied, and revised [1];

as more complex products of learning, such as interpretations of information, beliefs about cause-effect relationships, or know-how [29];

as more complex and valuable than information; (as information about a particular topic that is organized to be useful) [23];

as know-how concerning process and product technology, as found in equipment, employees, files, operator manuals, job descriptions, etc. such that technology is tantamount to an "organizational mind" or the repository of organizational knowledge [31]; and, as symbolic descriptions of definitions, symbolic descriptions of relationships and the procedures to manipulate both types of descriptions [24].

In this paper, organizational knowledge refers to a product of collective problem solving and learning. Organizational knowledge is held in mental and structural artifacts that can affect the behavior (problem solving and learning) of an organization [59].

Nowadays information technology can construct quasi-mental and structural artifacts by utilizing its storage and representation techniques. Both hard and soft information can be captured in information technology to increase the expertise of an organization [29]. Information technology is unique as a repository of organizational knowledge [30] in that it both seeks and encapsulates know-how [31].

3. Organizational memory

A critical component of a learning and problem solving system is an organizational memory consisting of mental and structural artifacts that can affect performance [59]. The **shared and stored knowledge** from previous problem solving can be called organizational memory [59].

Huber [29] argues that organizational memory exists in three form — humans, papers, and computer-resident — and that humans need the support of information technology ranging from databases to expert systems in order to prevent inaccurate learning and incomplete recall. Information researchers, who have a data and representation-oriented perspective on organizational memory, conceptualized the organizational memory as framework, stored information, hypertext, and formalized expertise, and stored data and expertise [50].

Organizational memory is a fundamental component of organizational learning because learning basically updates and revises the organizational memory. The organizational memory comprises a schema data base and a script data base. A schema is a cognitive structure composed of a network of expectations learned from experience and stored in memory [56]. It provides a basis for the interpretation of information, events, and actions. Organizational schema covers of the functions, the ideas, and the technical attributes of an organization as found in equipment, people, electronic and manual catalogs, files and databases, the organizational structure, job descriptions and other documents.

A script schema is a cognitive structure devoted to the retention of context-specific knowledge about event sequences and guides action [18]. Organizational scripts refers to the sequence of steps used to convert input into output. Organizational scripts are found in operator manuals, job descriptions, and managers. They are recipes, flexible schema, for the transformation process.

Organizational memory is accomplished through the systemic processing of knowledge or information. Information technology, then, can fairly be thought of as an organizational "mind." The question is how to utilize emerging knowledge representation technology to develop automated schema and scripts for intelligent organization.

4. Learning and problem solving systems

The foundation for an intelligent organization is of a network of learning and problem solving systems. An organization learns if any of its units acquires knowledge that it recognizes as potentially useful to the organization [28]. Organizational learning thus involves acquiring, distributing, or interpreting information which finally contributes to script and schema (organizational memory) revision [29]. The generic architecture of any learning and problem solving system is illustrated in Figure 1.

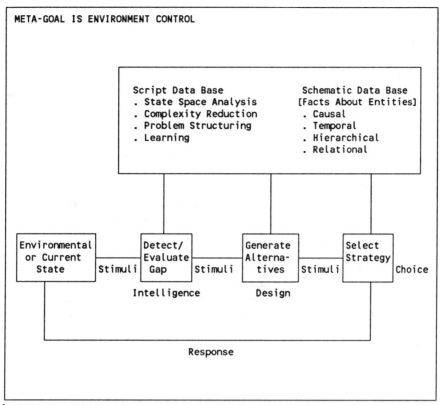

Hunt and Sanders [1989]

Figure 1. Learning and problem system architecture

The meta-goal of the learning and problem solving meta-script is environmental control through problem resolution. This involves reducing the difference between some ideal and an existing environmental state by invoking an appropriate script [5, 39, 40, 43]. An important outcome of the problem solving process is script and schema revision as the system "learns." Learning occurs as the problem solving system updates or modifies its schematic and scriptural knowledge bases. In essence the environmental context of the situation is "memorized" along with the behaviors which were found to assist in controlling it.

Many types of scripts are evoked by a problem solving meta-script including [cf. 31]:

> state-space analysis scripts, which aid in perception, interpretation, problem identification and diagnosis;

> complexity reduction scripts, which assist in problem decomposition and the decreasing or filtering of choices or alternatives;

> problem structuring scripts, which aid in selecting a process for solving a problem; and

> learning scripts (congenital learning, experiential learning, vicarious learning, grafting, rote learning, learning by being told, learning from examples, learning by analogy, and learning by investigating causal relationships) which provide the LPSS with a means for modifying the contextual knowledge contained in the scripts and schemas [8, 15, 29, 45].

Along with script revision, the knowledge in the schematic database will be also updated and revised during the learning process.

5. The evolution of the group cognitive structure

As members of a group in an organization begin to interact and solve problems, the organizational "mind" or memory is activated to acquire knowledge, distribute information, and interpret the shared information. Combining knowledge or information from participants leads not only to new information but also to new interpretation and understanding [29].

If a learning and problem solving system is to be effective, it must have a dynamic modeling process for scanning its environment and evaluating and detecting gaps by pooling knowledge from organizational memory. And it must have a means of changing or adapting to that environment and for retaining its lessons. Problem solving and learning are key components of survival and if an organization remains rooted in its past without updating its knowledge structures, it does not learn and it might well be buried in its obsolete knowledge.

The challenge is to develop learning and problem solving systems which are capable of acquiring, developing, and representing new knowledge in an organizational mind capable of computation and representation. Answering this challenge depends on understanding how organizations learn to model problems in dynamic worlds. Some of the thinking processes which control the evolution of a group cognitive structure are described below after which we shall describe the possible role of information technology as an agent in the learning and problem solving network.

5.1 Knowledge sharing in group problem solving

Researchers in psychology have studied problem solving in the context of interpersonal relationships. Those studies have shown that there is an association between the problem conceptualization script and the effectiveness of the problem solving process [3, 22].

The biased sampling model of group problem solving suggests that group members usually fail to pool their information effectively because discussion tends to be dominated by information that members held in common before discussion (pre-decision schema) and by information that supports members' current preferences. This model places importance on the role of the pregroup information distribution [54]. According to the biased sampling model, unshared information will tend to be omitted from discussions, and will therefore have little effect on member's preferences during group discussions. Shiflett [51] suggests that the extent to which unique resources or unshared information are considered in a group's final judgment can be a major criterion for measuring group productivity. Increasing the effectiveness of information systems requires mechanisms and tools which reduce biased information sampling.

Stasser and Titus [54] found that unique or unshared information had little effect on a group's final decision. That result corresponds to Shiflett's [51, p. 67] observation that "The fact that two or more individuals possess the same resource does not increase the total set of available resources but does increase the probability of that resource being used." Initial shared knowledge, or shared scripts, might not act to detect a problem state in the LPSS network. Filtered information creates a problem for the LPSS network because members come from different areas of expertise, and any unshared information might be critical to the success of the final outputs.

5.2 Group cognition

Recently groups have been conceptualized in terms of Gestalt notions, with the group members acting in concert as a *thinking entity*. Some researchers have observed that groups suffer from information processing biases caused from "solution-mindedness," which results in unintended or poor outputs [27] and "groupthink" [33]. Group cognition can be defined as convictions that group members are aware that

230

they share and consider as defining their "groupness." Group cognition provides a basis for uniting group members as a single thinking entity [2].

Groups differ with regard to the control mechanisms that they use to maintain common beliefs or cognition among group members. In some groups, there are no control mechanisms. But, most groups develop mechanisms for controlling and maintaining group cognition. For example, regular meetings, newsletters, tools, and methodologies control groups' beliefs during problem solving processes.

Typically, group cognition changes with time. Changes can take place either by the addition and/or omission of cognitions, and by reformulation of old cognitions. Changes in group cognitive structures reflect a process of adaptation to environmental conditions as well as to group norms and values. The important idea here is that group beliefs, a thinking entity's script, might be transformed by structural changes caused by human or machine agents.

5.3 The emergent cognitive structure of the group

The resulting group cognitive structure is ultimately related to the level of intragroup communication and the way in which the group engages in joint problem solving. Guilford [20] suggests two fundamental thinking operations in group problem solving. Convergent group thinking leads to singular solutions with identifiable criteria for correctness. Such operations can be expected to predominate in solving well-structured problems. Divergent group thinking refers to cognitive operations that are directed at generating a large number of disparate solutions that typically meet no singular criterion of correctness. Group problem solving depends on both types of operations. These two thinking processes ultimately determine the group cognitive structures. Walsh and Fahey [57] acknowledged that each individual group member's knowledge structure represents a fundamental element in a group's collective knowledge structure. But they posit that political processes within a group will determine whose knowledge structures are represented in the collective knowledge structure. The notion of a negotiated belief structure recognizes both the potential schematic endowment of a particular problem (pre-decision schema) and the influence patterns evident around any particular problem [58].

Each group cognition for a problem domain is different in terms of dimensions represented in its schema. *Coverage* is the breadth of knowledge possessed by all of the participants for solving a particular problem. It is the aggregate level of knowledge possessed by the group. The *level of coverage* can be increased by divergent thinking processes in the group. These processes accommodate cognitive operations that are directed at generating a large number of disparate solutions. For example, different individual views from different departments can be aggregated or pooled to increase problem coverage, therefore giving the group the ability to solve a large unstructured problem. In a design problem, broad and diverse participation and combination of diverse sources of expertise were recommended [42]. Cooperative design emphasizes the importance of bringing together the competence of designers and users [37]

Consensus is the common or shared set of knowledge representations of a problem domain among participants. The *level of consensus* can be increased or decreased depending upon convergent thinking processes among participants. In collaborative work environment, collaborators can share not only the results of work but also the dynamic process of working to support a broader range of dynamic collaboration activities [32].

Coverage and consensus are independent in the sense that there is no predetermined relationship between the two cognitive structures. Consensus and coverage activities can be facilitated by learning, knowledge acquisition, information distribution, and information interpretation [cf. 29]. The final product of the cognitive activities will be the cognitive representation of revised schema and/or scripts [learning] in the organizational memory.

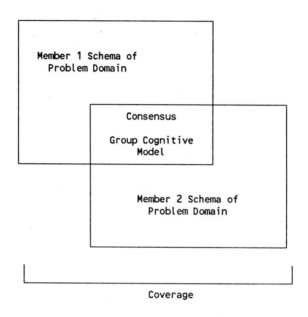

Coverage

Figure 2. Venn diagram illustrating the distribution of cognitive resources within a two person group. Note that there is a possibility to overlap between Member 1 Schema and Member 2 Schema. But, multiperson decision support systems have more interests in human and computerized problem solvers with different cognitive schema [30]

If a group is to be effective, in dealing with complex problems, then the group should employ a negotiated cognitive structure marked by highly realized coverage. This means that group members have almost completely pooled and exchanged their respective knowledge among the group members [58]. In this case, the high level of coverage means that there has been divergent discussion and deliberation on a solution. When well-structured problems are analyzed by groups, the emphasis should be on convergent thinking process. That is the organization of knowledge and decision models and the evaluation of the solution. In this context, interaction among group members will focus on trading facts, on answering questions, and on evaluating each alternative. Differences in the information exchanged across problem types imply corresponding differences in the underlying cognitive operations that contribute to solution quality [52].

The group cognitive structure and thinking process can be facilitated by three different types of distributed decision support environments including distributed computing, distributed decision support, and distributed communications[55]. The goal of each distributed decision environment can be described with respect to the resultant group cognitive structure (See Figure 3).

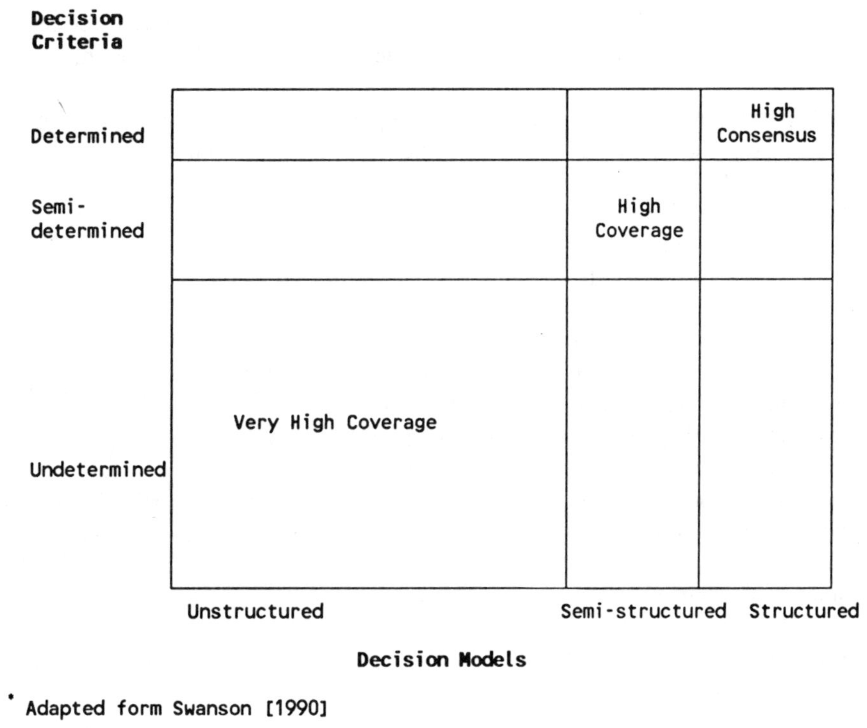

Decision
Criteria

	Unstructured	Semi-structured	Structured
Determined			High Consensus
Semi-determined		High Coverage	
Undetermined	Very High Coverage		

Decision Models

* Adapted form Swanson [1990]

Figure 3. The appropriate cognitive structure for different problem situations

6. Technology as an agent in a network

Information technology can be designated the preserver of knowledge and agent of cognitive evolution [38]. Organizational intelligence can be facilitated by manipulating coverage and consensus among participants around a problem in the learning and problem solving network. A technological agent in the learning and problem solving network can dynamically select one of the distributed decision environment according to problem type. Thus a technological agent can control the emergence of the *thinking entity's* cognitive structure. For example, in large ill-structured problems, cooperation among nodes in a network is necessary because a single node often has a provincial viewpoint, insufficient expertise, and limited resources for dealing with problem complexity.

The cooperative distributive problem solving (CDPS) researchers, who are studying how a loosely-coupled network of problem solvers can work together to solve problems that are beyond their individual capabilities, are trying to develop the knowledge and reasoning techniques that loosely-coupled networks of sophisticated problem-solving nodes require in order to cooperate effectively in solving complex and distributed problems. The CDPS concept is useful for illustrating how cooperation and interaction occurs between machines and human beings to affect the group cognitive structure. Each node shares a high-level partial solution and these agents can collaborate to solve the global problem. The nodes in this environment cooperatively solve a problem by using their local expertise, resources, and information to individually solve subproblems, and then integrate these subproblem solutions into an overall solution [16].

This framework recognizes the necessity of cooperation (consensus) and integration of views (coverage) among nodes composed of human and machine experts. Also, this framework imposes two constraints; one is that the distributed sub-solutions of the overall solution must be mutually consistent, and the other is that nodes must rely on sophisticated local reasoning to decide on appropriate action and interactions. In essence, this notion of CDPS emphasizes consensus among nodes by imposing the constraint of mutual consistency among sub-solutions. Also, it emphasizes coverage in the sense that it requires sophisticated local reasoning and any necessary expertise at least in one node for solving a problem.

To establish final consensus or coverage among group members, the CDPS concept suggests three approaches [16]: negotiation, functionally-accurate cooperation, and organizational structuring. Negotiation relies on dialogue among nodes to resolve inconsistent views. Functional cooperation involves exchanging tentative solutions to resolve inconsistent problem views. Organizational structuring uses common knowledge about general problem solving roles and communication patterns to decrease uncertainty about patterns of cooperation.

The difference between negotiation and functionally-accurate cooperation is that negotiation takes a top-down view of problem solving whereas the functionally-accurate cooperation approach takes a bottom-up view. The organizational structuring approach involves a compromise between the top-down and bottom-up approaches. It gives more general, long-term information about the relationships between nodes. With this general and high level view, nodes can ensure that they meet conditions that are essential to successful problem solving, including coverage of related expertise. In dynamic domains where the problem-solving situation is frequently changing, the organizational structuring approach is appropriate. Agents can perform meta-level reasoning, and change their goals according to their assumptions about the beliefs of other agents.

Information processing theory [17] has hypothesized that structures reflect and store information about an organization's perceptions of its environment. Organizations have been observed to have a tendency toward biased information sampling [54] and group thinking or solution-mindedness [33]. By applying high-level meta-goals among nodes, the organizational structuring approach can encourage divergent and/or convergent thinking processes among nodes in a network. An organizational structuring approach can specify authority and connectivity for view integration among nodes in terms of such topologies as hierarchical, lateral, matrix organization or market systems [16]

7. Implications for the design of the intelligent organization

A network of learning and problem solving systems can be made more effective by utilizing an organizational structuring approach in a CDPS environment. This high-level meta-goal for marshalling the interaction process among human and machine agents can be capsulized in intelligent controller and resolver (ICOR). According to changes in the problem context, the ICOR can dynamically link three supporting environments (distributed communications, distributed decision support, and distributed computing) [55]. The ICOR can be used to make decisions about information sharing, to assist in negotiation and cooperation, to facilitate inter-group communication, and to set the authority structure among human and machine nodes. These functions are of particular importance in environments where goals change and problem solutions unfold as the territory is mapped [45].

The meta-goal for the network of learning and problem solving systems is environmental control whereas the meta-goals for the ICOR in group problem solving environments are to facilitate consensus and coverage according to a problem type (Figure 4). Because unshared information or knowledge will not be part of the emergent group's cognitive structure and should be pooled and shared to reduce sampling bias, one of the primary duties of the ICOR is to facilitate the development of a group cognitive structure. As an agent in the learning and problem solving systems, ICOR dynamically involves knowledge processing or learning activity. It assists in revising and updating the organizational memory from knowledge acquisition, information distribution, and information interpretation.

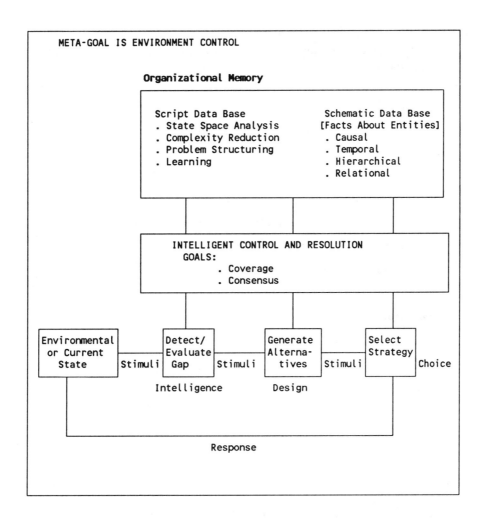

Figure 4. Learning and problem system architecture with ICOR

It is in this context that the ICOR should provide access to organizational memory as embodied in equipment, people, electronic and manual catalogs, files and databases, the organizational structure, job descriptions, operator manuals, job descriptions, and managers. This requires a search engine capable of navigating through the organizational knowledge repository.

The ICOR can control and maintain group cognition by scheduling meetings, distributing pertinent information, and identifying models germane to the problem solving task. When there is insufficient knowledge about the problem domain, the ICOR should also have the ability to add machine and human agents with diverse views. This requires pointers to expertise as well as to individuals with varying psychosocial profiles.

The ICOR should have a bargaining and mediation mechanism to assist in developing the group negotiated belief schema. Intelligent agents in group decision support systems (GDSS) can assist in this task [cf. 12] by encouraging communication, providing idea generation and synthesis, and even utilizing an intelligent rule-base to filter, structure, and monitor communication and to suggest changes of content. As yet there are few examples of intelligent GDSS [6] but with increased sophistication they could also be used to facilitate the development of the group schema.

As noted by Hirschheim and Newman [26] many organizational assumptions are actually symbolic myths, metaphors, and magic which oversimplify complex tasks. As such the system should occasionally generate "surprise" or random solutions and have built in obsolescence for strategies, actions, and procedures, possibly via "sunset" rules that would stop systems from running beyond a certain date [30]. The idea here is to discourage over-reliance on standard routines and to question assumptions of causality that might not be valid.

Table 1. Features of ICOR

```
. Facilitates coverage and consensus according to a problem situation

. Specifies authority and connectivity for flow of information

. Reduces biases in information sampling

. Facilitates information and knowledge sharing

. Assists in negotiation and cooperation

. Facilitates communication

. Provides access to organizational memory

. Adds machine and human agents with diverse views

. Generates "surprise" or random solution
```

8. Conclusion

This paper has discussed several ways in which the effectiveness of a network of learning and problem solving systems can be improved by controlling the emergence of the group cognitive structure. We assume organization as a problem solving system which can be configured as a set of machine and human problem solvers. Traditional GDSS researches have focused on the interaction principles among problem solvers, but the real contribution of technology should be found in the contribution to the problem solving capability of a system.

The group schema of the *thinking entity* can be facilitated using multiple viewpoints, pooling and sharing information, and by having automated support for mediation, modeling and search. In particular, the ICOR can increase the ability to evaluate and detect gaps (problem finding capability) and assist in selecting a strategy or solution by the aggregation of individual models found in human and machine nodes. Even though the ICOR cannot suggest any solution for a specific problem, it can facilitate and evaluate the whole problem solving process within group members.

The final contribution of an organizational decision support system should be evaluated in terms of cognitive contribution to the intelligent organization. Having broad-based coverage suggests that a *thinking entity*'s cognitive structure is also broad-based and complex. However, group cognitive models which are thorough and extensive might be unsuitable. Chapanis [7] outlines two primary criteria that can be used to judge the effectiveness of a model. The first question to ask is whether the model provides for economy of description. The second question to ask is whether the model has the power to suggest implications at first sight. Occam's razor [1836] suggests that the simpler approach should win out. "What can be done with fewer is done in vain with more." The same razor can be used to judge the effectiveness of the thinking entity's cognitive model. But this presents a dilemma. Perhaps coverage leads to a group cognitive model which is not parsimonious, but is rather unwieldy. This notwithstanding, if the model represents the problem space adequately it would be difficult to pass inferior judgment for reasons of cognitive complexity. The question is whether an economical group cognitive model results in **more** decisions with the same level of effectiveness as a complex cognitive model. Fostering the development of a group cognitive schema (consensus) which has sufficient coverage to deal with problem complexity will present a continuing challenge to designing intelligent organizations.

1. Note that the meaning of "group" in this paper has a slightly different meaning from the one used in group decision support systems (GDSS) research. In this paper, a group is composed of participants in organizational decision processes in which there is a higher level of formality than found in GDSS. King and Star [36] state that decision making processes in the organizational decision support systems context are very formal and structured. Thus individual and social factors, such as personality, persuasion, tacit knowledge, and cohesion, are not so critical and the decision making process among participants is "articulated due process." Norms and protocols govern the process and are invoked in it.

References

[1] Barr, Avron and Feigenbaum, E.A., *The Handbook of Artificial Intelligence*, Reading, Massachusetts, Addison-Wesley Publishing Company, Inc. (1989).

[2] Bar-Tar, Daniel, *Group Beliefs: A Conception for Analyzing Group Structure, Process, and Behavior*, New York, Springer-Verlag (1990).

[3] Bougon, Michel, Weick, Karl, and Binkhorst, Din, "Cognition in Organization: An Analysis of the Utrecht Jazz Orchestra," *Administrative Science Quarterly*, Vol. 22 (December, 1977), pp. 606-639.

[4] Brix, V.H., "Action Learning and Control Theory," *Omega*, 11 (1983), pp. 491-500.

[5] Cerveny, R.P., Garrity, E.J., and Sanders, G.L., "A Problem Solving Perspective on Systems Development," *Journal of Management Information Systems*, Vol. 6, No. 4, (Spring 1990) pp. 102-122.

[6] Cerveny, R.P., Wang, C. and Sanders, G.L., "A Framework for Research in Group Decision Support Systems," *Proceedings of the 24th Hawaii International Conference on Systems Sciences*, 1991.

[7] Chapanis, A., "Men, Machines, and Models," *American Psychologist*, Vol. 16, (1961), pp. 113-131.

[8] Courtney, J.F., Paradice, D.B. and Ata Mohammed, N.H., "A Knowledge-Based DSS for Managerial Problem Diagnosis," *Decision Sciences*, Vol. 18, No. 3 (Summer 1987), pp. 373-399.

[9] Davis, G.B., "Strategies for Information Requirements Determination," *IBM Systems Journal*, 21 (1982), pp. 4-30.

[10] Dery, D., "Decision-Making, Problem Solving, and Organizational Learning," *Omega*, 11 (1983), pp. 321-328.

[11] Dery, D. and Mock, T.J., "Information Support Systems for Problem Solving," *Decision Support Systems*, Vol. 1, (1985), pp. 103-109.

[12] Desanctis, G. and Gallupe, R.B., "A Foundation for the Study of Group Decision Support Systems," *Management Science*, 33 (5), (1987), pp. 589-609.

[13] Dhar, Vasant, "On the Plausibility and Scope of Expert Systems in Management," *Journal of Management Information Systems*, Summer 1987, Vol. 4, No. 1, pp. 25-41.

[14] Diaper, Dan, *Knowledge Elicitation: Principles, Techniques, and Applications*, Chichester, England, Halsted Press (1989).

[15] Dietterich, T.G., "Learning and Inductive Inference," *The Handbook of Artificial Intelligence*, P.R. Cohen and E. Feigenbaum (eds.) William Kaufman Inc., Los Altos, CA, (1982), pp. 323-511.

[16] Durfee, Edmund H., Lesser, Victor R., and Corkill, Daniel D., "Trends in Cooperative Distributed Problem Solving," *IEEE Transactions on Knowledge and Data Engineering*, Vol. 1, No. 1, (March 1988), pp. 61-83.

[17] Galbraith, J., *Organization Design*, Reading, MA, Addison-Wesley, 1977.

[18] Gioia, D.A. and Manz, C.C., "Linking Cognition and Behavior: A Script Processing Interpretation of Vicarious Learning," *Academy of Management Review*, 1985, 10, pp. 527-539.

[19] Gioia, D.A. and Poole, P.P.,"Scripts in Organizational Behavior," *Academy of Management Review*, 9, 3 (1984) pp. 449-459.

[20] Guilford, J.P., "The Structure of Intellect," *Psychological Bulletin*, 53 (1956), pp. 267-293.

[21] Hale, David P. and Kasper, George M., "The Effect of Human-Computer Interchange Protocol on Decision Performance," *Journal of Management Information Systems*, Vol. 6, No. 1 (1989) pp. 5-20.

[22] Hall, Roger I., "The Natural Logic of Management Policy Making: Its Implications for the Survival of an Organization," *Management Science*, Vol. 30, No. 8, (1984), pp. 905-927.

[23] Harmon, Paul, Maus, Rex, and Morrissey, William, *Expert Systems: Tools and Applications*, New York, John Wiley & Sons, Inc. (1988).

[24] Hayes-Roth, *Building Expert Systems*, Reading, MA, Addison-Wesley (1983).

[25] Hedberg, B. & Johnsson, S., "Designing Semi-confusing Information Systems for Organizations in Changing Environments," Database, 13 (Winter/Spring 1982) pp. 12-24.

[26] Hirschheim, R. and Newman, M., "Symbolism and Information Systems Development," Information Systems Research, Vol. 2, No. 1, (March 1991), pp. 29-62.

[27] Hoffman, L.R. and Maier, N.R.F., "Valence in the Adoption of Solution by Problem-Solving Group: Quality and Acceptance as Goals of Leaders and Members," *Journal of Personality and Social Psychology*, 6 (1967), pp. 175-182.

[28] Huber, G.P., "A Theory of the Effects of Advanced Information Technologies on Organizational Design, Intelligence, and Decision Making," *Academy of Management Review*, 15, pp. 47-71.

[29] Huber, G.P., "Organizational Learning: The Contributing Processes and the Literatures," *Organizational Science*, Vol. 2, No. 1, February 1991, pp. 88-115.

[30] Hunt, R.G. and Sanders, G.L., "Propaedeutics of Decision-Making Supporting Managerial Learning and Innovation," *Decision Support Systems*, Vol. 2, (1986), pp. 125-134.

[31] Hunt, R.G. and Sanders, G.L., "Supporting Intelligent Organizations: Problem Solving and Learning," *Proceedings of the 22nd Hawaii International Conference on System Science*s, 1989.

[32] Ishii, Hiroshi and Miyake, Naomi, "Toward an Open Shared Workspace: Computer and Video Fusion Approach of Teamworkstation," *Communications of the ACM*, December 1991, Vol. 34, No. 12.

[33] Janis, I.L., *Groupthink: Psychological Studies of Policy Decision and Fiascos*, Boston, Houghton Mifflin (1982).

[34] Jarke, M., "Knowledge Sharing and Negotiation Support in Multiple-person Decision Support System," *Decision Support System*, 2, 1, 1986, pp. 93-102.

[35] Jaskolka, Gabriel A., "A Study of the Relation of Level of Agreement on Cognition in Groups with Certain Organizational Outcomes," Unpublished doctoral dissertation, State University of New York, Buffalo, New York, 1989.

[36] King, John L. and Star, Susan L., "Conceptual Foundations for the Development of Organizational Decision Support Systems," *Proceedings of Twenty-third Annual Hawaii International Conference on System Sciences*, Vol. III, 1990, pp. 143-151.

[37] Kyng, Morten, "Designing for Cooperation: Cooperating in Design," *Communications of the ACM*, December, 1991, Vol. 34, No. 12.

[38] Levinson, P., *Mind at Large: Knowing in the Technological Age*, Greenwich, CN:JAI Press, (1988).

[39] MacCrimmon, K.R. and Taylor, R.N., "Decision Making and Problem Solving," *Handbook of Industrial and Organizational Psychology*, Marvin D. Dunnete (ed.), Rand McNally, Chicago, (1976), pp. 1397-1454.

[40] Minch, R.P. and Sanders, G.L., "Computerized Information Systems Supporting the Multicriteria Decision Making," *Decision Sciences*, Vol. 17, No. 3, (1986), pp. 395-413.

[41] Mitroff, I., *Stakeholder of the Organizational Mind*, Jossey-Bass, San Francisco (1983).

[42] Muller, M. "Participatory design in Britain and North America: Responding to the Scandinavian Challenge," *In Reaching Through Technology*, CHI '91 Conference Proceedings, Edited by G.M. Olson and J.S. Olson , ACM, pp. 389-392.

[43] Newell, A. and Simon, H.A., *Human Problem Solving*, Prentice Hall, Englewood Cliffs, NJ, (1972).

[44] Paradice, D.B. and Courtney, J.F., "Controlling Bias in User Assertion in Expert DSS," *Journal of Management Information Systems*, Vol. 3, No. 1 (Summer 1986), pp. 52-64.

[45] Paradice, D.B. and Courtney, J.F., "Dynamic Construction of Statistical Models in Managerial DSS," *Annals of Operation Research*, Vol. 12, (1988), pp. 321-336.

[46] Pegels, C.C. and Sanders, G.L., "Information System Technology Transfer and Diffusion in China," Working Paper, School of Management, State University of New York at Buffalo, 1988.

[47] Rao, H.R., Cerveny, R.P., Sanders, G.L, Sridhar, R., Garrity, E.J., and Pakath, R., "Intelligent Control and Resolution of a Network of Learning and Problem Solving Processors," *Proceedings of the Twenty-third Annual Hawaii International Conference on System Sciences*, 1990.

[48] Robey, D.R. and Taggart, W., "Human Information Processing in Information and Decision Support Systems," *MIS Quarterly*, 6 (1982) pp. 61-73.

[49] Salaway, Gail, "An Organizational Learning Approach to Information Systems Development," *MIS Quarterly* (June 1987), pp. 244-264.

[50] Sandoe, K., Olfman, L., and Mandviwalla, "Meeting in Time: Recording the Workgroup Conversation," *Proceedings of International Conferences on Information Systems*, 1991, pp. 261-271.

[51] Shiflett, S.C.,"Toward a General Model of Small Group Productivity," *Psychological Bulletin*, 86 (1979), pp. 67-79.

[52] Silver, Steven D., Cohen, Bernard P., and Rainwater, Julie, "Group Structure and Information Exchange in Innovative Problem Solving," *Advances in Group Process*, Edited by Edward J. Lawler and Barry Markovsky, 5, (1988) pp. 169-194.

[53] Sims, R.R., "Kolb's Experiential Learning Theory: A Framework for Assessing Person-Job Interaction," *Academy of Management Review*, 8 (1983) pp. 501-508.

[54] Stasser, Garold and Titus, William, "Pooling of Unshared Information in Group Decision Making: Biased Information Sampling During Discussion," *Journal of Personality and Social Psychology*, 48, 6 (1985), pp. 1467-1478.

[55] Swanson, E. Burton, "Distributed Decision Support Systems: a Perspective," *Proceedings of Twenty-third Annual Hawaii International Conference on System Sciences*, Vol III, 1990.

[56] Taylor, S.E. and Crocker, J., "Schematic Bases of Social Information Processing," In E.T. Higgins, C.P. Herman, and M.P. Zanna (ed.), *Social Cognition*, Vol. 1 Hillsdale, N.J., Erlbaum, 1981.

[57] Walsh, James P.and Fahey, L., "The Role of Negotiated Belief Structures in Strategy Making," *Journal of Management*, 12 (1986), pp. 325-338.

[58] Walsh, James P., Henderson, Caroline M., and Deighton, John, "Negotiated Belief Structures and Decision Performance: An Empirical Investigation," *Organizational Behavior and Human Decision Processes*, 42 (1988), pp. 194-216.

[59] Walsh, James P. and Ungson, G.R., "Organizational Memory," *Academy of Management Review*, January 1991, pp. 57-91.

About the authors

Robert W. Blanning is a professor at the Owen Graduate School of Management, Vanderbilt University. He obtained his BS in physics from Pennsylvania State University, his MS in operations research from the Case Institute of Technology, and his PhD from the University of Pennsylvania, specializing in operations research and management information systems. He has been a faculty member in the Business Schools of New York University and the University of Pennsylvania's Wharton School. His teaching and research interests are model management systems, information economics, and the management applications of artificial intelligence. He has published in *Management Science, Decision Sciences, Communications of the ACM,* the *Naval Research Logistics Quarterly, Decision Support Systems, Information and Management, Omega, Policy Analysis and Information Systems,* the *International Journal on Policy and Information, Human Systems Management,* the *Journal of Information Science, Long Range Planning, Technological Forecasting and Social Change,* and the *Concise Encyclopedia of Information Processing in Systems and Organizations* published by Pergamon Press. He is an editorial board member of *Decision Support Systems* and *Information Systems Research,* and is an associate editor of *Information and Decision Technologies* and a board member of the *Journal of Management Information Systems.* He is editor of *Foundations of Expert Systems for Management,* published by Verlag Reinhland in 1990.

David R. King is director of Comshare's Applied Research Section. He has been responsible for the design and development of a number of AI-related DSS and EIS products. Currently, he is working on next-generation enterprise intelligence systems. He obtained his PhD in sociology and mathematical statistics from the University of North Carolina, and has authored over 40 articles and an upcoming book on decision support and knowledge base systems. He is past president of the Institute of Management College on Artificial Intelligence, and serves on the editorial boards of *Management Science* and the *International Journal of Expert Systems.*

NEW RELEASES

ARCHITECTURAL ALTERNATIVES FOR EXPLOITING PARALLELISM
edited by David J. Lilja

This tutorial surveys the fine-grain parallel architectures that exploit the parallelism available at the instruction set level, the coarse grain parallel architecture that exploit the parallelism available at the loop and subroutine levels, and the single instruction, multiple-data (SIMD) massively parallel architectures that exploit parallelism across large data structures.

It includes over 37 articles that discuss the potential of parallel processing for reducing execution time, available parallelism in application programs, pipelined processors, multiple-instruction issue architectures, decoupled access/execute architectures, dataflow processors, shared memory multiprocessors, distributed memory multicomputers, reconfigurable and massively parallel architectures, and comparing parallelism extraction techniques.

464 pages. March 1992. ISBN 0-8186-2642-9.
Catalog # 2642 $80.00 / $50.00 Member

KNOWLEDGE-BASED SYSTEMS:
Fundamentals and Tools
edited by Oscar N. Garcia and Yi-Tzuu Chien

This book emphasizes the characteristics of knowledge-based systems that make this technology particularly attractive, including rapid prototyping, knowledge engineering, representation paradigms, logical foundations, inferencing modes, verification and validation of knowledge bases, and languages, shells, and tools. Its 35 papers explore recent research and the rapid evolution of the field and provide a brief account of the status of today's KB systems.

It is organized into ten chapters that follow a structured path from general and fundamental issues to more specific topics, culminating in an examination of some popular commercial and research-oriented tools and a brief survey of current applications. The tutorial examines the subject of knowledge engineering and considers how to match the appropriate method to an existing problem.

512 pages. December 1991. ISBN 0-8186-1924-4.
Catalog # 1924 $65.00 / $45.00 Member

BROADBAND SWITCHING:
Architectures, Protocols, Design, and Analysis
edited by C. Dhas, V. K. Konangi, and M. Sreetharan

This tutorial investigates the latest information and research on broadband switching and provides supporting material and insight into the correlated areas of networking, performance analysis, and alternate technologies. It also describes broadband switching architectures, performance modeling techniques, multistage interconnection networks, experimental architectures for ISDN and ATM techniques, architectural options available for switches.

The text examines numerous trends in network architectures intended to meet the user's high bandwidth requirements, packet replication and switching in broadcast switching systems, bandwidth allocation and flow and congestion control, performance modeling, and photonic switching techniques and technology.

528 pages. August 1991. Hardbound. ISBN 0-8186-8926-9.
Catalog # 1926 $75.00 / $50.00 Member

COMPUTER COMMUNICATIONS:
Architectures, Protocols, and Standards (3rd Edition)
edited by William Stallings

This third edition is a major revision surveying the motivating factors and design principles for a communication architecture. The tutorial devotes considerable attention to the OSI model, discusses the framework used to develop protocols, and explores communication system design.

The book contains 29 papers, including 24 new articles, that provide a broad overview of communication protocols. Among the new topics are Signaling System Number 7, frame relay, and ISDN call control. Other new articles cover the IEEE 802.6 MAN standard, lightweight transport protocols, internetwork routing protocols, and application-level protocols and standards, and more current articles on protocols have replaced earlier versions from the second edition.

368 pages. March 1992. ISBN 0-8186-2712-3.
Catalog # 2712 $70.00 / $40.00 Member

from IEEE COMPUTER SOCIETY PRESS

To order any of these titles or for information on other books,
call 1-800-CS-BOOKS or order by FAX at (714) 821-4010

(in California call 714-821-8380)

Other IEEE Computer Society Press Titles

MONOGRAPHS

Analyzing Computer Architectures
Written by Jerome C. Huck and Michael J. Flynn
(ISBN 0-8186-8857-2); 206 pages

Branch Strategy Taxonomy and Performance Models
Written by Harvey G. Cragon
(ISBN 0-8186-9111-5); 150 pages

Desktop Publishing for the Writer:
Designing, Writing, and Developing
Written by Richard Ziegfeld and John Tarp
(ISBN 0-8186-8840-8); 380 pages

Digital Image Warping
Written by George Wolberg
(ISBN 0-8186-8944-7); 340 pages

Integrating Design and Test —
CAE Tools for ATE Programming
Written by Kenneth P. Parker
(ISBN 0-8186-8788-6); 160 pages

JSP and JSD —
The Jackson Approach to Software Development
(Second Edition)
Written by John R. Cameron
(ISBN 0-8186-8858-0); 560 pages

National Computer Policies
Written by Ben G. Matley and Thomas A. McDannold
(ISBN 0-8186-8784-3); 192 pages

Optic Flow Computation: A Unified Perspective
Written by Ajit Singh
(ISBN 0-8186-2602-X); 256 pages

Physical Level Interfaces and Protocols
Written by Uyless Black
(ISBN 0-8186-8824-2); 240 pages

Protecting Your Proprietary Rights in Computer
and High-Technology Industries
Written by Tobey B. Marzouk, Esq.
(ISBN 0-8186-8754-1); 224 pages

X.25 and Related Protocols
Written by Uyless Black
(ISBN 0-8186-8976-5); 304 pages

TUTORIALS

Advanced Computer Architecture
Edited by Dharma P. Agrawal
(ISBN 0-8186-0667-3); 400 pages

Advances in Distributed System Reliability
Edited by Suresh Rai and Dharma P. Agrawal
(ISBN 0-8186-8907-2); 352 pages

Architectural Alternatives for Exploiting Parallelism
Edited by David J. Lilja
(ISBN 0-8186-2642-9); 464 pages

Autonomous Mobile Robots:
Perception, Mapping and Navigation — Volume 1
Edited by S. S. Iyengar and A. Elfes
(ISBN 0-8186-9018-6); 425 pages

Autonomous Mobile Robots:
Control, Planning, and Architecture — Volume 2
Edited by S. S. Iyengar and A. Elfes
(ISBN 0-8186-9116-6); 425 pages

Broadband Switching:
Architectures, Protocols, Design, and Analysis
Edited by C. Dhas, V. K. Konangi, and M. Sreetharan
(ISBN 0-8186-8926-9); 528 pages

Computer and Network Security
Edited by M. D. Abrams and H. J. Podell
(ISBN 0-8186-0756-4); 448 pages

Computer Architecture
Edited by D. Gajski, V. Milutinovic, H. Siegel, and B. Furht
(ISBN 0-8186-0704-1); 602 pages

Computer Arithmetic I
Edited by Earl E. Swartzlander, Jr.
(ISBN 0-8186-8931-5); 398 pages

Computer Arithmetic II
Edited by Earl E. Swartzlander, Jr.
(ISBN 0-8186-8945-5); 412 pages

Computer Communications:
Architectures, Protocols, and Standards (Third Edition)
Edited by William Stallings
(ISBN 0-8186-2710-7); 368 pages

Computer Graphics Hardware: Image Generation and Display
Edited by H. K. Reghbati and A. Y. C. Lee
(ISBN 0-8186-0753-X); 384 pages

Computer Graphics: Image Synthesis
Edited by Kenneth Joy, Nelson Max, Charles Grant,
and Lansing Hatfield
(ISBN 0-8186-8854-8); 380 pages

Computer Vision: Principles
Edited by Rangachar Kasturi and Ramesh Jain
(ISBN 0-8186-9102-6); 700 pages

Computer Vision: Advances and Applications
Edited by Rangachar Kasturi and Ramesh Jain
(ISBN 0-8186-9103-4); 720 pages

Digital Image Processing (Second Edition)
Edited by Rama Chellappa
(ISBN 0-8186-2362-4); 400 pages

Digital Private Branch Exchanges (PBXs)
Edited by Edwin Coover
(ISBN 0-8186-0829-3); 394 pages

Distributed Computing Network Reliability
Edited by Suresh Rai and Dharma P. Agrawal
(ISBN 0-8186-8908-0); 357 pages

Distributed-Software Engineering
Edited by Sol Shatz and Jia-Ping Wang
(ISBN 0-8186-8856-4); 294 pages

Domain Analysis and Software Systems Modeling
Edited by Ruben-Prieto Diaz and Guillermo Arango
(ISBN 0-8186-8996-X); 312 pages

Formal Verification of Hardware Design
Edited by Michael Yoeli
(ISBN 0-8186-9017-8); 340 pages

Groupware:
Software for Computer-Supported Cooperative Work
Edited by David Marca and Geoffrey Bock
(ISBN 0-8186-2637-2); 500 pages

Hard Real-Time Systems
Edited by J. A. Stankovic and K. Ramamritham
(ISBN 0-8186-0819-6); 624 pages

For further information call 1-800-CS-BOOKS or write:

IEEE Computer Society Press, 10662 Los Vaqueros Circle, PO Box 3014,
Los Alamitos, California 90720-1264, USA

IEEE Computer Society, 13, avenue de l'Aquilon,
B-1200 Brussels, BELGIUM

IEEE Computer Society, Ooshima Building, 2-19-1 Minami-Aoyama,
Minato-ku, Tokyo 107, JAPAN

Integrated Services Digital Networks (ISDN)
(Second Edition)
Edited by William Stallings
(ISBN 0-8186-0823-4); 406 pages

Knowledge-Based Systems:
Fundamentals and Tools
Edited by Oscar N. Garcia and Yi-Tzuu Chien
(ISBN 0-8186-1924-4); 512 pages

Local Network Technology (Third Edition)
Edited by William Stallings
(ISBN 0-8186-0825-0); 512 pages

Microprogramming and Firmware Engineering
Edited by V. M. Milutinovic
(ISBN 0-8186-0839-0); 416 pages

Modeling and Control of Automated Manufacturing Systems
Edited by Alan A. Desrochers
(ISBN 0-8186-8916-1); 384 pages

Nearest Neighbor Pattern Classification Techniques
Edited by Belur V. Dasarathy
(ISBN 0-8186-8930-7); 464 pages

New Paradigms for Software Development
Edited by William Agresti
(ISBN 0-8186-0707-6); 304 pages

Object-Oriented Computing, Volume 1: Concepts
Edited by Gerald E. Petersen
(ISBN 0-8186-0821-8); 214 pages

Object-Oriented Computing, Volume 2: Implementations
Edited by Gerald E. Petersen
(ISBN 0-8186-0822-6); 324 pages

Parallel Architectures for Database Systems
Edited by A. R. Hurson, L. L. Miller, and S. H. Pakzad
(ISBN 0-8186-8838-6); 478 pages

Reduced Instruction Set Computers (RISC)
(Second Edition)
Edited by William Stallings
(ISBN 0-8186-8943-9); 448 pages

Software Engineering Project Management
Edited by Richard H. Thayer
(ISBN 0-8186-0751-3); 512 pages

Software Maintenance and Computers
Edited by David H. Longstreet
(ISBN 0-8186-8898-X); 304 pages

Software Quality Assurance:
A Practical Approach
Edited by T.S. Chow
(ISBN 0-8186-0569-3); 506 pages

Software Reuse — Emerging Technology
Edited by Will Tracz
(ISBN 0-8186-0846-3); 400 pages

Software Risk Management
Edited by Barry W. Boehm
(ISBN 0-8186-8906-4); 508 pages

Standards, Guidelines and Examples on System
and Software Requirements Engineering
Edited by Merlin Dorfman and Richard H. Thayer
(ISBN 0-8186-8922-6); 626 pages

System and Software Requirements Engineering
Edited by Richard H. Thayer and Merlin Dorfman
(ISBN 0-8186-8921-8); 740 pages

Test Access Port and Boundary-Scan Architecture
Edited by Colin M. Maunder and Rodham E. Tulloss
(ISBN 0-8186-9070-4); 400 pages

Visual Programming Environments: Paradigms and Systems
Edited by Ephraim Glinert
(ISBN 0-8186-8973-0); 680 pages

Visual Programming Environments: Applications and Issues
Edited by Ephraim Glinert
(ISBN 0-8186-8974-9); 704 pages

Visualization in Scientific Computing
Edited by G. M. Nielson, B. Shriver, and L. Rosenblum
(ISBN 0-8186-8979-X); 304 pages

Volume Visualization
Edited by Arie Kaufman
(ISBN 0-8186-9020-8); 494 pages

REPRINT COLLECTIONS

Distributed Computing Systems:
Concepts and Structures
Edited by A. L. Ananda and B. Srinivasan
(ISBN 0-8186-8975-0); 416 pages

Expert Systems:
A Software Methodology for Modern Applications
Edited by Peter G. Raeth
(ISBN 0-8186-8904-8); 476 pages

Milestones in Software Evolution
Edited by Paul W. Oman and Ted G. Lewis
(ISBN 0-8186-9033-X); 332 pages

Object-Oriented Databases
Edited by Ez Nahouraii and Fred Petry
(ISBN 0-8186-8929-3); 256 pages

Validating and Verifying Knowledge-Based Systems
Edited by Uma G. Gupta
(ISBN 0-8186-8995-1); 400 pages

ARTIFICIAL NEURAL NETWORKS
TECHNOLOGY SERIES

Artificial Neural Networks —
Concept Learning
Edited by Joachim Diederich
(ISBN 0-8186-2015-3); 160 pages

Artificial Neural Networks —
Electronic Implementation
Edited by Nelson Morgan
(ISBN 0-8186-2029-3); 144 pages

Artificial Neural Networks —
Theoretical Concepts
Edited by V. Vemuri
(ISBN 0-8186-0855-2); 160 pages

SOFTWARE TECHNOLOGY SERIES

Computer-Aided Software Engineering (CASE)
Edited by E. J. Chikofsky
(ISBN 0-8186-1917-1); 110 pages

Software Reliability Models:
Theoretical Development, Evaluation, and Applications
Edited by Yashwant K. Malaiya and Pradip K. Srimani
(ISBN 0-8186-2110-9); 136 pages

MATHEMATICS TECHNOLOGY SERIES

Computer Algorithms
Edited by Jun-ichi Aoe
(ISBN 0-8186-2123-0); 154 pages

Multiple-Valued Logic in VLSI Design
Edited by Jon T. Butler
(ISBN 0-8186-2127-3); 128 pages

COMMUNICATIONS TECHNOLOGY SERIES

Multicast Communication in Distributed Systems
Edited by Mustaque Ahamad
(ISBN 0-8186-1970-8); 110 pages

ROBOTICS TECHNOLOGY SERIES

Multirobot Systems
Edited by Rajiv Mehrotra and Murali R. Varanasi
(ISBN 0-8186-1977-5); 122 pages

IEEE Computer Society

IEEE Computer Society Press Publications

Monographs: A monograph is an authored book consisting of 100-percent original material.

Tutorials: A tutorial is a collection of original materials prepared by the editors, and reprints of the best articles published in a subject area. Tutorials must contain at least five percent of original material (although we recommend 15 to 20 percent of original material).

Reprint collections: A reprint collection contains reprints (divided into sections) with a preface, table of contents, and section introductions discussing the reprints and why they were selected. Collections contain less than five percent of original material.

Technology series: Each technology series is a brief reprint collection — approximately 126-136 pages and containing 12 to 13 papers, each paper focusing on a subset of a specific discipline, such as networks, architecture, software, or robotics.

Submission of proposals: For guidelines on preparing CS Press books, write the Editorial Director, IEEE Computer Society Press, PO Box 3014, 10662 Los Vaqueros Circle, Los Alamitos, CA 90720-1264, or telephone (714) 821-8380.

Purpose

The IEEE Computer Society advances the theory and practice of computer science and engineering, promotes the exchange of technical information among 100,000 members worldwide, and provides a wide range of services to members and nonmembers.

Membership

All members receive the acclaimed monthly magazine *Computer*, discounts, and opportunities to serve (all activities are led by volunteer members). Membership is open to all IEEE members, affiliate society members, and others seriously interested in the computer field.

Publications and Activities

Computer **magazine:** An authoritative, easy-to-read magazine containing tutorials and in-depth articles on topics across the computer field, plus news, conference reports, book reviews, calendars, calls for papers, interviews, and new products.

Periodicals: The society publishes six magazines and five research transactions. For more details, refer to our membership application or request information as noted above.

Conference proceedings, tutorial texts, and standards documents: The IEEE Computer Society Press publishes more than 100 titles every year.

Standards working groups: Over 100 of these groups produce IEEE standards used throughout the industrial world.

Technical committees: Over 30 TCs publish newsletters, provide interaction with peers in specialty areas, and directly influence standards, conferences, and education.

Conferences/Education: The society holds about 100 conferences each year and sponsors many educational activities, including computing science accreditation.

Chapters: Regular and student chapters worldwide provide the opportunity to interact with colleagues, hear technical experts, and serve the local professional community.